GENDER AND POLICING IN EARLY MODERN ENGLAND

This book traces the beginnings of a shift from one model of gendered power to another. Over the course of the seventeenth and early eighteenth centuries, traditional practices of local government by heads of household began to be undermined by new legal ideas about what it meant to hold office. In London, this enabled the emergence of a new kind of officeholding and a new kind of policing, rooted in a fraternal culture of official masculinity. London officers arrested, searched, and sometimes assaulted people on the basis of gendered suspicions, especially poorer women. *Gender and Policing in Early Modern England* describes how a recognisable form of gendered policing emerged from practices of local government by patriarchs and addresses wider questions about the relationship between gender and the state.

JONAH MILLER is a Research Fellow at King's College, Cambridge.

CAMBRIDGE STUDIES IN EARLY MODERN BRITISH HISTORY

SERIES EDITORS

MICHAEL BRADDICK
Professor of History, University of Sheffield

KRISTA KESSELRING
Professor of History, Dalhousie University

ALEXANDRA WALSHAM
Professor of Modern History, University of Cambridge, and Fellow of Emmanuel College

This is a series of monographs and studies covering many aspects of the history of the British Isles between the late fifteenth century and the early eighteenth century. It includes the work of established scholars and pioneering work by a new generation of scholars. It includes both reviews and revisions of major topics and books which open up new historical terrain or which reveal startling new perspectives on familiar subjects. All the volumes set detailed research within broader perspectives, and the books are intended for the use of students as well as of their teachers.

For a list of titles in the series go to
www.cambridge.org/earlymodernbritishhistory

GENDER AND POLICING IN EARLY MODERN ENGLAND

JONAH MILLER
University of Cambridge

Shaftesbury Road, Cambridge CB2 8EA, United Kingdom

One Liberty Plaza, 20th Floor, New York, NY 10006, USA

477 Williamstown Road, Port Melbourne, VIC 3207, Australia

314–321, 3rd Floor, Plot 3, Splendor Forum, Jasola District Centre, New Delhi – 110025, India

103 Penang Road, #05–06/07, Visioncrest Commercial, Singapore 238467

Cambridge University Press is part of Cambridge University Press & Assessment, a department of the University of Cambridge.

We share the University's mission to contribute to society through the pursuit of education, learning and research at the highest international levels of excellence.

www.cambridge.org
Information on this title: www.cambridge.org/9781009305143

DOI: 10.1017/9781009305174

© Jonah Miller 2023

This publication is in copyright. Subject to statutory exception and to the provisions of relevant collective licensing agreements, no reproduction of any part may take place without the written permission of Cambridge University Press & Assessment.

First published 2023

A catalogue record for this publication is available from the British Library.

A Cataloging-in-Publication data record for this book is available from the Library of Congress.

ISBN 978-1-009-30514-3 Hardback

Cambridge University Press & Assessment has no responsibility for the persistence or accuracy of URLs for external or third-party internet websites referred to in this publication and does not guarantee that any content on such websites is, or will remain, accurate or appropriate.

For mum and for dad

Contents

List of Tables	*page* viii
Acknowledgements	ix
Abbreviations and Conventions	xi
Introduction	1
PART I PATRIARCHY	21
1 Office and Household	23
PART II REMAKING OFFICE	59
2 The Law of Office	61
3 Office and Manhood	103
PART III POLICING	135
4 Arrests	137
5 Searches	173
Conclusion	205
Appendix A	219
Appendix B	223
Select Bibliography	230
Index	249

Tables

1	Official involvement in arrests recorded at the Old Bailey and Middlesex Quarter Sessions, 1674–1750	*page* 145
2	Official involvement in arrests by decade, 1681–1750	147
3	Prompts for arrests recorded at the Old Bailey and Middlesex Quarter Sessions, 1674–1750	163
4	Prompts for arrests by officers and non-officers, 1674–1750	164
5	Grounds for suspicion in arrests recorded at the Old Bailey, 1674–1750	167
6	Gender of arrestees in general and on suspicion in the records of the Old Bailey and Middlesex Quarter Sessions, 1674–1750	168
7	Official involvement in house searches recorded at the Old Bailey and Middlesex Quarter Sessions, 1674–1750	184
8	Gender of house searchers in the records of the Old Bailey and Middlesex Quarter Sessions, 1674–1750	185
9	Official involvement in person searches recorded at the Old Bailey and Middlesex Quarter Sessions, 1674–1750	191
10	Gender of searchees in the records of the Old Bailey and Middlesex Quarter Sessions, 1674–1750	193
11	Location of goods found on people as recorded in the Old Bailey Proceedings, 1674–1750	195
12	Gender of searchers in the records of the Old Bailey and Middlesex Quarter Sessions, 1674–1750	199

Acknowledgements

This book took shape during a tumultuous period in the history of policing. Longstanding allegations of racism and misogyny have risen to prominence in the aftermath of widely reported homicides. For the first time in a generation, discussions of the fundamental nature of policing and its possible alternatives have attracted considerable media attention. This context has undoubtedly influenced the pages that follow. More straightforwardly, the book is a product of many conversations with friends, colleagues, and mentors. It began as a doctoral thesis at King's College London, supervised by Laura Gowing and Hannah Dawson. I am extremely grateful for their unerring guidance and support through a project that became more complicated the longer it went on. For invaluable advice on turning the thesis into a book, I thank Mike Braddick, Laura Gowing, Cynthia Herrup, Mark Knights, Lyndal Roper, and Alex Walsham. For friendly criticism, discussion, and support along the way, I am grateful to Richard Bell, Dom Birch, Esther Brot, Fred Carnegy-Arbuthnott, Pippa Carter, Molly Corlett, Ben James, Charmian Mansell, Hannah Murphy, Joan Redmond, Charlie Taverner, Sonia Tycko, and Emily Vine. For references and research suggestions, I am indebted to John Baker, Alice Blackwood, Paul Cavill, Dave Churchill, Paul Halliday, Cynthia Herrup, Krista Kesselring, Bob Shoemaker, Brodie Waddell, and Tim Wales. The book has been much improved by comments from the series editors and from Liz Friend-Smith. Needless to say, all errors of fact or judgement are my own.

The London Arts and Humanities Partnership, the Institute of Historical Research, the Andrew W. Mellon Foundation, and the Provost and Fellows of King's College, Cambridge, have given financial and intellectual support without which the project would have been impossible. Chris Lippard and Jonny Newhouse generously offered sofas to sleep on within walking distance of archives. King's Fellows and colleagues in the

History Faculty provided a warm welcome to Cambridge in the strangest of circumstances.

Policing is not a cheerful subject, and I could not have kept thinking about it without the love and talk, at home and abroad, of Elle Crossley. Finally, I would never have attempted or finished this book without the encouragement of both my parents. It is dedicated to them.

Abbreviations and Conventions

BIA	Borthwick Institute for Archives, York
BL	British Library, London
CRO	Cheshire Record Office, Chester
CUL	Cambridge University Library, Cambridge
ER	*English Reports, Full Reprint 1220–1865*, 176 vols (Edinburgh and London, 1900)
ERO	Essex Record Office, Chelmsford
KHLC	Kent History and Library Centre, Maidstone
LMA	London Metropolitan Archives, London
LPL	Lambeth Palace Library, London
NRO	Norfolk Record Office, Norwich
OBP	*Old Bailey Proceedings* [oldbaileyonline.org]
Seipp's Abridgement	*An Index and Paraphrase of Printed Year Book Reports, 1268–1535* [bu.edu/law/faculty-scholarship/legal-history-the-year-books]
TNA	The National Archives, Kew

Printed law reports are cited in the conventional format: case name, year in brackets, volume number, name of reporter, and page on which the report starts, followed by a reference to the same page in the collected *English Reports* in the same format. For example, Olive v Ingram (1738), 2 Strange 1114, 93 *ER* 1067. Quotations from reports in Law French are given in the author's translation.

Introduction

On New Year's Eve, 1610, Margaret Willshere played a prank on the local constable. She was working as a servant in the Worcestershire village of Chaceley and plotted the enterprise with the help of her mistress and master. As night fell, she 'attired herself in man's apparrell', tore a sheet of paper from a book at random, and set off with 'a pike staffe on her shoulder'. When she knocked at the constable's door, Willshere claimed to have come from the nearby village of Bushley with news of 'a great robbery' and instructions (here she handed over the folded paper covered in writing) to raise the neighbourhood in pursuit of the thieves. There was, of course, no such robbery. Leaving the constable's door, she returned laughing to her accomplices, who 'made themselves merry thereat'.[1] It was not the most sophisticated joke, but it provides a striking illustration of the nature of law enforcement in early modern England. Margaret Willshere's instruments of disguise – the torn page, the staff, the men's clothes – were also, by necessity, the instruments of genuine policing. As a female servant, she was near the bottom of the social hierarchy and cut off from most sources of formal authority. The worlds of law enforcement and officeholding were not her worlds. To enter them, she thought, you needed special scraps of paper and special bits of wood, and you had to be a man.

Law enforcement was a male dominated activity in early modern England. Almost all of those tasked with keeping the peace or apprehending suspected offenders were men. This may seem quite obvious. There is a long history of entanglement between state power and male power. Male domination in this area might appear to be just another aspect of the broader male domination of early modern society. It might even be seen as inevitable, a universal feature of societies which have not undergone feminist revolution. But gendered hierarchy is not inevitable, and it is not

---

[1] J. W. Willis Bund (ed.), *Worcestershire County Records: Calendar of the Quarter Sessions Papers 1591–1643* (Worcester, 1900), 161.

always the same.[2] The predominance of men in the offices and activities of law enforcement was produced and sustained by particular circumstances, ideas, and practices. More importantly, the relationship between manhood and this kind of state power was not constant. Over the course of the early modern period, new forms of office were created with new and different links to masculinity. These changes gave rise to practices of policing which continue to cast long shadows over the present.

This book traces the emergence of a distinctive kind of gendered policing out of older structures of law enforcement and local government, a process which took place in fits and starts over the seventeenth and eighteenth centuries. It does not provide a comprehensive account of the ways in which early modern law enforcement was shaped by gender. The focus is narrower but it is set in a wide analytical frame, drawing inspiration from feminist scholarship on the shifting relationship between gender and the state, especially Carole Pateman's idea of a transition from paternal to fraternal forms of male power.[3] The history of policing is part – a crucial part – of wider histories of state formation. For much of the early modern period, policing was not clearly distinguished from other aspects of local government. Local government itself was not clearly distinguished from the operation of other kinds of social power – the power of landlords over tenants, husbands over wives, parents over children, mistresses or masters over servants. All of these structures combined to form a wide and complex system of patriarchy.[4] The process of differentiating one form of power from another involved increased specialisation and a move away from patriarchy towards fraternal models of male authority. Policing was not the only aspect of government to undergo this transformation, but it was one of the most consequential. The new style of specialised fraternal policing only emerged towards the end of the period – in the late seventeenth and early eighteenth centuries – and was concentrated in London. Its roots, however, stretched back to the

---

[2] Judith M. Bennett, 'Confronting Continuity', *Journal of Women's History* 9.3 (1997); Terry Lovell, 'Thinking Feminism with and against Bourdieu', *Feminist Theory* 1.1 (2000); Pierre Bourdieu, *Masculine Domination* tr. Richard Nice (Cambridge, 2001).

[3] Carole Pateman, *The Sexual Contract* (Cambridge, 1988); Hilda Smith (ed.), *Women Writers and the Early Modern British Political Tradition* (Cambridge, 1998). For an illustration of how these models can be applied to social history, see Karen Harvey, 'Ritual Encounters: Punch Parties and Masculinity in the Eighteenth Century', *Past & Present* 214.1 (2012). For a recent application of the model to the history of policing from the perspective of social and criminological theory, see Francis Dodsworth, *The Security Society: History, Patriarchy, Protection* (London, 2019).

[4] Susan Dwyer Amussen, *An Ordered Society: Gender and Class in Early Modern England* (Oxford, 1988); Antony Fletcher, *Gender, Sex & Subordination in England 1500–1800* (New Haven, 1995). On the use of 'patriarchy' to describe early modern power dynamics, see the essays in 'Forum: Early Modern Patriarchy', *Gender & History* 30.2 (2018).

earlier seventeenth century, while its legacies stretched forward into the decades and centuries that followed, as practices originating in the capital came to characterise policing across much of urban Britain.

The central argument of *Gender and Policing in Early Modern England* can be understood in two ways. First, it provides a new origin story for certain aspects of modern policing in which gender plays a central role. Second, it presents that story as an integral part of a much bigger process: the gendered differentiation of the state from other forms of social authority. This is clearly a more abstract argument and is set out in more detail below. Policing is a practice in which grand abstractions and concrete realities come together, or, sometimes, crash into one another.[5] On the one hand, policing is about government, law, political ideas, and the state. On the other, it is about individuals, bodies, and their experiences of power. Historians of early modern England have been aware of these connections for some time, but they tend to organise their analysis around a different concept: not policing but officeholding.

Policing and Officeholding

The history of early modern policing overlaps extensively with the history of officeholding. The most recognisable law enforcement officers of the period – constables and night watchmen – were part of an officeholding system which covered all aspects of local government. In the absence of a professional police force and large central bureaucracy, many routine activities of government could only be carried out by recruiting large numbers of people to hold office at a local level.[6] Just as constables and night watchmen kept the peace and enforced the law, so churchwardens and overseers of the

---

[5] Jonah Miller, 'The Touch of the State: Stop and Search in England, c.1660–1750', *History Workshop Journal* 87 (2019).

[6] This was not, as is sometimes suggested, a specifically English phenomenon. Government relied on widespread local officeholding across later medieval and early modern Europe: Beat A. Kümin, 'The English Parish in a European Perspective' in Katherine L. French, Gary G. Gibbs, and Beat A. Kümin (eds.), *The Parish in English Life 1400–1600* (Manchester, 1997); Cristina Julian Perez-Alfaro, 'The King's Face on the Territory: Royal Officers, Discourse and Legitimating Practices in Thirteenth- and Fourteenth-Century Castile' in Isabel Alfonso Anton, Hugh Kennedy, and Julio Escalona Monge (eds.), *Building Legitimacy: Political Discourses and Forms of Legitimation in Medieval Societies* (Leiden, 2004); Joachim Eibach, 'Burghers or Town Council: Who Was Responsible for Urban Stability in Early Modern German Towns?', *Urban History* 34.01 (2007); Glenn Burgess, 'Office-Holding, Participation and England's "Monarchical Republic"' in Jan Hartman, Jaap Nieuwstraten, and Michel Reinders (eds.), *Public Offices, Personal Demands: Capability in Governance in the Seventeenth-Century Dutch Republic* (Newcastle-upon-Tyne, 2009); María Ángeles, Martín Romera, and Hannes Ziegler (eds.), *The Officer and the People: Accountability and Authority in Pre-Modern Europe* (Oxford, 2021).

poor raised and distributed poor relief, surveyors of the highways kept roads in good repair, scavengers cleaned the streets, sextons dug graves, and swineherds prevented pigs from damaging private property. The list goes on, from beadles to bailiffs and pinders to parish clerks. The activities of these officers at the level of parish, manor, and ward were supervised and coordinated by a pyramid of official managers operating at city or county level, who also held various kinds of courts. These were sheriffs, mayors, coroners, royal commissioners of one sort or another, and justices of the peace. From the top of this system to the bottom, many tasks were shared between different groups of officers. Officers responsible for a particular aspect of government enforced laws relating to that area. No single set of officers held a monopoly on early modern policing, which can be best understood as a diffuse set of practices embedded in wider structures of local government.

Taken together, this panoply of officeholders comprised the early modern English state. If 'the state' is an abstraction, officers were the physical manifestation of it. Monarchs and chief ministers came and went, parliaments gathered and dispersed, but through interregnums, prorogations, revolutions, and all manner of constitutional crises what remained constant was the presence of thousands of officeholders, doing the business of government at ground level. This is both a way to understand the early modern state historically and a view held by some people at the time. The day after Elizabeth I died in 1603, a Catholic gentleman went to his local parish church and attempted to persuade his neighbours that they should not attend divine service until James VI&I had arrived in England and settled his religious policy. For this, he was summoned to the court of Star Chamber and condemned for committing such a heinous offence 'againste the state'. As the judges informed him, 'there is no *interregnum*, as the ignoraunte dothe suppose'; the state and its laws persisted beyond Elizabeth's death for two reasons. One, familiar to political historians, was that 'the verye instaunte that the breathe was oute of her Ma[jes]tie's bodye, Kinge James was lawfull & rightefull kinge'. The second was that although the crown was temporarily without a head to rest on there were still large numbers of officers carrying out their duties and embodying the state at a local level: 'Justices of peace are determyned' and 'Constables & Coroners, & suche pettie officers, remaine still'.[7] It is with constables and other such petty officers that this book is concerned.

---

[7] Attorney-General v Carew (1603) in William Paley Baildon (ed.), *Les reportes del cases in Camera Stellata, 1593 to 1609: from the Original MS. of John Hawarde* (London, 1894), 163–4. On the disruption of local government during the royal succession of 1603, see Susan Doran, '1603: A Jagged Succession', *Historical Research* 93.261 (2020).

Historians of officeholding have argued that the particular forms of early modern offices indicate particular features of the early modern state. As Michael Braddick put it, 'the state is embodied in offices, and differences between states over time and between places are differences in the forms of office'.[8] To modern eyes, it is the low-level officers of this period who are especially distinctive. Constables, churchwardens, overseers of the poor, and others who kept the wheels of government turning were unsalaried, untrained, part-time amateurs. Many were elected by their communities rather than appointed from above. Most held office for just a year or two, without payment beyond compensation for expenses and the occasional fee, before passing on their duties to a neighbour and returning to their ordinary lives. In fact, they never ceased to live their ordinary lives, serving as officers while simultaneously producing goods, farming land, running shops, or pursuing whatever means of getting a livelihood they happened to have. This system of short-term amateur service meant that significant numbers of people in any given village, town, or city held office at one time or another. As one pamphleteer wrote, 'tis hard to find a Man who has not sometime been call'd to bear Office in his Parish or Borough'.[9] Several historians have suggested that local officeholding was a powerfully participatory form of government, or rather self-government. According to Patrick Collinson and Mark Goldie, whatever the pretensions of English monarchs, the realities of rule bore less resemblance to absolutism than to a kind of 'monarchical republic', or 'self-government at the king's command'.[10] There has been some dispute about exactly what proportion of the population held office: was it one in twenty men per year, one in ten householders, one in four ratepayers, half of all men over the course of a lifetime?[11] Regardless, it is clear that early modern government required the participation of large numbers of officeholding amateurs.

---

[8] Michael J. Braddick, *State Formation in Early Modern England c.1550–1700* (Cambridge, 2000), 21.
[9] *The Claims of the People of England, Essayed. In a Letter from the Country* (London, 1701), 16.
[10] Patrick Collinson, 'The Monarchical Republic of Queen Elizabeth I', *Bulletin of the John Rylands University Library of Manchester* 69 (1987); Mark Goldie, 'The Unacknowledged Republic: Officeholding in Early Modern England' in Tim Harris (ed.), *The Politics of the Excluded, c.1500–1850* (Basingstoke, 2001). These studies represent a more sophisticated revival of an older tradition which presented medieval and early modern local government as proto-democratic: Eleanor Trotter, *Seventeenth Century Life in the Country Parish, with Special Reference to Local Government* (Cambridge, 1919); Albert Beebe White, *Self-Government at the King's Command: A Study in the Beginnings of English Democracy* (London, 1933); Arthur Bryant, *Humanity in Politics* (London, 1937), 86.
[11] Valerie Pearl, *London and the Outbreak of the Puritan Revolution* (Oxford, 1961), Chapter 2; Valerie Pearl, 'Change and Stability in Seventeenth-Century London', *The London Journal* 5.1 (1979), 16;

Historians of law enforcement have reached a similar conclusion by a different route. Their focus has been on the scale of participation in the administration of criminal law, especially at the beginning and end of the legal process: apprehension of suspects and trial by jury. Led by Cynthia Herrup, scholars in this field have emphasised the involvement of people who held no office in pursuing and capturing suspected offenders. Victims and bystanders were often the key (or even the only) participants in this core aspect of law enforcement.[12] As Sir Thomas Smith wrote in his account of the government of Elizabethan England, 'everie man is a seriant to take a theefe'.[13] At the same time, the involvement of juries at various stages of a prosecution – grand juries and trial juries for both Quarter Sessions and Assizes, as well as juries of matrons, manorial juries, and coroner's juries – allowed substantial numbers of people to take part in making decisions about innocence and guilt.[14]

Historians of both policing and officeholding have interpreted this widespread participation in law enforcement and local government as indicative of the nature of the early modern state. A highly participatory state was, in the language of social theory, an 'undifferentiated' state.[15] There was no clear distinction between state and society. The state relied on and was in many ways part of the wider social order. In the case of

---

Jeremy Boulton, *Neighbourhood and Society: A London Suburb in the Seventeenth Century* (Cambridge, 1987), 267–8; James Sharpe, *Early Modern England: A Social History 1550–1760* (2nd edition, London, 1997), 109–10; Goldie, 'The Unacknowledged Republic', 162; Henry French, *The Middle Sort of People in Provincial England 1600–1750* (Oxford, 2007), 120.

[12] Cynthia B. Herrup, *The Common Peace: Participation and the Criminal Law in Seventeenth-Century England* (Cambridge, 1987), 67–92; Cynthia B. Herrup, 'New Shoes and Mutton Pies: Investigative Responses to Theft in Seventeenth-Century East Sussex', *Historical Journal* 27.4 (1984). See also James Sharpe, 'Enforcing the Law in the Seventeenth-Century English Village' in V. A. C. Gatrell, Bruce Lenman, and Geoffrey Parker (eds.), *Crime and the Law: The Social History of Crime in Western Europe since 1500* (London, 1980); Malcolm Gaskill, *Crime and Mentalities in Early Modern England* (Cambridge, 2000); Sharon Howard, 'Investigating Responses to Theft in Early Modern Wales', *Continuity & Change* 19.3 (2004).

[13] Thomas Smith, *De Republica Anglorum: The Maner of Governement or Policie of the Realme of England* (London, 1583), 71.

[14] Herrup, *Common Peace*, 93–164; Thomas A. Green, *Verdict According to Conscience: Perspectives on the English Criminal Trial Jury, 1200–1800* (Chicago, 1985); J. S. Cockburn and Thomas A. Green (eds.), *Twelve Good Men and True: The Criminal Trial Jury in England, 1200–1800* (Princeton, 1988), Chapters 5–10; Brodie Waddell, 'Governing England through the Manor Courts, 1550–1850', *Historical Journal* 55.2 (2012); Matthew Lockwood, *The Conquest of Death: Violence and the Birth of the Modern English State* (New Haven, 2017), 146–96; Jane Bitomsky, 'The Jury of Matrons: Their Role in the Early Modern English Courtroom', *Lilith: A Feminist History Journal* 25.4 (2019).

[15] Gianfranco Poggi, *The State: Its Nature, Development and Prospects* (Stanford, 1990), 20–1. See also Michael Mann, *The Sources of Social Power I: A History of Power from the Beginning to A.D. 1760* (Cambridge, 1986), 1–18; Michael Mann, *The Sources of Social Power II: The Rise of Classes and Nation-States, 1760–1914* (Cambridge, 1993), 44–91.

officeholding, this is presented as the result of a period of dramatic social change. Local officers were simultaneously servants of the crown and of the local community. Sometimes, their loyalties were torn between these two, especially when it came to enforcing laws which did not align with the priorities of their neighbours. Officers found themselves caught between 'two concepts of order', between their duty to uphold the letter of the law and the pressure exerted by the people they lived among.[16] An influential school of social history, led by Keith Wrightson, has argued that the balance of officers' loyalties tilted away from their communities towards the crown over the late sixteenth and early seventeenth centuries. This was part of a broader process in which the 'middling sort of people' got richer and increasingly aligned themselves with the interests of their social superiors and the central government, rather than those of their poorer neighbours.[17] The social status of the middling sort both justified and derived from their participation in law enforcement and other areas of state activity. As Steve Hindle has argued, state power rested on and reinforced social hierarchy.[18]

The intermingling of state power and social power meant that offices were as much social roles as political or legal positions.[19] The authority of an officer was a product of both their personal identity – as a gentleman, yeoman farmer, or master artisan – and their official status. The two were inextricable from each other. To be a justice of the peace was to be a gentleman, and vice versa. To be a constable or churchwarden or overseer of the poor was to belong to the middling sort, and vice versa. It has become commonplace among historians of the early modern period to say that there were no clear distinctions between the official and the personal.[20]

---

[16] Keith Wrightson, 'Two Concepts of Order: Justices, Constables and Jurymen in Seventeenth-Century England' in John Brewer and John Styles (eds.), *An Ungovernable People: The English and Their Law in the Seventeenth and Eighteenth Centuries* (London, 1980); Ethan Shagan, 'The Two Republics: Conflicting Views of Participatory Local Government in Early Tudor England' in John F. McDiarmid (ed.), *The Monarchical Republic of Early Modern England: Essays in Response to Patrick Collinson* (Aldershot, 2007).

[17] Keith Wrightson, 'Aspects of Social Differentiation in Rural England, c. 1580–1660', *The Journal of Peasant Studies* 5.1 (1977); Keith Wrightson, *English Society 1580–1680* (London, 1982), 222–8; Steve Hindle, 'The Political Culture of the Middling Sort in English Rural Communities, c.1550–1700' in Harris (ed.), *The Politics of the Excluded*; French, *The Middle Sort*; Andy Wood, *Faith, Hope and Charity: English Neighbourhoods, 1500–1640* (Cambridge, 2020). For a critique of this argument, see Richard Hoyle, '"Wrightsonian Incorporation" and the Public Rhetoric of Mid-Tudor England', *History* 101.344 (2016).

[18] Steve Hindle, *The State and Social Change, 1550–1640* (Basingstoke, 2000).

[19] Braddick, *State Formation*, 27–37, 77, 82–4. See also Conal Condren, *Argument and Authority in Early Modern England: The Presupposition of Oaths and Offices* (Cambridge, 2006).

[20] Recent examples include: Fiona Williamson, '"A Fured Mutton Wolde Contayne As Much Good Doctrine": Social Politics in the Seventeenth Century Parish' in Fiona Williams (ed.), *Locating Agency: Space, Power and Popular Politics* (Newcastle-upon-Tyne, 2010), 78; Malcolm Gaskill,

Such distinctions are said to be characteristic of a 'modernity' which had not yet arrived, or which was only just beginning to take shape. Anglophone historians tend to be less explicit than others about the theoretical underpinnings of this idea, but there is a clear debt to the sociology of Max Weber.[21] Weber argued that unlike modern 'bureaucratic' officeholding, pre-modern 'patrimonial' officeholding did not distinguish between the office and the person who held it: 'The patrimonial office lacks above all the bureaucratic separation of the "private" and the "official" sphere'.[22] Only modern officeholding regimes, Weber thought, drew distinctions between the official and the personal.

Historians of officeholding and law enforcement are more or less in agreement that most aspects of early modern government were closer to the patrimonial than the bureaucratic. They differ, however, in their account of how, when, and where 'differentiation' – the separation of the official from the personal or social – began to take place. Historians of policing tend to locate the early stages of differentiation in the decades either side of 1700, specifically in London. Here, as John Beattie showed, the old system of law enforcement by constables and night watchmen who were unpaid amateurs, doing their duty for a short time before passing the burden to a neighbour, began to break down. A range of factors conspired to introduce increasingly long-term, specialised, and paid forms of officeholding into the capital's structures of law enforcement. Constables and watchmen began to serve for longer periods, received payment for their work, and were increasingly seen as specialists with a more important role in catching suspected offenders than anyone else.[23]

'Little Commonwealths II: Communities' in Keith Wrightson (ed.), *A Social History of England 1500–1750* (Cambridge, 2017), 92; Wood, *Faith, Hope and Charity*, 212, 218, 223.

[21] Robert Frost, 'Early Modern State-Building, The Scandinavian *Machstaat*, and the Shortcomings of Anglo-Saxon Scholarship', *Journal of Early Modern History* 7.1 (2003). For direct applications of Weber's models to early modern continental Europe, see Roland Axtmann, 'The Formation of the Modern State: A Reconstruction of Max Weber's Arguments', *History of Political Thought* 11.2 (1990); Julia Adams, *The Familial State: Ruling Families and Merchant Capitalism in Early Modern Europe* (Ithaca, 2005); Manon van der Heijden, *Civic Duty: Public Services in the Early Modern Low Countries* (Newcastle-upon-Tyne, 2012). Anglophone medievalists have engaged with Weber more directly than their early modernist colleagues, especially David D'Avray, *Rationalities in History: A Weberian Essay in Comparison* (Cambridge, 2010).

[22] Max Weber, *Economy and Society: An Outline of Interpretive Sociology* ed. Guenther Roth and Claus Wittich (Berkeley, 1978), 1028. Weber saw bureaucratic and patrimonial forms of office as ideal types rather than historical realities, but he explicitly linked bureaucracy with modernity, writing that 'The bureaucratic structure is everywhere a late product of historical development. The further back we trace our steps, the more typical is the absence of bureaucracy and of officialdom in general': *Economy and Society*, 1002.

[23] J. M. Beattie, *Policing and Punishment in London, 1660–1750: Urban Crime and the Limits of Terror* (Oxford, 2001), 114–256; Faramerz Dabhoiwala, 'Sex and Societies for Moral Reform, 1688–1800',

Historians of officeholding, by contrast, have presented the late seventeenth and early eighteenth centuries as a period of consolidation rather than change. The middling sort continued to dominate local offices across rural England (towns and cities rarely feature in these accounts) so state power and social authority continued to go hand in hand.[24] Such change as there was had taken place earlier in the seventeenth century. According to Michael Braddick, who has engaged directly with Weber's analytical framework, English government was 'still predominantly patrimonial' in 1700, but the civil wars of the 1640s and the fiscal demands of continental warfare in the 1690s had prompted the creation of new kinds of officers to collect new kinds of taxation. Officers of the new excise tax, in particular, bore a closer resemblance to Weberian bureaucrats than any of their predecessors had done. Excisemen were trained, salaried, full-time, and wielded a form of authority which 'depended on knowledge, precision and the application of impersonal norms, rather than on a broadly conceived "natural" and personal authority'.[25] In a recent study of corruption in the higher offices of politics and administration, Mark Knights also found a key turning point in the mid-seventeenth century. In 1600, he writes, 'the distinction between public and private roles was blurred'. This began to change in the 1640s with 'a conceptual and discursive shift' in which the notion of 'fiduciary "trust"' became routinely applied to office, starting with the monarch and rapidly becoming applicable more broadly'. Officers defined as trustees, whether they were monarchs or ministers or members of parliament, drew their authority from whoever or whatever entrusted them with power, not from their own personal status. Describing officers as trustees placed them

---

Journal of British Studies 46.2 (2007); Tim Hitchcock and Robert Shoemaker, *London Lives: Poverty, Crime and the Making of a Modern City, 1690–1800* (Cambridge, 2015), 29, 34–42, 56–60, 107–21. David Lemmings argues that this development was symptomatic of a broader decline of participation in legal processes: *Law and Government in England during the Long Eighteenth Century: From Consent to Command* (Basingstoke, 2011).

[24] Joan Kent, 'The Centre and the Localities: State Formation and Parish Government in England, circa 1640–1740', *The Historical Journal* 38.2 (1995); Steve Hindle, 'Power, Poor Relief, and Social Relations in Holland Fen, c.1600–1800', *The Historical Journal* 41.1 (1998); Joan Kent, 'The Rural "Middling Sort" in Early Modern England, circa 1640–1740: Some Economic, Political and Socio-Cultural Characteristics', *Rural History* 10.1 (1999); Steve Hindle, 'The Growth of Social Stability in Restoration England', *The European Legacy* 5.4 (2000); Naomi Tadmor, 'The Settlement of the Poor and the Rise of the Form in England, c.1662–1780', *Past & Present* 236.1 (2017).

[25] Michael J. Braddick, 'The Early Modern English State and the Question of Differentiation, from 1550–1700', *Comparative Studies in Society and History* 38.1 (1996), 109; Braddick, *State Formation*, 261. The significance of the Excise is laid out in greater detail in John Brewer, *The Sinews of Power: War, Money and the English State, 1688–1783* (New York, 1989) and in Michael J. Braddick, *Parliamentary Taxation in Seventeenth-Century England* (Woodbridge, 1994), 168–230.

in a 'principal-agent relationship'. Officers became agents who acted on behalf of principals like the crown, the people, or the state. It was these principals which provided the source of their authority.[26]

This book bridges the gap between histories of officeholding and law enforcement on this point. It argues that the changes in London's policing in the late seventeenth and early eighteenth centuries were facilitated by changes which took place earlier in the seventeenth century, which had much in common with the developments described by Braddick and Knights. The history presented here, however, differs from their work in its chronology, its cast of characters, and its conceptual framing. It unfolds at an uneven pace, beginning in the early 1600s, accelerating with the civil wars, and reaching a climax in the later seventeenth and early eighteenth centuries. It is less concerned with monarchs and politicians than with constables and other low-level officeholders. It focuses on changes in law and legal practice more than high politics or administration, though both of these do feature. Above all, this book argues that changes in officeholding, law enforcement, and the early modern state were all deeply entwined with gender. Only by paying attention to gender can we properly understand how new practices of policing emerged from the old officeholding system and what it was that made them so distinctive. The process traced by this book forms a crucial chapter in the much longer history of gendered state power.

Arguments

Part I sets out the relationship between local officeholding and the central institution of gendered power in early modern society: the household. Most officeholders were also householders. This was the norm throughout the early modern period, though as subsequent parts of the book show, it was a norm from which particular groups of officers increasingly diverged. The domination of local offices by heads of household was a result of the lack of distinction between official and personal or social identity. According to much contemporary political thought, the only people qualified to wield official power were those who already governed others, or at least were not themselves governed by anybody else. 'Independence' was the key quality required of an officer. A person who depended on someone else for their position, livelihood, or general well-being could not make decisions

---

[26] Mark Knights, *Trust and Distrust: Corruption in Office in Britain and Its Empire, 1600–1850* (Oxford, 2021), 416, 108–9.

independently; they were always likely to defer to the wishes of those they depended upon. Heads of household, in theory, were independent of all such influence. They could make decisions for themselves alone, a personal attribute which rendered them suitable to exercise official power.

In practice, restricting officeholding to the 'independent' meant that almost all officers were middle-aged, married men of the middling sort – patriarchs. Single men, poorer men, married women, young people, and servants were deemed too dependent on their masters, husbands, or fathers to qualify. In this respect, officers fit neatly into what Braddick, in a discussion of early modern social policy and criminal justice, called 'the patriarchal state'.[27] On the other hand, householder status was not entirely monopolised by men. Single women who headed their own households held office in small numbers throughout the period. Their claim to competence was the same as that of their male counterparts: personal status as governors in their own homes provided the independence necessary for office. This intertwining of the personal and the official also underlay another aspect of the office-household connection. Offices were attached to official households almost as much as they were to officeholders themselves. Subordinate members of those households – children, servants, apprentices, and above all male officers' wives – sometimes participated in official business. As auxiliaries to their officeholding fathers, masters, or husbands, they helped to enforce the law, raise taxes, convey orders, distribute poor relief, and generally carried out many of the routine tasks of local government. As in many patriarchal power structures, the blurring of boundaries between public and private, the official and the personal, granted patriarchs' subordinates some degree of access to authority.

From the early seventeenth century, certain groups of offices began to break out of this mould. Part II uncovers this process and its consequences for the relationship between official and male power, especially in the offices of law enforcement. There had always been alternative ways of thinking about office. The merging of social status and official position at the centre of the householder model could be challenged, power could be separated from the person who wielded it, officers could be described as mere appendages of a higher authority which had nothing to do with their own identity. These were not new ideas, but in the reign of James VI&I they began to be given real legal force. In response to the social and economic crisis of the 1590s, successive parliaments had passed an array of new laws on welfare, crime, commerce, and personal behaviour. These laws gave

---

[27] Braddick, *State Formation*, 101–75.

local officeholders considerable discretionary powers of enforcement, prompting elite fears about the misuse of those powers and about the possibility of resistance against them. Legal historians have recently shown how, to address these issues, senior lawyers and judges found new ways to supervise and restrain officers' activities. This was only one side of the coin, however, as judges and parliamentarians also sought to strengthen officers' position against challenges and opposition. These efforts were based on a view of official authority as something separate from individual officeholders. New statutes gave special legal protection to officers when they 'acted by authority' rather than for themselves. Judges in the central law courts drew new distinctions between officers on the basis of whether or not they required any particular personal qualities. 'Judicial' officers had to exercise discretion, and as such had to possess the 'independence' deemed necessary for good decision-making. 'Ministerial' officers, on the other hand, did not need to exercise discretion and so did not require any particular qualities. Rather than making their own decisions, ministerial officers carried out orders based on the decisions of their superiors. Their personal identities and characteristics were irrelevant; they were mere agents of the law, guided and authorised by powers greater than themselves.

The new law of office simultaneously strengthened and restricted officers' authority. So long as they acted as authorised, they received powerful legal protection. Those who strayed beyond their authorisation, however, received no such protection and were generally treated as rogue individuals, not officers at all. Unauthorised arrests, forced entries, or confiscations could not be attributed to higher powers; instead, they were treated as civil wrongs or even crimes. The potential for officers to become offenders dramatically increased during the civil wars. Contests over the location of sovereignty played out in confrontations between officers and people who refused to accept the source of their authority, branding them as law-breakers rather than law enforcers. This was an intensified version of a more general problem: without uniforms, and given the frequent rotation of individuals into and out of office, how could officers show that they were acting as officers, not as ordinary people? In everyday interactions with others, officers had to conjure the authority of greater powers using a specific set of props and performances. They identified themselves and claimed authority to act as agents of the law by brandishing wooden staves and invoking the monarch's name. These actions had important legal consequences. Once officers had conjured authority in this way, they could justify using force to execute their duties, and any use of force against them was deemed especially culpable. Without such performances, any use of force by officers would be unauthorised, no different to violence carried out by anyone else. Here, as more broadly under the new law of office, authority depended on separating official actions from the individual who carried them out.

Distinguishing the personal from the official changed the relationship between office and gender. In the mid-seventeenth century, some lawyers attempted (unsuccessfully) to exclude the small number of female officeholders by insisting that no woman, regardless of her status as a head of household, should be permitted to serve. Office, they argued, was linked to manhood, not the household. Another mid-seventeenth century development accomplished this breach with the household far more effectively. Officers of the Excise, the new tax system created during the civil wars, represented a break from past in terms of gender as well as in the proto-bureaucratic features emphasised by other scholars. Excisemen were entirely detached from ordinary households. Unlike the established patriarchs who continued to hold most low-level offices, they were recruited as single young men and moved from place to place to prevent them from becoming embedded in local communities. If they married and had children – neither of which were encouraged by this peripatetic lifestyle – their family members were absolutely prohibited from taking part in their official duties. Like ministerial officers, excisemen were described as limbs of a greater body, with no authority in themselves. The Excise itself was described by Andrew Marvell as a 'Monster' with 'A thousand Hands… and thousand Eyes'.[28]

Officers who served as the monster's hands and eyes, and who were paid a salary for that service, could not claim to be independent in the manner of the traditional householding officeholder. Nor could they claim the authority of patriarchal manhood. Instead, they turned to each other for masculine affirmation, developing a fraternal official culture focused on homosociability, alcohol, misogyny, and violence. Several historians have already noted this tendency among excisemen, but none have spotted the parallel development taking place among another group of officers: London constables and night watchmen. Constables were among the first officers to be defined as ministerial in the early seventeenth century, meaning no special qualities – like being head of a household – were required to hold the office. Parishes and wards still tended to choose householders to serve as constables, but as ministerial officers they were

---

[28] Andrew Marvell, 'Last Instructions to a Painter' in H. M. Margoliouth and Pierre Legouis (eds.), *The Poems and Letters of Andrew Marvell, vol. 1: Poems* (Oxford, 1971), 150.

able to appoint deputies to carry out their duties for them. At first, few elected constables chose this option. It was only in the later seventeenth century, in towns and cities fractured by social and religious divisions, that the significance of permitting deputisation became clear. In London, a growing proportion of those elected as constables hired deputies. These were often unmarried younger men with no claims to independence. Like excisemen, they turned to each other for social validation, socialising, drinking, patrolling the streets, and fighting together as 'brother officers'. The history of London's officers of law enforcement illustrates the transition described by Carole Pateman and others from 'paternal' to 'fraternal' forms of male power.[29]

Part III shows how this shift in the practice of officeholding shaped policing in the capital. As outlined above, accounts of early modern policing, in London and elsewhere, have emphasised the extent to which the detection, pursuit, and arrest of suspects were carried out by victims and bystanders rather than officers. Law enforcement was a matter of popular participation, not official control. This is undoubtedly true, but a new dataset and a closer examination of the role of officers reframe the picture in several ways. First, participation was circumscribed by gender. Making arrests was thought to be men's work, and the vast majority of arrests were made by men, officers or otherwise. Second, different patterns of arrest for different categories of crime mean that the scale of officers' involvement in policing has been considerably underestimated. As Robert Shoemaker and others have shown, officers played a more prominent role in the policing of misdemeanours than in the policing of felonies, which has dominated most accounts of law enforcement despite accounting for a smaller proportion of arrests and prosecutions.[30] Moreover, the rise of deputisation and the culture of official fraternity in London coincided with a substantial increase in the proportion of arrests made by officers. At the same time, constables and their colleagues acquired greater powers to make arrests on the basis of suspicion. These 'ministerial' officers may have been portrayed by lawyers as lowly instruments for the performance of tasks delegated to them by others, but in reality they possessed extensive discretionary leeway in deciding who counted as a suspect. This brought their individual identities to the fore, as officers and as men. The suspicions of London's

---

[29] See above, note 3.
[30] Robert B. Shoemaker, *Prosecution and Punishment: Petty Crime and the Law in London and Rural Middlesex, c.1660–1725* (Cambridge, 1991); Faramerz Dabhoiwala, 'Summary Justice in Early Modern London', *English Historical Review* 121.492 (2006).

fraternities of law enforcers often came to rest on women, particularly poorer women, who they frequently arrested on ill-defined charges of vagrancy, night-walking, or suspected theft.

The gendered dynamics which influenced patterns of arrest also shaped another key policing action: searches. Historians of early modern law enforcement have noted the importance of searches for evidence of crime but have not previously studied them in detail. The law of searching primarily concerned houses, which were powerfully protected. House searches usually required the presence of officers with specific warrants, pitting the authority of ministerial officers against the well-established rights of householders to defend the domestic threshold. People who did not have houses of their own were much more vulnerable to searches of lodgings, boxes, and other possessions, by officers or by anyone else. Law had little to say about these searches, and even less to say about searches of people themselves. Searches of clothes and bodies took place in a legal vacuum, governed only by cultural norms which protected high status men from the indignity of being searched while leaving the poor entirely open to such intrusion. The same officers of law enforcement who arrested London women on suspicion of various crimes often searched them for evidence of those crimes, restrained only by a (sporadic) sense of what might exceed the bounds of modesty. Often, these searches were highly invasive, especially when conducted by groups of male officers. This book began with the story of Margaret Willshere's prank and its lessons about the maleness of official authority. It ends with the much darker experience of another woman, Margaret Webb, who was searched by three officers in a London watch-house in the early eighteenth century. This search was violent, extraordinarily intrusive to a modern eye, and unlike any of the recorded searches of men. It was a moment in which the abstract power of the state became tangible, embodied by male officers' hands on a woman's body.

The tales of these two Margarets were separated by a century in which a new kind of policing gradually emerged from the old system of officeholding, contributing to wider changes in the relationship between gender and state power. Those changes were piecemeal but profound. Patriarchs continued to predominate in many offices, especially outside large towns and cities. The ties that bound office and household were not entirely undone. But they did begin to loosen and fray, and in some cases were severed altogether. Freeing office from the household was the first in a series of steps which, taken together, led to the rise of highly gendered and specialised practices of policing. The conclusion follows these practices forward in time through the spread of fraternal forms of law enforcement, the continued rise of a ministerial notion of officeholding, and the persistence of gendered uses of discretionary power. From this perspective, the history of policing can be seen as a central thread in the ongoing entanglement between masculinity and the everyday exercise of state authority.

Sources

The officeholders who carried out law enforcement and other aspects of local government are a ubiquitous presence in early modern archives. They were the recipients of enormous numbers of orders, summons, warrants, and writs. The fiscal aspects of their activities were recorded, audited, and approved (or disapproved) in innumerable account books. Their signatures appear at the bottom of every page of vestry minutes, every manorial court roll, every report of offences to the courts. Those who organised and supervised their activities – magistrates, tax commissioners, city aldermen – left records of payment and punishment, promotion and demotion, exemption and discharge. These administrative documents can be used to establish who officers were, their status, and their place in the wider machinery of government. They offer an invaluable counterpart (and sometimes a corrective) to the accounts of officeholding left by contemporary writers. They do not, however, provide much evidence of officers in action. Orders are carried out, warrants are served, money is collected and distributed, but we rarely find details of *how* officers went about their business or how their activities were understood and experienced by others.

What is missing in administrative records is supplied by the records of law. This book does make extensive use of administrative evidence, especially in Parts I and II, but its core arguments are based on several types of legal sources. These can be roughly grouped into four categories: handbooks or treatises, lawyers' reports of cases heard in the central courts, published Old Bailey trial reports, and the papers of Quarter Sessions courts. Each of these categories brings its own challenges and possibilities. Together, they can be used to reconstruct officers' everyday activities, as well as the legal framework which shaped those activities and how they were understood.

Legal treatises and handbooks for officeholding, which proliferated rapidly over the course of the early modern period, were clearly prescriptive rather than descriptive.[31] From elaborate canonical statements of common

---

[31] Helen L. Hull, '"Lowe and Lay Ministers of the Peace": The Proliferation of Officeholding Manuals in Early Modern England' in Christopher Cobb (ed.), *Renaissance Papers 2009* (Martlesham, 2010).

law principles by judges like Edward Coke and Matthew Hale to obscure and ephemeral pamphlets like Vincent Prince's *Constables Calendar* – an almanack with a brief list of constables' powers and duties at the end – these texts set out the rules of the game for officers in their dealings with other people.[32] The kind of prescription on offer is itself important evidence. Early guides to officeholding, like William Lambarde's *Dueties of Constables*, claimed they would help 'well disposed men' to 'better behave themselves' in office.[33] This remained the stated aim of many handbooks for officers over the following 200 years, but from the mid-seventeenth century onwards authors advertised another, more specific benefit to be derived from their works. The genre had always been a legal one: most of the writers were lawyers or magistrates and many texts were largely composed of digested statute and common law. In the century after the civil wars, however, authors stated explicitly that their books were designed to ensure officers knew the nature and limits of their legal powers. There was much talk of what was or was not 'safe' for an officer to do, 'what they ought legally to do' and 'what they ought to avoid, as not warrantable'.[34] One book was described as 'a Pilot to steer him in his right course, whereby he may avoid those Rocks and Sands of Over-doing and Under-doing'. Others warned officers about 'low sollicitors' who would pounce on any 'Irregularity' in their conduct.[35] This lengthening shadow of litigation in guides to officeholding reflected the spread of a particularly legalistic way of thinking about office, which is one of the central themes of Chapter 2.

Law provided a common framework for official action in cities, towns, and villages across the country. Guides to office were published in London, Oxford, or Cambridge, but they discussed situations that might arise 'in the Village' and surviving copies bear the inscriptions of

---

[32] Vincent Prince, *The Constables Calendar* (London, 1660). Unlike many other texts in this genre, Prince's work does not appear to have been reprinted, possibly because it was published just before the collapse of the republican regime which rendered it almost immediately out of date.

[33] William Lambarde, *The Dueties of Constables* (London, 1582), 1. This text was reprinted in 1583, 1584, 1587, 1591, and 1594. An enlarged edition was published in 1599 and reprinted in 1601, 1602, 1604, 1605, 1610, 1614, 1619, 1624, 1626, 1631, 1633, and 1640. It was a standard point of reference (and plagiarism) for many subsequent guides to officeholding.

[34] William Sheppard, *The Offices of Constables* (London, 1650), A4; George Meriton, *A Guide for Constables* (London, 1669), 106; R. Turner, *Duty and Office of a High Constable* (London, 1671), A2v-A3v; Giles Jacob, *The Compleat Parish-Officer* (London, 1718), A4v; P.S., *A Help to Magistrates, and Ministers of Justice: Also a Guide to Parish and Ward-Officers* (London, 1721), A2v.

[35] Turner, *Duty and Office*, A2v; Saunders Welch, *Observations of the Office of Constable* (London, 1754), A3; John Fielding, 'A Treatise on the Office of Constable' in *Extracts from Such of the Penal Laws, as Particularly Relate to the Peace and Good Order of the Metropolis* (London, 1761), 245–6.

owners from elsewhere.[36] The same was supposed to be true of cases heard in the central courts and recorded by lawyers and judges as collections of precedent.[37] In theory, rulings handed down in the Westminster courts of King's Bench, Common Pleas, and the Exchequer radiated outward to officers all over England. The two principal vehicles for this transmission were handbooks for officeholding (along with other legal treatises) and the lower courts. Handbooks conveyed the latest developments in common law with variable reliability. Many authors claimed to have written 'the most Compleat of any Work of this Nature', comprehensively covering the most recent statutes and judicial rulings. They criticised rival publications for being out of date, warning readers against 'blind Guides to lead them into the by-paths and crooked Meanders of many Errors'.[38] In reality, limited access to law reports – most existed only as manuscripts or reached print long after they were first compiled – and extensive plagiarism meant the genre often adapted slowly to new developments, though frequent revision of the most widely read handbooks ensured reasonable accuracy. The impact of central court judgments was equally variable in the lower courts. As we shall see, some rulings were highly effective in reshaping the legal treatment of officers and the people who encountered them; others were simply ignored.

Officers whose actions were discussed in the central courts had often behaved in unusual ways or found themselves in novel situations, raising questions not previously settled by statute or common law. Evidence of more ordinary official activity can be found in the final two categories of legal records used in this book: Old Bailey trial reports and Quarter Sessions papers. The *Proceedings of the Old Bailey* were published eight times a year from the 1670s onward, comprising reports of trials which gradually expanded from brief summaries into detailed accounts complete with verbatim transcripts of testimony. Old Bailey trial reporters were selective, concentrating on the most sensational aspects of a case and omitting procedural information of less interest to a public audience, but comparison with other sources suggests the trial reports were generally accurate if not comprehensive.[39]

---

[36] Sheppard, *Offices of Constables*, E3v. For example, the British Library copy of John Layer's *The Office and Dutie of Constables* (Cambridge, 1641) is inscribed: 'Christopher White his Book Bought at Coulchest[er] at price 0.0.8' (BL, RB.23.a.29082).

[37] On early modern law reports, see John Baker, 'Law Reporting in England 1550–1650', *International Journal of Legal Information* 45.3 (2017).

[38] *A New Guide for Constables, Headboroughs, Tything-Men, Church-Wardens* (London, 1692), A1; Meriton, *Guide for Constables*, A2–3.

[39] John H. Langbein, 'The Criminal Trial before the Lawyers', *University of Chicago Law Review* 45.2 (1978), 267–72; John H. Langbein, 'Shaping the Eighteenth-Century Criminal Trial: A View from

The same cannot be said of the most useful material left by Quarter Sessions: depositions. These were drawn up on the basis of notes taken by magistrates who interviewed witnesses, prosecutors, and defendants in the early stages of criminal procedure. Both deponents and the magistrates (or their clerks) who drew up their depositions had an interest in selective presentation of the facts, with at least one eye on what might shape the outcome of a subsequent trial. Depositions were carefully crafted arguments in narrative form, not straightforward descriptions of events.[40] Nonetheless, as recent scholarship on the history of women's work has shown, these sources frequently contain incidental details, not important enough to be worth distorting, which offer evidence of practices which might otherwise have gone unrecorded.[41] The activities of officers may have been especially likely to be mentioned in this way, their involvement in policing and other aspects of government taken as a given. This book draws together many such passing references to official activity in Quarter Sessions depositions, principally from Middlesex, Kent, and Norwich in the seventeenth and early eighteenth centuries.[42] These were among the most densely populated and intensely governed parts of the country, with high ratios of officers and magistrates per head of population.[43] Some conclusions drawn from these areas may not hold for areas where the nearest officer was considerably further away. Nonetheless, throughout Parts I and II, depositions from these three jurisdictions provide a means of assessing the everyday influence of pronouncements on officeholding by judges and handbook writers. In turn, those prescriptive statements supply

---

the Ryder Sources', *University of Chicago Law Review* 50.1 (1983); Robert B. Shoemaker, 'The Old Bailey Proceedings and the Representation of Crime and Criminal Justice in Eighteenth-Century London', *Journal of British Studies* 47 (2008).

[40] Natalie Zemon Davis, *Fiction in the Archives: Pardon Tales and Their Tellers in Sixteenth-Century France* (Stanford, 1990); Malcolm Gaskill, 'Reporting Murder: Fiction in the Archives in Early Modern England', *Social History* 23.1 (1998); Frances E. Dolan, *True Relations: Reading, Literature, and Evidence in Seventeenth-Century England* (Philadelphia, 2013), Chapter 4.

[41] Sheilagh Ogilvie, *A Bitter Living: Women, Markets, and Social Capital in Early Modern Germany* (Oxford, 2003); Alexandra Shepard, 'Crediting Women in the Early Modern English Economy', *History Workshop Journal* 79.1 (2015); Maria Ågren (ed.), *Making a Living, Making a Difference: Gender and Work in Early Modern European Society* (Oxford, 2016); Jane Whittle and Mark Hailwood, 'The Gender Division of Labour in Early Modern England', *Economic History Review* 73.1 (2020).

[42] The Norwich Mayor's Court was one of a number of borough courts which acted as both Quarter Sessions and Court Leet. The depositions surviving in its files relate to the Quarter Sessions side of the court's business.

[43] Middlesex and Kent had higher numbers of magistrates per person than any other county: Landau, *Justices of the Peace*, 299. Norwich (like London) was divided into messily overlapping parishes and wards, all of which had their own officers, as did the various courts which exercised jurisdiction over them: Fiona Williamson, *Social Relations and Urban Space: Norwich, 1600–1700* (Woodbridge, 2014).

a legal framework through which the actions described in depositions can be understood.

Much the same method can be used to extract relevant information from the Old Bailey *Proceedings*. The sheer volume of these trial reports, combined with their digitisation, makes it possible to locate a substantial number of incidental details about official activity. Part III combines these details with comparable material from Middlesex Quarter Sessions to produce a statistical analysis of officers' role in law enforcement in and around London in the late seventeenth and early eighteenth centuries. It was at that time, in that place, that a new relationship between gender and policing took shape.

PART I
Patriarchy

CHAPTER I

Office and Household

Life in early modern England revolved around households. They were the basic units of economic, social, and religious activity, the primary sites of education and socialisation.[1] They were also central to political thought. Parliamentarians and royalists, and later Whigs and Tories, disagreed over exactly how the household was related to the state – was each an analogy for the other, or was the state formed by a gathering of households? – but few disputed its fundamental importance.[2] Across the political spectrum, almost everyone subscribed to one version or another of 'the axiom of householder-citizenship', according to which government was an activity reserved for heads of household.[3]

There were various explanations for this. The simplest was that God had given power to heads of household to rule in His name. More complex, and more important here, was the explanation resting on the principle of 'independence'. Only independent people could be entrusted with decision-making, the argument went, because they alone could act without regard to the wishes of anyone else. Those who depended on others – economically, socially, politically – would simply say and do as

---

[1] Lena Cowen Orlin, *Private Matters and Public Culture in Post-Reformation England* (Ithaca, 1994); Keith Wrightson, *Earthly Necessities: Economic Lives in Early Modern Britain* (New Haven, 2000), 27–68; Karen Harvey, *The Little Republic: Masculinity and Domestic Authority in Eighteenth-Century Britain* (Oxford, 2012); Laura Gowing, *Gender Relations in Early Modern England* (Harlow, 2012), 29–50; Brodie Waddell, *God, Duty and Community in English Economic Life, 1660–1720* (Woodbridge, 2012), 85–148.

[2] Gordon J. Schochet, *Patriarchalism in Political Thought* (Oxford, 1975); Constance Jordan, 'The Household and the State: Transformations in the Representation of an Analogy from Aristotle to James I', *Modern Language Quarterly* 54.3 (1993); Rachel Weil, *Political Passions: Gender, the Family and Political Argument in England 1680–1714* (Manchester, 1999); Rachel Weil, 'The Family in the Exclusion Crisis: Locke versus Filmer Revisited' in Alan Houston and Steve Pincus (eds.), *A Nation Transformed: England after the Restoration* (Cambridge, 2001); Ann Hughes, *Gender and the English Revolution* (London, 2012).

[3] Mark Goldie, 'The English System of Liberty' in Mark Goldie and Robert Wokler (eds.), *The Cambridge History of Eighteenth-Century Political Thought* (Cambridge, 2006), 69. For a recent reassessment of this idea, see Anna Becker, *Gendering the Renaissance Commonwealth* (Cambridge, 2020).

they were told. This idea applied as much to everyday life as to rarefied debates in political theory. People who appeared to be economically independent were seen as honest and trustworthy; people who relied on relatives, employers, friends, or anyone else for their livelihood were seen as the opposite. According to this line of thinking, the only legitimate political actors were heads of household. Householders were independent in the sense that they were not – or were not supposed to be – subject to the domestic authority of anyone else. By contrast, wives, children, servants, and any other subordinate members of a household were deemed dependent on the will and approval of the head. This made them incapable of independent decision-making and, by extension, unfit for participation in government.[4]

In keeping with this logic, early modern officeholding was closely connected to the idea of the independent householder. This chapter shows how that connection worked. The legal requirements for officeholding made it almost inevitable that those chosen to serve would be 'independent' heads of household. Most officers were husbands and fathers of the middling sort, archetypal early modern patriarchs. It is worth noting that this made officeholding highly exclusive. Most people in this period were not heads of household. Marriage, lawful parenthood, and independent residence required considerable economic resources, which were much more easily marshalled by the rich and the middling sort than by the poor.[5] Across the country, especially in urban areas, large segments of the population (both women and men) were single at any given time, living as lodgers, servants, or apprentices in other people's households, or in less conventional house-sharing arrangements with unmarried friends and relations.[6] Officeholding was the duty and privilege of a middling householder minority.

---

[4] Matthew McCormack, *The Independent Man: Citizenship and Gender Politics in Georgian England* (Manchester, 2005); Alexandra Shepard, *Accounting for Oneself: Worth, Status, and the Social Order in Early Modern England* (Oxford, 2015), chapter 2. Carole Pateman highlighted the gendered nature of 'independent' participation in political life in 'The Patriarchal Welfare State: Women and Democracy' in Amy Gutman (ed.), *Democracy and the Welfare State* (Princeton, 1988).

[5] Laura Gowing, *Common Bodies: Women, Touch and Power in Seventeenth-Century England* (New Haven, 2003), 177–203; Patricia Crawford, *Parents of Poor Children in England, 1580–1800* (Oxford, 2010); Alexandra Shepard, 'Brokering Fatherhood: Illegitimacy and Paternal Rights and Responsibilities in Early Modern England' in Steve Hindle, Alexandra Shepard, and John Walter (eds.), *Remaking English Society: Social Relations and Social Change in Early Modern England* (Woodbridge, 2013).

[6] Amy M. Froide, *Never Married: Singlewomen in Early Modern England* (Oxford, 2005); Vanessa Harding, 'Families and Housing in Seventeenth-Century London', *Parergon* 24.3 (2007); Vanessa Harding et al., *People in Place: Families, Households and Housing in Early Modern London* (London, 2008); Mark Merry and Philip Baker, '"For the house her selfe and one servant": Family and Household in Late Seventeenth-Century London', *The London Journal* 34.3 (2009).

Through its connection to the household, officeholding was gendered in a more complex way than historians have acknowledged. Some studies ignore gender altogether, or state that officeholding was the preserve of adult men and leave it at that. This fails to account for the centrality of patriarchy to officeholding and of officeholding to patriarchy. As patriarchs, officers were expected to be sober and self-controlled, and to discipline those who could not control themselves. Self-government and the government of others blended official duties with the patriarch's social role. It also brought them into conflict with other men who asserted their own manhood by other means, such as drinking, gambling, sexual predation, and unlawful violence. In this way, local government and law enforcement became arenas of competition between alternate forms of masculinity.[7]

The association between office and household also provided some opportunities for participation in government by non-patriarchs. Officers' children, servants, apprentices, and above all male officers' wives were involved in carrying out official duties, so that in some ways, offices were held by households as much as they were held by individual people. Women who headed their own households could sometimes hold office themselves. Historians of women's involvement in politics have highlighted examples of female officers alongside queens and powerful aristocrats.[8] This has served to emphasise that officeholders were not exclusively male, but also tends to miss the particular ways in which officeholding was shaped by its links to householding.[9] Households empowered some women and disempowered others. Feminist historians in the early twentieth century described the pre-modern household as an institution of what

---

[7] Key works on early modern masculinities include: Elizabeth Foyster, *Manhood in Early Modern England: Honour, Sex and Marriage* (London, 1999); Tim Hitchcock and Michèle Cohen (eds.), *English Masculinities 1660–1800* (London, 1999); Alexandra Shepard, *Meanings of Manhood in Early Modern England* (Oxford, 2003); Karen Harvey, *The Little Republic: Masculinity and Domestic Authority in Eighteenth-Century Britain* (Oxford, 2012); Henry French and Mark Rothery, *Man's Estate: Landed Gentry Masculinities, c.1660–c.1900* (Oxford, 2012).

[8] For example: Karl von den Steinen, 'The Discovery of Women in Eighteenth-Century Political Life' in Barbara Kanner (ed.), *The Women of England: From Anglo-Saxon Times to the Present: Interpretive Bibliographical Essays* (London, 1980); Rosemary Sweet, 'Women and Civic Life in Eighteenth-Century England' in Rosemary Sweet and Penelope Lane (eds.), *Women and Urban Life in Eighteenth-Century England: 'On the Town'* (Aldershot, 2003); Amanda L. Capern, *The Historical Study of Women: England 1500–1700* (Basingstoke, 2008), 150–1.

[9] It remains surprisingly common for authors surveying the political lives of early modern women to declare that only queens held any official position: Merry E. Wiesner, *Women and Gender in Early Modern Europe* (Cambridge, 2000), 288; Carole Levin and Alicia Meyer, 'Women and Political Power in Early Modern Europe' in Allyson M. Poska, Jane Couchman, and Katherine A. McIver (eds.), *The Ashgate Research Companion to Women and Gender in Early Modern Europe* (Farnham, 2013), 342.

Eileen Power called 'rough and ready equality' between married people, offering opportunities for women which industrialisation had subsequently removed.[10] Beginning in the 1980s, their successors argued that early modern households were, by contrast, highly authoritarian and repressive of women; the household was a mechanism for social control over all non-patriarchs.[11] More recently, scholars have moved back towards an emphasis on married women's activities and their authority as partners (albeit subordinate partners) in the running of the household.[12] Like householding, officeholding provided circumscribed opportunities for some women: those who were married to middling men and those who were middling heads of household in their own right. This was characteristic of an officeholding regime built on the idea of the independent householder.

Idoneus Homo: The Independent Ideal

The most important statement about who could hold local offices in this period was made by judges in a case heard at the court of Common Pleas in 1588. According to Edward Coke's report of the case, the judges drew on medieval precedents to declare that 'the common law requires, that every constable should be *idoneus homo* [a suitable person], *i.e.* apt and fit to execute the said office; and he is said in law to be *idoneus* who has these three things, honesty, knowledge, and ability'. The three essential qualities were elaborated as follows:

---

[10] Eileen Power, 'The Position of Women' in Charles G. Crump and Ernest F. Jacob (eds.), *The Legacy of the Middle Ages* (Oxford, 1926), 410; Alice Clark, *The Working Life of Women in the Seventeenth Century* (London, 1919).

[11] Lyndal Roper, *The Holy Household: Women and Morals in Reformation Augsburg* (Oxford, 1989); Susan Dwyer Amussen, *An Ordered Society: Gender and Class in Early Modern England* (Oxford, 1988); Sarah Hanley, 'Engendering the State: Family Formation and State Building in Early Modern France', *French Historical Studies* 16.1 (1989); Antony Fletcher, *Gender, Sex & Subordination in England 1500–1800* (New Haven, 1995); Laura Gowing, *Domestic Dangers: Women, Words, and Sex in Early Modern London* (Oxford, 1996).

[12] Garthine Walker, 'Expanding the Boundaries of Female Honour in Early Modern England', *Transactions of the Royal Historical Society* 6 (1996); Joanne Bailey, *Unquiet Lives: Marriage and Marital Breakdown in England, 1660–1800* (Cambridge, 2003); Helen Berry and Elizabeth Foyster (eds.), *The Family in Early Modern England* (Cambridge, 2007); Amy Louise Erickson, 'Married Women's Occupations in Eighteenth-Century London', *Continuity and Change* 23.2 (2008); Tim Reinke-Williams, *Women, Work and Sociability in Early Modern London* (London, 2014), 15–102; Alexandra Shepard, 'Provision, Household Management and the Moral Authority of Wives and Mothers in Early Modern England' in Michael J. Braddick and Phil Withington (eds.), *Popular Culture and Political Agency in Early Modern England: Essays in Honour of John Walter* (Woodbridge, 2017).

honesty, to execute his office truly without malice, affection, or partiality; knowledge, to know what he ought to do; and ability, as well in estate as in body, that he may intend and execute his office, when need is, diligently; and not for impotency or poverty to neglect it.

Coke's summary was quoted almost verbatim in Michael Dalton's highly influential 1618 treatise on *The Countrey Justice*, and from there became orthodoxy among writers on the subject of constableship.[13] The tri-partite qualification was repeated, often word for word, throughout the seventeenth and eighteenth centuries. Even where the label *idoneus homo* was absent, honesty, knowledge, and ability were regularly cited as the essential characteristics of constables and of local officeholders in general.[14]

Some people were more likely to meet these requirements than others. 'Ability, as well in estate as in body' ruled out the poor and the sick. The records of Quarter Sessions provide numerous examples of constables and other officers who, lacking ability 'in body', were discharged for being 'lame', for failing eyesight, or for an unspecified 'infirmity'.[15] Legislation required certain levels of ability 'in estate' as a prerequisite to service in some offices. Surveyors of the highways, for example, had to be worth £30 a year under an Act passed in 1691.[16] Mostly, however, wealth was an informal qualification for officeholding, indirectly enforced by the two remaining criteria.

The type and extent of 'knowledge' needed varied from office to office, but all demanded some degree of literacy and legal competence. These qualities became increasingly widespread over the early modern period, but they remained socially stratified. Many women and men could read well enough to deal with warrants and instructions from superiors, but fewer were able to write well enough to produce the reports of local events

---

[13] Griesley's Case (1588), 8 Co. Rep. 38a, 77 *ER* 530; Michael Dalton, *The Countrey Justice* (London, 1618), 37.

[14] John Layer, *The Office and Dutie of Constables* (Cambridge, 1641), 3–4; Nicholas Collyn, *A Briefe Summary of the Lawes and Statutes of England* (London, 1655), 29–30; William Sheppard, *A Sure Guide for His Majesties Justices of the Peace* (London, 1663), 322; R. Turner, *Duty and Office of a High Constable* (London, 1671), 12; Henry Care, *English Liberties* (London, 1680), 209–10; J. P. Gent, *A New Guide for Constables, Headboroughs, Tything-Men, Church-Wardens …* (London, 1692), 7–8; Giles Jacob, *The Compleat Parish-Officer* (London, 1718), 4; Joseph Shaw, *Parish Law, or, a Guide to Justices of the Peace* (London, 1733), 314; Joseph Ritson, *The Office of Constable* (London, 1791), 3–4; Patrick Colquhoun, *A Treatise on the Functions and Duties of a Constable* (London, 1803), xiii.

[15] For example: KHLC, Q/SB/24/5; KHLC, Q/SB/26/67; LMA, WJ/SP/1644/9; LMA, MJ/SP/1690/12/011; LMA, MJ/SP/1696/10/017; LMA, MJ/SP/1722/07/014; LMA, MJ/SP/1722/07/033; LMA, MJ/SP/1723/01/011; LMA, MJ/SP/1724/10/042; LMA, MJ/SP/1725/04/029.

[16] Mark Goldie, 'The Unacknowledged Republic' in Tim Harris (ed.), *The Politics of the Excluded, c.1500–1850* (Basingstoke, 2001), 171–2.

and offences frequently demanded of officeholders. In the mid-sixteenth century, about 20 per cent of men could sign their own names, but only 5 per cent of women. These figures rose to 45 per cent and 25 per cent by the early eighteenth century. Literacy was exceptionally widespread in London, where about two-thirds of adults could sign their names by the 1720s, but even in the capital writing ability correlated with social status.[17] Like literacy, knowledge of the law was commonplace in this period; as Tim Stretton recently put it, 'almost everyone in the country had direct experience of the law, whether as litigant, witness, juror or curious observer'.[18] The level of expertise gained from this experience, however, was not necessarily sufficient for officeholding. The need for detailed information on, for example, exactly when it was or was not lawful for a constable to arrest a suspected criminal outside their own jurisdiction, fuelled the flourishing market in printed guides to various offices.

In the first half of the twentieth century, many historians assumed that local officeholders, especially constables, were profoundly incompetent. This was largely due to a reading of Shakespeare's buffoonish constables Elbow and Dogberry as accurate social commentary, combined with a broader reliance on materials produced by elite writers.[19] Evidence of gentry scorn for officers they considered lowly was not difficult to find. Even the lawyers who wrote handbooks for officeholders were unable to refrain from insulting their readers' intelligence. They addressed 'unlearned men' or 'the Plebeian, unacquainted with our Laws and Statutes', noting, for example, the 'large extent of the Constables Office, and how little skill or knowledge many of you have'.[20] In her comprehensive 1986 study of *The English Village Constable*, Joan Kent set out to rescue her subject's reputation, showing that most constables appear to have been as literate and

---

[17] Adam Fox, 'Words, Words, Words: Education, Literacy and Print' in Keith Wrightson (ed.), *A Social History of England, 1500–1750* (Cambridge, 2017), 137; David Cressy, *Literacy & the Social Order: Reading & Writing in Tudor & Stuart England* (Cambridge, 1980). Ongoing work by Mark Hailwood suggests literacy was more widespread but also more variable than previous scholarship allows.

[18] Tim Stretton, 'The People and the Law' in Wrightson (ed.), *A Social History of England*, 201; Christopher W. Brooks, *Law, Politics and Society in Early Modern England* (Cambridge, 2008); Paul Griffiths, 'Punishing Words: Insults and Injuries, 1525–1700' in Angela McShane and Garthine Walker (eds.), *The Extraordinary and the Everyday in Early Modern England* (Basingstoke, 2010).

[19] See, for example, A.M.P., 'The Old-Time Constable: As Portrayed by the Dramatists', *Police Journal* 2.4 (1929); Louise D. Frasure, 'Shakespeare's Constables', *Journal of English Philology* 58 (1934). A late example of this approach is Phoebe S. Spinrad, 'Dogberry Hero: Shakespeare's Comic Constables in Their Communal Context', *Studies in Philology* 89.2 (1992).

[20] William Lambarde, *The Dueties of Constables* (London, 1582), 2; Jacob, *The Compleat Parish-Officer*, A4v; George Meriton, *A Guide for Constables* (London, 1669), A2.

generally competent as their office required. They were, for example, often able to write and sign their own reports to magistrates and the courts.[21] Tasks like these, repeated over and over, may even have served as an informal education, widening the divide between those who qualified for office and those who did not.

That divide was greatest in the case of offices which demanded specific expertise. Parish clerks, for example, had to have a high level of literacy and 'competent Skill in Singing' in order to keep the parochial books and lead the congregation in Sunday service. Writing in a 'scrabling hand' might cause trouble when it became necessary to consult parish records. Musical ineptitude risked bringing inappropriate mirth into holy proceedings, like the clerk who 'did comitte many mistakes in his responses and other parts of his dueties that Caused severall persons to laugh and did give great discontent to others'. In a closely fought election for parish clerk in St Botolph without Aldgate (London), the supporters of one candidate hired a singing teacher to listen and pass judgment on the abilities of his opponent, who was duly condemned as being 'very much addicted to excursions & running from his tune'. In another, more unusual case, the terms of a bequest required the parish clerk of Skipton (Yorkshire) to give local children a grounding in literacy, religion, and classics, which ruled out Edward Goodgion, who was 'a Barber by p[ro]fession & farr unfit & unable to teach Latine'.[22]

The requirements of literacy, legal knowledge, and in some cases more rarefied skills, went some way to restricting officeholding to the middling sort of people. But the last of the *idoneus homo*'s three qualities was the most important in this respect. 'Honesty, to execute his office truly without malice, affection, or partiality' might refer to general moral character. Night watchmen, for example, were supposed to be 'honest and ablebodied Men' or 'able, active and honest Men' who would not go 'sotting in night cellars' while on duty. Candidates for election to various offices were, according to their supporters, of 'good life & conversation' or, more specifically, 'sober life & conversation'. The author of one handbook for constables complained that the office was 'frequently exercised by men

---

[21] Joan R. Kent, *The English Village Constable 1580–1642: A Social and Administrative Study* (Oxford, 1986), 130–9. For examples of reports written by officers in their own hands, see BL, Egerton MS 2985, 250–59, 271.
[22] Shaw, *Parish Law*, 43; LMA, DL/C/0239, Deposition of Francis Beech, 17 Feb 1679, 133v-36; LPL, Arches, Ee 6, Answers of Samuel Stretch, 2 Nov 1685, 38–43; LMA, DL/C/0253, Deposition of John Newcome, 25 June 1713, 228–9; BIA, GB 193, CP.H.2618, Allegations against Edward Goodgion, 19 Jan 1661, 2–3.

of low character, and worse morals'.[23] 'Honesty' could also be taken in a more literal sense: the quality of truth-telling. As well as making routine reports to their superiors, local officeholders were often called upon to provide testimony in court or in the form of certificates about a person's character or personal history.[24] The word of an officer was supposed to carry considerable weight. Pamphlets describing extraordinary events and apparitions carried the endorsements of churchwardens and constables as badges of veracity.[25]

This kind of honesty was, as Alexandra Shepard and Hillary Taylor have shown, strongly associated with hierarchies of wealth and gender. In a culture of 'closely aligned moral and material hierarchies', those with money or property were deemed ethically superior to those without. Women, in part because they were more likely to be poor and in part due to well-established misogynistic tropes, were seen as especially prone to dishonesty. In general terms, most early modern elites seem to have felt that truth came out of the mouths of the rich; the poor told nothing but lies. This way of thinking was based on the idea that moral virtue was linked to independence and independence required wealth. Only those who did not depend on others for a livelihood and were not economically vulnerable to the whims of another person had sufficient autonomy to speak their own minds. People who worked for others, rented their homes from others, received wages from others, or were subject to another's domestic authority were, according to this logic, stooges who would say and do whatever their masters wanted. They would also, out of a desire for money which richer people apparently lacked, be open to bribery.[26]

This helps to explain why, as Andy Wood recently argued, the early modern state 'depended on the institutional and informal participation of the

---

[23] 10 Geo II c.22; Saunders Welch, *Observations on the Office of Constable* (London, 1754), 12; BIA, GB 193, CP.I.667, Allegations against Charles Catton, 1–2; LMA, DL/C/0258, Deposition of John Verdon, 16 June 1719, 260-1v; John Paul, *The Compleat Constable* (London, 1785), 88.

[24] KHLC, Q/SB/1725/Misc, Certificate of John Sands' good character, unfoliated, dated 1 Oct 1725; *OBP*, May 1693, trial of Ann Harris, Esther King (t16930531-28); *OBP*, Feb 1719 (t17190225-28); *OBP*, Oct 1715, trial of Grace Prior, Lewis Clifton (t17151012-47); *OBP*, Apr 1718, trial of Edward Williams, Elizabeth Williams, Elizabeth Simmerton, Mary Roberts (t17180423-1); *OBP*, Dec 1744, trial of Elizabeth Williamson, Sarah Jackson (t17441205-23).

[25] See, for example: *A Strange and True Relation of a Wonderful and Terrible Earth-Quake* (London, 1661); *The Birth and Burning of the Image Called S. Michael* (London, 1681); *A Wonderful Prophesie, Declared by Christian James a Maid of twenty Years of Age* (London, 1684–86).

[26] Alexandra Shepard, *Accounting for Oneself: Worth, Status, and the Social Order in Early Modern England* (Oxford, 2015), ch. 2; Hillary Taylor, 'The Price of the Poor's Words: Social Relations and the Economics of Deposing for One's "Betters" in Early Modern England', *Economic History Review* 72.3 (2019); Alexandra Shepard, 'Worthless Witnesses? Marginal Voices and Women's Legal Agency in Early Modern England', *Journal of British Studies* 58 (2019).

middling sort – but, emphatically, not of the poor'.[27] A poor person could not hold office because a poor person was not an *idoneus homo*. They would, inevitably, act with 'affection, or partiality' towards those they depended on. Honest service could only be guaranteed by the impartiality of moderate wealth.[28] Handbook writers often glossed their descriptions of the *idoneus homo* with warnings about the perils of choosing poor people to serve. 'If he be poore', one early manual claimed, 'it is to be suspected he will abuse his office for benefit sake'. The 'meaner sort of inhabitants', another wrote, had a tendency to avoid carrying out certain duties 'for fear of displeasing those they depend upon'. They 'stand in awe of the greater; so that they dare not do what they ought', undone by the fear that 'if he commaunds the rich, They'le threaten him with unkindnes'. As Patrick Colquhoun put it as late as 1803, in an updated version of the original phrase, an officer needed 'Ability, as well in estates as in body, to enable him to act with firmness and independence'.[29]

Some contemporary writers seem to have felt that the 'meaner sort' were put into office far too often. The constableship, according to the seventeenth-century diplomat Guy Miege, 'does commonly fall into the hands of Tradesmen and Artificers, and men of small experience and ability', while Daniel Defoe wrote that most parish officers were 'Impudent, Illiterate, Upstart Fellows'. This was the cause, some thought, of endemic corruption. According to Defoe, churchwardens who 'went in as poor as Rats, have come out too rich ever to be poor again'. Corruption was the greatest of 'the Evils which may accrue by admitting mean and dissolute Persons' to hold local offices. The only way to root it out, one commentator argued, was to replace them with 'Persons of Substance' because, after all, 'substantial Men are less liable to the Temptations of Dishonesty, than those of low Circumstances'. The author of a pamphlet in praise of those 'Gentlemen of Property' who controlled the vestry of St Paul's Covent Garden thought it 'scarcely possible that these Gentlemen shall be tempted for a little dirty Lucre to stain Indelibly their Honour in the Abuse of their Office'.[30] They were simply too rich to want money.

---

[27] Andy Wood, *Faith, Hope and Charity: English Neighbourhoods, 1500–1640* (Cambridge, 2020), 220.
[28] On justifications for government by the middling sort in more general terms, see Ethan Shagan, *The Rule of Moderation: Violence, Religion and the Politics of Restraint in Early Modern England* (Cambridge, 2011), chapter 6.
[29] *An Ease for Overseers of the Poore* (Cambridge, 1601), 9–10; Layer, *The Office and Duties*, 161; Turner, *Duty and Office*, 12–13; 'The Song of a Constable: Made by James Gyffon, Constable of Alburye, Anno 1626', appended to Ritson, *The Office of Constable*, 47; Colquhoun, *A Treatise on the Functions and Duties*, xiii.
[30] Guy Miege, *The New State of England* (London, 1691) III, 79; Andrew Moreton [Daniel Defoe], *Parochial Tyranny: Or, the House-Keeper's Complaint against the Insupportable Exactions, and Partial*

Patriarchy

Evidence of official corruption is not hard to find. Stories told by contemporary authors about constables and watchmen who extorted bribes from those they encountered on the streets at night are corroborated by numerous cases in the records of Quarter Sessions and Assizes.[31] Carnivalesque vestry corruption, in which churchwardens and others spent huge amounts of poor relief money 'in Feastings and extravagant Expences', is apparent in the repeated entries those officers made in their account books for lavish dinners over which parish affairs were decided.[32] Court records also corroborate contemporary literature on bailiffs' habits of 'extorting & taking of … excessive Fees' from people they arrested or threatened with arrest.[33]

There is, however, no evidence to suggest that this corruption was the work of poor officeholders, or indeed that many such people existed. The pronouncements of contemporaries and quantitative analyses of officers' wealth both point to a solidly middling set of personnel. Guides to officeholding used a variety of euphemisms to convey the idea of moderate wealth: 'the able sort', 'men of discretion', 'sufficient Persons', and 'credible, honest, substantial Men'.[34] The most extravagant descriptions were reserved for overseers of the poor: 'as God himselfe hath a speciall respect to the miseries of the poore, so they be like God, which

---

Assessments of Select Vestries (London, 1727), 17–18, 9; A Short View of the Frauds, Abuses, and Impositions of Parish Officers (London, 1744), 8–9; Joseph Phipps, The Vestry laid Open; Or, a Full and Plain Detection of the Many Gross Abuses, Impositions, and Oppressions of Select-Vestries (London, 1739), 60, 9; The Select Vestry Justified (London, 1754), 35.

[31] Samuel Butler, Characters and Passages from Note-Books ed. A. R. Waller (Cambridge, 1908), 209; Edward Ward, The London Spy Compleat (London, 1703), 37; KHLC, Q/SB/1718/Examinations, Information of Elizabeth Toke, 5 Jul 1718, unfoliated; Q/SB/1725/Correspondence, Petition of Owen Davis, 5 Oct 1725, unfoliated; OBP, Apr 1732, trial of Showland Wright (t17320419-27); OBP, Sep 1735, trial of Ann Maund, Rachel Needham (t17350911-10); OBP, Sep 1736, trial of Sarah Andrews, Alice King, Sara Hutchinson, Isabel Walters, Elizabeth Gutheridge, Susan Anthill (t17360908-4); OBP, Jun 1738, trial of Richard Marks (t17380628-35).

[32] The Report of the Committee Appointed by a General Vestry of the Parish of St Botolph Without, Aldersgate (London, 1733), 18. Ongoing work by Jeremy Boulton promises to reveal the extent of corruption in the administration of parish workhouses, which Matthew Marriott attacked at length: A Representation of Some Mismanagements by Parish-Officers in the Method at Present Followed for Maintaining the Poor (London, 1726).

[33] KHLC, Q/SB/11/19, Information of William Kirby, 24 Jun 1670; KHLC, Q/SB/10/33, Petition of Henry Hatcher and Richard Hammon, undated; KHLC, Q/SB/28/263, Presentment of Thomas Slaney, 8 Oct 1706; KHLC, Q/SB/29/74, Deposition of Henry Tilby, 8 Sep 1707; Twelve Ingenious Characters: Or, Pleasant Descriptions of the Properties of Sundry Persons & Things (London, 1686), 10–12; Alexander Smith, The Comical and Tragical History of the Lives and Adventures of the most Noted Bayliffs in and about London and Westminster (London, 1723), 58.

[34] William Sheppard, The Offices of Constables (London, 1641), C1r; Layer, The Office and Duties, 12; John Fielding, 'A Treatise on the Office of Constable' in his Extracts from Such of the Penal Laws as Particularly Relate to the Peace and Good Order of This Metropolis (London, 1761), 256; P. S., Gent,

provide for the necessities of the poor'. Two Kentish overseers described as 'poore & very unfit p[er]sons' were duly discharged from their offices at the Quarter Sessions.³⁵ Those who supported particular candidates for local office described them as 'a substantiall Man' or 'a rich Man', while members of select vestries were consistently given the label 'Gentleman'. Some officers made public displays of their prosperity, like the London churchwardens who modified their pews with curtains and cupboards full of books.³⁶

This picture of solidly middling officeholding is borne out by numerous studies of officeholders' social and economic status. In seventeenth-century Terling (Essex), Keith Wrightson and David Levine found that 'parish office and participation in local institutions was restricted to the wealthier sections of village society'. Evidence to support this claim comes from details of officers' occupations and the rates at which they were taxed. Joan Kent showed that between the late sixteenth and mid-seventeenth centuries, most rural constables were either wealthy or middling farmers, while those in towns tended to be substantial crafts- and tradespeople. The same was true of eighteenth-century Hertfordshire, where most of those who served were the middling heads of 'business households' – farmers, artisans, and tradespeople.³⁷ Local rate-books show that churchwardens and former churchwardens in Chester were taxed at a higher level of poor rate than most of their fellow parishioners. A study of parish officeholding in north Norfolk made it clear that the vast majority of officers were at least rich enough to be assessed for poor rates and that most churchwardens and overseers were prosperous farmers or even gentry.³⁸

Larger scale studies present a similar picture, with little evidence of change over time. An investigation of officeholding in the 1630s, based

---

A Help to Magistrates, and Ministers of Justice: Also a Guide to Parish and Ward-Officers (London, 1701), 150.

³⁵ *Ease for Overseers*, 8; Meriton, *Guide for Constables*, 157; P. S., Gent, *A Help to Magistrates*, 149–50; Shaw, *Parish Law*, 112; KHLC, Q/SB/22/29.

³⁶ LMA, DL/C/0634, Deposition of Cater Fowler, 19 Jan 1721, 27–30; DL/C/0634, Deposition of Godfrey Cunningham, 26 Jan 1721, 33–35; *OBP*, Ordinary's Account, Oct 1732 (OA17321016); *OBP*, Jan 1743, trial of Mary Lowe (t17430114-13).

³⁷ Keith Wrightson and David Levine, *Poverty and Piety in an English Village: Terling, 1525–1700* (New York, 1979), 104; Kent, *The English Village Constable*, 82–122; Elaine Saunders, '"Men of good Character, strong, decent and active": Hertfordshire's Petty Constables, 1730–1799' (Open University PhD thesis, 2017), 38, 141–2, 156–60, 304–7.

³⁸ Nick Alldridge, 'Loyalty and Identity in Chester Parishes 1540–1640' in S. J. Wright (ed.), *Parish, Church and People: Local Studies in Lay Religion 1350–1750* (London, 1988), 108; Jan Pitman, 'Tradition and Exclusion: Parochial Officeholding in Early Modern England, A Case Study from North Norfolk, 1580–1640', *Rural History* 15.1 (2004), 34–38. See also Beat A. Kümin, *The Shaping of a Community: The Rise and Reformation of the English Parish c.1400–1560* (Aldershot, 1996), 32–37.

on almost 500 sets of parish accounts and scores of tax lists, showed that most officers were ratepayers and that many owned their own land. Henry French compiled data on twenty-one parishes from 1600 to 1750, finding that officers and vestry members were taxed for poor relief at a median or higher rate, which suggests that most belonged to the richer parts of their communities.[39] In eighteenth-century Norwich and Newcastle, almost every constable was either an artisan or a shopkeeper. The churchwardens and overseers of late eighteenth-century Essex were farmers and gentry who paid substantial sums towards the poor rates.[40] Work on the same subject by medievalists suggests this pattern of middling sort officeholding went back at least as far as the fifteenth century.[41]

Officers were expected to be – and generally were – relatively wealthy. That wealth was understood to qualify them to exercise authority independently, without corruption. The same concern for independence ruled out a large majority of the population according to age, gender, and marital status. The *idoneus homo* who could be trusted to wield authority honestly and impartially was a patriarchal head of household. Married women, servants, apprentices, lodgers, and children were all, like the poor, deemed unable to act as autonomous decision-makers; all their actions would be subject to the will of the head of household.

Courts routinely discharged people from office on the grounds that they were 'no housekeeper'. Sometimes, this had to do with the scale of a person's domestic establishment: one man was ruled exempt from the constableship because he was 'noe House Keeper, haveing but two Rooms up one payr of Stayres'.[42] But most of these cases concerned servants, lodgers, and children living as subordinates to a head of household. Several people were discharged from office because they were 'onely an hired servant and not a Householder'[43] Those who petitioned for exemption from office

---

[39] Henrik Langelüddecke, '"The pooreste and sympleste sorte of people"? The Selection of Parish Officers during the Personal Rule of Charles I', *Historical Research* 80.208 (2007); Henry French, *The Middle Sort of People in Provincial England 1600–1750* (Oxford, 2007), 112–14.

[40] Kathleen Wilson, *The Sense of the People: Politics, Culture and Imperialism in England, 1715–1785* (Cambridge, 1995), 301; Peter King, *Crime, Justice and Discretion in England 1740–1820* (Oxford, 2000), 66–70.

[41] J. A. Raftis, 'The Concentration of Responsibility in Five Villages', *Mediaeval Studies* 28 (1966); R. B. Goheen, 'Peasant Politics? Village Community and the Crown in Fifteenth-Century England', *The American Historical Review* 96.1 (1991); Christopher Dyer, 'The Political Life of the Fifteenth-Century English Village' in Linda Clark and Christine Carpenter (eds.), *The Fifteenth Century IV: Political Culture in Late Medieval Britain* (Woodbridge, 2004); A. S. Gibbs, 'Manorial Officeholding in Late Medieval and Early Modern England, 1300–1600' (University of Cambridge D.Phil thesis, 2018).

[42] LMA, MJ/SP/1694/04/007-14.

[43] LMA, MJ/SP/1735/06/020; LMA, MJ/SP/1730/04/038; LMA, COL/CA/01/01/94, f.83.

on these or similar grounds used the word 'inhabitant' as a synonym for householder. They claimed to be 'noe inhabitant but a Lodger only', 'no Inhabitant of the said Ward, but only an Inmate', or 'no Inhabitant but only an Inmate and lodged with his Mother'.[44]

It was not unusual for a young man to be granted exemption from office as 'a Servant to his Mother' or 'a Lodger in his Mothers house'.[45] In 1599, a resident of Greenstead (Essex) complained to an ecclesiastical court that he had been chosen as churchwarden despite being 'a bachelor and servant to his mother and by no means fit to the office'. The court discharged him and ordered 'another honest neighbour being a married man to be called in his place'.[46] In 1684, a Kentishwoman complained to justices of the peace that her son had been chosen constable 'notwithstanding he is my servant'. One unusually well-documented case involved a 'young man co-inhabiting with his mother' as a 'lodger' who was nonetheless chosen as churchwarden of his Welsh parish. A fellow resident wrote to the registrar of the local archdeaconry describing the young man as a 'sparke' and 'one that is wild and will not take the necessary care to discharge the duty incumbent for such an office'. The nominee himself declared an intention to enlist in the navy rather than hold any office 'during the time he is not a settled inhabitant'.[47] The number of young men discharged from office on the grounds that they were their mothers' servants or lodgers may suggest that those who voted for officers sometimes tried (unsuccessfully) to avoid electing female heads of household by choosing their sons instead.

Overseers of the poor had to be householders under statute. Every writer on the subject agreed that, in accordance with the Elizabethan poor laws, these officers ought to be 'substantial householders'.[48] In the summer of 1690, several inhabitants of Hornsey petitioned Middlesex justices to enforce this rule. At a vestry meeting on 22 April, Robert Moore had been chosen as overseer for the parish. He received the poor relief book

---

[44] LMA, COL/CA/01/01/91, f.29; COL/CA/01/01/142, f.122; COL/CA/01/01/148, ff.104–5, 151; COL/CA/01/01/154, f.114.
[45] LMA, COL/CA/01/01/85, f.82v; LMA, COL/CA/01/01/148, ff.104, 151; LMA, MJ/SP/1715/04/029; LMA, MJ/SP/1717/10/060.
[46] F. G. Emmison, *Elizabethan Life: Morals & the Church Courts* (Chelmsford, 1973), 232.
[47] KHLC, Q/SB/16/5, petition of Mildred Netter, 7 Oct 1684; W. T. Morgan, 'Disputes before the Consistory Courts of St Davids Concerning Elections of Churchwardens', *Journal of the Historical Society of the Church in Wales* 3.8 (1953), 93–94.
[48] 43 Eliz. I c.2 (1601); Layer, *The Office and Dutie*, 99; Sheppard, *The Offices of Constables*, K4r; Robert Gardiner, *The Compleat Constable* (London, 1692), 121; J. P., Gent, *A New Guide for Constables*, 107–8; Shaw, *Parish Law*, 194; Richard Burn, *The Justice of the Peace and Parish Officer* (London, 1755), vol. II, 188.

on 14 May, but no money had been collected or distributed since. Moore refused to serve, insisting that he was only a tenant in his house in the parish – his brother, a doctor, was the real owner. The petitioners, however, were less interested in legal ownership than the practicalities of residence, especially resident families. Moore's brother, they argued, was 'a singleman, & hath noe family of his owne resident in the sayd howse'. Moore, by contrast, 'inhabiteth & possesseth the howse with his family', so he 'is the Inhabitant, & not the doct[o]r whoe keeps noe family there'.[49] Similar disputes over the office of churchwarden were heard by the ecclesiastical courts. Here too, the aim was to secure an officer who lived in the parish 'with his wife and Family', regardless of title to property.[50] Officeholding was the duty of husbands and fathers.

As far as it is possible to tell, most officeholders were exactly that. In print, office was presented as something a person qualified for upon marriage, a signifier of patriarchal manhood. An early seventeenth-century ballad described a newly married woman telling her husband that now he had left bachelorhood behind, 'The chiefe men of the Parish / his quaintance will request: / And then he shall be called / to office with the rest'. Over a century later, the author of a tract against marriage included serving as scavenger, watchman, and constable among the burdens it would bring.[51] The available data suggest he was right to be worried: a large majority of those who held office were married. In northern Norfolk, almost half of those who held parish office between 1580 and 1640, and whose marriage dates can be traced, became officeholders for the first time within three years of tying the knot. The same was true of churchwardens in the diocese of Ely.[52] In Earls Colne (Essex), between 1603 and 1750, about 78 per cent of churchwardens were married before they took office. The figure is around 71 per cent for constables and overseers of the poor. Most of these were also already fathers of children: about 70 per cent of the churchwardens and 67 per cent of the constables and overseers. These numbers are based on Earls Colne parish records; the real proportions were probably higher, given that some officers may have married and had children elsewhere before moving

---

[49] LMA, MJ/SP/1690/July/014. For Moore's counter-petition, see MJ/SP/1690/July/015. The following year, Middlesex magistrates received another petition for exemption from office on the grounds that the petitioner 'never was a Housekeeper' in the parish in question: MJ/SP/1691/April/037.
[50] LPL, VH 77/20/1, Stancliffe v Allhallows Bread St (1684); VH 77/50, Brooks v Wowen (1717).
[51] *The Lamentation of a New Married Man* (London, 1619–29?); Henry Carey, *Cupid and Hymen: Or, a Voyage to the Isles of Love and Matrimony* (London, 1742), 50.
[52] Pitman, 'Tradition and Exclusion'; Eric Carlson, 'The Origins, Function, and Status of the Office of Churchwarden, with Particular Reference to the Diocese of Ely' in Margaret Spufford (ed.), *The World of Rural Dissenters, 1520–1725* (Cambridge, 1995), 192.

into the parish.⁵³ In the 1750s, when Sussex diarist Thomas Turner served as an overseer and churchwarden, he observed that his fellow officers were 'all masters of families and fathers of many children'.⁵⁴

By the standards of the time, most officers were middle-aged – somewhere between thirty and fifty. As Keith Thomas wrote many years ago, early modern England was in many ways a gerontocracy: 'the young were to serve and the old were to rule'. This statement should be qualified by the work of Alexandra Shepard, who has shown that contemporary understandings of the male body made middle age a moral and medical ideal – the 'firmest age' in which a man could 'control youthful energies without yet being threatened by their debilitating decline'.⁵⁵ Constables, according to the handbooks, were supposed to be over twenty-one and under seventy; parish clerks had to be thirty or older.⁵⁶ Here and there an officer is referred to as 'old', 'an elderly man', or 'the old gentleman', but older officers were frequently discharged for being 'infirme & sup[er]annuated and unfit to serve'.⁵⁷ Similarly, while writers of the period might refer in passing to a constable as 'a young Man', a Kentish case in which the youth chosen as constable refused to take up office is far more representative of the norm: 'he being a young man did say he would not serve'.⁵⁸

Finding the actual ages of people who held office requires time-consuming record linkage, which may explain why the question has received little scholarly attention. The only previously published works on the subject showed that between 1560 and 1640 Chester churchwardens were generally in their thirties and forties, while Essex constables at the end of the eighteenth century and the beginning of the nineteenth were almost all between the ages of thirty and sixty.⁵⁹ The same age group dominated

---

⁵³ These figures are based on data derived from an online collection of Earls Colne records: Sarah Harrison, Charles Jardine, Tim King, Jessica King, Alan Macfarlane, *Earls Colne, Essex. Records of an English Village 1375–1854* (2008) [dataset], www.dspace.cam.ac.uk/handle/1810/195838. For a full breakdown, see Appendix A.
⁵⁴ *The Diary of Thomas Turner 1754–1765* ed. David Vaisey (Oxford, 1985), 126.
⁵⁵ Keith Thomas, 'Age and Authority in Early Modern England', *Proceedings of the British Academy* 62 (1976), 5; Shepard, *Meanings of Manhood*, 23.
⁵⁶ Sheppard, *The Offices of Constables*, C1v; Edmund Wingate, *The Exact Constable* (London, 1660), 11; Shaw, *Parish Law*, 43. An Act of 1758 made it impossible to compel anyone over the age of 63 to serve as a constable in Westminster: 31 Geo II c.17 s.13.
⁵⁷ NRO, NCR Case 12b/7, Information of Mary Dawber, 21 Feb 1750; *OBP*, May 1750, trial of Ambrose Smith (t17500530-32); KHLC, Q/SB/22/176v. See also, for example, LMA, WJ/SP/1644/9, MJ/SP/1690/July/001; LMA, DL/C/0236, Deposition of Thomas Rewse, 23 Nov 1669, 23–26.
⁵⁸ Thomas Ellwood, *The History of the Life of Thomas Ellwood* (London, 1714), 92–98, 146–51; KHLC, Q/SB/16/5, petition of Mildred Netter, 7 Oct 1684.
⁵⁹ Alldridge, 'Loyalty and Identity', 107–8; King, *Crime, Justice, and Discretion*, 73.

officeholding in Earls Colne. On average, constables were 35.5 years old when they entered office, overseers were 39.8 and churchwardens 45.5, all firmly within the 'firmest age'.[60]

Taken together, the evidence drawn from parish and tax records, officeholding manuals, and discharges by various courts shows that local officers were generally middling-sort, middle-aged, married heads of household. This, once the euphemisms of 'honesty, knowledge, and ability' were stripped away, was the true identity of the *idoneus homo*. The principle that only the independent were fit to rule meant, in practice, that only heads of household were fit to rule. Official power and domestic power rested in the same hands. Local government and law enforcement were, in a sense, extensions of household discipline; or, to put it differently, what officers did in society was what patriarchs did at home. That, at least, was the patriarchal ideal. Such neat analogies broke down in the face of a more complex reality. Moving from who officers were to what they did, it becomes clear that officers governing the world beyond the household faced a variety of challenges to their patriarchal authority. First, they had to successfully govern their own less respectable impulses. Second, they clashed with other patriarchs who resented intrusions into their own households. Finally, and most significantly, they were directly opposed by men who behaved in accordance with a radically different mode of masculinity, one aspect of which was explicit defiance of officers. The everyday business of government was a battleground on which competing forms of masculine authority were asserted, disputed, and defined.

Officers as Patriarchs

Male officeholders were described by some contemporaries as 'civil fathers'. Like natural fathers, they were to be obeyed and respected as representatives of divine or political authority. In return, they provided paternal care and control over those who lived under their jurisdiction, especially the poor.[61] Thomas Turner, the Sussex diarist who served as churchwarden and overseer, orchestrated marriages between the parents of illegitimate children at which he gave away the bride, 'I being what is commonly called "father"'. As respectable heads of household, officers

---

[60] Appendix A.
[61] Richard Allestree, *The Whole Duty of Man* (London, 1658), 278; Humphrey Brailsford, *The Poor Man's Help* (London, 1689), 40; Patricia Crawford, *Parents of Poor Children in England, 1580–1800* (Oxford, 2010), 194–218.

dined together with their wives, sat together in church, and generally had a place in parish vestries.[62] Patriarchy linked official and domestic authorities, so that husbands, fathers, masters, and officers could be seen as almost interchangeable. According to statute, if a child under twelve years old was convicted of profane swearing, they were 'to be whipped by the Constable, or by the Parent, or Master, in the Constable's presence'. In Defoe's *Family Instructor*, a woman who has left her marriage waits apprehensively for a patriarchal reaction, 'expecting every Minute her Husband, or the Constable, should come up and take her away by force'.[63]

Like other patriarchs, male officers were expected to conform to a particular kind of masculinity. This was primarily based on self-control. A patriarch's mastery of himself was the grounding for his mastery of others, both in the household and in society at large.[64] As the author of *An Ease for Overseers of the Poore* put it, 'neither is he fit to be made Governour over others, which wants discretion to governe himselfe'. In the same vein, puritan moralists John Dod and Robert Cleaver wrote that 'it is impossible for a man to understand how to govern the common-wealth that doth not know how to rule his own house, or order his own person; so that he that knoweth not [how] to govern, deserveth not to reign'.[65]

Whether or not officers fulfilled this ideal is difficult to say. In 1704, a London constable was described by one of his neighbours as 'a housekeeper ... and a p[er]son of good substance repute & credit and is a man of civill conversations & quiet & peaceable in his temper and dispositions'. This description was prompted by the fact that the officer in question was being sued for defamation, which may raise questions about his quiet and peaceable disposition.[66] At the funeral of another constable killed in the course of duty in 1709, the minister of his parish described the perfect patriarch, restrained and respectable, honest and impartial:

---

[62] *Diary of Thomas Turner*, 94, 118. For officers and their wives dining together, see *OBP*, Apr 1718, trial of Mary Ipsley, Elizabeth Rickets (t17180423-29). On officers' pews, see Amanda Flather, *Gender and Space in Early Modern England* (Woodbridge, 2007), 144–8.

[63] Sheppard, *Offices of Constables*, F7; Meriton, *Guide for Constables*, 98; Gardiner, *Compleat Constable*, 51; Daniel Defoe, *The Family Instructor* vol. II (8th edition, London, 1766), 142.

[64] Katharine Hodgkin, 'Thomas Whythorne and the Problems of Mastery', *History Workshop Journal* 29 (1990); Susan D. Amussen, '"The part of a Christian man": The Cultural Politics of Manhood in Early Modern England' in Tim Harris (ed.), *Popular Culture in England, c.1500–1850* (Basingstoke, 1995); Anthony Fletcher, *Gender, Sex & Subordination in England 1500–1800* (New Haven, 1995), 411; Anthony Fletcher, 'Manhood, the Male Body, Courtship and the Household in Early Modern England', *History* 84 (1999); Tim Reinke-Williams, 'Manhood and Masculinity in Early Modern England', *History Compass* 12.9 (2014).

[65] *Ease for Overseers*, 10; John Dod and Robert Clever, *A Godly Forme of Household Government* (London, 1612), A8v.

[66] LMA, DL/C/0248, Deposition of John Crosby, 14 Feb 1704, f.234.

> he was of a sweet, gentle and courteous Temper, and of a very modest, and humble Behaviour; very good-natured, and always ready to serve and assist every one, even his very Enemies, and he had a singular Plainness and Sincerity shining thro' all his Actions; he was very courageous, and feared no Encounter, yet had great Calmness and Presence of Mind in Danger.[67]

A similar encomium announced the death of one long-serving churchwarden in a London newspaper: 'a Person of Integrity, and well-belov'd by his Neighbours; but the close Application to the Affairs of the Parish, and the frequent Troubles he met with in his Office, brought upon him the Disorder, of which he died'. A clergyman who had had some dealings with this churchwarden took a different view. He tore the obituary out of the newspaper, pasted it into a report on parish corruption, and annotated the clipping accordingly:

> He was of a fiery temper, very Peevish, Quarrelsome & bigotted ... & it is thought that he throw'd himself into a fever by Overheating himself with Passion & Quarrelling ... & the troubles he met with, were entirely owing to his own Mismanagement & Obstinacy.[68]

'Passion & Quarrelling' were the antithesis of self-control. A man who could not govern his own temper was incapable of governing others.[69]

Governing others could, in itself, be an assertion of patriarchal manhood. In late medieval London, Stephanie Tarbin has argued, the citizens and aldermen who ruled the city pursued a kind of 'civic manliness' based on controlling the moral and sexual lives of their neighbours. 'The reproof and correction of sin', Tarbin writes, 'demanded a specifically masculine virtue'.[70] In the seventeenth and eighteenth centuries, men of the middling sort displayed a similar masculinity of interference through their involvement in Societies for the Reformation of Manners. These societies operated as fund-raising bodies for the pursuit and prosecution of drinking,

---

[67] Thomas Bray, *The Tryals of Jeremy Tooley, William Arch, and John Clauson, Three Private Soldiers* (London, 1732), 64–5.
[68] *The Report of the Committee Appointed by a General Vestry of the Parish of St Botolph Without, Aldersgate* (London, 1733), BL, General Reference Collection, 796.g.31.
[69] Bernard Capp, '"Jesus Wept" But Did the Englishman? Masculinity and Emotion in Early Modern England', *Past & Present* 224.1 (2014); Jennifer C. Vaught, *Masculinity and Emotion in Early Modern English Literature* (Abingdon, 2016).
[70] Stephanie Tarbin, 'Civic Manliness in London, c.1380–1550' in Susan Broomhall and Jacqueline Van Gent (eds.), *Governing Masculinities in the Early Modern Period: Regulating Selves and Others* (Farnham, 2011), 34. See also Shannon McSheffrey, 'Men and Masculinity in Late Medieval London Civic Culture: Governance, Patriarchy and Reputation' in Jacqueline Murray (ed.), *Conflicted Identities and Multiple Masculinities: Men in the Medieval West* (New York, 1999); Shannon McSheffrey, *Marriage, Sex, and Civic Culture in Late Medieval London* (Philadelphia, 2006), 150–63.

gambling, and extramarital sex, providing their members with an opportunity to extend patriarchal control of other people's morals beyond the walls of the home.[71] Those who undertook such moral policing insisted they did so for purely public-spirited reasons. In 1663, a Cheshire constable, who was sued for defamation after he informed the churchwarden of sex between an unmarried couple, claimed to have acted as a dutiful, impartial *idoneus homo*: 'being at that time a constable and sworn officer and having taken his oath to present and make known all misdemeanours [he] did hold it his duty to make this lewd fact of theirs known … not of any malice that [he] bore to either of the parties'.[72]

Officers who engaged in this kind of meddlesome masculinity inevitably came into conflict with people who, for one reason or another, resented their intrusions. Many of these conflicts can be understood as clashes between overlapping or competing codes of manhood. For example, officers who tried to prevent husbands from abusing their wives were effectively intruding on the jurisdiction of another patriarch.[73] This may explain why John Haywood, a Kentishman who had 'beaten Maim'd & wounded his wife', also 'threatned to beat the office[er]s' who were sent to arrest him. In London, a constable who saw a male neighbour chasing his wife to beat her – 'He wanted her to dress his Supper, which she refused' – was killed when he tried to intervene. The neighbour declared 'You have no business between me and my wife', and then hit the constable in the face with an earthenware pot. When another London husband confined his wife to an attic and starved her to death, the local beadle sat by her bedside for a fortnight but did nothing to help; as the dead woman's brother put it, 'no Body could hinder him from locking his Wife up if he had a mind to it, for she was his Goods, and he might do what he would with her'.[74]

As John Locke pointed out in his critique of Robert Filmer's patriarchalist political thought, one of the problems with equating patriarchal and political power was that 'there will be as many kings as there are fathers',

---

[71] Margaret R. Hunt, *The Middling Sort: Commerce, Gender, and the Family in England 1680–1780* (Berkeley, 1996), 102–22. On these Societies, see Robert B. Shoemaker, *Prosecution and Punishment: Petty Crime and the Law in London and Rural Middlesex, c.1660–1725* (Cambridge, 1991), 238–72; Faramerz Dabhoiwala, 'Sex and Societies for Moral Reform, 1688–1800', *Journal of British Studies* 46.2 (2007).
[72] CRO, EDC 5/1663/17, Deposition of William Thorniley, 19 Nov 1663, unfoliated.
[73] Marianna Muravyeva, '"A King in His Own Household": Domestic Discipline and Family Violence in Early Modern Europe Reconsidered', *The History of the Family* 18.3 (2013).
[74] KHLC, Q/SB/29/95, Order to constable of Upper Hardres, 22 Aug 1707; *OBP*, Sep 1735, trial of Samuel Hutchins (t17350911-99); *OBP*, Jan 1732, trial of Corbet Vezey (t17320114-12).

'as many monarchs as there are husbands', and royal authority would be rendered meaningless in any individual patriarch's domain. This argument highlighted a genuine problem in early modern English society: where did the authority of officers end and that of the patriarch begin, and which was to take priority when the two came into conflict? According to Christopher Brooks, most lawyers thought 'there should be scope for civil intervention in the private lives of families, even if this was at the expense of fathers'.[75] Many non-lawyers appear to have thought differently. A striking illustration of this comes from Norwich in 1704, where the constable and watch found Thomas Braborne and the wife of JamesRamply in bed together in a notorious alehouse. They took Braborne to the stocks and would have done the same with Ramply's wife (whose name is not given in the constable's account of this episode) but Ramply himself appeared, 'strooke them and Rescued his wife'.[76] The cuckolded husband refused to allow officers to punish his wife for him. There were many other situations in which officeholders had the legal right to bypass the authority of patriarchs, some of which are discussed in Chapter 5, but not all patriarchs were willing to accept this.

Interfering officers were, however, less likely to collide with reputable patriarchs than with men who rejected self-control in favour of drinking, gambling, and extramarital sex as core signifiers of manhood. Hostility to officeholders was a key component of what Alexandra Shepard has called 'alternative' masculinity or 'the counter-code of manhood'.[77] In December 1721, a group of constables (under orders from JPs associated with the campaign for a reformation of manners) set out to shut down a 'noted Gaming House' known as Vandernan's, just off Drury Lane. One of the gamblers, seeing about twenty men approaching 'with Constables Staves', told his fellow gamesters to 'Put the Candles out, and draw your Swords, which they did'. A short siege commenced, in which the gamblers held the constables at bay by throwing 'Brickbats, drinking Pots, and a Chamber Pot full of Piss' from the windows, but their resistance collapsed when the officers sent for troops to help them break in. In the aftermath, as they were dragged away, one gamester derided the men arresting him in gendered terms: 'There's not a Man among ye, you're all a pack of informing

---

[75] John Locke, *Two Treatise of Government* ed. Peter Laslett (3rd edition, Cambridge, 1988), 193, 174; Christopher W. Brooks, *Law, Politics and Society in Early Modern England* (Cambridge, 2008), 384.
[76] NRO, NCR Case 12b/4, Information of Arthur Well, 18 Apr 1704.
[77] Shepard, *Meanings of Manhood*, 93–113; Alexandra Shepard, '"Swil-bols and Tos-pots": Drink Culture and Male Bonding in England, c.1560–1640' in Laura Gowing, Michael Hunter, and Miri Rubin (eds.), *Love, Friendship and Faith in Europe, 1300–1800* (Basingstoke, 2005).

Rogues'. The constables, he claimed, were too cowardly to face a fair fight outside their jurisdiction, where they would not have any special legal protection. 'Come but over the Kennel in Drury-lane', he challenged them, 'and I'll give you what you deserve ... half a dozen lusty Fellows would beat you all!'[78] According to this gambler, risk-taking and violence were the measure of manhood, and interfering constables reliant on military backup fell far short.

Similar confrontations took place over the policing of London's sex workers. At a May Fair in 1702, one man was overheard proclaiming that 'if the Rogues the Informers [constables] did Come into the faire to take any women out of his Company he would Chop them as small as Pott Herbs'. When the officers inevitably appeared, they were met with swords and brickbats, and a constable was killed.[79] In 1743, the City's Court of Aldermen offered a reward for information on anyone involved in an attack on the constable who arrested 'Unity Kelly a Notorious Night-Walker'. 'Great Numbers of Rude and Disorderly Persons unknown, several of them in Sailors Habits' had violently rescued Kelly from custody and 'insulted and abused' the constable and his assistants 'in so much that their Lives were in Danger'.[80] Female pickpockets and shoplifters, often associated by the authorities with sex work, were also repeatedly rescued from officers by groups of men ranging from three sword-wielding brothers to 'twenty Ruffians ... armed with Bludgeons and other Weapons'.[81]

In some of these cases, rescuers claimed the woman arrested was wife or sister to one of their number; they were responsible men protecting their families. On other occasions, however, it is clear that the primary

---

[78] *OBP*, January 1722, trial of Edward Vaughan, Philip Cholmley (t17220112-43); *OBP*, February 1722, trial of Charles Mac-cave, Edward Dun, Edward Galloway (t17220228-65). For the context of this altercation, see Tim Hitchcock and Robert Shoemaker, *London Lives: Poverty, Crime and the Making of a Modern City, 1690–1800* (Cambridge, 2015), 107–21; Heather Shore, '"The Reckoning": Disorderly Women, Informing Constables and the Westminster Justices, 1727–33', *Social History* 34.4 (2009).

[79] LMA, MJ/SP/1702/07/048, Information of Letticia Browne, 22 May 1702; LMA, MJ/SP/1703/07/021, Information of John Deering, 2 Jul 1703; *OBP*, Jul 1703, trial of Thomas Cook (t17030707-2); *OBP*, Oct 1703, trial of William Wallis (t17031013-21); Josiah Woodward, *A Sermon Preach'd ... At the Funeral of Mr. John Cooper, a Constable* (London, 1702); R v Wallis in *A Report of all the Cases Determined by Sir John Holt* (London, 1738), 484.

[80] LMA, COL/CA/01/01/147, f.206.

[81] LMA, MJ/SP/1699/02/042, Information of George Abbott, 16 Feb 1699; LMA, COL/CA/01/01/154, f.277. See also LMA, MJ/SP/1749/05/017, Information of John Steward, 15 Apr 1749; LMA, MJ/SP/1749/07/128, Information of John Lambert, 22 Jun 1749. On the links between these forms of theft and sex work, see Faramerz Dabhoiwala, 'The Pattern of Sexual Immorality in Seventeenth- and Eighteenth-Century London' in Paul Griffiths and Mark S. R. Jenner (eds.), *Londinopolis: Essays in the Cultural and Social History of Early Modern London* (Manchester, 2000), 99; Shelley Tickell, *Shoplifting in Eighteenth-Century England* (Woodbridge, 2018), 180–4.

motivation was hostility to the officers of law enforcement, regardless of who they happened to have in their custody.[82] As one rescuer confessed in court, 'If we met a man with a Constable in the Street, though we did not know him, we went to rescue him'. His companions, referred to by one officer as 'a Heap of Irishmen', allegedly rescued a man while shouting 'D——n the Constable, Murder him, Kill him', knocked the officer down and took the money in his pockets.[83] The printed *Proceedings* of the Old Bailey provide numerous examples of officer-hating. A thief 'had such a Spite and Hatred against' one particular constable 'that I was determined if ever I met him to have his Life'. A member of the so-called 'Black-Boy Alley gang' declared in the course of beating up a headborough that if his victim had been the constable 'I would poke those two eyes of yours out, cut your head off and carry it away in triumph'.[84] Beadles and constables were said to be hated by the residents of Bowl Yard ('as bad as Drury-Lane, or Black-Boy-Alley') who 'have a spight against the Parish Officers, because they have disturbed them' in their disorderly lives. In some areas, there were drinking establishments which officers were too afraid to enter: 'we dare not go down into his Cellar for Fear of being knocked on the Head; when the Constable and Beadles go down, the Candles are all put out, and they are beaten almost to Death'.[85]

This kind of opposition was associated with a youthful, anti-marital, bachelor style of manhood. According to longstanding comic tradition, all married men were cuckolds, so officeholders – as quintessential patriarchs – were inevitably portrayed in this way. A fake warrant for the arrest of London sex workers, printed to mock the Societies for the Reformation of Manners, claimed to enforce the wishes of a Privy Council 'Learned in the Laws of Cuckoldom' and was signed by constables John Falshort, William Wantool & Adam Lost-yard at their office 'by Cuckolds Point'. In similar style, the Grub Street satirist Ned Ward described watchmen as

---

[82] On the significance of opposition to officers and others involved in the campaign for a reformation of manners, see Hitchcock and Shoemaker, *London Lives*, 40, 60, 121, 177.

[83] *OBP*, Feb 1741, trial of Robert Hunt, James Timms (t17410225-7). On the crimes and criminalisation of Irish Londoners, see Peter King, 'Ethnicity, Prejudice, and Justice: The Treatment of the Irish at the Old Bailey, 1750–1825', *Journal of British Studies* 52 (2013); Adam Crymble, 'How Criminal Were the Irish? Bias in the Detection of London Currency Crime, 1797–1821', *The London Journal* 43.1 (2018).

[84] *OBP*, Sep 1741, Ordinary's Account (OA17410916); *OBP*, Oct 1744, trial of Thomas Wells, Theophilus Watson, Joshua Barnes, Thomas Kirby, Ann Duck (t17441017-6). On the 'Black-Boy Alley gang', see Hitchcock and Shoemaker, *London Lives*, 180–91.

[85] *OBP*, Oct 1744, trial of Edmund Long, Henry Townley, Charles Savage (t17441017-24); *OBP*, Sep 1737, trial of William Clark (t17370907-40); *OBP*, Sep 1744, trial of Luke Ryley, John MackEvoy (t17440912-48).

a 'Crazy Crew of Cornigerous [horn-wearing] Halberteers'. Officeholders were aligned with middle-aged patriarchy against the riotousness of male youth. Ward called one constable a 'Grey headed lump of grave Ignorance' and an early seventeenth-century ballad suggested that officers only paid attention to the drunken misbehaviour of bachelors, leaving their fellow householders to pass unhindered: 'No Constable nor watch feare I', says a married man, 'I doe not reele, but soberly / can passe them void of care'.[86]

Clashes between disorderly young men and patriarchal officers intersected with a kind of class conflict when the young men in question were members of the social elite. Officeholders of the middling sort were instructed to treat their superiors with special respect. According to one handbook for officers, a constable who arrested a man for breaking the peace 'may for a Time imprison the Offender (being a Man of Quality) in the Constable's own House', while poorer offenders were to be put in the stocks. A gentleman suspected of criminal activity should be issued with a summons to court, not arrested like anyone else. Former high constable Saunders Welch advised watchmen 'not to be impertinent, nor squabble with those they ought to protect, I mean people of credit heated by liquor'. This was especially important, because 'members of the house of commons themselves have been exposed to the insolence of watchmen, and for want of discernment or thro' wantonness of power in the constable of the night, have suffered improper confinement'. As a general rule, Welch wrote, officers should remember that 'tho' the law makes no distinction of persons, prudence doth'.[87]

Henry Fielding, who worked with Welch as a magistrate, imagined officeholders as the embodiment of deference. In his *History of Tom Jones*, one constable 'stood trembling with his Hat off' before Tom, the adopted son of the local squire, and 'would have surrendered his Prisoner, had Tom demanded her, very readily'. When, later in the story, Tom is arrested for murder, the constable hearing 'the Accident had happened in a Duel' – that is, an honourable fight between elite men – 'treated his Prisoner with great Civility'.[88] There is evidence that some officers did live up to this ideal. In 1690, when the night watchmen of Ashford (Kent) discovered the man they had stopped was Charles Wheeler Esq (a wealthy lawyer and member of the town corporation), 'then the afores[ai]d watchmen hereing

---

[86] John Smith, *The Constables Hue and Cry After Whores & Bawds* (London, 1701), 4, 5; Ward, *London Spy*, 78, 38; *Tis Not Otherwise: Or, the Praise of a Married Life* (London, 1617).
[87] P.S., *A Help to Magistrates*, 93; Welch, *Observations*, 13, 14–15, 36.
[88] Henry Fielding, *The History of Tom Jones I* (Dublin, 1749), 180; Henry Fielding, *The History of Tom Jones III* (Dublin, 1749), 230.

whome he was they desired him to go home' without any further questions about his presence on the streets at night. In cases like these, social status trumped official authority. As one parish reformer wrote, officeholders rarely used the full extent of their powers against those with money: 'the Rich seldom feel the Pinch of these Oppressions; those petty Tyrants dare not impose upon and abuse them, as they do the poor, and middling Sort of People'.[89] Whether or not that was true, it did not stop elite men complaining about interference in their lives by officeholders who – as they saw it – were encouraged by their position to meddle with matters above their proper station.

The most common point of tension was night-walking. Like Charles Wheeler, many gentlemen felt they were entitled to walk or ride at night without obstruction. Watchmen, empowered and instructed by common law to challenge any stranger on the streets at night, tried to stop them. In 1672, Greenwich watchmen failed to stop a horseman who, as he rode away, 'bid them kis his arse'. One London gentleman who was unable to escape arrest was indignant when the beadle escorted him to a nearby watch-house: 'Go with you, you Black-guard Dog! says he. Do you know who you talk to? I'd have you know, Sirrah, that I have got Money, and a 5 l. Note in my Pocket'. This kind of defiance of official power extended to the very top of the social order. In 1691, a group of unfortunate watchmen were beaten up by the Earl of Danby and his retinue, and in the following year a watchman was killed on duty by servants of Lord Salisbury.[90]

Fighting with officers was an important aspect of 'rake' identity – a version of elite masculinity based on sex, violence, and excess which became increasingly prominent after the Restoration.[91] In some respects, this was a hangover from the rowdy ideal of cavalier manhood cultivated by royalists during the civil wars. As one ballad described: 'The Constable flies, / And his Club-men withdraw, / When they hear the fierce cries / of the dreadful Huzza'.[92] A common trope in post-Restoration songs

---

[89] KHLC, Q/SB/22/71, Informations of John Ansell, William Buckhurst, Gilburd Norton, William Trench, Daniel Morton, 8 Jan 1690; Phipps, *Vestry laid Open*, A3.

[90] KHLC, Q/SB/12/1, Information of Thomas Tudor, 12 Oct 1672; *OBP*, Dec 1733, trial of John Beach (t17331205-31); LMA, MJ/SP/1691/02/036-37, Informations of William Burrowes, William Burnham, Thomas Farnel, Lawrence Nichols, Thomas Ben; LMA, MJ/SP/1692/12/003, Petition of Susan Matson, undated.

[91] Erin Mackie, 'Boys Will Be Boys: Masculinity, Criminality, and the Restoration Rake', *The Eighteenth Century* 46.2 (2005); Erin Mackie, *Rakes, Highwaymen, and Pirates: The Making of the Modern Gentleman in the Eighteenth Century* (Baltimore, 2009).

[92] *The Night-Walkers; Or, the Loyal Huzza* (London, 1672–96). On royalist masculinity, see Hughes, *Gender and the English Revolution*, chapter 3; Angela McShane, 'Roaring Royalists and Ranting

saw a heroic 'gallant' wager that he could pass through London at night without being stopped by the watch, duping an array of idiotic constables along the way.[93] This youthful elite antagonism towards officers was still alive and well in the mid-eighteenth century, when Tobias Smollett described Roderick Random with his drinking companions Wagtail, Ranter, Chatter, and Bragwell, the last of whom proposes as an evening's entertainment 'that we should scour the hundreds, sweat the constable, maul the watch, and then reel soberly to bed'.[94]

At least some young aristocrats genuinely lived the rake lifestyle. Philip Herbert, the seventh earl of Pembroke, was known to contemporaries for duelling, drunken assaults, possible blasphemy, and his enormous number of hunting dogs. In 1678, aged twenty-five, he was convicted of manslaughter but granted a reprieve under 'privilege of peerage'. Two years later, in an episode publicised by several sensationalist pamphlets, he fought and killed a constable and his assistant when they stopped his carriage after a night of drinking. On being stopped, Herbert apparently said 'God Dam um ... they would make um know who they were' and emerged with sword drawn. An account sympathetic to the earl emphasised 'the insolent behaviour of an ignorant Constable', with his 'impertinent Questions' about what Herbert was doing on the road after dark, and concluded that a man of such 'Gallantry and Honour' could not be expected to 'bear the insolent Affronts of the Mobile [the mob] without Resentment'. He was tried and found guilty of murder but received a royal pardon.[95]

At the heart of rake masculinity, alongside class, was the idea of 'wit'. One night in 1708, a pair of Norwich watchmen stopped two horsemen riding through the city streets. One of the horsemen 'Called out & said these are the Rogues that unhorst Norford on Satterday Last', then dismounted, drew his sword and – swearing 'he would Sacrafice them' – chased one of the watchmen and stabbed him. Later that night, the same man (a gentleman called John Mingay) was overheard complaining that

---

Brewers: The Politicisation of Drink and Drunkenness in Political Broadside Ballads from 1640 to 1689' in Adam Smyth (ed.), *A Pleasing Sinne: Drink and Conviviality in Seventeenth-Century England* (Cambridge, 2004).

[93] For example *The Jolly Gentleman's Frollick: Or, the City Ramble* (London, 1675–96); *The Frollicksome Wager: Or, the Ranting Gallant's Ramble through the City* (London, 1683–1703).

[94] Tobias Smollett, *The Adventures of Roderick Random II* (London, 1748), 106.

[95] David L. Smith, 'The infamous seventh earl of Pembroke, 1653–1683', Subsection of 'Herbert, Philip, first earl of Montgomery and fourth earl of Pembroke', *ODNB* (Oxford, 2004); *A True and Sad Relation of Two Wicked and Bloody Murthers* (London, 1680), 1; *Great and Bloody News from Turnham Green* (London, 1680); *An Impartial Account of the Misfortune that Lately Happened to the Right Honourable Philip Earl of Pembrook and Montgomery* (London, 1680), 1–2.

the watch 'had abused him' and expressing his regret at failing to kill the watchman 'to have Learnt him more witt'. A 1640 play called *Wit in a Constable* revolves around the notion that officeholders, unlike the gallants they encountered on their rounds, were devoid of wit. The hero, constable Busy, sets out to overturn this assumption by showing himself 'a true sparke, that Constables / Hereafter may be thought to have some wit'. If his various schemes succeed, 'Time shall report some Constables have wit'. At the close, when Busy has triumphed in arranging his daughters' marriages to wealthy gentlemen, another character ends the play by declaring 'We should confesse this Constable had wit'.[96]

Tensions between rakes and officers were particularly intense in the spring of 1712. A series of unprovoked attacks on Londoners by groups of young gentlemen were attributed by the press to an organised club calling themselves the 'Mohocks'. Whether or not they really went by that name, the swirling rumours were taken seriously enough for Middlesex justices of the peace to demand that every constable in the Holborn-Finsbury area send a detailed report of all the assaults and batteries which had taken place in their jurisdiction over the previous two months. These reports suggest that there was a burst of violence associated with elite men, in particular one George Wigmore of Gray's Inn and several other law students. Windows were broken, people were knocked down for no particular reason, and their possessions were thrown into the street. The attacks on women were especially vicious, involving gendered rituals of violent shaming. One constable's report described how the unnamed wife of Richard Fisher was assaulted by five or six men as she carried a drink from her husband's shop to the nearby post house. They 'Threw the Drink in her face and upon her Cloaths' and then 'Threw her all alonge upon the Stones pulling her Hedcloathe off'.[97] Pulling off a woman's headdress was widely understood to suggest she had lost her sexual virtue, and episodes in which men flung liquids at women's faces or genitals have been interpreted by some scholars as metaphorical ejaculations, emphasising masculine potency. Similarly sexualised motives may have been behind the practice of cutting women's lips. One servant reported that two gentlemen 'seized this Informant by her head and with a violent force thrust a penknife or

---

[96] Raymond Stephanson, *The Yard of Wit: Male Creativity and Sexuality, 1650–1750* (Philadelphia, 2004); NRO, NCR Case 12b/4, Informations of John Sparrow, Peter Mathews, James Pettitt, Alexander Wade, 8–9 Mar 1708; Henry Glapthorne, *Wit in a Constable* (London, 1640).

[97] Daniel Statt, 'The Case of the Mohocks: Rake Violence in Augustan London', *Social History* 20.2 (1995); LMA, MJ/SP/1712/04/002-32; LMA, MJ/SP/1712/04/004, Return of Joseph Eagleton, 1 Apr 1712.

some other instrum[en]t through the lower part of her face at some small distance from her lower lip into the mouth'. Another woman was also 'cut threw hear lower lipe'. None of the Mohocks' male victims were subjected to this.[98]

Several constables reported that they or their watchmen had been attacked, like Robert Howard of St Margaret's, whose laconic report read: 'I met 2 men which apeerd to be gentle men which did bete me with there sticks in St James street'. As one historian of the Mohock episode put it, 'The watch represented the lowest echelon in the hierarchy of official order, and as such would naturally attract the attention of young rakes who sought to rebel against authority'.[99] In John Gay's dramatic recreation of these events, *The Mohocks*, one of the gentlemen opens the play in a tavern, announcing that

> In vain th'embattell'd Watch in deep array,
> Against our Rage oppose their lifted Poles;
> Through Poles we rush triumphant, Watchman rolls
> On Watchman; while their Lanthorns kick'd aloft
> Like blazing Stars, illumine all the Air.

The Mohocks then sing a drinking song, which includes the lines 'We will scower the Town, / Knock the Constable down, / Put the Watch and the Beadle to flight'. When they encounter and inevitably overpower the night watch, the leader of the Mohocks (known as the 'Emperor') mocks the constable in distinctly rakish, anti-patriarchal terms:

EMP. The Constable is my Prisoner – hark ye, Sirrah, are you married?
CONST. Yes, an please your Honour.
EMP. Then you are a Cuckold, Coxcomb.

Humiliated, the officers are left clinging to their manhood. In an effort to cheer up his companions, the constable says 'The Mohocks are but men and we be Men as well as they be and a Man is a Man'.[100] This appeal to the most basic equality of maleness belies the gendered defeat they have experienced. As patriarchs, the officers have collided with – and been overwhelmed by – an alternative model of manhood. Sobriety and self-control are defeated by drunkenness, riot, and wit.

---

[98] Patricia Simons, *The Sex of Men in Premodern Europe: A Cultural History* (Cambridge, 2011), 45–51; LMA, MJ/SP/1712/04/027, Information of Mary Ann Kilby, 5 Apr 1712; LMA, MJ/SP/1712/04/028, Report of Thomas Lowen, 31 Mar 1712.
[99] LMA, MJ/SP/1712/04/022, Return of Robert Howard, undated; Statt, 'The Case of the Mohocks', 193.
[100] W. B. [John Gay], *The Mohocks. A Tragi-Comical Farce* (London, 1712), 1, 9, 7.

In the course of their duties, officeholders came into conflict with men who claimed authority from various sources: the household, social class, or a willingness to use violence. Because most officers were patriarchs, these conflicts took on specifically gendered dimensions; they were contests between patriarchal men over the boundaries of their respective jurisdictions, or contests between patriarchal and alternative modes of manhood. Office was aligned with a particular kind of masculinity, and challenges to official power merged with challenges to the dominance of the patriarchal model. As we shall see in Chapter 3, the introduction of new kinds of officeholding from the mid-seventeenth century onward disrupted this alignment and created new kinds of official manhood. The various conjunctions of office and masculinity were an inevitable consequence of the fact that officers were almost exclusively male. But this is not the whole story. The relationship between office and household, as well as producing a preponderance of patriarchs, made room for some participation in official life by non-householders, and by householding women.

Official Households

Apart from the general association created by the requirements of the *idoneus homo*, households were important to particular offices in particular ways. For constables, the house itself was an essential asset. In London, a constable was 'obliged to put the Kings Arms and the Arms of the City over his Door ... to signifie, that a Constable lives there'. The Court of Aldermen repeatedly ordered officers to comply with this, demanding they display staves of office or painted lathes on their houses as identification.[101] This was to ensure 'they may be more easily found when wanted', which might be at any time of day or night – one constable described being 'call'd out of his Bed and charg'd with the Prisoner about five in the morning' – so a person might be discharged or exempt from holding office if their work took them out of the house too often.[102] An urban officer's night-time beat was usually close to where they lived ('the Fact was committed in my Walk, and very near my Door') and one Norwich constable seems to have stored a set of staves at home for emergencies, which he rushed to collect when there was 'a very great uproar' at the watch house.

---

[101] Gardiner, *Compleat Constable*, 112; J. M. Beattie, *Policing and Punishment in London, 1660–1750: Urban Crime and the Limits of Terror* (Oxford, 2001), 122.

[102] Shaw, *Parish Law*, 318; TNA, ASSI/45/2/1/200, Deposition of Nicholas Hobson, 18 Aug 1647; *OBP*, Sept 1719, trial of Elizabeth Jakes (t17190903-49); Beattie, *Policing and Punishment*, 142.

Office and Household 51

Another constable, serving in a Kentish coastal parish, stored the thirteen horse loads of wool he had confiscated from smugglers in his own house.[103]

As a place to go in search of justice and a storage space for evidence or weaponry, the officer's household was in some ways a domestic precursor to the police station. This impression is strengthened by the habit constables and other officers had of detaining suspected law-breakers in their own homes. In Smollett's *Roderick Random*, a sex worker called Nancy Williams is arrested by a bailiff (Mr Vulture) who offers her a choice of imprisonment in gaol or in his house. Numerous cases in the Old Bailey *Proceedings* show Smollett was not being fanciful; constables and beadles, as well as bailiffs, took suspects 'to my own House' to be held until they could be brought before a magistrate. One London constable, arresting a woman charged with pickpocketing, presented her and the man who accused her with almost exactly the same choice Mr Vulture offered Nancy Williams: he 'put 'em to their Choice, to go to my House or the Watchhouse, till the Justice was up'. Another had his house specially set up for the purpose; when he brought a suspect home, he 'took care to secure him in the cage till morning'.[104] Like prison-keepers, officers charged the people they detained for their hospitality, which may have made the practice popular but drew sharp criticism from the authorities. The author of a 1641 handbook wrote that suspects should always be held in local gaols or in the stocks. A century later, Saunders Welch was still complaining about officers who imprisoned people in their homes 'for the little consideration of taking a few dirty shillings'.[105]

The economic aspect of householding had a more complex relation to office. Lower down the official hierarchy, a large household signified neediness, which might qualify a person to serve in a salaried post. Sextons were often expected to be heads of household who had fallen on hard times and needed an additional income to support their families. The same seems to have applied to beadles, one of whom was given a pay rise due to the

---

[103] *OBP*, Sept 1737, trial of William Clark (t17370907-40); NRO, NCR Case 12b/7, Information of Margaret Bishop, 9 Aug 1750; BL, Egerton MS 2985, Information of John Impett, March 1661, 67.

[104] Tobias Smollett, *The Adventures of Roderick Random I* (London, 1748), 202; OBP Apr 1726, trial of William Brown (t17260425-7); OBP Jul 1732, trial of Mary Sullivan (t17320705-12); OBP Jul 1744, trial of William Quarendon (t17440728-13). For more examples of officers' holding suspects at home, see OBP Mar 1720, trial of Michael Dobson (t17200303-48); OBP Jan 1728, trial of William Hodges (t17280117-16); OBP Aug 1741, trial of James Heater (t17410828-6). For more literary examples, see Ellwood, *History of the Life of Thomas Ellwood*, 146–51; *The Midnight-Ramble: Or, the Adventures of Two Noble Females* (London, 1754), 22.

[105] Sheppard, *Offices of Constables*, D1r; Welch, *Observations*, 19. Judicial complaints about constables imprisoning suspects in their own houses go back at least as far as 1482: *Seipp's Abridgement* 1482.133 (Michaelmas 22 Edw IV 16, f.35b).

'Largeness of his Family'. The exact number of domestic dependents could be disputed when two candidates vied for the same office. Supporters of Charles Dymond, who wanted to be parish clerk of St Botolph Aldgate in 1713, pointed to the fact that 'hee has six or seven Children'. His opponents argued, however, that several of these children were 'growne up & provided for', so could not qualify as reasons to employ him.[106] In the higher offices which traditionally received only fees and expenses, the cost of maintaining a family took on the opposite meaning. Supporting a family demanded time which service as a constable, churchwarden, or overseer might not allow. In 1660s Kent, justices received petitions for discharge from one man who begged for time to 'better follow his labours for the Releife of himselfe and Familie' and another who 'being a poore man and having a great Charge of Children is not able to execute the same'. In 1695, a man petitioned Middlesex justices for exemption from the office of overseer in Mile End on the grounds that he was only visiting England briefly from Nevis, where he had a plantation and 'a family of whites and blacks in the said island of one hundred and ten persons'. The demands of such a large 'family', the petitioner claimed, were incompatible with holding office.[107]

Officeholders' families functioned as more than symbols of need. On paper, offices were held by heads of household, but in practice, other members of the same household sometimes took part in official business. In her work on late medieval churchwardens, Katherine French has shown that 'the responsibilities of the office might be shared among family members, even if the husband was the formal office holder'.[108] This continued into the early modern period. In court records, we find a constable's male apprentice helping to pursue and arrest a suspected thief in Hull in 1647 and another doing the same in London a century later.[109] A young resident of a riverside London ward was sworn in as a constable 'to Assist his Father

---

[106] LPL, Arches, Eee 14, Deposition of Henry Harrill, 9 Nov 1738, 374; LMA, DL/C/0253, Deposition of Michael Drewitt, 18 Jun 1713, 218–19; Deposition of Valentine Bevis, 2 Jul 1713, 241-3v. Dickens mocked the competitive enumeration of candidates' children in the election of a beadle in *Sketches by Boz*, as discussed in William F. Long and Paul Schlicke, 'Bung against Spruggins: Reform in "Our Parish"', *Dickens Quarterly* 34.1 (2017).

[107] KHLC, Q/SB/8/67, petition of Andrew Usher, undated; Q/SB/10/35, petition of John Bradley, undated; W. J. Hardy (ed.), *Middlesex County Records. Calendar of Sessions Books 1698–1709* (London, 1905), Book 521, May 1695, p.34.

[108] Katherine L. French, 'Women Churchwardens in Late Medieval England' in Clive Burgess and Eamon Duffy (eds.), *The Parish in Late Medieval England* (Donnington, 2006), 313.

[109] TNA, ASSI/45/2/1/19, Deposition of Robert Ellington, 22 August 1647; *OBP* May 1744, trial of John Saunders (t17440510-5).

in taking Care of the Keys' (the quays). The sons of parish clerks in the capital and in York helped their fathers take notes of parish affairs and even officiated for them during church services. The son of a bailiff helped to collect debts and acted more generally as 'an Assistant to his Father in the Execution of his Office'. A Kentishman was 'Deputy & under bayliffe to his brother'.[110] Beyond these male partnerships, court records reveal a sexton's daughter who 'assists her Father in the Execution of his Office' and a Norwich constable who went on the beat at midnight with his mother.[111]

Above all, male officers' wives were frequently involved in their husbands' activities. The puritan preacher William Gouge was alarmed by what he saw as unwelcome female interference at the highest level of local government:

> more petitions and suites are made to the wives of Magistrates in the cases of Justice then to the Magistrates themselves: and the favour of their wives is more esteemed then their owne: so as the power of governing, and the maine stroke in determining matters, is from their wives, they are but the mouthes and instruments of their wives, in so much as among the common people the title of their places and offices is given to their wives.[112]

Gouge may have been exaggerating, but at a less exalted level there is plentiful evidence of officers' wives playing a part in legal processes and the administration of poor relief, as well as more menial tasks on which the smooth running of local government depended. This appears to have happened across the country throughout the seventeenth and eighteenth centuries, sometimes but not always drawing hostile male commentary. In the 1630s in Sileby (Leicestershire), the involvement of a churchwarden's wife in her husband's parish duties prompted one neighbour to comment that the parish effectively had an extra churchwarden, 'for I thinke Mrs Church will take upon her the state of a Churchwarden'. In 1663, a Norfolk magistrate issued a pair of arrest warrants at the request of a local constable's wife. In 1667, Lancashire pauper Elizabeth Goodson complained that the overseers did not 'take any care but rather threaten me with discourageble words ... especially one of the overseers wife'. In 1717, a London woman got a writ to arrest the father of her illegitimate baby from 'a Bailiff's

---

[110] LMA, COL/CA/01/01/143, f.462; BIA, GB 193, CP.H.2450, Deposition of Henry Penrose, 29 Jan 1664, 10; LMA, DL/C/0251, Deposition of John Shelley, 29 Mar 1710, 448–50; *OBP*, February 1682, trial of George Pye (t16820224-1); KHLC, Q/SB/11/19, Information of William Kirby, 24 Jun 1670.
[111] LPL, Arches, Eee 14, Deposition of Jane Singleton, 9 Nov 1738, 373; NRO, NCR Case 12b/1 1690–1700, Information of Mary Burman, 5 November 1699.
[112] William Gouge, *Of Domesticall Duties* (London, 1622), 355–6.

Wife'.¹¹³ In 1738, a widow applying for poor relief in Lewisham 'was put in to the Watch house there by order of the Church-Wardens Wife'. In 1739, a beadle's wife in Isleworth, west of London, took the lead in finding the father of a pregnant arrival's child. In 1740, when the vestrymen of St Laurence Pountney in the City wanted to call a parish meeting, the sexton's wife 'carried out printed Summons's and delivered them at the Parishioners Houses'. Women's involvement in their husbands' officeholding continued into the following century: a pamphlet published in Manchester in 1800 complained that 'Overseers wives acted as magistrates, they signed passes [and] relieved the poor'.¹¹⁴

These examples contradict Naomi Tadmor's statement that officers' wives 'were not included in parish governance'.¹¹⁵ They align closely, however, with recent studies of gender and officeholding in continental Europe. In the case of Swedish customs officers, for example, Maria Ågren argues that 'wives shared with their husbands the quotidian responsibility for the state office ... this even went so far as to involve the women in the core tasks of customs administration'. Similarly, in Portugal, Darlene Abreu-Ferreira has shown that 'public offices – officially held by men – were in fact family affairs'.¹¹⁶ These accounts have something in common with the idea of women's 'power through the family', first developed by medievalists and adopted by historians of early modern England in studies of the informal influence of royal, aristocratic, and other elite women. Women whose male relatives held positions of power could use their familial connections to shape the way in which that power was exercised.¹¹⁷ Married women's involvement in officeholding, however, reveals women not only influencing

---

¹¹³ Quoted in Bernard Capp, 'Life, Love and Litigation: Sileby in the 1630s', *Past & Present* 182 (2004), 65; James M. Rosenheim (ed.), *The Notebook of Robert Doughty 1662–1665* (Norwich, 1989), 27; Jonathan Healey, *The First Century of Welfare: Poverty and Poor Relief in Lancashire 1620–1730* (Woodbridge, 2014), 97; *OBP*, September 1717, trial of Elizabeth Arthur (t17170911-50).

¹¹⁴ KHLC, Q/SB/1738/Examinations, Examination of Mary Laffever, 6 March 1738; *OBP*, September 1739, trial of Elizabeth Harrard (t17390906-8); LMA, DL/C/0636, Deposition of Elizabeth Godfrey, 13 Feb 1740, 384-v; T Battye, *A Concise Exposition of the Tricks and Arts Used in the Collection of Easter Dues* (Manchester, 1800), 26.

¹¹⁵ Naomi Tadmor, 'Where Was Mrs Turner? Governance and Gender in an Eighteenth-Century English Village' in Hindle, Shepard, and Walter (eds.), *Remaking English Society*, 109.

¹¹⁶ Maria Ågren, *The State as Master: Gender, State Formation and Commercialisation in Urban Sweden, 1650–1780* (Manchester, 2017), 115; Darlene Abreu-Ferreira, 'Women and the Acquisition, Transmission and Execution of Public Offices in Early Modern Portugal', *Gender & History* 31.2 (2019), 383.

¹¹⁷ Jo Ann McNamara and Suzanne Wemple, 'The Power of Women through the Family in Medieval Europe: 500–1100', *Feminist Studies* 1.3/4 (1973); Barbara J. Harris, 'Women and Politics in Early Tudor England', *The Historical Journal* 33.2 (1990); Elaine Chalus, *Elite Women in English Political Life c.1754–1790* (Oxford, 2005); Elaine Chalus, '"Ladies are often very good scaffoldings": Women and Politics in the Age of Anne', *Parliamentary History* 28.1 (2009).

those who wielded formal authority, but also wielding it directly as subordinate members of official households. In this respect, they were not so different to those women who, as head of their own households, held office in their own right.

Scholars have uncovered examples of female officeholding from the fourteenth century to the eighteenth and beyond. Some offices, generally ignored by legal writers, were dominated by women. These were usually low down in the parish hierarchy and sometimes attached to receipt of poor relief. Female 'searchers of the dead' fell into this category, granted pensions in return for examining corpses for signs of plague or other causes of death.[118] Many sextons were women, especially in London, keeping the capital's churches clean and overseeing burials in their churchyards. The parish of St John's Hackney, for example, employed Rebecca Dowse as sexton from 1714 until 1738, when she died and was replaced by John Singleton. When he died in 1745, his daughter Jane took her father's place. The parish also had its own midwife, who appears in the minutes of vestry meetings at the end of every list of parish officers. In the early eighteenth century, this was always a woman.[119]

Women also held higher, more powerful offices in law enforcement and local government.[120] There were female beadles and reeves on late medieval English manors and female churchwardens in the parishes.[121] In the sixteenth century, women served as churchwardens across the country, from Morebath in Devon to Tynemouth in Northumberland.[122] Women held

---

[118] Diane Willen, 'Women in the Public Sphere in Early Modern England: The Case of the Urban Working Poor', *Sixteenth Century Journal* 19.4 (1988); Richelle Munkhoff, 'Searchers of the Dead: Authority, Marginality, and the Interpretation of Plague in England, 1574–1665', *Gender & History* 11.1 (1999); Wanda S. Henry, 'Women Searchers of the Dead in Eighteenth- and Nineteenth-Century London', *Social History of Medicine* 29.3 (2016); cf. Manon van der Heijden and Ariadne Schmidt, 'Public Services and Women's Work in Early Modern Dutch Towns', *Journal of Urban History* 36.3 (2010).

[119] LMA, P79/JN1/139-142. Women continued to hold office as sextons throughout the eighteenth and nineteenth centuries: Wanda Henry, 'Hester Hammerton and Women Sextons in Eighteenth- and Nineteenth-Century England', *Gender & History* 31.2 (2019).

[120] Ongoing work by Alice Blackwood will provide a much fuller picture of parish officeholding by women in the sixteenth and seventeenth centuries.

[121] Mark Forrest, 'Women Manorial Officers in Late Medieval England', *Nottingham Medieval Studies* 57 (2013); Gibbs, 'Manorial Officeholding', 77; Christine Peters, *Patterns of Piety: Women, Gender and Religion in Late Medieval and Reformation England* (Cambridge, 2003), 33–8, 178–83; Katherine L. French, *The Good Women of the Parish: Gender and Religion after the Black Death* (Philadelphia, 2008).

[122] Sara Mendelson and Patricia Crawford, *Women in Early Modern England 1550–1720* (Oxford, 1998), 52–8; Eamon Duffy, *The Voices of Morebath: Reformation & Rebellion in an English Village* (New Haven, 2001), 191–99; Amanda L. Capern, *The Historical Study of Women: England 1500–1700* (Basingstoke, 2008), 150.

a wide range of offices throughout the seventeenth and eighteenth centuries. There were female overseers and churchwardens in Essex, Suffolk, and Dorset in the 1690s and early 1700s, and in Cambridgeshire and Hertfordshire in the 1750s, 1760s, and 1770s. A woman was surveyor of the highways in Nottinghamshire in 1750. Anne Sigsworth went to court for reimbursement of the money she had spent as a constable in the North Riding in 1695, as did Isabel Eyre in Derbyshire in 1712.[123] One Elizabeth Wood owned a copy of *The Universal officer of justice*, a guide to local officeholding published in 1730, and wrote her name on the inside cover.[124] These women were, however, undoubtedly unusual. Where it is possible to tell, they were invariably single or widowed heads of their own households, often living in relatively small rural settlements which may not always have had enough patriarchs to choose from. The records of most parishes and manors yield long lists of uninterrupted male names. Earls Colne elected 212 constables between 1603 and 1750, and all of them were men. Every churchwarden of the parish whose name survives in the records was a man. One woman, the widow Ann Sandall, served as overseer of the poor in 1722–3, but before and after her the parish chose 151 men.[125]

Men dominated most local offices throughout the early modern period, but the form of that domination was changing. In 1738, Sarah Bly was elected sexton of St Botolph Aldersgate, narrowly defeating her rival candidate, a man named Olive. For several reasons – including Bly's gender and the fact that she had won on the strength of female parishioners' votes – Olive claimed the result was illegitimate and launched legal proceedings. The case eventually made its way to King's Bench, where Olive's counsel argued that 'This election is void because she is unfit for the office, and is *persona minus idonea*' – a less than suitable person. The obvious defence for Bly's lawyers would have been that as a householder, Bly *was* an *idoneus homo*, regardless of her gender. But this was not the path they chose. Instead, they argued that women could be sextons because this was 'an office which may be executed by any persons whatsoever, and requires no capacity or judgment at all'. It was, they claimed, 'a servile ministerial office, which requires neither skill nor understanding'. It did not matter

---

[123] Goldie, 'The Unacknowledged Republic', 172; French, *Middle Sort of People*, 107–8; Saunders, 'Men of good character', 90; Eleanor Trotter, *Seventeenth Century Life in the Country Parish, with Special Reference to Local Government* (Cambridge, 1919), 104 n. 3; W. E. Tate, *The Parish Chest: A Study of the Records of Parochial Administration in England* (4th edition, Chichester, 1983 [first published 1946]), 34.
[124] *The Universal Officer of Justice* (London, 1730), BL, General Reference Collection, RB.23.a.35572.
[125] Appendix A.

who held the office of sexton because a sexton had no real decision-making power; there was no need for the independent discretion of the *idoneus homo*.[126]

This argument proved successful: the court ruled in Bly's favour and upheld her election. The logic it rested on, however, emerged from a kind of legal thinking which, over the previous century, had begun to redefine certain kinds of officeholding. The sextonship was neither the first nor the last office to be described as 'servile', 'ministerial', and requiring 'no capacity or judgment'. The same ideas that persuaded the eighteenth-century King's Bench justices to allow a woman to be sexton had been used by their predecessors to foster a new kind of officeholding within and alongside the old system. The power of these offices was increasingly separated from the individual officer's personal virtues. They no longer had to possess honesty, knowledge, and ability. The monopolisation of officeholding by the *idoneus homo*, the independent householder, was coming to an end. This did not, as Bly's case suggested, open the door to widespread female participation in office. Instead, it facilitated the emergence of a different mode of official masculinity and a different understanding of official power.

---

[126] *Olive v Ingram* (1738), 7 Mod. 263, 87 *ER* 1230. Reported more briefly at 2 Strange 1114, 93 *ER* 1067. On the significance of Bly's case in the history of women's suffrage, see Hilda Smith, 'Women as Sextons and Electors: King's Bench and Precedents for Women's Citizenship' in Hilda Smith (ed.), *Women Writers and the Early Modern British Political Tradition* (Cambridge, 1998).

PART II

Remaking Office

CHAPTER 2

The Law of Office

A key premise of government by independent heads of household was that the official was not separate from the personal. Officers' authority rested in large part on their unofficial power as patriarchs, their position as the generally acknowledged rulers of domestic and communal life. There was, however, another way of thinking about office which drew sharp distinctions between the official and the personal. This was the notion that officers were representatives, that they exercised an authority granted to them by others which had nothing to do with their own identities. A play about a constable named Blurt, printed in 1602, captured this idea perfectly. It is set in a Spanish town governed by a duke and revolves around Blurt's futile efforts to prevent people from walking the streets at night. His attempts to exercise authority take the form of claims to represent or even embody the duke. 'I am the Dukes own Image', he declares, 'and charge you in his name to obey me'. When other characters insult him, he says 'you abuse the Duke, in me that am his Cipher'. When he is derided as a peasant, he warns 'you have called the Dukes owne ghost Peasant, for I walke for him i'th night'. His orders should be followed, he insists, because 'the Dukes tongue ... lyes in my mouth'. Blurt's embodiment of the duke gives him a kind of dual personhood; on the one hand, he is an official representative of authority, on the other, he is an ordinary man. As he puts it, 'I have two voices in any company: one, as I am Master Constable: another, as I am Blurt'.[1] Later in the seventeenth century, the poet Samuel Butler described officers as people who, like Blurt, lived a double life as both private individuals and representatives of higher power. An officer, Butler wrote, was 'a mungrel of mixt generation – Nature meant him for a man, but his office intervening put her out, and made him another thing'. This other thing tended to overwhelm an officer's own identity: 'The

---

[1] *Blurt Master-Constable. Or The Spaniards Night-Walke* (London, 1602), B2, F4v, H1. The play is usually attributed to Thomas Dekker or Thomas Middleton.

most predominant part in him is that in which he is something beside himself … having no intrinsic value he has nothing to trust to but the stamp that is set upon him'.[2]

This chapter argues that a similar view of officeholding began to be used by lawyers, judges, and parliamentarians in the seventeenth century to redefine certain kinds of official authority. Through statutes and judicial rulings, they developed a new law of office which clearly distinguished the official from the personal. This was an important phase in the history of state formation, the separation of state power from other kinds of social power.[3] In the long run, that separation undermined the association between office and household. It also had more immediate consequences for the exercise of official power on an everyday basis. Particular groups of officers, especially those involved in law enforcement like constable Blurt, justified their actions by claiming to act as impersonal representatives of higher authorities. This brought them powerful legal protection and the right to use serious violence. On the other hand, if they failed to act in this impersonal fashion, if they allowed their own intentions and identities to interfere, those legal powers and protections disappeared. In other words, the law adopted the notion that office was a kind of double personhood and gave it teeth. Chief justice Matthew Hale, writing at about the same time as Samuel Butler, thought that officers 'consist not only of natural Persons, as they are such, but of Persons constituted in some Degree of Empire, Power, or Jurisdiction'.[4] Officers, when they acted by authority, were not ordinary people but embodiments of state power.

There is an obvious objection to these arguments. Lawyers are sometimes said to see the world through the prism of a courtroom, reducing complex realities to a series of abstract propositions. In taking early modern lawyers' pronouncements on officeholding seriously, there is a risk of reproducing their own distorted point of view. This challenge can be met by making connections between the law of law books and the law as disseminated and acted upon in society at large. The principles laid down by judges in the central courts and by MPs in statutes could have broad social significance, shaping the behaviour of officers and those who encountered them across the country. This chapter treats the law as a framework which gave particular meanings to officers' actions and through which people

---

[2] Samuel Butler, *Characters and Passages from Note-Books*, ed. A. R. Waller (Cambridge, 1908), 243.
[3] Michael J. Braddick, 'The Early Modern English State and the Question of Differentiation, from 1550–1700', *Comparative Studies in Society and History* 38.1 (1996).
[4] Matthew Hale, *The Analysis of the Law: Being a Scheme or Abstract of the Several Titles and Partitions of the Law of England Digested into Method* (3rd edition, Savoy, 1739), 34.

understood and responded to those actions. In doing so, it responds to Michael Braddick's recognition that 'much more could be said about the development and everyday use of political languages and about the representation of authority in face-to-face contexts'.[5] It was in these everyday face-to-face contexts that the law of office really mattered.

Action by Authority

Seventeenth-century lawyers and legislators remade office by treating certain categories of officers as representatives of something outside themselves.[6] This was not an original idea. In England, some writers (especially legal scholars) had described officers as representatives of their political masters since the end of the twelfth century. In continental Europe, some civil lawyers had portrayed officers as delegates of the crown for almost as long.[7] An English civil lawyer, John Cowell, defined an office in 1607 as 'that function, by vertue whereof a man hath some imploiment in the affaires of another, as of the King or other common person'.[8] To hold office, on these terms, was to act on behalf of someone else and so to represent them.

The dictionary in which Cowell's definition appeared was burnt by order of parliament for its alarmingly expansive account of the royal prerogative.[9] His definition of office was not specifically targeted, but it did contrast sharply with the thinking of many contemporary elites. Much of the early seventeenth-century gentry tended to see office as roughly synonymous with personal duty.[10] Every student at grammar school, public school, or university learnt from Cicero's *De Officiis* that

---

[5] Michael J. Braddick, *State Formation in Early Modern England, c.1550–1700* (Cambridge, 2000), 432.
[6] For discussions of other forms of representation and delegation in early modern English society and culture, see Holga Syme, *Theatre and Testimony in Shakespeare's England: A Culture of Mediation* (Cambridge, 2011); Jason Peacey, '"Written according to my usual way": Political Communication and the Rise of the Agent in Seventeenth-Century England' in Chris R. Kyle and Jason Peacey (eds.), *Connecting Centre and Locality: Political Communication in Early Modern England* (Manchester, 2020); Mark Netzloff, *Agents Beyond the State: The Writings of English Travelers, Soldiers, and Diplomats in Early Modern Europe* (Oxford, 2020).
[7] John Sabapathy, *Officers and Accountability in Medieval England 1170–1300* (Oxford, 2014), 238, 248; Myron Piper Gilmore, *Argument from Roman Law in Political Thought 1200–1600* (2nd edition, New York, 1967).
[8] John Cowell, *The Interpreter: Or Booke Containing the Signification of Words* (London, 1607), Zz 2r. 'Common' in this context meant something like 'public' or 'relating to the commonwealth', rather than non-noble.
[9] Johann P. Somerville, *Politics and Ideology in England, 1603–1640* (London, 1986), 122–7.
[10] For dictionary definitions along these lines, see the entries for 'office' in Randle Cotgrave, *A Dictionary of the French and English Tongues* (London, 1611); Thomas Wilson, *A Christian Dictionary* (London, 1612); John Bullokar, *An English Expositor* (London, 1616).

there is no Condition of Life, either Publique, or Private; from Courts of Justice, to Particular Families; either Solitary, or in Society; but there is still a place for Humane Duty: And it is the Well, or Ill discharging of This Office, that makes our Character in the World, either Glorious, or Shameful.

The merging of 'office' and 'duty' made 'office-talk' a staple of seventeenth-century political discourse. In his work on this subject, Conal Condren provides a definition of office as capacious as Cicero's: 'an office was an identifiable and discriminate constellation of responsibilities'. On these terms, 'there was little that might not be made into an office'.[11] In a society saturated with notions of religious, communal, political, and patriarchal obligation, equating office with duty in this way created an almost infinitely applicable concept. Everyone had their place, and every place had its duties. Shepherds were to care for their flocks, parents to govern and instruct their children, citizens to serve their cities. The duty of subordinates was to obey their superiors, that of superiors to rule over their subordinates with wisdom and justice. The duty of husbandry – to cultivate the land entrusted to humans by God – and the duty of monarchy could equally be described as 'offices'. Mothers, millers, midwives, and magistrates all had their duties and were, on these terms, officeholders.[12]

From the early seventeenth century, a growing number of lawyers and legislators began to reject all of this. Like Cowell and their predecessors in the common and civil law traditions, they saw office – or at least certain kinds of office – as something much narrower, much more specific, and much less personal. If holding office meant representing a higher power, then it had nothing to do with individual social duties. To act on behalf of someone (or something) else was emphatically different to fulfilling personal responsibilities. What lawyers thought about this question mattered, not because their ideas were new, but because they began to give them real legal force. In the first decade or so of the reign of James VI&I, a series of statutes and judicial rulings drew clear distinctions between officers' actions as representatives of higher powers and their actions as private individuals. These legal interventions simultaneously restricted

---

[11] *Tully's Offices in Three Books* tr. Roger L'Estrange (London, 1680), 4; Conal Condren, *Argument and Authority in Early Modern England: The Presupposition of Oaths and Offices* (Cambridge, 2006), 29, 19.

[12] John Rider discussed 'the Middwifes office' in his *Biblioteca Scholastica* (London, 1589), 'Obstetricor, obstetrico'. An anonymous feminist tract of the mid-eighteenth century described motherhood as an 'office': *Woman Not Inferior to Man: Or, a Short and Modest Vindication of the Natural Right of the Fair-Sex to a Perfect Equality of Power, Dignity, and Esteem, with Men* (London, 1749), 13–15.

the scope of officers' discretion and bolstered their authority as impersonal instruments of the state.[13]

Changes to the law of office were prompted by a combination of legal and extra-legal developments.[14] The decades either side of 1600 witnessed rapid demographic and economic change. This brought spiralling poverty, a series of bad harvests, frequent grain and enclosure riots, and a dramatic spike in prosecutions for property crime.[15] In response, successive parliaments passed new laws on poor relief, market supply, alehouse licensing, vagrancy, and many other aspects of social and economic life.[16] The burden of enforcing these laws fell on royal commissioners, local magistrates, and the lower-level officeholders who reported offences to them and carried out their commands.[17] From the point of view of judges and politicians in Westminster, this created a problem. Officers had wide discretion in the implementation of these new laws, so there was a great deal of room for biased, excessive, or negligent enforcement.[18] Misuse or abuse of legal authority stirred up resentment and reflected badly on central government. To address this danger, senior judges attempted set limits to the discretionary powers wielded by commissioners, magistrates, and others. As Paul Halliday, John Baker, and David Chan Smith have shown, justices of King's Bench and Common Pleas increasingly reviewed and restrained the actions of those who were granted legal authority. That authority, in the judges' eyes, was delegated from the crown and therefore required supervision by the crown's courts.[19] With a slightly dubious astronomical simile,

---

[13] These developments took place in parallel with judicial and parliamentary efforts confine the power of the monarch and crown servants to legal channels: Alan Cromartie, *The Constitutionalist Revolution: An Essay on the History of England, 1450–1642* (Cambridge, 2006), Chapters 6–8.

[14] On different models of causation in legal history, see Charles Barzun, 'Causation, Legal History, and Legal Doctrine', *Buffalo Law Review* 64.1 (2016); Simon Stern, 'Proximate Causation in Legal History', *History & Theory* 60.2 (2021).

[15] The classic account is Keith Wrightson, *English Society 1580–1680* (London, 1982), esp. 121–82.

[16] Joan R. Kent, 'Attitudes of Members of the House of Commons to the Regulation of "Personal Conduct" in Late Elizabethan and Early Stuart England', *Bulletin of the Institute of Historical Research* 46.113 (1973); David Dean, *Law-Making and Society in Late Elizabethan England: The Parliament of England, 1584–1601* (Cambridge, 1996), 188.

[17] Joan R. Kent, *The English Village Constable 1580–1642: A Social and Administrative Study* (Oxford, 1986), 24–56; Anthony Fletcher, *Reform in the Provinces: The Government of Stuart England* (New Haven, 1986).

[18] Keith Wrightson, 'Two Concepts of Order: Justices, Constables and Jurymen in Seventeenth-Century England' in John Brewer and John Styles (eds.), *An Ungovernable People: The English and Their Law in the Seventeenth and Eighteenth Centuries* (London, 1980); J. A. Sharpe, 'Enforcing the Law in the Seventeenth-Century English Village' in V. A. C. Gatrell, Bruce Lenman, Geoffrey Parker (eds.), *Crime and the Law: The Social History of Crime in Western Europe since 1500* (London, 1980).

[19] Paul D. Halliday, *Habeas Corpus: From England to Empire* (Cambridge, MA, 2010), 18–30; David Chan Smith, *Sir Edward Coke and the Reformation of the Laws* (Cambridge, 2014); John Baker, *The Reinvention of Magna Carta 1216–1616* (Cambridge, 2017), esp. Chapters 5–9.

one chief justice argued that 'all jurisdiction of inferior courts and officers are derived of the crown ... they are well compared to stars that receive all their light of the sun'. This meant, as another King's Bench ruling held, that 'no wrong or injury, either public or private, can be done but that it shall be (here) reformed or punished by due course of law'.[20]

Increasing supervision, however, was only one side of the story. Judges and legislators also worried that officers enforcing the new laws would face resistance, either in the form of direct obstruction by violence or through litigation. Officers who misused their authority had to be punished, but those who acted properly had to be supported and protected. The restraint of officers' discretionary powers described by Halliday, Baker, and Chan Smith was accompanied by a simultaneous reinforcement of those powers, provided they were used in the manner authorised by law. Both restraint and reinforcement followed from what was, in effect, a view of official action as action authorised by the state. Officers who acted by authority needed – and increasingly received – legislative and judicial protection. In particular, MPs and judges set out to strengthen the position of officers who were sued for carrying out authorised actions, and to discourage lawsuits against officers by threatening litigants with financial penalties. On the flipside, these measures would not protect officers who acted beyond the limits of their authority. The distinction between authorised and unauthorised actions, between acting as an officer and as a private person, became the foundation for a new law of office.

Officers were mostly likely to be sued for using their coercive powers: making arrests or confiscating property ('distraint'). People who felt they had been wrongfully arrested or distrained could sue for damages in the civil courts. Before the beginning of the seventeenth century, officers had to choose between two strategies of defence.[21] Either they could deny the allegations altogether by pleading the 'general issue' ('not guilty') or they could admit the substance of the allegation – they had arrested or distrained the plaintiff – but introduce new information to cast the manner in a different, more favourable light (pleading 'specially' by 'justification'). An officer who pleaded the general issue would have to prove that they had not arrested or distrained the plaintiff at all, or at least not in the manner alleged. They could not, however, argue that their actions were justified by authorisation from above. This was not usually the best option. Even

---

[20] Fleming CJKB quoted in Smith, *Edward Coke*, 270; James Bagg's case (1615), 11 Co. Rep. 98a, 77 *ER* 1278.
[21] On pleading, see John Baker, *Introduction to English Legal History* (Oxford, 2019), Chapter 5.

courts which allowed more flexible forms of pleading looked unfavourably on officers who pleaded the general issue. In a case before the court of Star Chamber, a Welsh JP charged with offences concerning 'his publike offices' decided to represent himself rather than taking legal counsel. He then 'pleaded in generall wordes the generall pardon, w[hi[ch by th'opinion of the Judges was nothinge, for that he oughte to have pleaded it speciallye'.[22] In the judges' view, officers should plead 'justifications' to explain that their actions were carried out under orders from a superior or in accordance with their own legal powers.

Justifications, however, brought their own difficulties. In response to a plea of justification, plaintiffs could reply that the officer had acted *de injuria sua propria absque tali causa* ('of their own wrong without such cause'). In other words, that they had acted in a personal rather than an official capacity.[23] The case would then proceed to a trial of whether or not this was true. Alternatively, the plaintiff could 'demur', arguing that the officer's justification was technically deficient or raised legal questions requiring consideration by judges. In the last decades of Elizabeth I's reign, the increasingly assertive courts of King's Bench and Common Pleas ruled against many justifications by officers on technical or legal grounds. Justifications had to explain an officer's authority for a given action from start to finish – from the rights of a town to elect a mayor, for example, through the mayor's capacity to act as a justice of the peace, down to the officer's lawful arrest of the plaintiff under a mayoral warrant. Making these long explanations in precisely the right way required considerable skill. Officers' legal counsel often made accidental omissions or errors of wording which led to their justification being ruled insufficient.[24]

Beginning in 1601, a group of MPs attempted to make things easier for officers facing lawsuits. Many of these were the same MPs who had drafted and supported the new laws on personal, social, and economic behaviour.[25]

---

[22] Stepnie v Warren (1607) in William Paley Baildon (ed.), *Les reportes del cases in Camera Stellata, 1593 to 1609: From the Original MS. of John Hawarde* (London, 1894), 334.
[23] For example: Gray v Hansaker (1557) in John Baker (ed.), *Reports from the Lost Notebooks of Sir James Dyer*, vol. 2 (London, 1994), 410.
[24] Collet v Well & others (1587), BL Add. MS 35948 ff.99–101, 2 Leonard 34, 74 *ER* 336; Beale v Carter (1589), BL Harley MS 4814 f.98, Owen 98, 74 *ER* 927; Smith v Hillier & Clerke (1590), Cro. Eliz. 167, 78 *ER* 425; Sturton/Smith/Stretton v Browne (1590), BL Harley MS 4814 f.114v, BL Add. MS 35948 ff.98v–99, Cro. Eliz. 204, 78 *ER* 460; Cowleigh/Congley v Edwards (1601), BL Add. MS 35948 ff.101–2, Cro. Eliz. 184, 78 *ER* 441; Godbye v Knight (1602), BL Add. MS 25203 ff.619–21.
[25] Key figures involved in both efforts were Francis Darcy, Nicholas Fuller, Francis Hastings, Thomas Hoby, Sir Robert Johnson, Sir George More, and Sir Robert Wroth. On the role these MPs played in legislation relating to personal conduct, see Kent, 'Attitudes of Members'. Much of the legislation discussed below was introduced by these men or modified by them in committee, as recorded

At first, their method was straightforward. To discourage litigation against officers, and to compensate officers who were wrongly accused, they introduced heavy financial penalties for people who sued officers and lost.[26] From 1610 onwards, they adopted a more ambitious approach. This involved changes to the pleas with which officers defended themselves. Under the new legislation, the dichotomy between pleading the general issue and pleading justifications was abolished. Officers could now make both arguments at once, simultaneously denying a plaintiff's claim in its entirety and justifying their actions by reference to a higher authority. Furthermore, they could do this with a simple plea of 'not guilty', so the risk of losing a case through mistakes in pleading disappeared.

The first phase began with the 1601 Poor Law. Most of this Act simply confirmed the provisions of the 1598 Poor Law, including powers granted to churchwardens and overseers of the poor to distrain property in lieu of unpaid poor rates. This was the most straightforwardly coercive aspect of the new poor relief system, and the most likely to meet with opposition from ratepayers who could afford to take officers to court (the paupers who faced coercion under other sections of these Acts were, by definition, less likely to have the resources to litigate). Those who drafted the 1601 law may have been influenced by a case heard after the passage of the 1598 Act, in which judges ruled against royal commissioners who had distrained property in lieu of unpaid taxes.[27] MPs decided that officers who distrained people's goods when they failed to pay legally mandated dues should be better protected from lawsuits. To that end, a new clause was introduced stating that any officer sued for distraint 'done by Authoritie of this Acte' could 'recover Treble Damages, by reason of his wrongfull vexacon in that behalf, with his Costs also'.[28] Ratepayers who sued churchwardens or overseers of the poor would have to prove the officer had acted not by authority of the Act but 'of his owne wronge'. Failure to prove this would be extremely expensive. The threat of significant financial losses, MPs hoped, might make people think twice about suing officers.

---

by the Commons *Journals* and by parliamentary diarists: T. E. Hartley (ed.), *Proceedings in the Parliaments of Elizabeth I*, vol. 3 (London, 1995), 436; David Harris Willson (ed.), *The Parliamentary Diary of Robert Bowyer, 1606–1607* (Minneapolis, 1931), 137.

[26] There was precedent for this in earlier legislation which awarded multiple damages to commissioners of sewers and enclosure commissioners who successfully defended themselves against civil suits: 23 Hen. VIII c.5 s.7 (1532); 2&3 Ph&Mar c.1 s.8 (1555).

[27] Rooke's Case (1598), 5 Co. Rep. 99b, 77 *ER* 209.

[28] 43 Eliz. c.2 s.18 (1601). There was no similar provision in the 1598 Poor Law: 39 Eliz. c.3 (1598).

More clauses requiring unsuccessful plaintiffs to pay heavy penalties appeared in two statutes of 1606, both of which also concerned officers distraining for unpaid taxes. The first was an Act allowing JPs to levy rates to pay for conveying offenders to gaol. This included a provision that anyone who carried out distraint for non-payment of such rates could claim triple legal costs should they be unsuccessfully sued. The second statute raised taxes to repair an important highway from Nonsuch to Kingston. To sue a tax collector who distrained 'by authority of this p[re]sent Acte' would be to risk significant losses. In this case, the provisions of the 1601 Poor Law were reproduced exactly: victorious defendants would recover triple damages as well as legal costs.[29] These were powerful protections, though at this point they only covered a limited range of official activities. Subsequent legislation was both broader in scope and intervened more directly in litigation procedure.

In 1610, parliament passed 'An Acte for ease in pleading against troublesome and contencious Suites, p[ro]secuted against Justices of the Peace Maiors Constables and c[er]taine other his Majesties Officers, for the lawfull execution of their Office'. The statute referred specifically to civil suits of trespass, battery, and false imprisonment, brought against officers 'for or conc[er]ning any Matter Cause or Thing by them or any of them done by vertue or reason of their or any of their Office or Offices'. As in the Acts discussed above, there was an attempt to discourage lawsuits by threatening plaintiffs who lost their case with an extra financial penalty, in this case double legal costs. There was also, however, a new provision for officers to 'plead the Gen[er]all Yssue that he or they are not Guiltie, and to give such speciall Matter in Evidence' as would offer 'good and sufficient matter in Lawe' to clear them of wrongdoing.[30] This meant officers could avoid the risk of defeat on a technically deficient justification without losing the opportunity to justify their actions as authorised by higher powers. They could make the simple plea of not guilty (the 'general issue') and introduce their justification later in the proceedings as 'speciall Matter in Evidence', not as a plea. Plaintiffs would then have to prove their case as a whole *and* prove that the officer had acted 'of their own wrong' rather than 'by authority'.

This statute gave officers a significant advantage in any lawsuit brought against them. Its intention, one parliamentary diarist wrote, was 'that justices of peace and constables shall not be troubled for doing their offices'. According to Michael Dalton, the Act provided 'better encouragement'

---

[29] 3 Jac. I c.10 s.3 (1606); 3 Jac. I c.19 s.4 (1606).
[30] 7 Jac. I c.5 (1610).

for officers who were 'discouraged from doing their offices' by 'causelesse suits commenced by contentious persons'. Exactly how much 'causeless' litigation there was against officers is questionable. It is clear, however, that MPs had decided to grant officers special protection. The value of this protection is illustrated by the fact that during the bill's passage through the House of Lords, archbishop Richard Bancroft attempted 'very vehemently', albeit unsuccessfully, to include officers of the ecclesiastical courts as well as their secular counterparts.[31]

At first, the 1610 statute was set to run for seven years, but an Act of 1624 extended it to 'be p[er]petuall and have contynuance for ever'. The same 1624 Act also fulfilled the archbishop's wishes by extending its protections to churchwardens and overseers of the poor alongside constables and justices of the peace. This was just the beginning. Early in the reign of Charles I, parliament allowed any officer enforcing the laws against breaches of the sabbath to 'pleade the generall issue, and to give the speciall matter in evidence' on much the same terms. One of the last statutes passed before the outbreak of civil war provided the same protection for officers involved in the regulation of weights and measures.[32] After the restoration of monarchy in 1660, the number of these general issue clauses in legislation exploded. Nineteen Acts passed in the 1660s supported officers' authority in this way, most of them requiring the payment of double or triple legal costs by plaintiffs who failed to overcome the disadvantages they now faced. Successive parliaments repeatedly used this device throughout the later seventeenth century, reaching a peak in the 1690s, which saw forty-five general issue clauses added to the statute book. By the beginning of the eighteenth century, the total number was approaching a 100.[33]

These laws covered a wide range of official activities. Some were part of major legislative interventions: officers enforcing the Corporation Act, the Settlement Act, and the Conventicle Acts were permitted to plead the general issue and give special matter in evidence if sued for anything they did under those statutes. Even the 1679 Habeas Corpus Act included a clause allowing officers brought to court on suspicion of unlawful imprisonment to plead and argue in this way.[34] Then there were the Acts

---

[31] Elizabeth Read Foster (ed.), *Proceedings in Parliament 1610* (New Haven, 1966), vol. 1, 121, 242; Michael Dalton, *The Countrey Justice* (1618), 306. In fact, the justices of King's Bench extended the Act's provisions to churchwardens acting under the Poor Laws almost immediately after it was passed: Salter v Oketry (1610), BL Add. MS 25213 f.97.

[32] 21 Jac. I c.5 ss.1–2; 3 Car. I c.2 (1627); 16 Car. I c.19 s.7 (1640).

[33] A full list of seventeenth-century general issue clauses is provided in Appendix B.

[34] 13 Car. II c.1 s.12 (1661); 14 Car. II c.12 s.20 (1662); 16 Car. II c.4 s.6 (1664); 22 Car. II c.1 s.11 (1670); 31 Car. II c.2 s.19 (1679).

reinforcing officers' powers to crack down on poachers, unlicensed hackney coaches and hawkers, or people who set off 'Squibbs Serpents & other Fire-works'.[35] Most of all, there were dozens of clauses protecting the officers who collected various kinds of taxes: customs, parliamentary subsidies, excise taxes, poll taxes, emergency taxes to cover military spending, and innumerable local taxes for the repair of specific roads, the navigation of rivers, the rebuilding of gaols. In part, this reflects the huge expansion of parliamentary taxation – and legislation more generally – in the later seventeenth century.[36] It is worth noting, however, that more statutes brought with them more legal support for the officers who acted under their authority.

Alongside all of these specific measures, the Act of 1610 continued to provide a wide and robust legal shield. As late as the 1770s, a lawyer reviewing the jurisdiction of the University of Cambridge over the policing of 'common women' bemoaned the fact that its officers did not come under the statute. After consulting counsel on the precise meaning of the university's charters, he wrote that 'It were indeed much to be wish[e]d that the particular Privileges & Protection given by several Acts of Parl[iamen]t' to constables, JPs, and other officers 'were extended to the officers of the university exercising the Powers under these Charters'. In particular, he noted that other officers 'are permitted to plead the general Issue & give the special Matter of Justification in Evidence. If the officers of the university c[oul]d do the same they w[oul]d have no Occasion to set forth the Charters specially in their Plea, which requires some nicety & frequently occasions some Risque in the success of the defence'. Without these advantages in pleading, university officers faced the same problems other officers had confronted before 1610. They also lacked the deterrent against litigation provided by the threat of double costs. All in all, he thought those who governed the university should consider 'How far it may be worthwhile to apply to Parl[iamen]t to extend all or some of these privileges to the Vicechanc[ellor], Proctors &c acting under this Charter'. Nothing came of this suggestion, but it illustrates the long-term significance of the special privileges granted to officers in the early seventeenth century.[37]

---

[35] 3 W&M c.10 s.6 (1691); 4 W&M c.23 s.7 (1692); 6&7 W&M c.22 s.12 (1694); 8&9 Wm III c.25 s.6 (1696–7); 9 Wm III c.27 s.6 (1697–8); 9 Wm III c.7 s.6 (1697–8).
[36] Michael J. Braddick, *The Nerves of State: Taxation and the Financing of the English State, 1558–1714* (Manchester, 1996), 95–109; Julian Hoppit, 'Patterns of Parliamentary Legislation, 1660–1800', *Historical Journal* 39.1 (1996), 109.
[37] Cambridge University Library, GBR/0265/UA/CUR37.5/58, 'Opinions of Counsel respecting University Jurisdiction as to Common Women by Mr Pemberton, 1770 & 1771', p. 5.

While MPs developed this novel form of legislative protection for officers, judges were working along similar lines. To begin with, they too became concerned with the position of officers sued for actions carried out under orders from above. If the order itself was defective, was the officer at fault? This was not a new problem, but decisions made in the first decade of the seventeenth century clarified the law and served as precedent for many years to come. In 1602, a justice of Queen's Bench declared that a gaoler who imprisoned someone on the orders of a mayor should not held liable if those orders turned out to be unlawful: 'he must be obedient to his superior and as such he will be excused'. This was related to the nature of the gaoler's office. His duty was to do as the mayor instructed, not to 'examine the authority of his superior'.[38] But what if the order given to an officer was not only unlawful but entirely beyond the jurisdiction of the person or body issuing it? In a case heard in 1606, an officer of the Council of Marches was sued for false imprisonment in the course of property litigation which, according to the justices of King's Bench, was outside the Council's jurisdiction. Two of the judges 'thought the defendant not punishable because he did nothing without a court order', but two others argued that this principle did not hold where the court acted beyond its jurisdiction.[39] The question was resolved in a 1613 case by a long and elaborate judgment. This confirmed that 'it would be against reason' to punish officers for carrying out the orders of courts and other authorities because if they did not do so those authorities 'would have punished them for their disobedience'. Conversely, officers who acted under an authority which had no jurisdiction were not obliged to obey that authority and so could be held liable for their actions: 'it is not of necessity to obey him who is not a Judge of the cause, no more than it is a mere stranger'. In these circumstances, an officer's actions were not attributable to a higher power, only to themselves.[40]

This distinction was related to a broader problem judges were grappling with in the Jacobean period: deputisation.[41] Could officers appoint deputies to act for them? If so, did those deputies have the same authority and protection under law? More importantly, if an officer was supposed to be *idoneus homo*, as discussed in the previous chapter, what would

---

[38] Gobye v Knight (1602), BL Add. MS 25203 f.620v, my translation. For a case addressing related questions in the court of Exchequer, see Doillie v Joiliffe, Lane 48, 145 *ER* 289 (1610).

[39] Whitherley v Huninges (1606), translated and reproduced in Baker, *Reinvention*, 516.

[40] The Case of the Marshalsea (1613), 10 Co. Rep. 68b, 77 *ER* 1027. The extent of the Marshalsea court's jurisdiction had been debated at length a few years before: Cox v Gray (1610), BL Add. MS 25213 f.127v. Legal protection of officers acting under warrant was later enshrined in a 1751 statute 'indemnifying Constables and others acting in Obedience to their Warrants': 24 Geo. II c.44.

[41] Chan Smith, *Sir Edward Coke*, 275.

happen if they chose deputies who did not possess the required qualities of honesty, knowledge, and ability? How could the appointment of deputies be squared with a model of officeholding which valued the personal identity of the officer? If it could not, how could office be redefined to accommodate deputisation? To resolve these questions, judges distinguished between different types of officeholding. Some officers continued to require the personal characteristics of the *idoneus homo*. For them, the personal was inextricable from the official. Other officers, however, no longer had to be *idoneus homo* or possess any particular qualities at all. These officers could appoint deputies because their own identities were irrelevant to their position. For them, in theory, the official became clearly separate from the personal.

Judges began by ruling against deputisation in particular circumstances. Bailiffs, for example, could sometimes appoint deputies but could not deputise someone to hold confiscated property on their behalf.[42] Royal purveyors, who requisitioned supplies for the crown, could not lawfully appoint deputies because 'the office of purveyor is one of trust' and because such officers ought to be 'men of sufficiencie to aunsweare the kinge & the state'.[43] In other words, the personal identity (and wealth) of purveyors mattered too much to their office for deputisation to be allowed. Similar objections were made to deputisation by manorial stewards: the 'qualities of his mind, science, fidelity, and diligence ... are so individually annexed to him that he cannot make a deputy'.[44] The logic of these arguments was clarified by a ruling on deputisation by sheriffs, who could and frequently did appoint under-sheriffs to deputise for them in many tasks. This was acceptable, but only up to a point. In 1613, justices of Common Pleas resolved that 'a sheriff in making an under-sheriff did implicitly give him power to execute all the ordinary offices of the sheriff himself, that might be transferred by the law ... but he could not deal with a writ of redisseisin, because in that the sheriff is a Judge'.[45] The nature of a writ of redisseisin is less important than the justices' reasoning: sheriffs could delegate many of their powers to deputies, but not those powers which allowed them to act as judges. Judicial acts could only be performed by the original officer.

---

[42] Taylor v James (1607), Godbolt 150, 78 *ER* 91.
[43] Richards Case (1605) in Baildon (ed.) *Les reportes*, 248. Also reported at Moore (KB) 762, 72 *ER* 890.
[44] The Earl of Shrewsbury's Case (1610), 9 Co. Rep. 48a, 77 *ER* 801. In fact, King's Bench decided in favour of stewards appointing deputies. This was confirmed the following year in an unnamed case reported at BL Add. MS 25213, f.126, and much later in Howard v Wood (1678), 2 Show. KB 21, 89 *ER* 767. Similar concerns were raised about deputisation by an auditor of the court of wards: Auditor Curle's Case (1610), 77 *ER* 1149.
[45] Norton v Simmes (1613), Hobart 12, 80 *ER* 163. Also reported at Godbolt 212, 78 *ER* 129.

Official actions could be divided into two types: judicial and ministerial. In his 1581 handbook for justices of the peace, William Lambarde explained that JPs could command a person to find sureties for the peace 'either as a Minister when hee is willed to do it by a higher auctoritie: or as a Judge when he doth it of his owne power derived from his Commission'. This division could be applied well beyond sureties for the peace. Michael Dalton's later handbook divided all of a JP's powers between the two categories. 'The Power and Authoritie of the Justices of Peace', he wrote, 'is in some cases Ministeriall or Regular and limited, as a Minister onely; And in some other cases Judiciall or Absolute, and as a Judge'.[46] To act ministerially was to obey the commands of a higher authority. To act judicially was to exercise the powers of office independently.[47]

In their efforts to decide who could appoint deputies, judges applied these categories of official action to some offices in their entirety. The most important case concerned the office of constable, the 1610 general issue statute, and the ideal of the *idoneus homo*. In 1615, a man called Phelps sued a constable named Winchcombe in the court of King's Bench for false imprisonment.[48] Winchcombe claimed the benefit of the 1610 statute: he wanted to plead the general issue and bring special matter in evidence to show that he had arrested Phelps by authority, in this case the authority of a warrant. If he won the case, he expected to receive double legal costs, as the statute provided. The problem was that Winchcombe's status as a constable was uncertain. The warrant for Phelps' arrest had been sent to another man, the elected constable, but he had been too sick to execute it and appointed Winchcombe to act as his deputy. Phelps' counsel argued that this made the arrest unlawful. By law, they said, a constable had to be *idoneus homo*, a suitable person with the requisite levels of honesty, knowledge, and ability. Anyone elected to the office who did not meet those qualifications was, as shown in the previous chapter, promptly discharged. Winchcombe had not been elected, merely chosen by the arbitrary will of the elected constable to deputise for him, so there was no guarantee that he (Winchcombe) was *idoneus homo*. As such, he could not be entrusted with the powers of office, should not have

---

[46] William Lambarde, *Eirenarcha: Or, of The Office of Justices of the Peace* (London, 1581), 83; Dalton, *Countrey Justice*, 17.

[47] Matthew Hale later drew parallels between this distinction and the distinction between *merum imperium* and *mixtum imperium* in Roman law: *Analysis of the Law*, 33–38; *The Digest of Justinian, Vol. 1* tr. Alan Watson (Philadelphia, 1985), 40.

[48] There are several printed reports of this case. What follows is based on Phelps v Winchcombe, Moore (KB) 845, 72 *ER* 944; Phelps v Winchcomb, 3 Bulstrode 77, 81 *ER* 66; Phelpe v Winscombe, 1 Rolle 274, 81 *ER* 485. There is a very brief manuscript report at BL Add. MS 25213 f.178v.

executed the arrest warrant, and certainly should not have the benefit of statutory protection designed specifically for constables.

The justices of King's Bench disagreed. Their ruling rested on a distinction between judicial and ministerial offices. As one of the judges explained, 'Of officers there are these two kinds, a judicial officer, and ministerial; a judicial officer cannot make a deputy, because he is called to do justice; otherwise it is of a ministerial officer, who may make his deputy'. Constables, the court decided, were ministerial officers and so capable of making deputies. Those deputies would have the full legal powers and protections of a constable, including those provided by the 1610 Act; as Edward Coke put it, 'a deputy is the person of the constable, and so within the statute'.

Judicial officers could not appoint deputies because independent judgement – discretion – required qualities particular to the individual officer, which a deputy might not possess. Ministerial officers, by contrast, did not need to possess any special characteristics. Their function was simply to perform the tasks they were authorised to carry out by higher powers. They did not need to make judgements or exercise discretion, only to act exactly as they were required to act by statute, common law, or instructions from a superior. There was no need for any particular qualities of mind or character, so a deputy could do the job just as well as the officer originally chosen.[49] In 1629, in a high-profile case before King's Bench, the attorney general argued that gaolers, like constables, were ministerial officers. The case involved the imprisonment of several MPs who had criticised royal policies in the House of Commons. The warrant for their imprisonment had not stated a particular cause, and when the MPs brought a writ of habeas corpus, their gaoler was unable to provide a specific reason for their detention. Labelling the gaoler a ministerial officer was part of the attorney general's attempt to justify this: 'it is not fit that the gaoler, which is but a ministerial officer, should be acquainted with the secrets of the cause'.[50] Ministerial officers followed orders; they did not need to know why they did what they did.

---

[49] Curiously, writers in the civil law tradition came to exactly the opposite conclusion about the relationship between discretion and deputisation. Bartolus of Sassoferrato and others who were influenced by his work (including Jean Bodin) argued that discretionary powers *belonged* to individual magistrates and so could be granted to deputies to wield on their behalf, whereas non-discretionary powers belonged to the law, the prince, or the state, so magistrates had no right to delegate them to anyone else: Gilmore, *Argument from Roman Law*, 38, 76–78, 98–103.

[50] T. B. Howell, *A Complete Collection of State Trials and Proceedings for High Treason and other Crimes and Misdemeanors from the Earliest Period to the Present Time*, vol. 3 (London, 1816), 281. For a general account of these proceedings, see John Reeve, 'The Arguments in King's Bench in 1629 Concerning the Imprisonment of John Selden and Other Members of the House of Commons', *Journal of British Studies* 25.3 (1986).

This notion of a ministerial officer was little more than a legal fantasy. In practice, almost every officer (including constables and gaolers) exercised some degree of discretionary power.[51] The caricature of an entirely servile officer could, however, be polemically useful. It suggested a kind of lowliness and subordination. In 1614, senior members of the legal profession (counsel, serjeants, and judges) attempted to exclude attorneys and solicitors from residing at the inns of court, issuing an order which described them as 'but ministeriall persons and of an inferior nature'.[52] This vocabulary was not restricted to lawyers. During the 1640s, political writers of all stripes described those whose powers they wished to undercut as ministerial officers. For William Prynne, 'Parliament is the Superiour Soveraigne power, the King but the Ministeriall; and it is more rationall and just, that the inferiour should condescend to the greater Power, the Ministeriall to those hee serves, then they to him'. The Scottish Presbyterian Samuel Rutherford called royal authority 'a ministeriall power' borne by an 'honourable servant and watchman appointed by the community'. On the other side, royalists argued that 'the Judges of Inferiour Courts of ministeriall Justice' had no right to exercise any powers other than those 'issued from the King' or his predecessors.[53] Radical critics of both royal and republican government argued that 'The power of the Magistrate is not absolute, his authority is ministeriall', extending only to those tasks delegated by God or by the people.[54]

Those who used the concept of ministerial officeholding for political purposes wanted to emphasise that such officers represented and served the authority of others. They were less interested in the legal niceties of discretion and deputisation than in the model of official authority as delegated rather than inherent in the office. According to Thomas Hobbes, 'The word *Minister* in the Originall signifieth one that voluntarily doth the businesse of another man'.[55] On these terms, to define someone as a ministerial officer

---

[51] As attorney general in 1582, John Popham argued that 'a constable is like a judge' when deciding whether or not to arrest someone for a breach of the peace: Attorney-General v Joiners' Company of London (1582), translated and reproduced in Baker, *Reinvention*, 470. According to one admiralty court judge, constables and jurors were 'judges' in the same category as justices of the peace: Charles George Cock, *English-Law: Or, A Summary Survey of the Houshold of God on Earth* (London, 1651), 138.
[52] C. W. Brooks, *Pettyfoggers and Vipers of the Commonwealth: The 'Lower Branch' of the Legal Profession in Early Modern England* (Cambridge, 1986), 162.
[53] William Prynne, *The Soveraigne Power of Parliaments and Kingdomes* (London, 1643), part II, 39; Samuel Rutherford, *Lex, Rex: The Law and the Prince* (London, 1644), 398; *Reasons of the Present Judgment of the University of Oxford, Concerning the Solemne League and Covenant* (London, 1647), 30.
[54] Enoch Grey, *Vox Coeli, Containing Maxims of Pious Policy* (London, 1649), 21; John Warr, *The Priviledges of the People, or, Principles of Common Right and Freedome* (London, 1649), 8.
[55] Thomas Hobbes, *Leviathan* ed. J. C. A. Gaskin (Oxford, 1996), 356.

was to argue that there was a power above them, from which their own authority derived. The most consequential deployment of this idea was to label the monarch a ministerial officer, someone who did not act for themselves but did the business of others – in this case, the sovereign people. Theorists of popular sovereignty in continental Europe had long argued that no monarch (or pope) was anything more than 'a mere minister of the people' or 'a minister of the commonwealth'.[56] After the trial and execution of Charles I in 1649, defenders of the new republican regime announced to the English people that 'The power is originally, really, and fundamentally in themselves; it is but Ministerially in the King, as a Publick servant'. Parliament had done to the king what judges had already done to the constable: they had treated him as an officer whose authority was separable from his person, and who could be held accountable for misuses of the authority delegated to him by a higher power.[57] Oliver Cromwell paid lip-service to this notion of a ministerial ruler when he described the office of lord protector as that of 'a good constable to keep the peace of the parish'. After 1660, of course, apologists for the restored monarchy turned the tables once again, arguing that MPs were 'only Ministerial Servants'.[58]

In law, unlike politics, the specific meanings of the ministerial-judicial division made it difficult to simply separate offices into one category or another. Almost all officers possessed some discretionary powers, and almost all sometimes acted on instructions from above. Distinctions between ministerial and judicial *acts* rather than *offices* were far easier to sustain. In 1650, the chief justice of King's Bench (temporarily renamed the Upper Bench) ruled that 'a judicial Act' could not be delegated to a deputy, whereas 'a ministerial act' could be; in each case of deputisation, it had to be established whether the actions performed by the deputy required any particular ability or discretion. More broadly, ministerial and judicial acts held different positions in law. Ministerial acts had to be carried out in the prescribed manner and failure to do so could be punished. Judicial acts, being discretionary, could be carried out as the officer saw fit, without any threat of punishment. One of the arguments in a well-known ruling on the independence of juries was that giving a trial verdict

---

[56] Quentin Skinner, *The Foundations of Modern Political Thought: Volume 2, The Age of Reformation* (Cambridge, 1978), 117–21, 133.
[57] *Anglia Liberata, or, The Rights of the People of England, Maintained against the Pretences of the Scottish King* (London, 1651), 47; D. Alan Orr, *Treason and the State: Law, Politics and Ideology in the English Civil War* (Cambridge, 2002), 171.
[58] W. C. Abbott (ed.), *The Writings and Speeches of Oliver Cromwell* vol. 3 (Cambridge, MA, 1947), 470; Cimelgus Bonde [Giles Duncombe], *Salmasius His Buckler, or, A Royal Apology for King Charles the Martyr* (London, 1662), 314.

'is not an act ministerial, but judicial ... for which they are not finable, nor to be punisht'. On the other hand, claiming to act ministerially could allow officers to avoid taking responsibility for their actions. In the 1684 treason trial of Algernon Sidney, chief justice George Jeffries was at pains to emphasise that his refusal to grant Sidney professional legal representation was not a vindictive personal act, but the inescapable procedure of the law, which he, as a ministerial officer, dutifully performed. 'We are the Ministers of the Law', he declared, 'tis the Law says we are not to allow you Counsel ... Therefore don't go away and say that we as men sitting here impose upon you, we sit here only to administer the Justice of the Nation'.[59] Like an officer who pleaded the general issue and claimed to have acted 'by authority', an officer acting ministerially disavowed any personal motive and insisted they were merely serving the state.

Over the course of the late seventeenth and eighteenth centuries, the ministerial-judicial distinction was both widely applied and increasingly contested. Constables, for example, were said to act ministerially when they reported information about possible conventicles to justices of the peace: 'the Constable ... is not Judge of the truth of the Fact, he is only a Ministerial Officer or Servant in this Case'.[60] Similarly, they had a 'purely ministerial' power to prevent voting in parliamentary elections by people who did not hold the franchise, though one justice suggested that 'the officer in this case, though not properly and strictly a judge, yet he is *quasi* a judge; for he has a distinguishing power who shall be admitted to vote, and who not'.[61] The precedent of Phelps v Winchcombe was cited in numerous cases relating to the appointment of deputies and the amount of discretionary power vested in particular offices,[62] but the basic logic of its distinctions came under increasing pressure. In a case involving a deputy parish clerk, one lawyer argued that 'the distinction that has been made between judicial and ministerial officers must not be received in so great

---

[59] Cater v Startute (1650), Style 217, 82 *ER* 659; Bushell's Case (1670), Vaughan 135, 124 *ER* 1006; *The Arraignment, Tryal & Condemnation of Algernon Sidney* (London, 1684), 7.
[60] Edmund Saunders, *Observations upon the Statute of 22 Car. II. Cap. I* (London, 1685), 84.
[61] This is an understudied aspect of the well-known case of Ashby v White (1703), which was widely reported: 6 Mod. 45, 87 *ER* 810; 1 Salkeld 19, 91 *ER* 19; 2 Ld. Raym. 938, 92 *ER* 126. For a full account of the politics surrounding this case, see E. Cruickshanks, 'Ashby v. White: The Case of the Men of Aylesbury, 1701–4' in C. Jones (ed.), *Party and Management in Parliament, 1660–1784* (Leicester, 1984).
[62] For example: Sir Walter Vane's Case (1668), 1 Sid. 355, 82 *ER* 1153; Colvin v Fletcher (1722), 8 Mod. 43, 88 *ER* 33; R v Simpson (1724), 1 Strange 609, 93 *ER* 731; R v Harwood (1725), 8 Mod. 380, 88 *ER* 270; Nott v Long (1735), Cas. t. Hard. 181, 95 *ER* 117; Olive v Ingram (1738), 7 Mod. 263, 87 *ER* 1230; R v Clarke (1787), 1 T.R. 679, 99 *ER* 1317; Milward v Thatcher (1787), 2 T.R. 81, 100 *ER* 45; R v Bristow (1795), 6 T.R. 168, 101 *ER* 492; Schinotti v Bumsted (1796), 6 T.R. 646, 101 *ER* 750.

a latitude; for there is a difference between some ministerial officers and others. Those that require skill and judgment cannot make a deputy'. The chief justice of King's Bench agreed, saying that 'it was certain, that even a ministerial office, which requires skill, cannot be executed by deputy'. He expressed 'some doubts, how that was to be understood of a constable's making a deputy'. Later in the eighteenth century, however, another chief justice pushed the law towards allowing more rather than less deputisation by refusing to accept that all discretionary acts were 'judicial'. 'It is taking the definition too large', he argued, 'to say "that every act where the judgment is at all exercised, is a judicial act": a judicial act is supposed to be done *pendente lite* [during litigation] … This construction is the most convenient, and agreeable to the rule of law in cases of appointing deputies'.[63] On these terms, any officer who did not actually sit in court as a judge could appoint a deputy.

In 1788, Alice Stubbs, a widowed householder in Staffordshire, was chosen to be her parish's overseer of the poor. Some local men who opposed this took her to court, eventually to King's Bench, arguing that women could not hold such an office. As in the case of Sarah Bly, discussed at the end of the previous chapter, one of the arguments in favour of Stubbs was that the office in question was a ministerial one, which anyone could hold regardless of their qualities as an individual. In making this argument, Stubbs' counsel made one of the clearest surviving statements on the difference between judicial and ministerial offices. It was true that overseers exercised some discretion, but this did not undermine the ministerial character of the office, or the possibility of appointing a deputy. 'There is no foundation for any such objection', her counsel argued, 'for it can only hold in cases where the office is strictly judicial … where the duty consists in an original exercise of office, not in obeying the mandate of another'. The office of overseer, they claimed, 'is wholly ministerial, for he acts in almost all instances under the control and direction of justices of the peace'. The judges accepted this argument, and Stubbs retained her office, but only on the understanding that it was a ministerial office, involving ministerial acts; she held no 'original' authority of her own, only obeyed 'the mandate of another'.[64]

---

[63] Peake v Bourne (1732), 2 Strange 942, 93 *ER* 956; Speak v Bourn (1732), 2 Barn. KB 52, 94 *ER* 351; Midhurst v Waite (1761), 3 Burr. 1259, 97 *ER* 821.
[64] R v Stubbs and others (1788), 2 T.R. 395, 100 *ER* 213. For a full account of the case, see Hilda Smith, 'Women as Sextons and Electors: King's Bench and Precedents for Women's Citizenship' in Hilda Smith (ed.), *Women Writers and the Early Modern British Political Tradition* (Cambridge, 1998).

For all the confusion over the exact nature of the division between ministerial and judicial, the binary remained in use throughout the period and into the nineteenth century.[65] The notion of ministerial officeholding, of acting on behalf of a higher authority, was a legally useful one. For officers who wanted to appoint deputies – a rapidly growing number, as we shall see in Chapter 3 – it offered a way around the obstacle of the requirement that officers should be *idoneus homo*. More broadly, it chimed with legislators' efforts to protect officers who acted 'by authority' rather than for themselves. A ministerial officer's actions were not their own; they were, in a sense, the actions of whoever or whatever had authorised them. As Hobbes put it, 'Public ministers are those, that have authority from the sovereign ... For every act they do by such authority, is the act of the commonwealth'.[66]

An instructive parallel can be drawn with contemporary servant law. One of the central issues in early modern servant law was liability. If a servant committed an offence, were they liable for it, or was their master? It was a longstanding legal principle that, as William Blackstone put it, 'the master is answerable for the act of his servant, if done by his command, either expressly given, or implied'. *Respondeat superior* – let the master answer. 'If a smith's man pricks my horse', chief justice John Holt explained in 1707, 'the master is liable for the damage'.[67] It was, however, important to note that the authorisation of servants had its limits. 'The act of the servant', one influential judgement stated, 'shall not bind the master, unless he acts by the authority of his master'.[68] If a smith's servant stole a horse, they were acting outside what they had been authorised to do, so the crime was theirs. It was only when servants acted by authority – as representatives – that their actions were attributable to their masters. When they acted without authority, their actions were their own.

---

[65] The distinction was particularly tricky to draw with regard to justices of the peace and sheriffs, whose status as ministerial or judicial officers was sometimes said to depend on whether they acted individually or as a group: Fitzwilliams' Case (1603), Cro. Eliz. 915,78 *ER* 1136; Rich v Player (1684), 2 Show. KB 286, 89 *ER* 943; R v Venables (1725), 3 Mod. 377, 88 *ER* 268; R v Inhabitants of Hamstall Ridware (1789), 3 T.R. 379, 100 *ER* 631. For nineteenth-century examples of the distinction, see Holroyd v Breare and Holmes (1819), 2 B. & Ald. 474, 106 *ER* 439; Walsh v Southwark and others (1851), 6 Ex. 150, 155 *ER* 492.

[66] Hobbes, *Leviathan*, 162.

[67] William Blackstone, *Commentaries on the Law of England*, vol. 1 (Oxford, 1768), 429; Sir Robert Wayland's Case (1707) in *A Digest of Adjudged Cases in the Court of King's Bench from the Revolution to the Present Period* (London, 1733), 654. See also Anthony Gray, *Vicarious Liability: Critique and Reform* (Oxford, 2018), 5–28.

[68] Ward v Evans (1703) in *Digest of Adjudged Cases*, 655. For an overview of early modern servant law, see Douglas Hay, 'England, 1562–1875: The Law and Its Uses' in Douglas Hay and Paul Craven (eds.), *Masters, Servants, and Magistrates in Britain and the Empire, 1562–1955* (Chapel Hill, 2004).

Ministerial officers operated under a similar structure of attribution and liability, with one important difference. Their master was, in effect, the state. This master could authorise actions but could not be held liable if those actions were in some way wrongful. According to the legal maxim that 'the king can do no wrong', the sovereign power could not be charged with a crime in its own courts.[69] Provided it was authorised by the state – via statute, common law, or judicial warrant – no action performed by a ministerial officer could be a civil or criminal offence. This, added to the deterrent of double or triple costs under general issue clauses, gave officers a remarkable degree of protection from prosecution. But the principle of sovereign immunity cut both ways. If the state was incapable of wrongdoing, then any wrongs committed by officers could not be attributed to the state, only to the officers themselves. If authorised acts were always lawful, unlawful acts could not have been authorised. This was the reason, according to Edward Coke, that the monarch should not make an arrest in person; if it turned out to be an unlawful arrest, there had to be someone else – an officer who made the arrest on the monarch's behalf – to take the blame.[70]

The difference between authorised and unauthorised action was at the centre of the law of office. This was often expressed as a contrast between action *virtute officii* (by virtue of office, i.e. authorised) and *colore officii* (under the colour or appearance of office, i.e. unauthorised). The entry for 'office' in a 1652 legal dictionary elaborated on this distinction:

> These words *colore officii* are always taken *in malam partem* [in a bad sense], and varie from these words *virtute officii*, or *ratione officii* [by reason of office], which are always taken *in bonam partem* [in a good sense], and imply that the Office is the just cause of the thing, and the thing is pursuing the office: but the other words signifie an act ill done by pretence and countenance of the Office, and it carrieth the counterfeit shew of dutie.[71]

The judges and politicians of the early seventeenth century had not invented this distinction, but they had given it teeth and made it central

---

[69] Janelle Greenberg, 'Our Grand Maxim of State, "The King Can Do No Wrong"', *History of Political Thought* 12.2 (1991). See also Louis L. Jaffe, 'Suits Against Governments and Officers: Sovereign Immunity', *Harvard Law Review* 77.1 (1963).
[70] Edward Coke, *The Second Part of the Institutes of the Laws of England* (London, 1642), 186–7. Coke made this argument by reference to a late fifteenth-century precedent: *Seipp's Abridgement*, 1485.005 (Mich. 1 Hen. VII 5 f.4b).
[71] Edward Leigh, *A Philologicall Commentary* (London, 1652), 168. The earliest example of this distinction is the first Statute of Westminster, which condemned royal officers who seized land 'per colour de son office': 3 Edw. I c.24 (1275). Early modern lawyers tended to refer, however, to Coke's gloss on this statute, which stated that 'Colore officii is ever taken in malam partem, as virtute officii is taken in bonam': Coke, *Second Part of the Institutes* (London, 1642), 206.

to the legal treatment of officeholders. An officer who did something *virtute officii* was under the powerful legislative and judicial protections granted to those who acted by authority. An officer who acted *colore officii*, on the other hand, acted outside authority altogether; what they did was not simply a bad official act, it was an unofficial act masquerading as an official one, when in reality it was not an official act at all. As one court ruling on the difference between judicial and ministerial actions put it, 'judicial acts misdone ... are but erroneous', whereas a ministerial act misdone was 'void' – it had no legal force whatsoever.[72] The unauthorised acts of ministerial officers could not be attributed to the state, only to themselves. Without any external legitimating authority, they were the acts of mere private individuals and, in some cases, could even be treated as crimes.

Constable or Criminal?

The law of office, despite its occasionally arcane technicalities, appears to have become increasingly prominent in many people's thinking about officeholding from the mid-seventeenth onwards. This is not to say that the entire population began debating whether or not a parish clerk could appoint a deputy. Rather, the central idea behind much of the legal innovation of the early seventeenth century – the difference between impersonal action by authority and personal action without authority – began to take root beyond lawyers' chambers at the inns of court. It was just as unoriginal an idea outside the legal profession as it had been inside it, but circumstances conspired to give the personal-impersonal distinction a new, broad, and immediate importance. The circumstance which seems to have done most to drive the spread of legalistic ideas of office was the confusion of civil war.

When the political and religious conflicts of Charles I's three kingdoms produced the first of the English civil wars, officeholders across the country found themselves acting on behalf of one of two rival governments.[73]

---

[72] Fitzwilliams' Case (1603), Cro. Eliz. 915, 78 *ER* 1136.
[73] Previous work on local officeholding in the mid-seventeenth century has tended either to emphasise the role of officers in maintaining stable government at a local level or to suggest that the nature of officeholding changed without specifying exactly how: John Morrill and John Walter, 'Order and Disorder in the English Revolution' in Anthony Fletcher and John Stevenson (eds.), *Order and Disorder in Early Modern England* (Cambridge, 1985), 153; Stephen K. Roberts, 'State and Society in the English Revolution' and Mark Knights, 'The Long-Term Consequences of the English Revolution: State Formation, Political Culture, and Ideology' both in Michael J. Braddick (ed.), *The Oxford Handbook of the English Revolution* (Oxford, 2015), 299, 520.

The Law of Office

This was, as Paul Halliday has put it, a 'jurisdictional nightmare'.[74] Parliament and the monarch both claimed to speak in the voice of the true sovereign, and each attempted to delegitimise actions carried out in the name of the other. As the conflict escalated in the summer of 1642, parliament announced that arrests made in the name of the king were unlawful and could, therefore, be resisted:

> if any Messenger or officer shall by coullour of any Command from his Majestie, or warrant under his Majesties hand, arest, take, or cary away any of his Majesties Subjects to any place whatsoever contrary to their wills … it is both against the Lawes of the Land, and the liberties of the Subject, and is to the disturbance of the publique peace of the Kingdome, and any of his Majesties Subjects so arested, may Lawfully refuse to obey such arests and commands.[75]

Controversies in high politics over who ruled the kingdom were played out in everyday struggles over the power of officeholders.[76] Which authority an officer represented became a pressing practical concern. Anyone confronted with an officer's attempts to tax, arrest, or otherwise command them necessarily adopted the legal view of officeholding as action on behalf of a higher power.[77] The question was: which higher power?

Most people's encounters with this question went unrecorded. A full account of interactions between officeholders and others during the years of civil war and republican rule is beyond the scope of this chapter.[78] Court records suggest that many of those who came face-to-face with officers responded to them as representatives of one government or another. The

---

[74] Halliday, *Habeas Corpus*, 161.
[75] *A Declaration by the Lords and Commons in Parliament Declaring that None Shall Aprehend, or Arest any of His Majesties Subjects or Servants that Obeyeth the Ordinance of Parliament, under Pretence of His Majesties Warrant* (London, 1642).
[76] Ann Hughes, 'The King, the Parliament, and the Localities during the English Civil War', *Journal of British Studies* 24 (1985); Rachel Weil, 'Thinking about Allegiance in the English Civil War', *History Workshop Journal* 61 (2006).
[77] John Cowell's dictionary was republished in 1658, the offensive definition of royal prerogative removed but that of office intact: *The Interpreter, or, Book Containing the Signification of Words* (London, 1658), Y4. His definition of office as 'imploiment in the affaires of another' was taken up by the mid-century barrister William Sheppard and remained current in legal dictionaries into the eighteenth century: William Sheppard, *The Offices of Constables* (London, 1641), A1; William Sheppard, *An Epitome of All the Common & Statute Laws of this Nation Now in Force, Wherein More then Fifteen Hundred of the Hardest Words or Terms of the Law Are Explained* (London, 1656), 780; Thomas Blount, *Nomo-Lexikon, a Law-Dictionary* (London, 1670), Aaa; Giles Jacob, *A New Law-Dictionary* (4th edition, London, 1739), 'Office'.
[78] The best account of this subject remains Ann Hughes, 'Parliamentary Tyranny? Indemnity Proceedings and the Impact of the Civil War: A Cast Study from Warwickshire', *Midland History* 11.1 (1986).

most striking evidence comes from cases in which officers were resisted. Resistance to officers was certainly not new; what is distinctive about these episodes is the particular form that resistance took. Assize and Quarter Sessions papers from the 1640s and 1650s are relatively sparse and unevenly distributed, but they offer frequent examples of people defying officers on the basis of the authority they claimed to represent.

In 1647, a gentleman in York refused to obey a summons under the authority of the (parliamentarian) lord mayor and Assize judges. As the officer who attempted to serve the summons deposed, 'he said in a scoffinge manner he cared not a pinn for the Lord Maior, the Judge, nor for this dep[onen]t, nor did he care a pinn for theire Warrants nor would hee obey them'. The gentleman promised vengeance should York ever return to royalist control, threatening the officer that 'If the other p[ar]ty came againe (meaninge the kings p[ar]ty) he would not leave this deponent worth a grote' and would sue the city rulers for false imprisonment. In the same year, an officer in Colchester presented a copy of the parliamentary ordinance which authorised his actions but was still defied by a man who answered 'Parliament, Parliament, I know noe such thing they are gone'. This kind of opposition to officers acting in the name of parliament continued during the period of republican government. In 1652, a Middlesex labourer resisted officers who tried to arrest him for drinking on the Sabbath, condemning 'the authority of Parliament by which they act'. The following year, a vintner told a constable who wanted to search his house that 'he should take his authority and wipe his breech'. In the chaotic atmosphere of January 1660, a Whitechapel publican told an officer who tried to shut down his alehouse that he 'had no Authority and that there was noe Authority in England'. As Caroline Boswell puts it, 'ordinary struggles for social authority intersected with the extraordinary tensions produced by civil war and revolution'.[79] At the centre of those struggles were officeholders and their claims to represent authority.

Further evidence of this mid-century dynamic comes from a wave of accusations that officers had committed crimes. To suggest that officeholders acted *colore officii* or 'by collour of any Command' given by an illegitimate regime was to argue that they acted not as bearers of higher authority but as private individuals who could be held liable for their actions in a court of law. This way of thinking was encouraged by propaganda produced

---

[79] TNA, ASSI 45/2/2/50, Deposition of Thomas Dayle, 21 Mar 1647; Caroline Boswell, *Disaffection and Everyday Life in Interregnum England* (Woodbridge, 2017), 184, 87–88, 25; Bernard Capp, *England's Culture Wars: Puritan Reformation and its Enemies in the Interregnum, 1649–60* (Oxford, 2012), 252.

on both sides. In 1655, a royalist London preacher labelled the representatives of the Protectorate 'a Company of Thieves and Robbers'. A few years earlier, a parliamentarian pamphlet relating the exploits of a notorious highwayman claimed that by joining the royalist army he 'did many robberies with authority'.[80] Throughout the 1650s, many officeholders and soldiers found themselves in court, charged with theft, trespass, battery, or false imprisonment. Most of these lawsuits targeted actions which had in fact been carried out on behalf of the parliamentary government, especially sequestrations of property. The accused officers sought help from parliament's Indemnity Committee, which granted protection from prosecution to anyone who could prove they were being sued, in one officer's words, 'for doinge his duty … in discharge of his said place, and according to the power given him by sev[er]all Ordinances of Parliam[en] t'.[81] The records of the Indemnity Committee reveal what one historian has called 'a massive legal assault on state officials from the beginning of the Civil War to the mid-1650s'. Long after the fighting was over (in England at least), officers remained vulnerable to the accusation that they were no better than criminals. In June 1653, two men came to the Warners' house in Peckham with a warrant to speak to Master Warner but were refused entry. The following week they came again, this time with a constable, but when Mistress Warner 'came and looked forth at a Window' she still refused to let them in, because 'for ought she knew wee came to robb her'.[82] Early in 1660, when the protectorate was on its last legs, a royalist pamphlet called a group of bailiffs who attempted to arrest one gentleman cavalier 'legall Thieves'.[83]

The forms of disobedience that took shape in the mid-seventeenth century persisted long after 1660. People who resisted officers continued to do so on the basis of the powers they claimed to represent. Residents of towns and cities who opposed officers derided the mayors who authorised their actions. A Colchester alehouse-keeper refused

---

[80] Lena Liapi, *Roguery in Print: Crime and Culture in Early Modern London* (Woodbridge, 2019), 130–1.
[81] TNA, SP 24/30, Petition of Hugh Aldred, 1 Feb 1647. For other petitions for indemnity from officeholders, see SP 24/30, Petition of William Aldridge, 20 Jan 1647; SP 24/30, Petition of John Abeares, 3 Nov 1647; SP 24/30, Petition of John Allison, 29 Jun 1653; SP 24/30, Petition of Robert Alford, undated; SP 24/30, Petition of Edward Anson and William Miller, undated; SP 24/30, Petition of Richard Alford, undated; SP 24/31, Petition of John Atkinson, 5 Jul 1647; SP 24/31, Petition of Richard Attenborowe, undated.
[82] John A. Shedd, 'Thwarted Victors: Civil and Criminal Prosecution against Parliament's Officers during the English Civil War and Commonwealth', *Journal of British Studies* 41.2 (2002), 140; TNA, SP 24/30, Deposition of John Parsons and Charles Bedford, 14 Jun 1653.
[83] *An Epistle Narrative of the Barbarous Assault and Illegall Arrest of Freder. Turvill, Esquire: By Sixteen Bailiffs, with the Death of One of Their Followers* (London, 1660), 5.

entry to constables in 1677, declaring that 'he did not care A turde for Mr Maior'; a Norwich publican, in a similar situation, announced that 'the Maior had nothing to do there' and 'he did not Care a pin for the Maior'.[84] National authorities were equally subject to challenge and abuse when people refused to comply with the officers who governed in their name. Jacobites and those with Jacobite-sympathies were prominent in this kind of resistance. In 1690, a man refused to pay a tax collector in Norwich because, he said, he doubted the legitimacy of the parliament which had raised the tax in the first place. When a Chelsea gatekeeper told a drunk man that 'he was the Kings Servant' and would not let him pass down the Kings Road at night, the man 'in his passion did say Damn the King'. On the other side of London, a man confronting the night watch on Ratcliffe highway in 1733 'declared that his present Majesty King George the Second and Sir Robert Wallpole Knight were Rogues and Villains like unto the Watchmen'.[85] To oppose officers was to oppose the powers they represented.

Some who resisted officers, rather than challenging the legitimacy of the power that authorised them, denied that they were authorised at all. In 1696, a Londoner resisted a bailiff's attempts to confiscate her horse, asking 'where was his Authority for doing so'. Two years later another woman resisted arrest by a man she claimed 'was noe officer', though he insisted that he was.[86] This approach led naturally to accusations of crime. Officers who did not act by authority were no different to other private individuals; their attempts to arrest people were merely assaults, their confiscations simply theft under the pretence of authority. In 1682, a butcher in Hollingbourne (Kent) accused several officers of stealing from him 'under pretence of a meane processe' (a lawful warrant). In 1716, several excisemen were charged with theft after 'seizeing and carrying off the Goods' of people who had refused to pay their taxes. A London constable, on trial in 1721 for theft and assault, was acquitted when the jury decided he had simply been trying to arrest a suspect: 'It appearing not to be a Robbery but a Lawful Action'.[87]

---

[84] ERO, Colchester Quarter Sessions: Examinations, T/A 465/2, Information of Giles Abbot, 28 Oct 1677; NRO, NCR Case 12b/4, Information of Charles Lucas, 16 Mar 1704.
[85] NRO, NCR Case 12b/2, Information of John Collings, 26 March 1690; LMA, DL/C/0261, Deposition of John King, 11 Jun 1723, 27–8; LMA, MJ/SP/1733/04/076, Information of John Davis, 3 Apr 1733.
[86] LMA, MJ/SP/1696/10/018, Petition of Mary Jolly, undated; LMA, MJ/SP/1698/10/043, Information of Sarah Miller, 13 Sep 1698.
[87] KHLC, Q/SB/14, Information of James Wills, 19 June 1682; TNA, CUST 47/81/71, 47/81/106; *OBP*, Jan 1721, trial of Edward Arnold (t17210113-35).

The distinction between crime and 'Lawful Action' could be difficult to draw. From the mid-seventeenth century onwards, handbooks for officers were full of advice on how to avoid prosecution for actions carried out in the course of duty.[88] There were, according to the author of a 1660 guide for constables, 'many causeless and contentious sutes commenced' against officers, especially for 'Trespass, Battery or false Imprisonment'. These were the same charges specified by the 1610 general issue statute, charges likely to arise from forcible entries and arrests when they were deemed illegitimate by the person on the receiving end.[89] Not all such lawsuits were 'causeless'. Court records provide many examples of straightforwardly criminal activity among officers, from extortion and embezzlement to burglary and theft.[90] One particularly common offence involved gaining entry to a person's house to confiscate or search for illicit goods, then robbing them of everything inside.[91] Those officers who stepped on to the wrong side of the law as corrupt thief-takers (orchestrating crimes and claiming rewards for prosecuting the criminals) were only the tip of the iceberg.[92]

---

[88] See introduction, notes 34–35.

[89] Edmund Wingate, *The Exact Constable* (London, 1660), 164, 169.

[90] For examples from in and around London, see LMA, MJ/SP/1696/12/057, Information of Francis Baynes, 15 Dec 1696; LMA, MJ/SP/1697/12/046, Information of Jane Smith, 24 Nov 1697; LMA, MJ/SP/1699/07/086, Informations of Ann Crook, William Holder and James Phillipps, 28 Jul 1699; LMA, MJ/SP/1703/04/042, Informations of William Goss and William Spicer, 18 Mar 1703; LMA, MJ/SP/1719/07/066, Petition from William Lee, 12 Jul 1719; LMA, MJ/SP/1732/07/073, Letter from James Cardonnel to Clerk of the Peace, 11 Aug 1732; LMA, MJ/SP/1750/04/016, Petition of Blanch Ratcliffe, undated; *OBP*, Dec 1699, trial of Thomas Rachey (t16991213-1); *OBP*, Apr 1732, trial of John Theobalds (t17320419-43); *OBP*, Apr 1743, trial of Robert Morris (t17430413-31); *OBP*, Dec 1747, trial of Benjamin Jewks (t17471209-54); LMA, COL/CA/01/01/80, ff.100, 106, 111; LMA, COL/CA/01/01/81, f.156. High constable William Smorthwait was the leader of a group of violent thieves in 1680s Yorkshire: Alan Macfarlane and Sarah Harrison, *The Justice and the Mare's Ale: Law and Disorder in Seventeenth-Century England* (Oxford, 1981).

[91] KHLC, Q/SB/12/5, Information of Mary Ellott, 21 Jan 1672; Q/SB/28/100, Information of Thomas Deakins, 18 Sep 1705; NRO, NCR Case 12b/2, Informations of Edward Quintin and John White, 11 July 1690; *OBP*, October 1693, trial of Walter Batson, Jeremy Bedford, William Dando (t16931012-10); *OBP*, October 1693, trial of Walter Batson, William Dando, Jeremiah Bedford (t16931012-42); *OBP*, October 1693, trial of Walter Batson, Jeremy Bedford, William Dando (t16931012-23); *OBP*, October 1693, trial of Walter Batson (t16931012-53); *OBP*, Apr 1714, trial of John Clap (t17140407-42); *OBP*, trial of Daniel Soams, Quilt Arnold (t17231016-19); *OBP*, July 1729, trial of William Jones (t17290709-14).

[92] Gerald Howson, *Thief-Taker General: The Rise and Fall of Jonathan Wild* (London, 1970); Ruth Paley, 'Thief-takers in London in the Age of the McDaniel Gang, c.1745–1754' in Douglas Hay and Francis Snyder (eds.), *Policing and Prosecution in Britain, 1750–1850* (Oxford, 1989); Tim Wales, 'Thief-Takers and Their Clients in Later Stuart London' in Paul Griffiths and Mark S. R. Jenner (eds.), *Londinopolis: Essays in the Cultural and Social History of Early Modern London* (Manchester, 2000). Paul Griffiths traces thief-taking back to the early seventeenth century: *Lost Londons: Change, Crime, and Control in the Capital City 1550–1660* (Cambridge, 2008), 308–12.

It could be genuinely challenging to tell constables from criminals and, in particular, bailiffs from burglars. In 1698, when a group of bailiffs climbed over a wall at 5 am to enter a house by the back door, some of the residents cried out 'Bailies and Rogues', others shouted 'Thieves and Murderers'. Sometimes the division between law enforcers and law breakers collapsed entirely, as when the landlady of a boarding house referred to the officers who came to arrest her lodger as 'a Parcel of Thieving Bailiffs'. Witnesses at several Old Bailey trials spotted groups of thieves standing around houses and highways but presumed they were bailiffs waiting to catch a debtor; 'knowing one of them to be a Bailiffs follower, I thought they were only setting somebody for an Arrest'. One winter night in 1725, when John Norton and John Hall 'saw 2 men and a Girl whispering together at the End of an Alley', Hall said to Norton 'I don't like the Looks of those Fellows; I believe they are Bailiffs. Prithee John, step over and observe 'em'. It was 'a Moon-light Night', so Norton could see their faces clearly as he passed and returned to tell his friend 'they looked more like Thieves than Bailiffs'. He was right, but how he could tell the difference is a mystery.[93]

Officers and criminals often did the same things. Both might turn up at a house to demand money or break down the door and take away valuables instead. Both had a capacity for violence if their commands were disobeyed.[94] Pamphlets complained of London's 'worse than High-waymen Watch' who, according to the publican and satirist Ned Ward, 'play more Rogues Tricks than ever they detect, and occasion more Disturbances in the Streets than ever they hinder'. As Horace Walpole put it in 1742, 'the greatest criminals in this town are the officers of justice; there is no tyranny they do not exercise, no villainy of which they do not partake'.[95] The difference between officers and criminals was, of course, that officers acted by authority. Authority from statutes, warrants, and common law was what made their actions lawful and their orders binding. In the words of John Locke,

---

[93] *OBP*, Jan 1698, trial of William Sickes, Mary Sickes, Thomas Barker, Elizabeth Stanley, Jane Greek (t16980114-31); *OBP*, Jun 1725, trial of Thomas Dowler, Thomas Jefferies (t17250630-28); *OBP*, Mar 1726, trial of Lawrence Simpson, William Swift (t17260302-49); *OBP*, Jul 1730, trial of Galamiel Bishop (t17300704-10); *OBP*, Jan 1725, trial of John Vaughan, Edward Quin, Frances Dun (t17250115-28). Maria Ågren found similar kinds of confusion in her recent study of customs officers in early modern Sweden: *The State as Master: Gender, State Formation and Commercialisation in Urban Sweden, 1650–1780* (Manchester, 2017), 32.

[94] For a theoretical account of these similarities, see Charles Tilly, 'War Making and State Making as Organized Crime' in Peter Evans, Dietrich Reuschemeyer, Theda Skocpol (eds.), *Bringing the State Back In* (Cambridge, 1985), 169–71.

[95] *An Impartial Account of the Misfortune That Lately Happened to the Right Honourable Philip Earl of Pembrooke and Montgomery* (London, 1680), 1; Edward Ward, *The London Spy Compleat* (London, 1703), 38; *The Letters of Horace Walpole, Early of Orford, Volume I* (London, 1846), 216.

the 'command of any magistrate, where he has no authority, being as void and insignificant, as that of any private man', it was 'authority, that gives the right of acting'.[96] Without authority, an arrest was a false imprisonment, a forcible entry a trespass. But how, practically speaking, did officers lay claim to authority? How did they identify themselves as officeholders, authorised to do things which, if anyone else did them, would be crimes?

Conjuring Authority

Without uniforms or badges, officers' claims to authority depended on other means of identifying themselves.[97] People accused of resisting officers sometimes said they had simply not known that the person they encountered was an officer. In 1641, for example, a man who stabbed a constable in the leg during a fight denied that he had seen 'any Constable' at all. The same plea was made by a vintner accused of 'obstructing an officer in the due execucion of his Office'; he insisted that 'he did it ignorantly, not knowing him to be an Officer'.[98] To avoid situations like these, officers identified themselves – and so laid claim to official authority – with an array of special props and performances.

Several historians have noted the theatricality of the routine activities of early modern English government. Justices of the peace, according to Michael Braddick, had to display judicial dignity and impartiality to retain the faith of their colleagues and those who were brought before them as prosecutors, defendants, and witnesses.[99] Outside the court room, especially at the lower levels of local government and law enforcement, officers relied on certain kinds of ritualised performance to show that they represented the state. Jonathan Healey describes these performances as 'moments of government', while recent work by Lucy Clarke draws attention to those occasions on which the performance failed and people refused

---

[96] John Locke, *Two Treatises of Government*, ed. Peter Laslett (3rd edition, Cambridge, 1988), 421. The view that a magistrate's power depended on specified legal authority was a feature of many early modern theories of resistance and limited monarchy.
[97] City of London marshals wore a special livery and parish beadles were sometimes provided with a particular kind of overcoat, but these were exceptions to the general rule.
[98] LMA, WJ/SP/1641/Jy/1, Information of John Drummond, 12 May 1641; TNA, CUST 47/45/37.
[99] Michael J. Braddick, 'Administrative Performance: The Representation of Political Authority in Early Modern England' in Michael J. Braddick and John Walter (eds.), *Negotiating Power in Early Modern Society: Order, Hierarchy and Subordination in Britain and Ireland* (Cambridge, 2001). See also Anthony Fletcher, 'Honour, Reputation and Local Officeholding in Elizabethan and Stuart England' in Fletcher and Stevenson (eds.), *Order and Disorder*; Richard Cust and Peter G. Lake, 'Sir Richard Grosvenor and the Rhetoric of Magistracy', *Historical Research* 54.129 (2007).

to accept an officer's claim to authority.[100] None of these scholars, however, has discussed the legal significance of official performances or their relationship to the wider law of office. Unlike displays of judicial impartiality, performances of authority by local officeholders involved concrete matters of legality rather than contestable notions of fairness and justice. In order to receive the legal protections granted by statute and common law from the early seventeenth century onwards, officers had to show the people they encountered that they acted by authority, not for themselves.

One group of people who were especially keen to make this distinction were criminals who pretended to be officers. Examples of people impersonating officers can be found throughout the early modern period.[101] In 1596, for example, five men from Lancashire were charged with having 'collected divers sums and deceived the Queen's people' by pretending to be tax collectors, 'wearing on their breasts a box with the Queen's arms'. A century later, three men caused chaos in an Essex alehouse by grabbing and beating up several customers, alternately 'swearing that one of them was Constable' or 'p[re]tending they were Press masters & had authoritie under the Kings seale'.[102] Deceptions like this became increasingly common in the late seventeenth and early eighteenth centuries, especially in London. Court records from Westminster, Middlesex, and the City contain dozens of cases of imposters who, on the pretence of official authority (*colore officii*), robbed, conned, and extorted residents of the capital.[103] In 1699, for example, Ann Cook was accosted on the street in Soho by a man who 'pretended that he had a Warrant to Arrest her', forced her into a coach, took her to an accomplice's house, and robbed her. It later emerged that 'He had no Warrant, neither was he any Officer'. Churchwardens and overseers of the poor were sometimes impersonated as well as constables and watchmen, though the powers of law enforcement officers do seem to have been especially attractive to imposters.[104] In the 1670s, one London

---

[100] For a discussion of the performance of one low-level officeholder in an earlier period, see Jonathan Healey, 'The Fray on the Meadow: Violence and a Moment of Government in Early Tudor England', *History Workshop Journal* 85 (2018); Lucy J. S. Clarke, '"I say I must for I am the kings Shrieve"': Magistrates Invoking the Monarch's Name in 1 Henry VI (1592) and The Downfall of Robert Earl of Huntingdon (1598)', *Historical Research* 95.268 (2022).

[101] Tobias B. Hug, *Impostures in Early Modern England: Representations and Perceptions of Fraudulent Identities* (Manchester, 2010), Chapter 2.

[102] Attorney-General v Nixen, Pepper, Ellis, Johnson & Anglesey (1596) in Baildon (ed.), *Les reportes*, 36–7; ERO, Q/SBb 3, Informations of Nathaniel Francis and Samuel Chaplin, 1 Sep 1694.

[103] Jennine Hurl-Eamon, 'The Westminster Imposters: Impersonating Law Enforcement in Early Eighteenth-Century London', *Eighteenth-Century Studies* 38.3 (2005).

[104] *OBP*, Oct 1699, trial of Henry Chapman (t16991011-23); LMA, WJ/SP/1691/07/004, Petition of the Overseers of St Martin's in the Fields, undated; *OBP*, Jan 1700, trial of John Littlehales (t17000115-29);

constable complained that night watchmen were constantly fooled by criminals masquerading as their counterparts from a neighbouring parish:

> it is a very evill and dangerous custom that the constables and watch men have to let all p[er]sons pass, if they have but a halbert or staff with a lanthorne in their hand like a watch man, That when the Constable or any of his men asketh who goeth theare they presently answer The Watch, nameing one watch or another, And soe they pas[s] saying good night Brother.[105]

One night in 1674, according to an anonymous pamphlet, a group of thieves dressed up 'in the mantle of Authority' and systematically burgled their way across the capital. They disguised 'a well experienced member of their Fraternity, in his Gown, Cap, Staff and all the formalities of a Constable, the rest being put into a suitable Garb, and reverently attending him as his watchmen'. On the prowl at 10 or 11 pm, they banged on the first promising door they came to, 'knocking furiously, as with authority', and produced a fake warrant to search for illegal coin forgers. Inside, they ransacked the place and took away more than £57 'for the Kings use'. The next stop was an alehouse, where they were let in 'at the sight of the Staff and Halberts' and carried away £20 worth of plate. Finally, after taking more than £100 worth of stock from an eminent shop keeper on the pretence of searching for 'French prohibited goods', they were caught by the real constable and watch.[106]

The tools of imposture – the cap and gown, staff and halberds – were, necessarily, the same as those used by real officers to claim lawful authority. Genuine officeholders might sometimes rely on warrants (though these too could be forged), but there were many situations in which officers were empowered and expected to act without written warrant. 'A sworn and known Officer', one handbook explained, 'needs not to shew his Warrant'.[107] To qualify as 'known', officers in smaller settlements might rely on personal acquaintance with their neighbours, but in larger towns and cities they had to identify themselves with the same props and performances used by those who impersonated them. Just as the imposter had his 'Gown, Cap, Staff and all the formalities of a Constable', so one Master

---

      OBP, May 1722, trial of Charles John, James Bradshaw (t17220510-38); *OBP*, Oct 1738, trial of Margery Stanton (t17381011-15); *OBP*, Dec 1747, trial of Elizabeth White, Ann Page (t17471209-40).

[105] LMA, City of London Police: Predecessors, CLA/048/PS/02/006, Petition of Robert Wilkins, undated.

[106] *The Counterfeit Constable, or, The Wicked Watch* (London, 1674), 4–6. Another 1670s pamphlet told a similar story: *Strange and Wonderful News from London: Or, A True Narrative of Several Most Remarkable Occurrences There* (London, 1679), 5–6.

[107] Meriton, *Guide for Constables*, 108. Some magistrates, like the London JP Thomas De Veil, thought officers should always carry warrants to justify their actions, but this was neither legally required nor widely practised: *OBP*, Dec 1738, trial of James Lyon (t17381206-26).

Rogers, a real constable, 'went home to put on his Cap and Gown' before he set about arresting members of a riotous London crowd in 1715. To the same effect, a real constable faced with a breach of the peace in 1723 'put through his Staff, to shew his Authority'.[108]

Staves were perhaps the most important implements of authority. Constables and beadles were sometimes referred to as 'staff-officers' or 'staff men'. The fictional constable in one eighteenth-century tract was actually named 'Staff'.[109] Samuel Butler called a constable's staff an 'ensign of his authority'; Samuel Johnson called it 'An ensign of office; a badge of authority'.[110] Different types of staff served different purposes. 'For a Badge of his Authority', wrote the diplomat Guy Miege, a constable 'carries a long Staff painted, with the Kings Arms; and, for a Surprise, sometimes he uses a short Staff, which he hides till he thinks it convenient to produce it'. When disorder seemed likely to break out, high constables summoned their subordinates 'to meet me with your long Staves'.[111] Bailiffs' staves were unpainted but tipped with silver, earning them the soubriquet 'Tipstaff'. An account of the life of Abraham Wood, a bailiff-cum-trickster, included an episode in which he confronted an indebted tailor: '[Abraham] pulling his Staff out of his Pocket, the Taylor seeing it tipt with Silver, instead of being painted, said, *you are no Constable, Sir. Right*, reply'd Abram, *but I'm a Bailiff, and arrest you*'.[112]

As emblems of authorisation, staves were almost definitive of office-holding; to wield a staff was, in some sense, to be an officer. In 1695, Thomas Stibbs – a Londoner who had held office before but did not at the time – saw a Jacobite crowd gathering near his house and rushed out of the door 'takeing his Constables Staffe in his hand (haveing formerly Executed that Office) with a designe to seize those who made the disturbance'.[113] Law breakers recognised the significance of these objects

---

[108] *OBP*, September 1715, trial of Thomas Cotton and Charles Warren (t17150907-13); *OBP*, John Lant, Richard Ayres, David Kite, John Ambler (t17231204-52).

[109] LMA, DL/C/0243, deposition of William Grey, 25 Sep 1691, 351v–52; *The Midnight-Ramble: Or, The Adventures of Two Noble Females* (London, 1754), 21; Henry Fielding, *The Coffee-House Politician: Or, The Justice Caught in His Own Trap* (London, 1730).

[110] Butler, *Characters*, 209; Samuel Johnson, *A Dictionary of the English Language* (London, 1755), 1919.

[111] Guy Miege, *The New State of England* (London, 1691) III, 77–8; LMA, MJ/SP/1725/06/026, Order from high constable Clifford Phillips, 8 Jun 1725; LMA, MJ/SP/1737/09/092, Letter from high constable Robert Yates, 16 Sep 1737.

[112] *OBP*, Dec 1732, trial of Jane Gale, Eleanor Walker (t17321206-40); Alexander Smith, *The Comical and Tragical History of the Lives and Adventures of the Most Noted Bayliffs in and about London and Westminster* (London, 1723), 37.

[113] MJ/SP/07/048, Information of Thomas Stibbs, 21 Jun 1695. Constables in some parishes were required to pass on the staff to their successor when they left office: Robert Henry Hadden, *An East End Chronicle: St George's in the East Parish and Parish Church* (London, 1880), 19.

and, when they confronted officers on the streets, often tried to wrench their staves from their hands or hack them to pieces.[114] In 1702, a soldier who clashed with officers during a fair 'took a Constables Staff & cryed; now I am High Constable'. A decade later, John Gay described a similar inversion in his play *The Mohocks*: taking the watchmen's staves for themselves, the eponymous elite troublemakers 'make them Mohocks, and our selves Constable and Watchmen'. As they later explain to a magistrate, by removing the officers' performative props 'they unconstabled the Constable' and 'unwatch'd the Watch'.[115]

The function of officers' staves was best captured, albeit mockingly, by Ned Ward. On his ramblings through the city, the narrator of Ward's periodical *The London Spy* was forever bumping into constables who were 'Arm'd with a Staff of Authority, Sealed with the Royal Arms' and who frequently brandished this 'painted Scepter' in an effort to command obedience. In another work of similar style, Ward wondered at the confidence and presumption of a constable who, in his day job, was cringingly deferent: 'Tis strange that a Painted *Staff* ... should change a Tunbelly'd *Tapster* into an Emperour of the *Moon*'. Thus transformed from a private person into an embodiment of authority, the constable was 'a *Midnight Magistrate*', 'a Prince of *Darkness*', a figure of great and mysterious power.[116] Constables were frequently derided in early modern literature ('little morsell of Iustice', 'a meere plot, a tricke', 'this shred of Authority'), but they also possessed a kind of magic and the glamour of the night. Ward was not the only writer to call the constable a 'prince of darkness'; others settled on 'King of the Night', 'Mr. nocturnal Justice' or 'fairy King'. In the words of one playwright, constables 'with staffe and lanthorn's light / Are like blacke Pluto Princes of the night'.[117]

With staves as their wands, constables practised what Pierre Bourdieu called 'social magic', the transformation of a text, object, or person (in this case the constables themselves) into something more than its material reality.[118]

---

[114] NRO, NCR Case 12b/2, Information of Randall King, 5 Nov 1699; NRO, NCR Case 12b/2, Informations of Michael Bishop, William Watts and Nicholas Chambers, 7 Aug 1750; *OBP*, Dec 1680, trial of Edward Townsend (t16801208-9); *OBP*, Ordinary's Account, Jul 1687 (OA16870715); *OBP*, Jan 1722, trial of Edward Vaughan (t17220112-43); *OBP*, Dec 1744, trial of William Harding (t17441205-60); LMA, MJ/SP/1691/07/042, Informations of Charles Green and John Ward, 2 Jul 1691.

[115] LMA, MJ/SP/1702/07/048, Information of William Sharpe, 4 Jun 1702; [John Gay], *The Mohocks* (London, 1712), 9–10.

[116] *London Spy*, 361, 36; *The London Terrae-Filius: Or the Satyrical Reformer* (London, 1708).

[117] *Blurt Master-Constable*, B2v, D2v; Ward, *London Spy*, 78; Butler, *Characters*, 209; Miege, *The new state* III, 79; Fielding, *The Coffee-House Politician*, 26; Henry Glapthorne, *Wit in a Constable* (London, 1640), H4.

[118] Pierre Bourdieu, *Language and Symbolic Power* tr. Gino Raymond and Matthew Adamson (Cambridge, MA, 1991), 125, 249.

Tun-bellied tapsters became emperors of the moon. For spells, officers had a vocabulary of authority revolving around invocations of the monarch. To make an arrest, for example, they needed only to declare 'I arrest you in the Kings Name'; according to most legal commentators, these words gave 'sufficient notice of what he is'. This explained why the figure of the bailiff, who carried out arrests for debt, was said to be 'an occasionner of disloyal thoughts in the commonwealth, for he makes men hate the king's name worse than the devil's'.[119] The same phrase worked more generally as a claim to official authority. In 1708, a Norwich watchman ordered two men on horseback 'in the Queens name to stand'. A decade earlier, a group of people who attacked a constable in the same city fled when he cried for help, 'Charging All in the Kings name to assist him'. Henry Carey's first play, *The Contrivances*, showed a constable called to a disorderly house: 'Who's within there'? he demanded, 'I Charge you to come out in the King's Name, and submit your selves to my Royal Authority'.[120]

On other occasions, officers simply stated the fact that they were officers to elicit compliance with their demands. Customs officers in early eighteenth-century Kent, attempting to search Dutch ships for contraband, declared that they 'did belonge to her Ma[jes]ties Customes' or that they 'were the Queenes officers'.[121] A Yorkshire constable, arriving at the scene of a homicide, initially received no response to his questions about 'who had done that bloodie deed'. It was only when he announced 'I am the Constable and I must know who hathe slaine the man' that witnesses began to cooperate. In 1744, a pair of excisemen were tried at the Old Bailey for highway robbery after seizing bootleg spirits from a man in the street. They were only acquitted when it became clear that, before carrying out the seizure, 'They told him, they were Excise-Officers'.[122] These words transformed assault and theft into lawful arrest and confiscation.[123] Like staves, they conjured authority, making possible what Bourdieu called 'the

---

[119] Robert Gardiner, *The Compleat Constable* (London, 1692), 64; Michael Dalton, *Officium Vicecomitum: The Office and Authority of Sherifs* (London, 1628), 42; Sheppard, *Offices of Constables*, C8v-D4r; John Earle, *Microcosmography; Or, A Piece of the World discovered; in Essays and Characters* (London, 1628), 'A Sergeant, or Catch-Pole'.

[120] NRO, NCR Case 12b/4, Information of John Sparrow, 8 Mar 1708; NRO, NCR Case 12b/2, Information of Randall King, 5 Nov 1699; Henry Carey, *The Contrivances: Or, More Ways than One* (London, 1715), 29–30.

[121] KHLC, Q/SB/31/22, Deposition of Richard Dawson, 30 Mar 1711; KHLC, Q/SB/31/24, Deposition of John Hazard, 28 Oct 1711.

[122] TNA, ASSI 45/1/4/26, Deposition of Christopher Richardson, 20 Jun 1642; *OBP*, Feb 1744, trial of Thomas Petty, Edmund Smith (t17440223-17).

[123] This is a classic instance of what J. L. Austin called a 'performative utterance': *How to Do Things with Words: The William James Lectures Delivered to Harvard University in 1955* (Oxford, 1962).

authorized imposture' of a person who acts 'with the authorization and the authority of an institution'.[124]

By conjuring authority in this way, officers claimed to represent the state, to attribute their actions to it, to bring its authority to bear on their dealings with other people. The constable's staff and the monarch's name were among the principal forms in which many people encountered state power. In such encounters, the state functioned as the great authoriser, turning speech, gestures, and violence into official actions. An officer who spoke the special words or waved a painted staff ceased to be a private individual and became instead an instrument of impersonal authority.

Authority and Homicide

This way of thinking about office was articulated most clearly in homicide law.[125] If officers were fundamentally different to other people, if they wielded a legal authority that was not their own, then killings involving officers had to be treated distinctly from all other killings. As representatives of the state, officers could sometimes be allowed to exercise legitimate violence, including lethal violence, without incurring any punishment. On the other hand, a person who killed such a representative committed a more serious offence than any ordinary killer and could be punished with particular severity. In both cases, this kind of special treatment was conditional on the officer having conjured authority before the homicide took place.

Aspects of this approach to killings by and of officers had existed since the medieval period, but the law crystallised into this form in the early seventeenth century.[126] A year after the passage of the 1610 general issue statute and just a few years before the key ruling in Phelps v Winchcombe, the justices of King's Bench heard a case which was to become the starting point for legal thinking on official homicide until the end of the century.[127] A London sergeant-at-mace, a kind of bailiff who served the City authorities, had been killed by a Scotsman named John Mackalley in the course of a fight over the arrest of Mackalley's friend for unpaid debts. The killing took place on a dark winter night, and the sergeant 'did not shew … any warrant, or his mace', but before the fight began he had spoken the magic words, 'I arrest

---

[124] Bourdieu, *Language and Symbolic Power*, 109.
[125] For a full account of early modern homicide law, see K. J. Kesselring, *Making Murder Public: Homicide in Early Modern England, 1480–1680* (Oxford, 2019).
[126] I hope to provide a full account the development of this strand of homicide law elsewhere.
[127] What follows is based on the most detailed report of this case, written by Edward Coke: Mackalley's Case (1611), 9 Co. Rep. 61b, 77 *ER* 824.

you in the King's name'. Several justices thought that Mackalley was only guilty of manslaughter; he had protected his friend from a sudden assault and, they argued, had not knowingly obstructed an arrest because he 'cannot know the officer or minister of justice in the night'. This was overruled by the majority, who felt that 'although he cannot see the officer, yet when he hears him say, I arrest you in the King's name, &c. he ought to obey him'. The final judgment included a broad statement of principle on this point:

> when the officer or King's minister by process of law ... arrests in the King's name, or requires the breaker of the peace to keep the peace in the King's name, and they notwithstanding disobey the arrest or command in the King's name, and kill the officer, or the King's minister, reason requires that this killing and slaying shall be an offence in the highest degree of any offence in this nature.

An officer who claimed to act in the monarch's name was a representative of the state. To kill such a person could only be murder, punishable by death. As the justices explained,

> the life of a man is much favoured in law, but the life of the law itself (which protects all in peace and safety) ought to be more favoured, and the execution of the process of law and the offices of conservators of the peace, is the soul and life of the law, and the means by which justice is administered and the peace of the realm kept.

Or, to put it more bluntly, 'if any magistrate or minister of justice, in execution of his office, be killed, it is murder, for their contempt and disobedience to the King, and to the law'. Like those who challenged officers by defying the powers that authorised them, the judges saw violence against officeholders as violence against the state itself.

The original purpose of this bombastic ruling may have been to assert the judges' status as highest authority in matters of law. James VI&I had attempted to intervene on behalf his countryman Mackalley, so the ruling sent an unambiguous message that, as Coke was reported to have said at the end of the proceedings, the king should 'not hinder Course of Justice'.[128] The killing featured in a widely circulated anti-Scottish ballad and one observer later wrote that the judgment was given 'more to satisfy the sheriffes of London, than justice'.[129] Regardless of these political concerns, Mackalley's case provided a clear framework for the treatment of those who

---

[128] BL Add. MS 25213, f.126.
[129] 'Upon the Scottes' in *Early Stuart Libels: An Edition of Poetry from Manuscript Sources*, eds. Alastair Bellany and Andrew McRae (2005); Francis Osborne, 'Traditional Memoirs' in Walter Scott (ed.), *The Secret History of the Court of James the First* (Edinburgh, 1811), vol. 1, 229–30.

killed officers. Provided the officer had given some 'notice' of their authority, anyone who killed them had, in the words of one early seventeenth-century handbook, set themselves against 'the law, the officers thereof, and the Justice of the realme'. There could be no lenience in punishing such a person; the verdict was murder and the sentence capital. This principle was confirmed in judicial rulings and legal commentary throughout the seventeenth century.[130] In a 1619 case involving forceful resistance to bailiffs, the chief justice stated that 'this resistance is not made to the bailiffs, but to the justice of the realm' because, as the judges had stated in the Mackalley ruling, 'executions [of legal process] are the life of the law'.[131] The hanging of a man who shot an officer's assistant in 1693 was marked by the publication of a ballad warning others not to resist arrest: 'Let my misfortunes teach the rest / obedience to the laws; / Let them not magistrates molest, / for that has been the cause / Of shedding blood, for which I die'. As the judges at the man's trial told the jury, homicide 'where any Lawful Authority shall be opposed' was always to be punished by death.[132]

Similar logic applied to killings *by* officers. As the lord chancellor put it a few years before Mackalley's case, 'whoever comes to arrest someone comes with the sceptre and sword of the king, which sceptre is that he ought to arrest the party peaceably, but if the party makes resistance then the sword should help the sceptre'.[133] The legal implications of this metaphor were laid out by chief justice Matthew Hale in his posthumously published treatise on criminal law. A person who resisted arrest could justifiably be killed by officers with no legal repercussions. This was because resisting officers meant resisting royal authority, an offence justly punished by death: 'by their resistance against the authority of the king in his officers they draw their own blood upon themselves'. Hale also spent some time discussing exactly what kind of 'notice' was required to make the killing of an officer automatically qualify as murder. For constables, he wrote, 'it is sufficient notice, if he declare himself to be the constable, or command the peace in the king's name'. In some cases, however, 'it seems there is no necessity for him to notify himself to be such by express words, but it

---

[130] Michael Dalton, *The Countrey Justice* (London, 1618), 210; Edward Coke, *Third Part of the Institutes of the Laws of England* (London, 1644), 52; R v Stanley/Standlie (1663), 1 Sid. 159, 82 *ER* 1031, Kelyng 86, 84 *ER* 1094; *OBP*, Jul 1681, trial of William Buckly (t16810706a-3).

[131] White v Whitshire (1619), 2 Rolle 137, 81 *ER* 709. Also reported at Palmer 52, 81 *ER* 973. The labelling of executions of process as 'the life of the law' makes an interesting contrast to Coke's better-known dictum that 'reason is the life of the law'.

[132] *Francis Winter's Last Farewel* (London, 1693); *OBP*, Apr 1693, trial of Francis Winter (t16930426-45).

[133] Ellesmere LC in Star Chamber (1606), BL Add. MS 35955 f.28v. Ellesmere's metaphor strikingly prefigures the frontispiece of Hobbes' *Leviathan*.

shall be presumed, that the offender knew him'. Here Hale referred to a 1630 case in which a man who shot a bailiff trying to break into his house was deemed to have known who the intruder was, despite the fact that no explicit notice had been given. The bailiffs who made arrests for debt on behalf of sheriffs and civil courts were said to be *jurus et conus* (sworn and known), regardless of whether the particular person they confronted knew who they were: 'it is not necessary, that he be known to the party arrested, but it is sufficient if he be commonly known'.[134]

On these terms, it was extremely difficult for a defendant to show that they had killed an officer without knowing who their victim was, or, more accurately, what they represented. Trials of officer-killers in the late seventeenth and early eighteenth century often revolved around the question of whether notice of official authority had been given. In a 1694 case, witnesses testified that the deceased officer had shown 'his Authority as a Constable, by producing his Staff, and very mildly desired him [the killer], in the King's Name, to yield and surrender himself quietly to his power'. The killer claimed, by contrast, that the officer 'came without a Staff or Warrant to seize him, therefore he thought him not to be a Constable'. Similar arguments were made by other defendants, generally without success.[135] A rare exception came in 1691, when an Old Bailey jury acquitted the killer of a bailiff who had burst into his lodgings with several other officers and grabbed him 'before they gave the word of Arrest to him'. The judges asked the jury to reconsider their verdict; they did so, but returned to reiterate that the man was not guilty of murder.[136] More typical was a case heard in 1703, in which two men were found to have murdered a constable who tried to arrest them after another officer had brandished a staff, 'Signifieing his Authority'. At the constable's funeral, the presiding clergyman denounced the 'Insult upon the Queen's Majesty' implied by such an attack on 'the very Face of Authority'.[137]

The constable's staff and the monarch's name turned private individuals into officers who benefited from special legal protection. But this

---

[134] Matthew Hale (1609–76), *Historia Placitorum Coronae* (London, 1736), vol. 2, 85–6; Hale, *Placitorum Coronae*, vol. 1, 458–61; R v Pew (1630), Cro. Car. 183, 79 *ER* 760.

[135] *OBP*, May 1694, trial of Drury Wake (t16940524-26); R v Noble (1713) in Howell, *State Trials*, 731–62; *OBP*, Feb 1713, trial of Christopher Bannister, Elizabeth Roberts (t17130225-28); *OBP*, Jun 1738, trial of Godfrey Walker (t17380628-16).

[136] *OBP*, Apr 1691, trial of S- F- (t16910422-27).

[137] LMA, MJ/SP/1702/07/048, Information of Stephen Smith, 29 May 1702; Josiah Woodward, *A Sermon Preach'd ... At the Funeral of Mr. John Cooper, a Constable* (London, 1702), 9; *OBP*, Jul 1703, trial of Thomas Cook (t17030707-2); *OBP*, Oct 1703, trial of William Wallis (t17031013-21); R v Wallis in *A Report of all the Cases Determined by Sir John Holt* (London, 1738), 484.

transformation relied on officers staying within the bounds of what they were authorised to do. So long as they acted by authority, killing them was a crime of the highest order and, in some circumstances, they were permitted to kill without legal consequences. As the existence of official imposters made clear, however, not everyone who waved a staff and invoked the monarch's name was acting by authority. Such props and performances were indispensable to the everyday operation of government but were not, in the end, failsafe. The impersonal authority created by early seventeenth-century statute and common law was attached to particular kinds of action. Magic words and bits of painted wood could be used to claim that such an action was taking place, but did they possess authority in themselves? If officers used those tools to give the appearance of authority to actions that were not entirely lawful, were they still under special legal protection?

This question arose in a 1709 case which produced the first major challenge to the logic of the Mackalley ruling. Three soldiers were tried for the killing of a constable in the course of a fight with officers in Covent Garden. The officers had unlawfully arrested a woman on suspicion of selling sex – exactly why this arrest was unlawful is explained in Chapter 4 – and the soldiers attempted to rescue her. One of the officers warned them not to interfere, saying 'Here is a Constable, and you are not to molest him in the Execution of his Office', but the soldiers replied 'G—d d—n me … how do we know that'? and drew their swords. The constable was urged by his colleague to 'pull out his short Staff, that they might see there was a Constable'. He then carried out a full invocation of official authority, announcing that 'he was the Queens Officer and about the Queens business and that the woman was his prisoner and shewed them his Constables Staff and charged them in the Queen's name to keep the Peace'. The men seem to have accepted this and backed down, saying 'if you are, we beg your Pardon' as they lowered their swords.[138] This ought to have been the end of the story, a potentially explosive encounter defused by a constable's conjuring of authority. The officers took the arrested woman to the watch-house and the soldiers kept their peace. But for reasons which remain obscure, the officers who arrived at the watch-house told others who were there that the constable was under attack and needed help, prompting several watchmen and constables – including the man who was eventually

---

[138] Thomas Bray, *The Tryals of Jeremy Tooley, William Arch, and John Clauson* (London, 1732), 26, 4, 12, 10, 20; LMA, MJ/SP/1709/04/010, Information of Samuel Bray, 19 Mar 1709.

killed – to rush out to Covent Garden with their staves.[139] Accounts of the confrontation between the three soldiers and this second group of officers varied: it is not clear how the fighting began or who began it. At some point, one of the constables found himself cornered. Well aware of his position under homicide law, he apparently 'expostulated with them one by one, explaining unto them the Danger they would draw upon themselves' by doing him harm, but the soldiers stabbed him nonetheless.[140]

The three men were found guilty of murder at the Old Bailey, but the judges decided there were complex legal questions at stake and arranged for the case to be passed on to Queen's Bench. Lawyers for the prosecution cited the precedent of Mackalley's case, arguing that the officer had been killed in the execution of duty after notice of his authority was clearly given. The defence claimed the constable had not been killed in the execution of duty, but in the course of an unlawful arrest. This, they insisted, removed any special protection from the officer's actions and opened the way to a verdict of manslaughter rather than murder.[141] The case was reserved for consideration by all twelve royal justices of the central courts who, after lengthy deliberations, were divided seven against five in favour of manslaughter.

Chief justice John Holt gave the majority ruling, in which he stated that conjuring authority was meaningless (or worse, misleading) in the case of an unauthorised action, and that an officer who carried out such an unauthorised action was not really an officer at all, but a private individual committing an offence – a criminal. One of the justices suggested that the fact a constable's staff had been displayed was enough to make the soldiers guilty of murder: it was 'Sufficient Warning and Manifestation of Authority and therefore ought to have restrained them from that Violence which they did Commit'. Holt disagreed. 'I do not know that any Authority is in the Staff', he replied. 'If the Constable hath an Authority the Shewing his Staff is a good Indication of it', but without lawful authority it was mere imposture, or, as Holt put it, 'a Fraud and an Aggravation of his Misdemeanour And indeed a Lye'. The conjuring of a false authority could not, according to Holt, turn a person's actions into lawful acts of authority. Instead, 'he acts not as Constable but as an Oppressor. A Constable, that acts out of the limits of his Jurisdiction, and out of his Office, must be taken as an Oppressor'. One of Holt's

---

[139] LMA, MJ/SP/1709/04/008, Information of Thomas Lovett, 19 Mar 1709; LMA, MJ/SP/1709/04/011, Information of Philip Cholmondley, 19 Mar 1709; LMA, MJ/SP/1709/04/013, Information of Foulk Withers, 19 Mar 1709.
[140] Bray, *Tryals*, 20–26, 3; LMA, MJ/SP/1709/04/008, Information of Thomas Lovett, 19 Mar 1709.
[141] 11 Mod. 246, 88 *ER* 1017; 2 Ld. Raym. 1297, 92 *ER* 350.

fellow justices made the same point more straightforwardly: 'if he is in the wrong he is no Constable or officer'.[142]

This judgment pushed the law of office to its logical conclusion. Where early seventeenth-century judges and legislators had distinguished between authorised and unauthorised actions in order to grant officers legal protection, Holt used the same distinction to reduce that protection's scope. His scepticism about the legal status of the constable's staff – on a previous occasion he had expressed similar reservations about the power of the monarch's name[143] – reopened the question of how a person on the street or in a field was to recognise an officer acting by authority. Later in the eighteenth century, some lawyers and judges rejected Holt's ruling for precisely this reason. Justice Michael Foster's 1762 treatise on criminal law included an extended commentary on the case, in which he disagreed violently with Holt. His central point was that the soldiers had no idea that the initial arrest was unlawful (it was 'a fact of which they were totally ignorant at that time') so mitigating the severity of their punishment on that basis made no sense. What they did know was that a constable had shown them his staff of office. 'I remember a saying of a very learned judge', Foster wrote, 'That a constable's staff will not make a constable. This is very true. But if a minister of justice ... produce his staff of office, or any other known ensign of authority: this, I conceive, will be a sufficient notification with what intent he interposeth'. On this basis, Foster called for 'a general submission to the known badges of authority', which would 'greatly conduce to the stability of government'.[144]

Foster's arguments on this point were cited in court and repeated by later legal writers.[145] This prevented the Mackalley ruling, and the law of official homicide it had shaped, from becoming obsolete. But Holt had highlighted a basic tension in the law of office which could not be argued away. However impersonal their authority, officers remained individual people prone, like others, to personal faults and errors. They might conjure

---

[142] BL, Add. MS 35979, 'Law Reports, being cases tried before Sir John Holt, Chief Justice', 70–70v; R v Tooley in *Report Of all the Cases*, 488; 11 Mod. 249, 88 *ER* 1019; BL, Add. MS 35994, 'Law Reports 1722–3 and Miscellaneous', 95–97, 99v.

[143] Genner v Sparks (1704) in *Digest of Adjudged Cases*, 112.

[144] Michael Foster, *A Report of Some Proceedings on the Commission for the Trial of the Rebels in the Year 1746, in the County of Surrey; And of Other Crown Cases: To Which Are Added Discourses upon a Few Branches of the Crown Law* (London, 1762), 316, 311, 317.

[145] R v Adey (1780), 1 Leach 206, 168 *ER* 205; *OBP*, Sep 1779, trial of Mary Adey (t17790915-74); *OBP*, Nov 1796, trial of Francis Dunn, William Arnold, William Ryan (t17961130-5); May 1799, trial of Timothy Brian, James Barry, Patrick Holland, Daniel Driscoll, George Romsey, Cornelius Donohough, John M'Carty, John Sullivan, Hannah Brian, Eleanor Hern (t17990508-21); Edward Hyde East, *A Treatise of the Pleas of the Crown* (London, 1803), vol. 1, 326, 314–5.

abstract powers to give force to their commands, but the reality of their own personhood was ultimately inescapable. This was all the more of a problem since the notion of ministerial officeholding had undercut the ideal of the *idoneus homo*. If certain kinds of office could be held by anyone, regardless of personal qualities, the contrast between an officer's claim to impersonal authority and their status as an individual could be stark. In 1735, a London watchman was ordered by the local constable to arrest a woman named Sarah How. As she later told the Old Bailey,

> This Fellow laid hold of me, and swore he'd carry me to the Compter; I asked him for what? he said he had Orders for it, and that was enough. Well then, says I, let me go quietly. D—Ye for B—, says he, I'll lug ye along as I think fit. You dirty Dog, says I, what do ye mean by that? I'll go as I please – Why how now ye B—? Do you resist Authority? I am the King's Servant – You the King's Servant, ye Scrub Rascal? – Then he took me a Knock. I told him he had no business to strike me. He said he would if he pleas'd. I assured him I should take the liberty of striking again, for all his Authority, and so I did.[146]

A man who could be described as a 'dirty Dog' or 'Scrub Rascal' did not command Sarah How's respect, 'for all his Authority' as 'the King's Servant' acting under orders from above.

The legal separation of the official and the personal was a powerful tool of government: it protected officers from litigation and violence, it allowed them to use force without fear of consequences, and it criminalised resistance against them. At the same time, it undid the ties binding office to household and official authority to social status. There was now no reason for officeholding to be restricted to independent heads of household. In the later seventeenth and early eighteenth centuries, a new kind of officer emerged. In place of the sober, reputable patriarch, fraternities of male law enforcement officers combined the exercise of lawful authority with a very different style of masculinity, turning the old alignment between official power and patriarchy on its head. This was made possible by the legal innovations of the early seventeenth century. Judges and legislators had changed the nature of official authority. Those changes opened the door to a new kind of official manhood.

---

[146] *OBP*, May 1735, trial of Sarah How (t17350522-33).

CHAPTER 3

Office and Manhood

One of the foundational narratives of feminist history described the seventeenth century as a major turning point in the relationship between gender and formal authority. In the medieval period, the story goes, women were able to participate in the structures of government. It was only in the seventeenth century that political activity was redefined as the exclusive preserve of men. Among the earliest historians of this process was the campaigner for women's suffrage Charlotte Carmichael Stopes. In her *British Freewomen: Their Historical Privilege*, published in 1894, Stopes argued that women had been sheriffs under the Plantagenets, justices of the peace under the Tudors, and voters under the early Stuarts. This era of relative openness had come to an end, she wrote, when 'early in the seventeenth century, men's views regarding women became much altered, and the liberties of women thereby curtailed'. So began 'The Long Ebb', a period of exclusion lasting until Stopes' own day when the movement for women's votes brought about 'The Turn of the Tide'.[1] Many among subsequent generations of feminist historians followed Stopes' lead.[2] In their magisterial survey of women's lives in early modern England, Sara Mendelson and Patricia Crawford wrote that 'By the end of the [seventeenth] century, both political theory and political institutions were more clearly defined as male'.[3]

---

[1] Charlotte Carmichael Stopes, *British Freewomen: Their Historical Privilege* (London, 1894), 99; Hilda L. Smith, '"No Leisure for Myself": C.C. Stopes and British Freewomen' in Hilda L. Smith and Melinda S. Zook (eds.), *Generations of Women Historians: Within and Beyond the Academy* (London, 2018). Annie Beatrice Wallis Chapman and Mary Wallis Chapman told a similar story in their *The Status of Women under the English Law* (London, 1909). Some of Stopes' evidence was challenged by Rose Graham, 'The Civic Position of Women at Common Law before 1800', *Journal of the Society of Comparative Legislation* 17.1/2 (1917).

[2] Patricia Crawford, '"The Poorest She": Women and Citizenship in Early Modern England' in Michael Mendle (ed.), *The Putney Debates of 1647: The Army, the Levellers and the English State* (Cambridge, 2001); Hilda Smith, *All Men and Both Sexes: Gender, Politics, and the False Universal in England, 1640–1832* (Philadelphia, 2002), 73–84, 109–33.

[3] Sara Mendelson and Patricia Crawford, *Women in Early Modern England 1550–1720* (Oxford, 1998), 428.

Several aspects of this narrative have been challenged. In particular, its association with long-standing ideas about the separation of public and private life has attracted extensive criticism.[4] The notion of a golden age for women followed by relegation to the private sphere has been systematically debunked.[5] Nonetheless, the old story retains some analytical power. Women may not have participated in medieval political life as freely as Stopes suggested, and that participation may not have been so entirely curtailed in the seventeenth century. But recent work by Ann Hughes and Jamie Gianoutsos has highlighted a different kind of gendered political transition, centred on the civil wars and revolution of the mid-seventeenth century. In these accounts, the triumph of parliamentarians over royalists brought about a 'masculinisation of politics'. Parliamentarians drew clearer distinctions between the state and the family as a means of escape from what they saw as emasculation and corruption under royal government. They envisaged a virtuous 'masculine republic', free from the interlinked threats of tyranny and feminised politics.[6]

In a very different way, officeholding also underwent a process of masculinisation by separation from the household. That separation excluded women who had held office themselves or participated in official activity by virtue of their status as subordinate members of officeholding families. At the same time, it put state authority into the hands of men who were not householders and who fell far short of the independent ideal described in Chapter 1. In fact, some of these new officers rejected the code of patriarchal independence altogether, instead asserting their manhood outside the household through fraternal sociability, drinking, violence, and sexual predation. This brand of masculinity was often (though not exclusively) associated with unmarried youth.[7] England did not have the organised fraternities of unmarried men described by historians of France and Germany,[8] but English print culture was full of similar associations

---

[4] Rachel Weil, *Political Passions: Gender, the Family and Political Argument in England 1680–1714* (Manchester, 1999); Rachel Weil, 'The Public, the Private, and Feminist Historiography', *Histoire Sociale/Social History* 40.80 (2007).

[5] Amanda Vickery, 'Golden Age to Separate Spheres? A Review of the Categories and Chronology of English Women's History', *Historical Journal* 36.2 (1993).

[6] Ann Hughes, *Gender and the English Revolution* (London, 2012), 149; Jamie A. Gianoutsos, *The Rule of Manhood: Tyranny, Gender, and Classical Republicanism in England, 1603–1660* (Cambridge, 2020).

[7] Alexandra Shepard, *Meanings of Manhood in Early Modern England* (Oxford, 2003), 93–126; Alexandra Shepard, '"Swil-bols and Tos-pots": Drink Culture and Male Bonding in England, c.1560–1640' in Laura Gowing, Michael Hunter, and Miri Rubin (eds.), *Love, Friendship and Faith in Europe, 1300–1800* (Basingstoke, 2005).

[8] Natalie Zemon Davis, 'The Reasons of Misrule: Youth Groups and Charivaris in Sixteenth-Century France', *Past & Present* 50 (1971); Merry E. Wiesner, 'Guilds, Male Bonding and Women's Work

between bachelorhood, alcohol, fighting, and misogyny.[9] This was the mode of manhood displayed by the gamblers, gallants, rakes, and rioters who, as discussed in Chapter 1, patriarchal officers tried to police. It was the disorderly underside of early modern masculinity, challenging the authority of husbands and fathers at the same time as it reinforced male domination over women.[10] From the mid-seventeenth century onward, a growing number of officers asserted their gendered identities in this way. Habits associated with misrule were adopted by those authorised to rule. Those who represented the state began to behave in ways which mirrored the activities of those who defied its authority. The separation of office from household, and the creation of novel forms of officeholding, produced a new official fraternalism which, in time, came to characterise a new style of policing.[11]

These changes were driven by forces which had uneven consequences for different offices and different parts of the country. The first attempt to exclude women from an office by separating it from the household was led by members of the legal profession. Compared to the legal redefinition of office described in the previous chapter, this effort was strikingly unsuccessful. A second attempt, orchestrated by central government administrators, had far more of an effect, though this was restricted to new offices created in the mid-seventeenth century. Perhaps the most significant steps towards changing the way in which office was gendered were taken by innumerable London householders who, in the later seventeenth and early eighteenth centuries, increasingly withdrew from direct participation in certain aspects of government. This was also a circumscribed development, which made only a limited impact beyond the capital. Nonetheless, it was here that a new relationship between gender and policing began to take shape.

---

in Early Modern Germany', *Gender & History* 1.2 (1989); Merry E. Wiesner, '"Wandervogels" and Women: Journeymen's Concepts of Masculinity in Early Modern Germany', *Journal of Social History* 24.4 (1991).

[9] Bernard Capp, 'English Youth Groups and the Pinder of Wakefield', *Past & Present* 76.1 (1977); Tim Reinke-Williams, 'Misogyny, Jest-Books and Male Youth Culture in Seventeenth-Century England', *Gender & History* 21.2 (2009).

[10] Mary Ann Clawson, 'Early Modern Fraternalism and the Patriarchal Family', *Feminist Studies* 6.2 (1980); Lyndal Roper, 'Blood and Codpieces: Masculinity in the Early Modern German Town' in *Oedipus and the Devil: Witchcraft, Religion and Sexuality in Early Modern Europe* (London, 1994).

[11] Wendy Brown has described the various masculinities associated with state power in the history of political thought: *Manhood and Politics: A Feminist Reading in Political Theory* (Totowa, NJ, 1988).

Legal Exclusion

Under the old system of officeholding by heads of household, there was no clear legal basis for the exclusion of women. A propertied singlewoman or widow could be an *idoneus homo* in much the same way as a propertied singleman, husband, or widower. The requirement for an officer to be a 'substantial householder' did not rule out women because, as one lawyer put it, 'substantial householder has no reference to sex'.[12] In a lecture given at Gray's Inn in 1622, a prominent barrister argued that although women were sometimes prevented from holding particular offices for which they were deemed unfit, this was not strictly legal: 'they are not in Law to be excluded as uncapable'.[13] The fact that officeholding by women was rare had less to do with law than with the gendered distribution of wealth and informal mechanisms of exclusion.

This makes it all the more striking that a number of common lawyers invented a legal prohibition on certain kinds of female officeholding in the seventeenth century. In 1634, royal justices put forward an explicitly gendered idea of qualification for office by dismissing the role of the household. The case itself was relatively innocuous. An attorney of King's Bench named Prouse had been chosen constable of Taunton according to the custom of 'houserow', whereby an office rotated among the heads of a particular set of households – whoever happened to be head of the next household in line would serve the following term. Prouse claimed exemption on the basis of his status as an officer of King's Bench, and this ought to have been a narrowly defined case on the subject of the court's privileges. In their ruling in favour of Prouse, however, the justices produced a broad condemnation of officeholding by rotation among households. 'Houserow', they argued, 'cannot be a good custom; for then a woman being an inhabitant in one of the said houses, it may come to her course to be constable, which the law will not permit'.[14] Gender, the justices argued, trumped householding as a qualification (or disqualification) for office. It is not clear what prompted the justices to make this novel declaration. The only published report of the case makes no reference to any statute or precedent. The Prouse judgment roughly coincided with a number of other legal attacks on female participation in politics, though there is no evidence

---

[12] R v Stubbs (1788), 2 T.R. 396, 100 *ER* 214.
[13] Robert Callis, *The Reading of That Famous and Learned Gentleman, Robert Callis Esq; Sergeant at Law, Upon the Statute of 23 H. 8. Cap. 5. Of Sewers: As It Was Delivered by Him at Gray's Inn, in August, 1622* (London, 1647), 202. I am grateful to Alice Blackwood for this reference.
[14] Prouse's Case (1634), Cro. Car. 389, 79 *ER* 940.

of any direct links between them. In 1634, Edward Coke had already written (though not yet published) his opinion that 'Women having freehold or no freehold' were not permitted to vote in parliamentary elections. In 1640, this principle was put into practice when the votes of several female freeholders in Ipswich were disallowed by the county sheriff.[15]

Whether or not the Prouse ruling represented one move in a broader exclusionary campaign, the idea that women should not hold office, even if they were householders, was soon taken up by lawyers and magistrates who publicised it through handbooks for officeholding. William Sheppard, a barrister who later advised Oliver Cromwell on legal reform, wrote in a 1641 guide for constables that 'the partie chosen, as he must be a lay person, so he must be a layman, not a lay-woman'. Like the judges in Prouse's case, he condemned the custom of 'houserow' on these grounds: 'a widow or maid, albeit she keep House of her self, and dwell in a House whose owner hath been used to serve in this Office, is not to be chosen to this Office'.[16] Sheppard's opposition to female officeholding proved influential within the handbook genre. In 1660, republican magistrate Edmund Wingate wrote that a constable should be, among other things, 'not a woman'. George Meriton, a lawyer who also wrote a guide to Yorkshire dialect, made the same assertion in his 1669 officeholding manual, as did legal hack Robert Gardiner in 1692. For these authors, the possibility that 'houserow' would put women into office was 'not sufferable'.[17] Several eighteenth-century writers echoed their concerns, and in some cases extended the exclusion of women to other offices.[18] As Richard Burn bluntly put it in his widely read guide for justices of the peace, 'A woman ought not to be appointed overseer'.[19]

These were prescriptive statements, not evidence of practice. Clearly, there was a desire among some legal professionals to exclude women from office. That desire was sometimes shared by judges in the lower courts, like the magistrates presiding at Derbyshire Quarter Sessions in 1684 who ruled that Mary Jacques should not serve as churchwarden because

---

[15] Edward Coke, *The Fourth Part of the Institutes of the Laws of England Concerning the Jurisdiction of Courts* (London, 1644), 4–5; BL, MS Harley 158, f.285v, 'A short and true relation of the carriage of the election of the Knights for the countie of Suffolke at Ipswich'.
[16] William Sheppard, *The Offices of Constables* (London, 1641), B8v. On Sheppard's career, see Nancy L. Matthews, *William Sheppard, Cromwell's Law Reformer* (Cambridge, 1984).
[17] Edmund Wingate, *The Exact Constable* (London, 1660), 8–9; George Meriton, *A Guide for Constables* (London, 1669), 6; Robert Gardiner, *The Compleat Constable* (London, 1692), 7–8.
[18] Giles Jacob, *The Compleat Parish-Officer* (London, 1718), 3; Richard Burn, *The Justice of the Peace and Parish-Officer* (London, 1755), vol. 1, 219; John Paul, *The Compleat Constable* (London, 1785), 2.
[19] Burn, *Justice of the Peace*, vol. 2, 188.

'she as a woman was not capable of the office'. A decade later, the same court declared Mistress Elizabeth Sleigh incapable of holding the office of overseer for the same reason. On the other hand, Derbyshire parishioners persisted in choosing women to serve as constables on the principle of 'houserow', in one case petitioning magistrates to allow the widow Elizabeth Taylor to 'officiate and execute the said office according to our ancient custom'.[20] Derbyshire was not the only county with a mixed record on this question. As shown in Chapter 1, women held a variety of offices across the country both before and after the mid-seventeenth century, often with the endorsement of courts of Quarter Sessions. Even King's Bench did not always pursue the exclusionary logic of the Prouse ruling, upholding the elections of Alice Stubbs and Sarah Bly, as discussed in previous chapters. It is possible, of course, that the pronouncements of handbook writers against female officeholding influenced the election and appointment of officers in ways which have left no trace in the archive. Some of those who had a voice in such decisions – parish ratepayers, manorial tenants, urban freemen – might have had copies of one manual or another which claimed female officeholding was unlawful. They might have persuaded their neighbours that it would not be right to choose a woman to hold office. Even if this were true, the evidence of female officeholding throughout the early modern period suggests that those who sought to outlaw the practice were at most partially successful, and perhaps not even that. Small numbers of women continued to hold office on the basis of their status as heads of household.

Excise and Independence

The link between officeholding and householding was broken far more decisively by a different mid-century development: the Excise. During the civil wars, both parliament and the king introduced indirect excise taxes on particular goods to fund their military endeavours. These emergency measures did not disappear in peacetime. In fact, more and more goods were subjected to excise taxation over the following decades and into the early eighteenth century.[21] Revenue collection on this scale required a growing establishment of dedicated officers, who numbered in the thousands by

---

[20] Mendelson and Crawford, *Women in Early Modern England*, 57; Graham, 'Civic Position of Women', 191–3.
[21] Michael J. Braddick, *Parliamentary Taxation in Seventeenth-Century England* (Woodbridge, 1994), 168–230; D'Maris Coffman, *Excise Taxation and the Origins of Public Debt* (London, 2013).

1700 and accounted for about half of all central government employees involved in fiscal administration. Most of these officers were 'gaugers', tasked with measuring the quantities of beer, malt, silk, soap, candles, and other commodities stored by producers and retailers. Historians have emphasised the formality of excise administration, its complex hierarchies, its elaborate training arrangements, and the highly technical skills required of its officers. 'The English Excise', according to John Brewer, 'more closely approximated Max Weber's idea of bureaucracy than any other government agency in eighteenth-century Europe'. The excise officer was a 'symbol of a new form of government' with, in Michael Braddick's words, 'an identity shaped by being a professional state official'.[22]

These accounts have concentrated on the highly specialised and 'professional' nature of excise officeholding. The level of technical expertise required of the new officers was undoubtedly new: recruits had to be highly literate and numerate, they were trained in algebra and the arcane symbols of elaborate record keeping, and some were dismissed for mistaken measurements or miscalculations.[23] Revenue agents were also full-time, salaried, and served continuously for many years, presenting a stark contrast to the part-time, amateur, rotational officeholding of churchwardens or overseers of the poor. This particular contrast can, however, be overdrawn. Largely unnoticed by historians, substantial numbers of offices were salaried long before the creation of the Excise. Beadles, sextons, scavengers, and parish clerks received fixed annual payments from their parishes throughout the early modern period. London's marshals were paid a regular salary by the City corporation. Many of these officers also served for long periods of time, often until death, as did sheriff's bailiffs, 'a body of men which changed little from year to year' according to one of the few scholars to study them.[24]

---

[22] John Brewer, *The Sinews of Power: War, Money and the English State, 1688–1783* (New York, 1989), 66–8, 114; Michael J. Braddick, *State Formation in Early Modern England c.1550–1700* (Cambridge, 2000), 262. See also Miles Ogborn, *Spaces of Modernity: London's Geographies, 1680–1780* (New York, 1998), 158–200.

[23] TNA, CUST 47/1, p. 37; 47/115, pp. 45–46; 47/159, p. 167; Michael J. Braddick, 'Public Office and Private Benefit in Early Modern England' in Juan Carlos Garavaglia, Michael J. Braddick, and Christian Lamouroux (eds.), *Serve the Power(s), Serve the State: America and Eurasia* (Newcastle-upon-Tyne, 2016), 212–18.

[24] T. E. Hartley, 'Under-Sheriffs and Bailiffs in Some English Shrievalties, c.1580 to c.1625', *Bulletin of the Institute of Historical Research* 47.116 (1974), 169. Salaries and long-term service among the lower parish officers is evident in books of vestry minutes, such as those of St John's Hackney, covering 1613–1771: LMA, P79/JN/137–142. On City marshals, see Donald Rumbelow, *I Spy Blue: The Police and Crime in the City of London from Elizabeth to Victoria* (London, 1971), 43–60.

What certainly was novel about excise officeholding was its disconnection from the household. A new recruit to the revenue service was supposed to be between the ages of twenty-one and thirty, male, and, according to an order from the Board of Commissioners, ought to be 'a single man'. Once in the Excise, a man might marry and have children, but this was often a source of tension with his employer, not something which bolstered his position as an officeholder. Marriage did not fit easily with the Board's practice of periodically 'removing' officers from one jurisdiction to another. Single officers were less able to object to being suddenly uprooted; in 1695, the commissioners wrote to a Staffordshire exciseman demanding 'to know why he being a single man should not be removed to Sudbury' (in Suffolk). Unlike other officers, an exciseman rarely used his house as a space for official business for the simple reason that he did not have one. Most officers lived in lodgings or rooms above 'offices' rented by the Board in public houses.[25] The women who featured most often in excise records were 'office-keepers', effectively landladies for resident excisemen, and the salaried 'housekeepers' who managed the London premises from which the Board of Commissioners ran the whole operation.[26] As Celia Davies has written of modern bureaucracies, 'the work can often only be accomplished in the requisite detached an impersonal manner by dint of a great deal of preparatory and servicing work which is carried out by women'. Landladies were a favourite subject of Thomas Chaloner, an exciseman turned poet, who poured invective on those he thought were scolding and ugly, praising the 'comely' and 'meek' to the skies.[27]

There were no female excise officers. Moreover, unlike the wives of male constables, churchwardens, overseers, and other traditional officeholders, excisemen's wives were forbidden to take part in their husbands' official business. These women only appear in the administrative documents when they were the source of a problem. Officers were often discharged

---

[25] John Brewer, 'Servants of the Public – Servants of the Crown: Officialdom of Eighteenth-Century English Central Government' in John Brewer and Eckhard Hellmuth (eds.), *Rethinking Leviathan: The Eighteenth-Century State in Britain and Germany* (Oxford, 1999), 144; TNA, CUST 47/46, p. 56; 47/1, p. 40.

[26] For female office-keepers, see: TNA, CUST 47/114, pp. 92, 96; 47/115, pp. 7, 72; 47/159, pp. 13, 20, 34, 87, 103, 105, 131, 162; 47/160, pp. 9, 20; 47/184, pp. 4, 133; 47/185, p. 28. For female housekeepers in the central office, see: TNA, CUST 47/46, p. 11; 47/115, pp. 46, 126; 47/159, p. 62; 47/160, pp. 58, 89; 47/184, p. 20; 47/185, pp. 14–15.

[27] Celia Davies, 'The Sociology of Professions and the Profession of Gender', *Sociology* 30.4 (1996), 671; Thomas Chaloner, *The Merriest Poet in Christendom* (London, 1732), 9, 35, 111. It is worth noting that older institutions of government also employed women to do this kind of service work, like the female housekeeper at Hick's Hall, where Middlesex justices held their Quarter Sessions: LMA, MJ/SP/1732/04/067.

for marrying women who worked, or had relatives who worked, in trades which came under excise jurisdiction. Such potential conflicts of interest led to the rapid removal of any officer who 'married a Woman whose Relations are under his survey', 'married the Daughter of a Trader under his survey', or was 'married to the sister of a Brewer under his survey'. When John Cannon, exciseman and autobiographer, married Susannah, his landlady's servant, they kept it secret from his superiors and both of their families for almost six months. Even after the marriage was made public, Susannah was unable to take an active part in John's excise life. One senior officer learnt this the hard way: summoned before the Board, his wife confessed that she had 'rec[eiv]ed 2 sev[era]ll sumes of money, & a note for paym[en]t of an other sume' owed to the revenue, a violation for which her husband was demoted to a position at the bottom of the official hierarchy. The ban on familial participation also applied to sons. In 1735, the commissioners discharged an officer who 'makes a frequent practice of trusting his Son w[i]th his Brandy Permit & Cyder Certificate Books & allowing him to grant permits & Certificates to the Traders'.[28] Offices in the Excise were attached to male individuals, not households.

The exciseman was, in some ways, the exact opposite of the independent householder. His position and salary depended entirely on his superiors, who could promote, remove, demote, or discharge him at any time. In the eyes of some contemporaries, this made excisemen mere tools of state power, unfree beings who had no choice but to do exactly as they were instructed, regardless of the consequences for the rest of society. From the moment of its creation in the mid-seventeenth century, officers of the Excise were said to be the embodiment of state tyranny over the liberties of the people.[29] The dependence of excisemen, some argued, threatened to crush the independence of the country as a whole.

Even people who served or had served in the Excise could portray its officers in this way. The poet Thomas Chaloner, who became a schoolmaster on his retirement from the revenue service, had never liked the job. In the preface to his only published work, he wrote that the business was 'too

---

[28] TNA, CUST 47/185, pp. 22, 104; 47/184, pp. 70–1; *The Chronicles of John Cannon, Excise Officer and Writing Master: Part 1 1684–1733* ed. John Money (Oxford, 2010), 121, 128; TNA, CUST 47/45, pp. 43–44; 47/160, p. 43.

[29] See, for example: *The Judicial Arraignment, Condemnation, Execution & Interment of the Late Pernicious Endenized Dutch Devil Excize, and Its Infernal Imps Excize-Men, Englands Grant Pests* (London, 1653); William Prynne, *A Declaration and Protestation against the Illegal, Oft-Condemned, New Tax and Extortion of Excise in General* (London, 1654). See also Braddick, *Parliamentary Taxation*, 168–230.

slavish' for him from the start. 'Slavery', for Chaloner, meant dependence on the will of another.[30] In a poem supposedly written on the back of one of the numerous journals and notebooks excisemen were required to fill, he berated himself and his colleagues for their lack of independence: 'O Ideots! you Excise-men that can be / Not Subject to your Wills, but Slavery'. Again and again, he challenged the gauger to 'retrieve thy Liberty' rather than be 'That dull insipid Thing, that can submit / To Slavery, and will be fond of it'. He was not, however, very optimistic about this: 'since Ambition cannot make him brave, / Let him be always Gauger, always Slave'. Another poem's subtitle announced 'the Business of Excise prescrib'd as a sovereign Antidote to Liberty'. In the lines that followed, Chaloner conjured the image of an exciseman dutifully trudging from one retailer to another, battling the wind and pouring rain, before telling him, bitterly, 'You'll not complain of too much Liberty'.[31]

Ezekiel Polsted, another literary exciseman, was equally aware of the problem of dependence. In 1697, having risen to the rank of supervisor, he published a satirical pamphlet in praise of life in the Excise, repeatedly pointing out that its officers were in some sense unfree. Gaugers, he wrote, had 'an *External Dependence*' on those who paid their salaries. This was so debilitating in terms of liberty that even their emotions were mere echoes of the master's will: 'if you weep he is sad; if you laugh he is merry; and all this while in reality neither, but in obliging those on which *insinuating observance* their *subsistence* does depend'. Polsted confirmed this characterisation by pretending to argue against it. Dependence, he announced, could be a virtue as well as a vice. It was, for example, a spur to honesty and diligence, because the exciseman sought to ensure 'that his great Master (to whom he is responsible for his well-being) is not defrauded'. Salaries, of course, secured an officer's obedience to the monarch because "Tis He only allows him that Competency he enjoys'. But salaries might, Polsted suggested, actually make a person more independent: 'Our *Excise-Man* having a *Compleat Maintenance* without *Charge*; a *Sufficiency* without *Dependence*'. In contrast to Chaloner's beleaguered officer struggling with the elements, he portrayed the rounds of stock inspections as a joyous – and subsidised – exploration of fields, forests, and cities. 'Our *Excise-Man*', Polsted wrote, 'is the only Person that can possibly enjoy these *Pleasures* without *Expence*; for what others purchase at a dear Rate, he receives with

---

[30] On this use of the word, see Mary Nyquist, *Arbitrary Rule: Slavery, Tyranny, and the Power of Life and Death* (Chicago, 2013).
[31] Chaloner, *The Merriest Poet*, C1v-D1, 2, 4–5, 45.

Interest; for whereas they are necessitated to *pay* for their Pleasures, he is *paid* for them'. Overall, work in the excise was not 'slavery' but 'that Incomparable Dependence'. Eventually, however, Polsted's tongue-in-cheek effort to rescue the reputation of excise life collapsed in the face of the facts. The exciseman 'is satisfied it lies in the Power of his Masters with or without Reason to reduce him' to a lower grade. The threat of demotion meant that, 'as an Officer, he is advis'd by Providence to devour less, considering the Scantness of his Fortunes, and (which is more) the frequent Vicissitudes that inevitably attend them'. It was necessary to be 'prepar'd for all imaginable Events' because, as a person dependent on the will of others, the exciseman's fate was not in his own hands.[32]

One major cause of uncertainty in excise life was the system of 'removes', under which officers were constantly moved from one posting to another. True to form, Polsted tried to make a virtue out of this constant upheaval: 'My Country is where're my *Bread* I get, / Not where I was *Bred*, but where I have *Meat*: / Where I am *known* not *Christen'd*; there I dwell / (And no where else) wherever I do well'. Removes were explicitly intended to keep officers detached from – and independent of – the people around them.[33] The minutes of the Board of Commissioners are full of references to officers who had to be relocated after they 'contracted too much Acquaintance there'. Forms of acquaintance involving the exchange of money were especially problematic. One exciseman was removed 'having a great inclination to gaming, & having contracted more acquaintance in his s[ai]d D[ivisio]n than is consistent with the performance of his Duty'. Another had to be transferred because he had bought an orchard producing cider, 'w[hi]ch must necessarily oblige him to deal with the Traders under his survey'. Many were removed or even discharged for borrowing money from people under their jurisdiction. It was often quite clear that removes were against the officers' wishes, the Board 'taking care that they be not placed in the Div[isio]ns which they respectively desire'. It is hardly surprising that some officers, when ordered to pack their bags for a new position, simply refused to go.[34]

One consequence of the 'removes' system was that excisemen were always outsiders. Unlike traditional householding officers, they were not

---

[32] Ezekiel Polsted, *Kaloz telonesantai or, The Excise-Man* (London, 1697), 7–8, 43, 75, 97, 82, 52, 68, 117. For Polsted's career, see TNA, CUST 47/2, pp. 44, 58.
[33] Polsted, *Kaloz telonesantai*, 11; Miles Ogborn, 'Wherein Lay the Late Seventeenth-Century State? Charles Davenant Meets Streynsham Master', *Journal of Historical Sociology* 15.1 (2002), 97–8.
[34] TNA, CUST 47/159, pp. 5, 167; 47/84, p. 79; 47/2, pp. 67, 13; 47/184, p. 111; 47/45, pp. 12, 49, 63; 47/185, pp. 102, 123; 47/80, pp. 83, 109; 47/81, p. 71.

long-term residents in the places where they worked, embedded in patterns of neighbourly reciprocity and reproach.[35] John Cannon wrote that he arrived at his first excise post to work 'amongst strangers'. At first, this had exactly the effect intended: he 'minded nothing else but how to oblige my superior officers'. Over time, his isolation diminished as '[I] associated myself in all my vacant hours in innocent games & diversions ... with several young gentlemen of good reputation whose friends were clergymen, gentlemen, or tradesmen'. Nonetheless, a few years later when he was sick with smallpox, he reflected on 'the distance I was from my native country & friends, abandoned wholly to strangers'. Cannon's family was in Somerset, near enough to his post in Oxfordshire to send letters frequently and occasionally get leave for a visit. This does not seem to have been enough, and in 1714 he unsuccessfully petitioned the Board for a transfer to Bristol or Sarum, 'being grown weary of my long absence from my native friends'. But years away from home left him at least as cut off from his 'native country' as his place of work. As he wrote of a 1717 trip to see his sick mother, after 'my long absence', 'the parish seemed quite strange'.[36] Alienated from both his home and his working environment, Cannon appears to have been the archetypal uprooted officer, disconnected from the society around him and existing only to serve the state.

The fear, for opponents of the Excise, was that the central government controlled an army of John Cannons. Criticism of the revenue administration reached a peak in 1733 when merchants dealing in wine and tobacco orchestrated a major political campaign against proposals to extend taxation to those commodities.[37] Nicholas Amhurst, editor of the opposition periodical *The Craftsman*, claimed that excisemen were 'absolutely dependent on the Crown, which hath the sole Power of putting Them in and turning Them out of their Employments'. This was dangerous, he thought, because excise officers might be 'either chosen Members of Parliament Themselves, or have a very great Influence in the Election of others'. The House of Commons – the great barrier against arbitrary government – would be filled up with people who owed their careers directly

---

[35] Henry French, '"Ancient inhabitants": Mobility, Lineage and Identity in English Rural Communities, 1600–1750' in Christopher Dyer (ed.), *The Self-Contained Village? The Social History of Rural Communities, 1250–1900* (Hatfield, 2007). Long residence could give a candidate for parish office an advantage over rivals: LPL, Arches, Personal Answers, Ee 6, answers of Samuel Stretch, 2 Nov 1685, 38; LMA, DL/C/0258, deposition of John Verdon, 16 Jun 1719, 260–1v; DL/C/0261, deposition of John King, 11 Jun 1723, 27–8.
[36] *Chronicles of John Cannon*, 83, 86–7, 101, 119, 117, 131–2.
[37] Paul Langford, *The Excise Crisis: Society and Politics in the Age of Walpole* (Oxford, 1975).

to the executive. Voters, dependent on excisemen for a fair assessment of their taxes, would be open to influence, while the officers themselves, dependent on the government paying their wages, would use that influence however their superiors desired. 'I cannot for my Life put it out of my Head', Amhurst wrote, 'that such an infinite Multiplicity of Officers, immediately under the Direction of the Crown, must have some Sort of Influence over Those, who lye at their Mercy'. Locked in a spiral of dependence, officers, taxpayers, and the country at large would be powerless to prevent the rise of tyranny. The Excise, as Thomas Chaloner put it, was a 'Plague to Mankind, and endless Slavery, / A perfect Antidote to Liberty'.[38]

On this view, excisemen resembled the legal model of the ministerial officer, discussed in the previous chapter. Existing solely to carry out the orders of superiors, without personal status or discretionary power, they were seen as officers of an entirely different kind to the heads of household who dominated the old structures of local government and law enforcement. In the later seventeenth and early eighteenth centuries, however, that contrast became less clear cut. The notion of ministerial officeholding allowed those who were chosen to serve in some of the old offices to appoint deputies. In London, especially in the offices of law enforcement, deputisation gradually became the norm rather than the exception. The deputy officers who came to dominate policing in the capital were, in many ways, more like excisemen than like the householders whose places they filled.

London's Deputies

The early seventeenth-century legal endorsement of deputisation in ministerial offices had profound consequences. Initially, only people who were sick, injured, or otherwise physically unable to carry out the duties of office were expected to appoint deputies to act for them. In London, however, people who were entirely capable of serving soon began to hire deputies anyway, especially in the ministerial offices of constable and watchman.[39] In 1630, the City corporation issued a proclamation against this practice, complaining that householders were delegating 'the services which themselves ought to performe, to inferiour ministers'. As a remedy, they insisted

---

[38] Caleb D'Anvers [Nicholas Amhurst], *An Argument Against Excises* (London, 1733), 24; Caleb D'Anvers [Nicholas Amhurst], *The Second Part of an Argument Against Excises* (London, 1733), 48; Chaloner, *The Merriest Poet*, 4.

[39] Paul Griffiths, *Lost Londons: Change, Crime, and Control in the Capital City 1550–1660* (Cambridge, 2008), 294–6, 300–1.

that anyone chosen as constable was required to 'undergoe and serve the same Office in his own person'. Whether or not this had any effect at the time, the problem did not go away. In 1661, a mayoral proclamation again complained that 'by admitting of Deputies, the office of Constable is, for the most part, slenderly supplied and served by mean persons'. Twenty years later, Middlesex justices of the peace were still condemning those 'able and substantial householders' who paid 'unfit mean & unable persons' to deputise for them. In 1682, the City's Court of Aldermen sued three men who had 'procured three other persons to bee Sworne as their Deputies contrary to the Custome of this City'. Later in the same decade, the aldermen made another order against deputisation and announced that the practice was 'contrary to the Lawes of this City'.[40]

For the City authorities, this was a losing battle. As John Beattie showed, the decades either side of 1700 saw a rapid expansion of deputisation in London officeholding. By the late 1720s, almost all of the serving constables in some inner city wards were deputies. Proportions were much lower in the outer wards, but the average across the City was about 40 per cent.[41] Opposition to the appointment of deputy constables faded away from the 1690s onward. In 1693, the Court of Aldermen decided to regulate rather than resist, ordering that 'noe person chosen Constable within this City be Admitted to put in a Dep[u]ty without the expresse order of this Court'. A year previously, the author of a handbook for officers had written that someone chosen to serve as a constable in London 'may hire a Deputy in his stead' without any special reason. Over the following decades, deputisation among constables became so common that by 1750 one man felt the need to petition the aldermen for permission *not* to hire a deputy and to 'have Liberty to serve the said Office' instead.[42]

Resistance to deputisation among watchmen also collapsed in the 1690s. By this time, almost every householder selected for watch duty was choosing to pay someone else instead.[43] In 1692, Middlesex magistrates proposed legislation under which householders would be replaced by paid deputies, funded by parish taxes, with those who contributed guaranteed exemption from watch duty. The Bill did not pass, but Elaine Reynolds has shown

---

[40] LMA, CLA/048/PS/01/005–6; MJ/SP/1682/02/001; COL/CA/01/01/87, f.144v; COL/CA/01/01/95, f.81v.
[41] J. M. Beattie, *Policing and Punishment in London, 1660–1750: Urban Crime and the Limits of Terror* (Oxford, 2001), 147–9.
[42] LMA, COL/CA/01/01/97, f.492v; Gardiner, *Compleat Constable*, 112; LMA, COL/CA/01/01/154, ff.148–9.
[43] Beattie, *Policing and Punishment*, 172–6.

that many metropolitan parishes developed a similar system informally, and much the same arrangements were eventually institutionalised in the capital by a series of Watch Acts of the early eighteenth century.[44] Similar patterns emerged in some other English cities, though never on the same scale. The corporation of Bristol began to appoint a number of salaried deputy watchmen in 1674 and Norwich residents frequently chose to pay others to serve for them in the same office. In 1691 Guy Miege wrote of all the towns in England that 'This Duty of Watching is commonly performed by Men hired for that purpose, and paid for't by the Citizens'.[45] This was an exaggeration: deputy watchmen only became the norm in Bath in the mid-eighteenth century and in Manchester and Birmingham from the 1790s.[46] Large-scale deputisation among constables remained primarily a London phenomenon.

The forces behind the shift towards deputisation in the capital are obscure. The legal category of ministerial officeholding provided the means, but what was the motive? Why did so many heads of household become determined to avoid their law enforcement duties? At the end of the eighteenth century, those calling for the reform of London policing suggested that deputisation was the logical consequence of a more commercial society. Householders were simply too busy with their own business to take up the duties of office. According to Patrick Colquhoun, 'the advanced state of society, and the important and useful occupations of individuals, who are engaged in pursuits of commerce, trade, and manufactures, render it impossible to expect that they would serve in their own persons'.[47] Some earlier writers saw officeholding in similar terms. Daniel Defoe, for example, wrote of the constableship that 'The Imposition of this Office is an insupportable Hardship; it takes up so much of a Man's time, that his own Affairs are frequently totally neglected, too often to his Ruin'. The idea that London householders turned away from officeholding because they could not spare the time

---

[44] LMA, MJ/SP/1692/12/018, 'Clauses abt the watche & ward to be inserted into an Act of Parliamt'; Elaine Reynolds, *Before the Bobbies: The Night Watch and Police Reform in Metropolitan London, 1720–1830* (Basingstoke, 1998).
[45] John Miller, *Cities Divided: Politics and Religion in English Provincial Towns, 1660–1722* (Oxford, 2007), 46; NRO, NCR Case 12b/6, Information of Bartholomew Nockolds, 26 Apr 1732; Guy Miege, *The New State of England* (London, 1691), vol. 3, 333.
[46] John Wood, *A Description of Bath* (London, 1765), 381; Arthur Redford, *The History of Local Government in Manchester* (London, 1939), vol. 2, 92–7; Beatrice Webb and Sidney Webb, *English Local Government: Statutory Authorities for Special Purposes* (London, 1922), 254–5.
[47] Patrick Colquhoun, *A Treatise on the Functions and Duties of a Constable* (London, 1803), 76. See also Joseph Ritson, *The Office of Constable* (London, 1791), xii.

is supported by the fact that deputisation was especially common in the richer inner city wards, which were dominated by prosperous merchants, artisans, and retailers – members of a commercial middling sort who increasingly thought of time as equivalent to money.[48] This group may also have sought to mark the distance between themselves and their poorer neighbours by withdrawing from the more mundane or unsavoury aspects of local government.[49]

Alternatively, rising deputisation could be seen as a more direct symptom of declining community. Religious and political divisions – the legacy of civil war and revolution – pulled apart neighbourhoods which had once (at least in theory) been governed by unified groups of householders.[50] There were no explicit requirements that low-level officeholders be loyal to the established church and state. The oaths of allegiance required of civic officers under the Clarendon Code of the 1660s were not demanded of officers below the level of high constable.[51] Nonetheless, officeholding by those who did not conform in political or religious matters attracted some controversy.[52] In the 1660s, senior clergy attempted to restrict membership of London vestries – generally made up of current and former officeholders – to Anglicans. The 1689 Toleration Act explicitly allowed Dissenting Protestants to appoint deputies to serve in their place as constables, churchwardens, or overseers of the poor.[53] In its aftermath, arguments arose in several London parishes over whether or not Dissenters

---

[48] Andrew Moreton [Daniel Defoe], *Parochial Tyranny: Or, The House-Keeper's Complaint Against The Insupportable Exactions, and Partial Assessments of Select Vestries* (London, 1727), 17; Beattie, *Policing and Punishment*, 148; Margaret R. Hunt, *The Middling Sort: Commerce, Gender, and the Family in England 1680–1780* (Berkeley, 1996), 53–6.

[49] On the increasing distinctiveness of London's middling sort in this period, see Peter Earle, *The Making of the English Middle Class: Business, Society and Family Life in London, 1660–1730* (Berkeley, 1989). A parallel might be drawn with the withdrawal of the upper gentry and aristocracy from county government at about the same time: James M. Rosenheim, 'County Governance and Elite Withdrawal in Norfolk, 1660–1720' in A. L. Beier, David Cannadine, and James M. Rosenheim (eds.), *The First Modern Society: Essays in English History in Honour of Lawrence Stone* (Cambridge, 1989).

[50] For the impact of these changes at a higher level of local government, see Paul D. Halliday, *Dismembering the Body Politic: Partisan Politics in England's Towns, 1650–1730* (Cambridge, 1998).

[51] 13 Car. II St. 2 c.1; *The Case of the Dissenters, and Others in Office, With Respect to the Laws Now in Force* (London, 1712), 9–10.

[52] Mark Goldie and John Spurr, 'Politics and the Restoration Parish: Edward Fowler and the Struggle for St Giles Cripplegate', *English Historical Review* 109.432 (1994). After 1715, Whig authorities in the City of London may have attempted to exclude Jacobites from holding office as constables: Beattie, *Policing and Punishment*, 144.

[53] Paul Seaward, 'Gilbert Sheldon, the London Vestries and the Defence of the Church' in Tim Harris, Paul Seaward, and Mark Goldie (eds.), *The Politics of Religion in Restoration England* (Oxford, 1990); 1 W&M c.18 s.5.

should be permitted to vote in the election of parish officers.⁵⁴ Similar disputes surrounded the position of London's growing Jewish population.⁵⁵ Some Jewish heads of household cast votes for local officers and some held office themselves, but others were excluded from both aspects of government or strongly encouraged to appoint Christian deputies.⁵⁶ Religious minorities may account for a substantial proportion of those who appointed deputy constables and watchmen. On the other hand, some were keen to serve in person in order to minimise the use of official powers against their co-religionists; this seems to have been the attitude of at least some London Quakers in the late seventeenth and early eighteenth centuries.⁵⁷ Meanwhile Anglican householders, no longer bound to all of their neighbours by the ties of shared religious practice, may have felt less and less of an obligation to dedicate time and energy to the government of their wards and parishes, preferring to hire deputies instead.

Neither of these explanations – the commercial or the religious – makes it clear why large-scale deputisation was concentrated in the offices of law enforcement. Why did London householders not pay their way out of the office of churchwarden or overseer of the poor? Both of these made heavy demands on a person's time, and both were more directly associated with notions of religious community than the constableship or service on the night watch. Yet deputy churchwardens were almost unheard of. When the churchwarden of St Paul's Shadwell arranged for a relative to serve on his behalf, he was confronted by an angry neighbour who insisted that 'every Man should act in his owne place or office'.⁵⁸ Deputy overseers of the poor were similarly unusual before the later eighteenth century.⁵⁹ According to

---

⁵⁴ For example: LMA, DL/C/0243, Challoner c. Harris, ff.111–122v; DL/C/0253, Dymond c. Barwell, ff.218–297v. I hope to write about disputed parish elections in more detail elsewhere.

⁵⁵ For one especially well-documented case, see LMA, DL/C/0265, Francia c. Myre, ff.144–53, 167–88; DL/C/0266, Francia c. Myre, ff.80–87v.

⁵⁶ The vestry of St Katherine Cree repeatedly chose Jewish overseers of the poor: LMA, P69/KAT2/B/001–002. On Jewish constables, see Karen A. Macfarlane, 'The Jewish Policemen of Eighteenth-Century London', *Journal of Modern Jewish Studies* 10.2 (2011).

⁵⁷ Simon Dixon, 'Quakers and the London Parish 1670–1720', *London Journal* 32.3 (2007), 237–43. Elsewhere, some Dissenters served in person as constables, churchwardens, and overseers in the 1660s and 1670s before being purged during the Tory reaction of the 1680s: Daniel C. Beaver, *Parish Communities and Religious Conflict in the Vale of Gloucester, 1590–1690* (Cambridge, MA, 1998), 310–312.

⁵⁸ LMA, DL/C/0263, Deposition of John Hendry, 11 Jul 1726, 186–7v. A man who appointed a deputy to serve for him as churchwarden of Middlewich in Cheshire was taken to court by his neighbours: BI, GB 193, CP.H.3441, 2–3; CP.H.3471, 2; CP.H.3448, 2–5.

⁵⁹ Beatrice Webb and Sidney Webb, *English Local Government from the Revolution to the Municipal Corporations Act: The Parish and the County* (London, 1906), 128. An early example comes from Hackney in 1751, when one resident paid another 10l. to take his place as overseer: Ruth Paley (ed.),

Beattie, the difference between these offices and those involved in metropolitan law enforcement was that constables and watchmen faced a specific and expanding set of difficulties in the late seventeenth and early eighteenth centuries. The growth of London's population, its traffic, its nightlife, and its levels of reported crime combined to produce 'policing problems' which led, in turn, to 'a flight from the office of constable' and the duty of participation in the night watch.[60] There may also be a more straightforward reason: the legality of deputisation was far better established for constables and watchmen than for other local officers. However reluctant City authorities were to accept it, the offices of law enforcement were repeatedly categorised as ministerial by the central courts. By contrast, there were no precedents to suggest that churchwardens fit into that category, and overseers of the poor were not categorised as ministerial until the late eighteenth century.[61]

Whatever the reasons behind it, deputisation, like the Excise, put large numbers of non-householders into office. In the absence of any requirement that deputies be *idoneus homo*, most of them came from below the ranks of the prosperous middling sort. In a comparison of 1690s tax assessments, Beattie showed that 'deputies were distinctly poorer than the men they replaced'. He also argued, without providing direct evidence, that 'constables, however poor, were householders' whereas 'watchmen were more likely to be lodgers'.[62] No lists of deputy watchmen survive, so the second claim is impossible to verify. Beattie's assurance that deputy constables were always householders, however, can be challenged. Those who worked as deputies were, it seems logical to presume, people who needed the money enough to accept relatively low rates of payment. Poverty was often closely connected to the life cycle; stable periods as a head of household were frequently preceded and followed by insecurity in unmarried youth and widowed old age.[63] The age and marital status of deputy constables cannot be established on a large scale, but what evidence there is suggests that many were indeed younger or older than the 'firmest age' associated with householding and mature masculinity.

This assessment is based on cautious record linkage. Deputy constables' names were recorded when they were sworn into office by the Court of

---

Justice in Eighteenth-Century Hackney: The Justicing Notebook of Henry Norris and the Hackney Petty Sessions Book (London, 1991), 181.
[60] Beattie, *Policing and Punishment*, 83, 86, 146–7.
[61] R v Stubbs (1788), 2 T.R. 395, 100 *ER* 213.
[62] Beattie, *Policing and Punishment*, 145, 205.
[63] Alexandra Shepard, *Accounting for Oneself: Worth, Status, and the Social Order in Early Modern England* (Oxford, 2015), 77–79, 131–33.

Aldermen. If these lists can be taken as more or less complete – which seems likely, given that constables possessed no powers in law unless they were sworn in – then it can be stated with some certainty that all of London's deputies were men. Linking their names to records of births and marriages is not straightforward. High levels of migration, considerable mobility between densely packed London parishes, and the frequent recycling of names across generations make this a hazardous business. Nonetheless, where a name is sufficiently unusual and does not appear to have been given to both fathers (or grandfathers) and sons, dates drawn from parish registers can be tentatively connected to particular individuals. Robert Christmas, for example, who Beattie found serving as a deputy constable in the ward of Bassishaw in the 1690s, appears to have been baptised in the church of St Michael Bassishaw in 1674, meaning he was barely twenty when he took office. There is no record of him marrying in the parish, or in any other parish within the ward of Bassishaw. He may, of course, have married elsewhere at a later date, but at the time of his deputy constableship it seems likely that Christmas was a young singleman, not a head of household.[64]

He was not unique in this respect, perhaps not even unusual. By the 1720s and 1730s, when deputisation was widespread in much of the City of London, a pattern appears to have emerged in which householders in their thirties or forties hired deputies who were significantly younger or older than themselves.[65] Among those elected to the constableship in Bridge ward between 1728 and 1731, the ages of two men can be calculated with some confidence. One was thirty when he was chosen, the other forty-five. Among those hired to deputise for these men and others, the ages of four can be identified. Two were young men like Robert Christmas, twenty-five and twenty-six when they took office. The other two were older: fifty-six and sixty-eight.[66] The last of these was well beyond what contemporaries considered middle age and may have contributed to the image conjured by Defoe in 1728 of city streets policed by 'superannuated Wretches, with one

---

[64] Beattie, *Policing and Punishment*, 145. Robert Christmas was baptised at St Michael Bassishaw on 13 Sep 1674: LMA, P69/MIC1/A/003/MS06988/001.

[65] The following is based on the Repertories of the Court of Aldermen and the registers of parishes within the wards of Bridge, Cornhill, Queenhithe, and Farringdon Without. The years 1728–31 are used because Beattie provided data on the scale of deputisation in each ward for that period: *Policing and Punishment*, 148. The relevant sections of the Repertories are: LMA, COL/CA/01/01/136, ff.65–9; 137, ff.121–25; 138, ff.91–95; 139, 71–75. The parish registers are accessible via ancestry.co.uk and have been checked against originals stored at the LMA, referred to in the notes below.

[66] Parish registers of St Magnus the Martyr and St Leonard Eastcheap: LMA, P69/MAG/A/001/MS11361, ff.91v–92; P69/LEN1/A/001/MS17607, ff.29–31.

Foot in the Grave, and t'other ready to follow ... Much fitter for an Almshouse than a Watch-house'.[67] It is, however, easier to find instances of young deputy constables than old ones, possibly because older men were more likely to have moved away from the wards where they were born. Between 1728 and 1731, unmarried men in their twenties or even their late teens can be found deputising for married men in their thirties and forties in wards across the City of London, from Cornhill (where almost all constables were deputies) to Queenhithe (where just over a third were deputies) to Farringdon Without (where only one constable hired a deputy in this period).[68] When Richard Cavey was elected constable in Farringdon Without in 1729, he had been a husband and father for over a decade. The man he hired to replace him, the aptly named Thomas Constable, was just nineteen and did not marry until his early forties.[69] Men like Thomas Constable and Robert Christmas often served as deputies repeatedly year after year, so that rotation among heads of household gave way to a more permanent corps of regular replacements.[70]

Like excise officers, London's deputies were seen by some contemporaries as dangerously lacking in independence. In place of substantial householders, whose wealth and status supposedly guaranteed their impartiality, the city's streets came to be policed by 'Desperate Characters' who, according to Ned Ward, 'undertake their Office, thro' no good Principle, but only for a Mercenary End of Twelve Shillings a Week Salary'.[71] Formally salaried constables had in fact first appeared in parishes north of the capital, where in the guise of specialised 'vagrant passers' they were employed to send migrants bound for London back to their home parishes.[72] But it was the more widespread and ad hoc payment of deputy constables and watchmen

---

[67] *Augusta Triumphans: Or, The Way to Make London the Most Flourishing City in the Universe* (London, 1728), 48.

[68] Parish registers of St Michael Cornhill, St Peter Cornhill, St Michael Queenhithe, Holy Trinity the Less, St Mary Somerset, St Mary Mounthaw, St Nicholas Cole Abbey, St Nicholas Olave, and St Peter near Paul's Wharf.

[69] Parish registers of St Bartholomew the Great, St Sepulchre-without-Newgate, and St Andrew Holborn: LMA, P69/BAT/A/002/MS06778/002, p. 2; P69/SEP/A/001/MS07219/003, p. 173; P82/AND/A/001/MS06667/010, f.214.

[70] Beattie, *Policing and Punishment*, 150–1.

[71] Edward Ward, *The London Spy Compleat* (London, 1703), 363.

[72] In 1713, Middlesex magistrates ordered the constables of Enfield and South Mimms to be paid a regular 'Sallary ... for passing & Relieving of Vagrants' out of the county treasury. The subsequent history of these 'vagrant passers' can be traced through the papers of the Middlesex Quarter Sessions until 1734, when this specialised form of constableship was either abolished or became so routine an aspect of county government as to no longer merit any special mention. Their first and last appearances in the records are MJ/SP/1714/01/19–20 and MJ/SP/1734/08/41. David Hitchcock found similar developments in Warwickshire and Hertfordshire at about the same time: *Vagrancy*

within the city itself which drew contemporary comment. Those who held office for profit rather than out of a sense of duty were thought to be more likely to take bribes, to embezzle from parish funds, to maliciously pursue and prosecute innocent people for the sake of a reward. Defoe railed against 'Mercenary Watchmen' and 'Hired Constables' who, he claimed, were more likely to collude with criminals than to catch them.[73]

There were, of course, many important differences between deputy officers and excisemen. Deputy constables and watchmen did not receive extensive technical training, they did not rise or fall through an elaborate official hierarchy, and they were not uprooted to serve far from their homes. They did, however, share something of excisemen's detachment from the people around them and the stigma of dependence on a salary. Both groups lacked the social authority associated with the householding amateur, the prestige of patriarchal manhood. The power exercised by deputies and excisemen came from the law of office, the impersonal authorisation of the state, not their standing as individuals. But this did not make them disembodied, genderless automata. Unable to assert their manhood through the household, they turned instead to an alternative mode of masculinity and to each other.

Official Fraternities

London's deputies and their counterparts in the Excise developed a new culture of official manhood. The emergence of this culture fits neatly into the shift described by Carole Pateman from paternal to fraternal male power, what one sociologist has called the 'fall of a patriarchalist social order and its replacement by fraternal forms of governance'.[74] The old association between office and household remained strong across much of the country, but excisemen and deputy officers of law enforcement embodied a different kind of masculinity: detached from the household and characterised by fraternal sociability and solidarity.

In his autobiography, John Cannon referred to his fellow excisemen as 'my brother officers'. He visited 'brother officers' in Henley and regularly

---

in *English Culture and Society, 1650–1750* (London, 2016), 109–111. On later 'vagrant contractors', see Audrey Eccles, 'The Eighteenth-Century Vagrant Contractor', *Local Population Studies* 85 (2010).
[73] Francis M. Dodsworth, '"Civic" Police and the Condition of Liberty: The Rationality of Governance in Eighteenth-Century England', *Social History* 29.2 (2004); Daniel Defoe, *An Effectual Scheme for the Immediate Preventing of Street Robberies* (London, 1731), 14.
[74] Carole Pateman, *The Sexual Contract* (Cambridge, 1988); Pavla Miller, *Transformations of Patriarchy in the West, 1500–1900* (Bloomington, 1998), ix.

went to an inn with 'brother officers' where 'we used to pass the time at cards over a glass of wine'. At the funeral of their supervisor, he and five other officers carried the coffin. In an echo of the language used by fraternities of journeymen in continental Europe, Cannon referred to the landlady of the excise office where he lodged as 'my Mother Winslow' and she, he claimed, referred to him as 'her son'. There were also sisterly connections between excisemen's spouses, in spite of the barriers preventing their involvement in official business. When John married Susannah, they found their first lodgings through another officer's wife who was a 'companion of my wife's', while two other officers' wives were the godmothers of their first child. Not long afterwards, a new supervisor and his family moved into the Cannons' house, with whom they lived 'in the greatest amity & friendship', Susannah and the supervisor's wife becoming 'like sworn sisters'.[75]

London's deputy officers used similarly fraternal vocabulary. In the published reports of trials at the Old Bailey, the first reference to a watchman calling his colleagues 'his Brother Watchmen' occurred in 1715. 'Brother Watchman' in the singular was more common, appearing 128 times between 1719 and 1836. 'Brother Officer' and 'Brother Constable' were later coinages, making their first appearances in 1740 and 1741, respectively, but these became even more common, with several hundred uses of 'brother constable' and over a thousand of 'brother officer' by the time of their last appearances in the trial reports in 1912.[76] These phrases also appear in the records of other courts in the capital, such as witness statements taken at Middlesex Quarter Sessions.[77] From the 1730s onwards, London's law enforcement officers increasingly used collective pronouns when they testified before the court: apprehended thieves 'told us' where to find stolen goods; 'we' searched suspected people and property.[78] Verbatim trial testimony began to be included in the Old Bailey *Proceedings* in the 1720s, so the emergence of this vocabulary in the 1730s does not appear to be an

---

[75] *Chronicles of John Cannon*, 101, 123–4, 114, 149, 130, 135, 139. On journeymen and their 'mothers', see Wiesner, '"Wandervogels" and Women'.

[76] *OBP*, searched for all cases where the transcription matches "brother watchmen", "brother watchman", "brother officer" and "brother constable". For the first uses, see: *OBP*, Jul 1715, trials Thomas Rye, Thomas Harvey, Thomas Stringer, William Harvey, Thomas Oven, John Tyler, Richard Cannon (t17150713-14); Sep 1740, trial of Abraham Izard (t17400903-50); Apr 1741, trial of Samuel Ellard (t17410405-54). See also Beattie, *Policing and Punishment*, 201, 203.

[77] See, for example, LMA, MJ/SP/1749/02/028, information of John Williams, 14 Jan 1749.

[78] See, for example: *OBP*, Sept 1732, trials of Edward Perkins, John Macgrady (t17320906-31); Dec 1732, trial of John Ingram (t17321206-34); Dec 1732, trial of William Green (t17321206-36); Apr 1738, trial of Margaret Wettley (t17380412-46); Dec 1738, trial of William Bullinbroke (t17381206); Apr 1741, trial of John Storer (t17410405-32).

illusion produced by the changing nature of the documents.[79] Deputy officers who served alongside each other year after year developed a sense of shared identity, mutual loyalty, and brotherly solidarity. In 1745, a watchman told the Old Bailey judges that he was attacked while pursuing a man who had dodged transportation. Asked if he was certain it was the suspect, now a prisoner in the dock, who had attacked him, he replied 'I saw nobody but the Prisoner and my partner, and I hope your Lordship don't think the watchmen would cut one another'. Near the end of his 1754 guidebook for constables, Saunders Welch wrote that 'union, secrecy and bravery, are the great points in the joint execution of our office'.[80]

Both excisemen and deputy officers spent a great deal of time with their colleagues. Much of that time was spent in excise 'offices' and in London's parish watch-houses. The latter were a creation of the civil wars, built by the City authorities in preparation for military assault. The temporary structures erected in the 1640s and 1650s were joined by many more substantial buildings from the 1670s onward. These watch-houses tended to consist of three rooms stacked one on top of the other, with a holding cell on the lower ground floor, a 'drinking room' above it, and the watch-house keeper's living quarters at the top.[81] Watch-houses were distinctively official spaces, not like the multi-purpose households of traditional officeholders. They were also, unlike the household, distinctively masculine: with the exception of watch-house keeper's wives, women rarely entered except as suspected law-breakers to be interrogated by the constable or held overnight in the cellar. Excise 'offices' were equally male dominated, again with the important exception of female 'office-keepers', the women whose work as landladies made homosocial officeholding possible. A fraternal culture took shape in these new official spaces. The centre of gravity in officeholding began to shift away from mixed-gender households, embedded in the wider social and economic life of the neighbourhood. Instead, a growing number of officers passed long hours in each other's company, separated by doors and walls from the world outside.

The principal way to pass the time in official spaces was to drink. Satirists portrayed constables and night watchmen as hypocrites who punished drunkenness in others despite constantly indulging in it themselves.[82] This

---

[79] Robert B. Shoemaker, 'The Old Bailey Proceedings and the Representation of Crime and Criminal Justice in Eighteenth-Century London', *Journal of British Studies* 47 (2008), 562.
[80] *OBP*, May 1745, trial of John Simmons (t17450530-14); Saunders Welch, *Observations of the Office of Constable* (London, 1754), 45.
[81] Griffiths, *Lost Londons*, 359; Beattie, *Policing and Punishment*, 186–7; Tim Hitchcock, *Down and Out in Eighteenth-Century London* (London, 2004), 153.
[82] Samuel Butler, *Characters and Passages from Note-Books* ed. A. R. Waller (Cambridge, 1908), 209; Ward, *The London Spy*, 78.

was not necessarily inaccurate. Old Bailey trial reports include numerous instances of drinking in London watch-houses. There were frequent errands to nearby alehouses to fetch more liquor and some officers clearly felt the effects. A constable called to the scene of a crime in 1735 was 'so drunk, he could not carry himself, much less the Prisoner'. A beadle who testified in another case thought it worth noting, apparently unprompted, that at the end of a night's work he departed the watch-house and 'left the constable and all the watchmen sober'.[83] Even during the daytime, official sobriety could not be guaranteed. In a deposition to the Bishop of London's Consistory Court, one witness explained that a group of constables instructed to keep the peace during a parish election created disorder rather than suppressing it: 'sev[era]l of them were Drunk & were very abusive & cust & Swore in the Church' until the churchwarden had them thrown out.[84] It may not have helped matters that in parishes which did not yet have a watch-house, alehouses were often the most obvious places for watchmen to stay warm through the night.[85]

Excisemen were equally drawn to drink. Alcohol was an integral part of what John Brewer called their 'boisterous male ethos'. Despite Ezekiel Polsted's warning 'against immoderate Drinking', officers were frequently discharged for 'debauchery drunkenness & Idlenes' or, more specifically, for being found 'in bed at a Vict[ualle]rs where he had been drunk 4 or 5 days successively'. One made it 'a comon practice in the Ride to get drunk, if he cou'd prevail upon the people, either at publick or private houses to let him have Liquor'. Another 'by drinking render'd himself incapable of doing Business and thereby also disorder'd his Senses in such a manner that the Revenue is not safe under his Care'.[86] Thomas Chaloner wrote several excise drinking songs, including one that began 'I Am a jolly Gauger, / It is my whole Delight / To trudge the City round all Day, / And to get Drunk by Night'. John Cannon spent many evenings drinking with his fellow officers, falling off his horse, stumbling through streets in the small hours. His companions were 'all bachelors' and upon marrying he gave up this kind of sociability. In fact, the mounting costs of social

---

[83] *OBP*, Dec 1735, trial of Burton Brace (t17351210-24); *OBP*, Dec 1744, trial of William Harding (t17441205-60). See also *OBP*, Feb 1738, trial of Mary Thomas (t17380222-33); *OBP*, Jul 1744, trial of Edward Moody, Edward Wandon (t17440728-12).

[84] LMA, DL/C/0268, Deposition of Henry Lister, 20 Oct 1731, f.142v.

[85] LMA, MJ/SP/1674/12/001, Petition from 'Officers and ancient Inhabitants' of Whitechapel, undated; *OBP*, Jun 1747, trial of Elizabeth Dennis, John Ryley (t17470604-1).

[86] Brewer, 'Servants of the Public', 134–5; Polsted, *Kaloz telonesantai*, 56; TNA, CUST 47/2, p. 37v; CUST 47/81, p. 47; CUST 47/185, p. 10; CUST 47/159, p. 73. See also CUST 47/45, pp. 15, 67; 47/81, p. 100; 47/160, pp. 30–1.

drinking were a significant factor in driving him towards marriage, which he saw as a cost-cutting manoeuvre: 'if she was with me [it] would altogether be far better & much cheaper'.[87]

The opposition between male sociability and marriage was linked to a broader anti-marital and misogynist discourse. This was exemplified by Chaloner's poetry. Alongside the drinking songs, there were verses insulting specific women ('So ugly too, her looks would make you Sh—te' or 'she's short, she's ugly, and she's old'), verses mocking a man who lived on the profits of his wife's sex work, and a warning about the health risks of paying for sex ('they're all of them Pox'd I'll give you my Oath'.) In a poem 'Upon Matrimony', he asked why anyone would undertake it when the chances of happiness were so small: 'Some few happy are, but there's ten to one / To the Contrary, ruin'd and undone; / If so, what Rational on Earth, ye Gods, / Would stand the Chance, or venture on such Odds?'[88] The exciseman, if he took Chaloner's advice, would stick to drinking with his brother officers and avoid marriage at all costs. For Chaloner, marriage was the antithesis of official manhood, not its essential prerequisite.

Anti-marital misogyny did not preclude sex. As Tim Hitchcock has shown, John Cannon's pre-marital sex life in the Excise was characterised by a predatory homosocial misogyny. He was encouraged to take part in group sex as 'an exciseman's qualification', bantered with his colleagues about sexual conquests, made numerous promises of marriage to get women into bed (sometimes getting them pregnant), kept up relationships with several women simultaneously, threatened violence when they pressed him to marry, and reacted with disgust when a woman he was interested in did anything so wanton as going to the theatre. Cannon was not the only one. In Norwich, in 1733, a drunken exciseman attacked a servant in the house he was assessing for tax. He 'fell to Kissing her' and, when she resisted, pulled up her clothes and 'exposed her nakedness'. The servant 'in her defence struck him with the fire shovell', giving him a wound on the head which he boasted about in a drinking cellar several days later, claiming 'he did take her by the private parts (which he spoke in a verry Lewd manner) … and after some other verry obscene expressions he swore he would not medle with it any more for he did not Like it'.[89]

---

[87] Chaloner, *The Merriest Poet*, 60; *Chronicles of John Cannon*, 123–4, 127.
[88] Chaloner, *The Merriest Poet*, 9–10, 14–15, 35, 43–44.
[89] Tim Hitchcock, 'Sociability and Misogyny in the Life of John Cannon, 1684–1743' in Tim Hitchcock and Michèle Cohen (eds.), *English Masculinities 1660–1800* (London, 1999); *Chronicles of John Cannon*, 75, 82, 93–4, 104, 109–13; NRO, NCR Case 12b/6, Informations of Margaret Leech and Robert Thacker, 2 Apr 1733.

Sexual violence was not restricted to excisemen. In fact, it was one of the continuities between the new forms of officeholding and the old. In 1647, a Yorkshire churchwarden was put on trial for, among other things, going into a woman's house where he 'offered violence unto her chastity, stripped her breast [and] threw her over a bed'. In 1699, Norwich constable Will Rutter (who was reputed to have survived multiple bouts of venereal disease) came to Ciscila Cragett's house while her husband was away and 'Did Importune her that he might have the Carnall Knowledge of her body And Told her that if she would lett him Lye with her that her husband should nott come into any Trouble', then attempted to rape her. In 1744, a Kentish overseer of the poor told a sick woman who received parish relief 'that if she would let him ly with her when she was well, he would take particular care of her and be kind to her'. He repeatedly solicited her, eventually paid her for sex and, when it became clear that she was pregnant, threatened 'to beat her Brains out, and to Shoot her, and Run her through with a Pitch Fork'.[90]

Bailiffs in particular seem to have taken advantage of their official powers to attack women. One talked his way into a woman's house in Kent by suggesting he was pursuing her husband: 'she Could not tell but that he had a Writt for her husband he having Arrested her Husband about two months before'. Once inside, 'he said he had noe writ for her Husband but offered to kisse her & put his tongue in her mouth his Hands in her Bossom & Likewise under her Coats' and would have raped her had the neighbours not heard her cry for help. A London bailiff made similar use of his authority as an officer. He arrested a woman for debt and said he would release her if she went with him to a 'Bagnio'. When she refused, he took her to 'the Bailiffs House', locked her in a room, and raped her at knifepoint.[91]

Bailiffs were in many ways precursors of the new official fraternalism. They held office for long periods of time, worked together in exclusively male groups and were known for their drinking. According to one writer, a bailiff in an alehouse would 'call for Drink as fast as men for Buckets of Water in a Conflagration'. They were also less straightforwardly tied to the household than other traditional officers. In an early eighteenth-century compilation of 'the Lives and Adventures of the most Noted Bayliffs'

---

[90] TNA, ASSI 45/2/1/52, Information of Ann Taylor, 24 Aug 1647; NRO, NCR Case 12b/2, Information of Ciscila Cragett, 20 Sep 1699; KHLC, Q/SB/1744/Informations/4, Information of Mary Starling, 5 May 1744.
[91] KHLC, Q/SB/30/189, Information of Elizabeth Hemmes, 3 Sep 1710; *OBP*, Mar 1720, trial of Michael Dobson (t17200303-48).

of the time, criminal biographer Alexander Smith described a range of unorthodox domestic arrangements, from happy bachelorhood to unmarried cohabitation to being caught 'in the Nooze of Matrimony' by 'an old Creature, who look'd more like an Hermaphrodite, than a Person of one single Sex'.[92]

Above all, bailiffs participated in a violent honour culture generally associated with the disorderly masculinity of men who, because of youth, poverty, or personal preference, had not attained patriarchal status.[93] Bailiffs were, in the words of one Old Bailey report, 'a sort of Men not very apt to take affronts'. In 1679, a group of London bailiffs fought with a debtor and his friends 'in a Braves do'. Many others fought, killed, and died with staves and swords. One notorious bailiff was said to have gone to arrest a man 'with a *Posse comitatus* of Rogues like himself', ensuring that 'a bloody Fight ensu'd' and 'a deal of Blood was spilt on both sides'.[94] This kind of violence may explain why bailiffs were so extremely unpopular. Known for their insolence and aggression, bailiffs and their assistants were 'worse than Dogs' and occasionally subjected to rough communal justice: 'd——m him he is a Bailiff's Follower, we will take him and duck him'. On the scaffold, a convicted felon 'inveigh'd against the Bailiffs: but declared that he died in Charity with all Mankind'.[95] Contemporary authors described the bailiff as 'a kind of *Excrescence* of the Law, like our Nails, made only to scratch and *claw*', or as 'Universally hated by Man, Woman, or Child'.[96] In court, defendants frequently claimed (with occasional success) that they had only hidden or fled from justice because they were 'afraid of Bailiffs', suggesting the hostility these officers inspired was at least tacitly accepted by some

---

[92] Hartley, 'Under-sheriffs and Bailiffs'; *Twelve Ingenious Characters: Or, Pleasant Descriptions of the Propertis of Sundry Persons & Things* (London, 1686), 10; Alexander Smith, *The Comical and Tragical History of the Lives and Adventures of the Most Noted Bayliffs in and about London and Westminster* (3rd edition, London, 1723), 12, 22, 45, 63.

[93] Pieter Spierenburg, 'Masculinity, Violence, and Honor: An Introduction' in Pieter Spierenburg (ed.), *Men and Violence: Gender, Honor, and Rituals in Modern Europe and America* (Columbus, 1998); Elizabeth Foyster, 'Boys will be Boys? Manhood and Aggression, 1660–1800' in Hitchcock and Cohen (eds.), *English Masculinities*; Robert Shoemaker, 'Male honour and the decline of public violence in eighteenth-century London', *Social History* 26.2 (2001); Shepard, *Meanings of Manhood*, 127–51.

[94] *OBP*, Dec 1675 (t16751208-1); Jan 1679, Ordinary's Account (OA16790121); Feb 1698, trial of Henry Harding, James Dancy (t16980223-21); Smith, *Comical and Tragical History*, 45. There is some discussion of bailiffs' violence in Myron C. Noonkester, 'Power of the County: Sheriffs and Violence in Early Modern England' in Joseph P. Ward (ed.), *Violence, Politics, and Gender in Early Modern England* (London, 2008).

[95] *OBP*, Sep 1739, trial of Richard Cox (t17390906); Apr 1737, trial of Richard Swift (t17470429-15); Jan 1725, Ordinary's Account (OA17250104).

[96] *Twelve Ingenious Characters*, 10; Smith, *Comical and Tragical History*, 66.

authorities.⁹⁷ That hostility, combined with bailiff's notorious touchiness, led inevitably to violence. In 1675, for example, a group of London bailiffs in pursuit of a debtor became 'incensed by the hissing and floutings of the Shop keepers and Apprentices thereabouts', drew their swords, and cut their way through the crowd, killing a surgeon who had stopped to see what all the fuss was about. One officer himself admitted that 'some thought a Sheriff's Bayliff ... an ungenteel Employment'.⁹⁸

Like bailiffs, excisemen and London's deputy officers took insults badly and were quick to use force. A brewer who got into a fight with several excisemen was forgiven by the Board of Commissioners when it emerged 'that he was provoked to it by the sawcy returns of the Officers, & their Smoaking in his Brewhouse'. Chaloner's song celebrating the drunken 'Jolly Gauger' includes the declaration that 'If any Man denies / To lend us Half a Crown / A Week before our Pay Day comes, / By Jove I'll knock him down'. Cannon recorded several excise-related fights. One was with a butcher he met on his rounds who called him 'Rogue, Rascal [and] Dog', one with a group of Irish excisemen over a game of ninepins, and one with his own supervisor. The last of these fights took place during a drinking session, when Cannon's supervisor 'began to play his pranks not only too familiar but rather too impudent ... which I could not take but grew in earnest & struck him a good blow'. He beat the man up and then paid for his drinks by way of compensation. After the encounter with the butcher, Cannon reflected that revenge was 'a pleasant cordial' but 'there is more bravery & disdain in slighting a private enemy & despising revenge than in cutting his throat; not that a man should be insensible of an injury or affront, for he that makes himself a sheep, the wolves will catch him'.⁹⁹

Such nuances were lost on many deputy law enforcement officers, who preferred to respond to perceived slights with violence. In 1688, the

---

⁹⁷ LMA, MJ/SP/1697/12/052, Examination of William Holliday, 30 Nov 1697; LMA, MJ/SP/1699/01/049, Information of Edward Overing, 12 Dec 1698; LMA, MJ/SP/1699/05/037, Information of Ann Finch, 25 Apr 1699; *OBP*, Dec 1712, trial of William White (t17121210-46); *OBP*, Mar 1720, trial of Mary North (t17200303-10); *OBP*, Mar 1720, trial of Hugh Kelley (17200303-24); *OBP*, Jul 1720, trial of John Howel (t17200712-23); *OBP*, Apr 1721, trial of Martha Blacklock (t17210419-26); *OBP*, Apr 1722, trial of George Watson (t17220404-53); *OBP*, Dec 1722, trial of John Flint (t17221205-17); *OBP*, Oct 1724, trial of Joseph Blake (t17241014-43); *OBP*, Dec 1724, trial of William Anderson (t17241204-34); *OBP*, Jan 1725, Ordinary's Account (OA17250104); *OBP*, Dec 1725, trial of John Austin (t17251208-70); *OBP*, Oct 1732, trial of John Booker (t17321011-31); *OBP*, Sep 1735, trial of William Phillips alias Clark (t17350911-72); *OBP*, Feb 1738, trial of James Lovell, William Staines (t17380222-54); *OBP*, Feb 1738, trial of Edward Brian (t17380222-57).
⁹⁸ *OBP*, Dec 1675 (t16751208-1); May 1722, Ordinary's Account (OA17220521).
⁹⁹ TNA, CUST 47/46, p. 99; Chaloner, *The Merriest Poet*, 60; *Chronicles of John Cannon*, 95–6, 163, 143, 96.

night watch of St Clement Danes in London pursued and attacked a group of servants who refused to doff their hats as they passed. Another London watchman fell to blows with several sailors after 'some fractious words; I might say some, and they said some again'. Night watchmen were referred to as 'brave Boys' in one late seventeenth-century pamphlet and, in Norwich, seem to have fought with each other in a drunken contest between the representatives of neighbouring wards, leaving one with a broken pipe and another in the stocks.[100] Constables could be equally violent. One was described by someone he attacked as 'a man of a factious turbulent and evill disposition'. In print, they were often portrayed as proud and over-sensitive to anything resembling a challenge to their authority. When a woman reprimanded a constable for urinating against her wall, he vowed 'he would revenge / This most outrageous wrong' and arranged to have her ducked as a scold. The gallants who insulted constables in contemporary ballads were met with indignation: 'Do I sit in this Chair of state, / and represent the way of King, / To be affronted at this rate?' The typical constable, wrote Samuel Butler, was 'implacable to those that rebel, or dispute his authority, which he will not endure to be scanted'.[101]

From the point of view of London's magistrates, law enforcement officers were far too touchy in matters of personal honour and far too ready to resort to blows. As Saunders Welch complained in 1754, 'officers totally forget the service of their warrants, upon being called by some silly fellow, fool and puppy'. They sometimes arrested 'the offender against themselves, under the mistaken notion of being insulted or obstructed in the execution of their office'. Officers, Welch wrote, should keep their private quarrels separate from their official business: 'If you have had any dispute or animosity with any person, I advise you to decline serving any warrant upon him' and instead 'refer it to a brother officer'. Pride had no place in policing. These thoughts were echoed in later treatises on the constableship by John Fielding and the barrister John Paul. Officers should always act 'with Caution, Integrity and Moderation', Fielding wrote. 'You must banish from your mind all partial prejudice or idle resentments', instructed Paul,

---

[100] *OBP*, Aug 1688, trial of Richard Vauson, John Ratteray, Nicholas Beck (t16880831-27); *OBP*, Oct 1744, trial of Edward Morgan (t17441017-27); *The Jolly Gentleman's Frollick: OR, The City Ramble* (London, 1675–96); NRO, NCR Case 12b/4, Informations of Charles Wen, Robert Baldwin, Thomas Browne and George Wen, 18 Jun 1704.

[101] LMA, WJ/SR/NS/002/B/048, Petition of Steven Hopgood, undated; *The Cucking of a Scould* (London, 1630); *The Frollicksome Wager; A Jest, or, Master Constable* (London, 1662); *Mark Noble's Frollick* (London, 1670); Butler, *Characters*, 209.

and instead proceed with 'temper and sedateness; coolly and deliberately considering the nature of every service you are called upon to perform'.[102]

Similar efforts were made to restrain the tempers of excisemen. 'He is not to be bias'd by his excited Passions', wrote Ezekiel Polsted, 'nor hector'd by Affronts and Clamor'. Polsted's ironically implausible exciseman did not drink or gamble, both of which led to 'Great engagements of the Passions' and left a man without 'a competent discretion for Self-government'. Those who managed the Excise wanted officers to be civil as well as dispassionate. Books of instructions for excisemen told them to behave 'civilly' or to 'take care by a Civil Behaviour to avoid giving any just Occasion of Complaint'.[103]

These pleas for civility, sobriety, and self-control were intended to draw deputy officers and excisemen away from the aggressive masculinity many of them displayed and push them back towards the old model of the officeholding householder, governing himself as he governed others. Deviation from that model, these authors recognised, made officers alarmingly similar to the people whose behaviour they were supposed to suppress.[104] As Welch put it (and Paul repeated almost verbatim), 'It ill becomes an officer called upon, and making use of the king's name to quell the unruly passions of others, instantly to fall into the same error himself'. Civility justified authority; incivility turned authority into hypocrisy.[105] It is unclear if these exhortations had any effect. For the most part, officers who restrained their passions did not leave traces in the archive. Exceptionally, an Old Bailey report from 1717 recorded the actions of three watchmen who, when they were challenged by a group of known troublemakers, did exactly what Welch and his fellow authors wanted: presuming the group were 'bent upon Mischief (having taken Notice of some of them before for such Enterprizes), to avoid a Fray [they] turned away from them'. It seems unlikely, however, that these watchmen were typical. In the later eighteenth and early nineteenth centuries, as deputisation

---

[102] Welch, *Observations*, 5, 39; John Fielding, 'A Treatise on the Office of Constable' in *Extracts from Such of the Penal Laws, as Particularly Relate to the Peace and Good Order of the Metropolis* (London, 1761), 290–91; John Paul, *The Compleat Constable* (London, 1785), 89.

[103] Polsted, *Kaloz telonesantai*, 33, 57–8; *Instructions for the Gagers of the Excise in the Country* (London, 1725), A2; *Instructions for Officers Who Survey Hop-Planters* (London, 1735), 13.

[104] An early instance of this problem was the proctor's watch in Cambridge. In the late sixteenth and early seventeenth centuries, this regulatory force made up of students and servants had such a tendency to violent excess that 'the distinction between the watch and unauthorized nightwalkers was often unclear': Shepard, *Meanings of Manhood*, 109.

[105] Welch, *Observations*, 4; Paul, *Compleat Constable*, 89; Michael J. Braddick, 'Civility and Authority' in David Armitage and Michael J. Braddick (eds.), *The British Atlantic World, 1500–1800* (Basingstoke, 2002).

spread still further and law enforcement began to be fully professionalised, magistrates, handbook writers, and eventually police commissioners spilt a great deal of ink trying to persuade constables and their colleagues to exert self-control, stay sober, and be civil.[106]

Deputisation and the rise of the Excise brought about a realignment between masculinity and state authority. Officeholding by heads of household did not disappear, but it was increasingly displaced in certain offices by a very different official style. In London, and wherever excisemen were to be found, state authority was carried by officers whose salaries made them dependent lackeys in the eyes of some, and whose gendered identities rested on male sociability, drinking, and violence. This official fraternalism was a new, hybrid version of masculinity, merging the disorderly manhood of rakes and gamblers with the law of office. There was no room here for female participation; the ambiguous opportunities provided by the household were overridden by a more straightforward identification of office with manhood. Many excisemen and deputy officers were not householding patriarchs. Their authority did not come from being husbands or fathers, but from the impersonal powers granted to them by law. The way they used those powers, however, was far from impersonal. In London, fraternities of male officers arrested and searched particular groups of people in accordance with hierarchies of gender and social status.

---

[106] *OBP*, Jan 1717, trial of Johnson Burdet, Thomas Winchurst (t17170111-21); Francis Dodsworth, 'Masculinity as Governance: Police, Public Service and the Embodiment of Authority, c.1700–1850' in Matthew McCormack (ed.), *Public Men: Masculinity and Politics in Modern Britain* (London, 2007), 46–7; David G. Barrie and Susan Broomhall, 'Policing Bodies in Urban Scotland, 1780–1850' in Susan Broomhall and Jacqueline Van Gent (eds.), *Governing Masculinities in the Early Modern Period: Regulating Selves and Others* (Farnham, 2011), 278; Francis Dodsworth, 'Men on a Mission: Masculinity, Violence and the Self-Presentation of Policemen in England, c.1870–1914' in David G. Barrie and Susan Broomhall (eds.), *A History of Police and Masculinities, 1700–2010* (Abingdon, 2012).

PART III

Policing

CHAPTER 4

Arrests

Changes in the nature of officeholding produced new practices of policing. Up to this point, this book has concentrated on who was granted state authority and how that authority was defined. In this chapter and the one that follows, the focus shifts to the use of state authority on an everyday basis. This requires a narrowing of geography and chronology. These chapters provide a picture of policing in the time and place where changes to officeholding were most extensive: London in the late seventeenth and early eighteenth centuries. How did London's fraternities of deputy officers choose to wield their legal powers? What impact did they have on the way the capital was policed? How did gender shape the dynamics of accusation and arrest, searches and suspicion? Answers to these questions come from a new dataset and a detailed study of the powers held by officers and others. What emerges is a practice of discretionary law enforcement which belies the myth of the impersonal ministerial officeholder. Constables and watchmen possessed increasingly wide discretionary authority to arrest and search suspects. They used that authority according to gendered notions of what was proper for women and men to do and what could legitimately be done to them.

The basic act of policing was the arrest. It was the archetypal encounter between state and subject, 'the beginning of Imprisonment', and 'the first Step to Justice'.[1] For historians of early modern England, arrests are emblematic of a broader system of participatory law enforcement. Before the creation of large professional police forces in the nineteenth century, the work of pursuing and apprehending suspected criminals was often carried out by victims and bystanders rather than by officers. In her landmark study of criminal justice in seventeenth-century Sussex, Cynthia Herrup stressed the role of victims and

---

[1] William Lambarde, *Eirenarcha: or, of The Office of Justices of the Peace* (London, 1581), 102; *The Law of Arrests in both Civil and Criminal Cases* (Savoy, 1742), A2.

other non-officers in searching for and arresting suspects.[2] Scholars of eighteenth-century policing have reached a similar conclusion: 'apprehension was the task of the victim of crime'.[3] The idea that law enforcement was taken over by agents of the state in the nineteenth century has recently been challenged by David Churchill, who showed that 'there was no police monopoly on apprehension in the early Victorian city' as private individuals continued to make a significant proportion of arrests.[4] Widespread participation by non-officers seems to characterise English policing over an extremely long period. For some historians, this provides evidence of a peculiarly English (or Anglo-American, or at least non-French) form of 'policing by consent'.[5] The fact that law enforcement in continental Europe was equally dependent on unofficial participation in this period does not seem to dent this confident assessment.[6]

There are, however, two more fundamental difficulties with the model of participatory policing. One is its failure to account for gender. With very few exceptions, scholars who emphasise the extent of unofficial participation in the capture of suspects ignore the fact that almost all of those unofficial participants were men. Secondly, although a great deal

---

[2] Cynthia B. Herrup, *The Common Peace: Participation and the Criminal Law in Seventeenth-Century England* (Cambridge, 1987), 67–92; Cynthia B. Herrup, 'New Shoes and Mutton Pies: Investigative Responses to Theft in Seventeenth-Century East Sussex', *Historical Journal* 27.4 (1984). See also James Sharpe, 'Enforcing the Law in the Seventeenth-Century English Village' in V. A. C. Gatrell, Bruce Lenman, and Geoffrey Parker (eds.), *Crime and the Law: The Social History of Crime in Western Europe since 1500* (London, 1980); Malcolm Gaskill, *Crime and Mentalities in Early Modern England* (Cambridge, 2000); Sharon Howard, 'Investigating Responses to Theft in Early Modern Wales', *Continuity & Change* 19.3 (2004).

[3] Douglas Hay and Francis Snyder, 'Using the Criminal Law, 1750–1850: Policing, Private Prosecution, and the State' in Douglas Hay and Francis Snyder (eds.), *Policing and Prosecution in Britain, 1750–1850* (Oxford, 1989), 18. See also J. M. Beattie, *Crime and the Courts in England 1660–1800* (Princeton, 1986), 35–41; Peter King, *Crime, Justice, and Discretion in England 1740–1820* (Oxford, 2000), 17–81; Robert B. Shoemaker, *The London Mob: Violence and Disorder in Eighteenth-Century England* (London, 2004), 27–50.

[4] David C. Churchill, *Crime Control and Everyday Life in the Victorian City: The Police and the Public* (Oxford, 2017), 174–5. See also Lucia Zedner, 'Policing before and after the Police: the Historical Antecedents of Contemporary Crime Control', *British Journal of Criminology* 46.1 (2006).

[5] Cyril D. Robinson, 'Ideology as History: A Look at the Way Some English Police Historians Look at the Police', *Police Studies* 2 (1979); J. A. Sharpe, *Crime in Early Modern England 1550–1750* (2nd edition, London, 1999), 57–8.

[6] For French and German examples, see David Garrioch, 'The People of Paris and their Police in the Eighteenth Century: Reflections on the Introduction of a "Modern" Police Force', *European History Quarterly* 24 (1994); B. Ann Tlusty, *The Martial Ethic in Early Modern Germany: Civic Duty and the Right of Arms* (Basingstoke, 2011). French and German observers have been no less prone to believing the myth of English policing by consent: Anja Johansen, 'Police-Public Relations: Interpretations of Policing and Democratic Governance' in Paul Knepper and Anja Johansen (eds.), *The Oxford Handbook of the History of Crime and Criminal Justice* (Oxford, 2016).

of law enforcement was carried out by non-officers, there were important differences between the kinds of arrests made by officers and others. Officeholders possessed wider discretionary powers of arrest than other people, and those powers were extended in the later seventeenth and eighteenth centuries. Their exercise of those powers produced highly gendered patterns of law enforcement.

Gendered Participation

Evidence for widespread participation in arrests is generally anecdotal. Unlike indictments or sentences, which lend themselves to quantification, no systematic records of arrests were kept in early modern England. Most of what is known about arrests comes from witness depositions in the papers of Assizes and Quarter Sessions. The survival of these materials is haphazard, as is the inclusion of detailed accounts of arrests. It is easy enough to produce examples of arrests by non-officers, but more difficult to give any precise sense of the balance between official and unofficial involvement, or the identities of those who participated. However, recent scholarship on the history of women's work has shown that qualitative materials like witness statements can, if collected in sufficient numbers, provide a basis for quantification.[7] Churchill's work on nineteenth-century policing adopts a similar methodology, aggregating mentions of arrests in Quarter Sessions depositions to produce data on the extent of unofficial participation.[8] This approach has its limits, particularly with regard to the types of crime dealt with by any given court, but it makes it possible to paint a far more detailed picture of participatory law enforcement.

This chapter draws on a dataset of 1,104 arrests mentioned in the published *Proceedings of the Old Bailey* and 195 arrests mentioned in depositions given by prosecutors, witnesses, and defendants at Middlesex Quarter Sessions in the last decades of the seventeenth century and the first half of the eighteenth.[9] These obviously represent a tiny fraction of the total number of arrests made in and around London in this period, but

---

[7] See introduction, note 41.
[8] Churchill, *Crime Control*, 24.
[9] The Old Bailey sample represents every appearance of the words 'apprehend' or 'apprehended' between 1674 (when the *Proceedings* were first published) and 1750, excluding cases unconnected to arrests. The word 'arrest' usually referred to arrest for debt and appears far less frequently. The Middlesex Sessions sample represents every apprehension mentioned in the surviving depositions over the same period: LMA, MJ/SP/1674–1750.

there is no reason to suppose that they are not representative.[10] The most obvious and most striking pattern revealed by these cases is in the gender of those who made arrests. It is not possible to identify the person (or people) making the arrest in every single instance, but of 525 identifiable arrestors in the Old Bailey *Proceedings*, 502 (95.6 per cent) were men. In the Middlesex Sessions records, 126 (85.7 per cent) of the 147 identifiable arrestors were men.

Why was this? Many women were victims of crime and women were no less likely than men to be passing by when a crime was committed. Some women were overpowered by suspects they tried to arrest, like the victim of a pickpocket who 'laid hold of him and struggled with him, but he got away'. Her mother then 'siezed him, and he throwing her down, got from her'. In a similar case, a woman pursued the suspect and 'laid Hold of him; but he being too strong got from her'. The suspects in both of these cases were eventually arrested by men.[11] But it was not only women who tried and failed to make arrests; these were dangerous and difficult physical encounters, regardless of gender. The disparity in who made arrests is more likely to have been a product of norms surrounding the act of arresting. Cases in which women called on men to act for them are significant in this regard. In 1696, a London shopkeeper recognised a man who had stolen from her two years earlier but did not attempt to arrest him herself. Instead, she looked for a (male) officer to make the arrest for her, and 'not finding a Constable to secure him then, he went away'. She saw the man again soon after and told her husband, who 'seiz'd him, and charged him with the suspicion of stealing'.[12] Many arrests made by men were prompted by their wives, mothers, daughters, mistresses, and other women who may have assumed that the apprehension of law-breakers was a masculine activity. Women who made arrests for themselves, in the eyes

---

[10] There is no obvious pattern to suggest that arrests were disproportionately mentioned in reports and depositions relating to any particular set of crimes, suspects, victims, or arrestors. The Old Bailey *Proceedings* provided considerably longer reports of the more sensational cases, typically homicides and violent robberies, but details of arrests were also frequently given in the brief reports of commonplace theft. On the general reliability of the *Proceedings*, see John H. Langbein, 'The Criminal Trial Before the Lawyers', *University of Chicago Law Review* 45.2 (1978); John H. Langbein, 'Shaping the Eighteenth-Century Criminal Trial: A View from the Ryder Sources', *University of Chicago Law Review* 50.1 (1983); Robert B. Shoemaker, 'The Old Bailey Proceedings and the Representation of Crime and Criminal Justice in Eighteenth-Century London', *Journal of British Studies* 47.3 (2008).

[11] *OBP*, Feb 1717, trial of John Lawrence (t17170227-20); *OBP*, Oct 1723, trial of Edward Glade (t17231016-7). For similar cases, see *OBP*, Jan 1724, trial of Joseph Hyde (t17240117-11); *OBP*, Dec 1748, trial of Charles Culley (t17481207-5).

[12] LMA, MJ/SP/1696/12/079, Information of Alice Evans, 27 Oct 1696. See also MJ/SP/1748/10/121, Information of Catherine Welsh, 13 Sep 1748.

of one witness at the Old Bailey, merited special commendation. In 1727, the judges were told that two women had robbed another of an apron and handkerchief as she hung out her laundry, 'but by the Industry and Courage of Sarah Bigs, they were both apprehended'.[13]

Male domination of arresting was not unique to London or to this period. Records of arrests in other parts of the country survive in much smaller numbers but these reveal much the same gendered patterns. In Kent, for example, depositions given to Quarter Sessions in the late seventeenth and early eighteenth century provide sufficient detail to identify twenty-two arrestors or groups of arrestors. All of them were men. Churchill found a similar gender imbalance in nineteenth-century Liverpool, and it seems plausible that this represented a long-term feature of English policing. In the Victorian press, arrests by unofficial men were 'celebrated as exemplary of masculine courage and assertion'.[14] No such celebratory accounts survive from the seventeenth and eighteenth centuries, but there was something specifically masculine in the manner of making an arrest and the tools used to do it.

Both officers and unofficial men were frequently said to have made arrests by hitting suspects with staves to 'knock them down'. In fact, 'knocking down' was almost synonymous with arrests. In John Gay's play *The Mohocks*, a constable tells his watchmen to 'knock down upon Suspicion'. A man who witnessed an arrest made by London bailiffs in 1741 said that 'it was strange they could not arrest a man without beating him'. Officers knocked people down as a matter of course. One suspect called before a magistrate said 'he had rather go without a Constable, than be knock'd down, and forc'd to go'. The potential severity of such beatings is illustrated by the case of a servant who 'was knock'd down and afterwards taken' by officers as a suspected thief, and later entered the Old Bailey courtroom 'in a very weak and helpless Condition as if not able to walk'.[15] Some officers denied they had knocked suspects down, claiming instead to have 'tapp'd him on the Shoulder' or politely presented a warrant.[16] But most appear to have admitted to it without

---

[13] *OBP*, Jul 1727, trial of Margaret Stoaks, Elizabeth Curd (t17270705-37).

[14] KHLC, Q/SB/8–33, Q/SB/1715–1750; Churchill, *Crime Control*, 182, 178–84.

[15] [John Gay], *The Mohocks. A Tragi-Comical Farce* (London, 1712), 5; *OBP*, Oct 1741, trial of William Westwood, Joseph Bellinger (t17411014-25); *OBP*, Apr 1738, trial of William Linton (t17380412-43); *OBP*, Jan 1719, trial of Thomas Cinnamon (t17190115-7). Even in the early twentieth century, an arrest was referred to by some police officers as a 'knock' or 'knock off': Clive Emsley, *The English Police: A Political and Social History* (2nd edition, Harlow, 1996), 219.

[16] *OBP*, Feb 1738, trial of Nathaniel Hillard (t17380222-4); *OBP*, Feb 1741 (t17410225-38); *OBP*, Dec 1730, trial of James Hall (t17301204-76).

hesitation, presumably considering knocking down an ordinary and acceptable way to make an arrest.[17]

The primary tools for knocking people down were staves, so much so that it was difficult to imagine how it could be done without one. In Defoe's *Colonel Jack*, the eponymous hero and his accomplice, Will, rob a man and later hear reports that they had knocked him down, 'which was not true, for neither Will, or I had any Stick in our Hands'.[18] Staves were not only important symbols of authority (as discussed in Chapter 2), they were also widely used as weapons. They accounted for a substantial proportion of homicides in seventeenth- and eighteenth-century England, and a large number of cases of non-lethal violence.[19] Many people used staves for many purposes, but when it came to the use of force, they seem to have been starkly gendered objects. In the assaults and other forms of violence reported to Quarter Sessions and borough courts, the use of staves matches a clear gender hierarchy. For example, in the records of Kent Quarter Sessions, Middlesex Quarter Sessions, and the Norwich Mayor's Court, there are many cases of men beating each other with staves, some cases of men beating women, a handful of women beating women, and no cases of women beating men.[20] This contrasts sharply with the violent use of knives, which was especially prevalent among women.[21] In contemporary ballads, staves were often phallic symbols, as in the story of a West Country miller who promises to please a woman with something 'As large, and as long as a Constables Staff'. This trope survived in songs about the new police of the nineteenth century, such as 'The Model Peeler', who

---

[17] LMA, MJ/SP/1708/02/023, Information of Charles Freely, 25 Jan 1708; *OBP*, Sep 1684, trial of Richard Burton, Martin Stevenson (t16840903-2); *OBP*, Oct 1695, trial of James Buffin (t16951014-27); *OBP*, Mar 1704, trial of William Barrow (t17040308-23); *OBP*, Apr 1718, trial of John Price (t17180423-24); *OBP*, Apr 1723, trial of Nathaniel Irish (t17230424-42); *OBP*, Aug 1727, trial of John Willsom (t17270830-28).

[18] Daniel Defoe, *Colonel Jack*, ed. Samuel Holt Monk (Oxford, 1989), 58.

[19] J. S. Cockburn, 'Patterns of Violence in English Society: Homicide in Kent 1560–1985', *Past & Present* 130.1 (1991), 80–1; James Sharpe, *A Fiery & Furious People: A History of Violence in England* (London, 2016), 640. Similar patterns of staff use have been found in records from the fourteenth and fifteenth centuries: Barbara A. Hanawalt, 'Violent Death in Fourteenth- and Early Fifteenth-Century England', *Comparative Studies in Society and History* 18.3 (1976), 319; Andrew J. Finch, 'The Nature of Violence in the Middle Ages: An Alternative Perspective', *Historical Research* 70.173 (1997), 267 n. 83.

[20] The figures for each court, based on depositions given between 1660 and 1750, are as follows: nine cases of male-male violence with staves in Kent, nine in Middlesex, twelve in Norwich; six male-female cases in Kent, three in Middlesex, three in Norwich; two female-female cases in Kent, none in Middlesex, and one in Norwich. KHLC, Q/SB/8–33, Q/SB/1715–1750; LMA, MJ/SP/1674–1750; NRO, NCR Case 12b/1–7.

[21] Garthine Walker, *Crime, Gender and Social Order in Early Modern England* (Cambridge, 2003), 79.

sings that 'all the little cook maids have a welcome for me, and no wonder for ... I always do my duty, and by the help of my trusty staff, I do it like a man'.[22]

With or without a staff, knocking down was a particularly patriarchal style of violence. Men knocked down women, masters knocked down servants, and husbands knocked down wives.[23] This was the violence of social discipline – or, in contemporary language, 'correction' – intended to coerce its victims into obedience.[24] Knocking someone down in order to arrest them was also a form of state violence: violence carried out under the protection of legal authority. Officers and other people who used force to make arrests could justify what they had done in court, and forceful resistance against them was deemed especially culpable. One lawyer explicitly connected the violence of arrests with other forms of patriarchal 'correction'. The use of force could be considered justified, he wrote, 'if an Officer, having a Warrant against one who will not suffer himself to be arrested, beat or wound him in the Attempt to take him; or if a Parent in a reasonable Manner chastise his Child, or a Master his Servant ... or even a Husband his Wife'.[25] On these terms, arrests were part of a continuum of lawful gendered violence in which the lines between official and unofficial uses of force were unclear.

Office and Arrests

In London, however, the balance between official and unofficial involvement in arrests was beginning to change. The sample of cases from the Old Bailey and Middlesex Sessions records provides a sense of who made arrests that goes beyond the anecdotal. Robert Shoemaker showed some

---

[22] *The West-Country Dialogue: Or, A Pleasant Ditty between Anniseed-Robin the Miller, and His Brother Jack the Plough-Man* (London, 1672–96); *Cheat upon Cheat, OR, The Debaucht Hypocrite* (London, 1664–1706); C. P. Cove, 'The Model Peeler', quoted in Wilbur R. Miller, *Cops and Bobbies: Police Authority in New York and London, 1830–1870* (2nd edition, Columbus, 1999), 126–7.

[23] Examples from Norwich and Kent include: NRO, NCR Case 12b/2, Information of John Thox, 18 Sep 1690; NRO, NCR Case 12b/2, Information of Elizabeth Lyton, 28 Jan 1691; NRO, NCR Case 12b/3, Information of Elizabeth Howlet, 5 Sep 1706; NRO, NCR Case 12b/7, Information of Mary Barker, 4 Jun 1750; KHLC, Q/SB/9/17, Examination of Mary Mecome, 3 Oct 1663; KHLC, Q/SB/24/208, Examination of Bennet Palmer, 9 Jul 1696.

[24] Susan Dwyer Amussen, 'Punishment, Discipline, and Power: The Social Meanings of Violence in Early Modern England', *Journal of British Studies* 34 (1995); Walker, *Crime, Gender and Social Order*, 23–74; Alexandra Shepard, *Meanings of Manhood in Early Modern England* (Oxford, 2003), 132–9; Elizabeth Foyster, *Marital Violence: An English Family History, 1660–1857* (Cambridge, 2005); Joseph P. Ward (ed.), *Violence, Politics, and Gender in Early Modern England* (London, 2008).

[25] William Hawkins, *A Treatise of the Pleas of the Crown*, vol. 1 (2nd edition, London, 1724), 130.

of the possibilities of these kinds of records in his work on the changing frequency of particular phrases in the Old Bailey *Proceedings*. The phrase 'Stop thief!' for example, appeared more and more often in the first half of the eighteenth century but dropped off after 1750. 'Cried watch' and 'called out watch' became increasingly common from the 1740s onward. Shoemaker interprets these trends as evidence of the changing patterns of unofficial participation in policing the capital. 'Ordinary Londoners played a growing role in apprehending criminals' in the first half of the century, as evidenced by the rising number of calls to bystanders to stop thieves. With the rise of the Bow Street Runners and other law enforcement initiatives in the second half of the century, he suggests, 'ordinary Londoners played a much reduced role in apprehending criminals'.[26] Shoemaker's method makes full use of the searchability of digitised records, but it is not clear that the frequencies of these particular phrases can be taken as proxies for shifting practices of law enforcement. A cry of 'stop thief!', for example, could just as easily lead to an arrest by an officer as by anyone else.[27] Close rather than distant reading of the Old Bailey reports, alongside the records of Middlesex Quarter Sessions, presents a slightly different picture. First, they reveal that the overall proportion of arrests made by officers was substantial, and higher than some accounts of participatory policing might suggest.

The figures shown in Table 1 are almost certainly underestimates. In many of the cases in which it is impossible to identify who made an arrest, what happened is described in the passive voice: suspects 'were apprehended', 'were taken', 'were secured', or 'were seized'. In the case of Quarter Sessions depositions, the use of this kind of phrase by one witness sometimes refers to an arrest which, in another witness's testimony, is attributed to an officer.[28] Even officers themselves sometimes used passive formulations to describe their own actions, like John Lavars, a watchman in St Martin's in the Fields who reported the confession made to him by a pair of thieves 'when they were apprehended'.[29] The number of arrests by officers which are hidden by this kind of language is unknowable. Similarly, non-officers sometimes deposed that they had arrested suspects themselves

---

[26] Shoemaker, *London Mob*, 27–49.
[27] Examples of arrests involving officers after someone cried 'stop thief!' include: *OBP*, Apr 1724, trial of John Winderam (t17240415-8); *OBP*, May 1728, trial of Joseph Johnson (t17280501-4); *OBP*, Jan 1729, trial of Daniel Crawfoot (t17290116-27); *OBP*, Jun 1731, trial of William Burroughs (t17310602-34); *OBP*, Dec 1742, trial of David Todd (t17421208-24).
[28] See, for example, LMA, MJ/SP/1748/10/123, Informations of William Draper and John Mason, 15 Sep 1748; LMA, MJ/SP/1748/10/124, Informations of John Anderson and Henry French, 19 Sep 1748.
[29] LMA, MJ/SP/1748/07/23, Information of John Lavars, 28 Jun 1748.

Table 1 *Official involvement in arrests recorded at the Old Bailey and Middlesex Quarter Sessions, 1674–1750*

Court	Total arrests	Arrests where un/official status of arrestor/s clear	Arrests involving officer/s
Old Bailey	1,104	508	209 (41.1 per cent)
Middlesex Sessions	195	153	48 (31.4 per cent)

when there had in fact been an officer involved. In 1749, a shoemaker of St James's told Middlesex justices that 'he saw the said James Hill drop the said [stolen] whig & he seized him', but a watchman of the parish deposed that in fact '*he* apprehended the said James Hill upon the outcry of stop thief'.[30] It seems likely that both men played a part; many arrests were carried out by more than one person, often mixed groups of officers and unofficial assistants. Officers were probably also responsible for at least some of the arrests which were described as being prompted or orchestrated by the victims of crime but not carried out by them. Deponents at both the Old Bailey and Middlesex Sessions said they 'had her apprehended', 'had them secured', or 'caused him to be apprehended'.[31] In 1728, for example, a man told the Old Bailey that he had been pickpocketed by a group of women and men and 'had them apprehended'. Further testimony clarified that a constable had made the arrest.[32] Many of the records from which it is impossible to identify arrestors may conceal further official involvement.

Another set of records – those relating to summary procedures – point to even more official activity. In summary courts, justices committed petty thieves, night-walkers, and vagrants to bridewells or houses of correction without trial by jury, a practice which became increasingly common in the late seventeenth and eighteenth centuries.[33] In these courts, officers were far more prominent among prosecutors than in the higher courts, typically because they had arrested the defendant themselves.[34] Summary

---

[30] LMA, MJ/SP/1749/05/112, Informations of Alexander Anderson and Valentine Roe, 17 May 1749. Italics added.
[31] *OBP*, Jun 1685, trial of Sarah Bedwell (t16850604-13); *OBP*, Dec 1721, trial of Robert Walton (t17211206-64); LMA, MJ/SP/1748/09/36, Information of Patrick Cannon, 9 Aug 1748; LMA, MJ/SP/1749/09/100, Information of Ann Crow, 21 Aug 1749.
[32] *OBP*, Jul 1728, trial of Peter Pemberton, Mary Pemberton, Mary Mason (t17280717-12).
[33] Joanna Innes, 'Prisons for the Poor: English Bridewells, 1555–1800' in Francis Snyder and Douglas Hay (eds.), *Labour, Law, and Crime: An Historical Perspective* (London, 1987); Peter King, 'The Summary Courts and Social Relations in Eighteenth-Century England', *Past & Present* 183 (2004).
[34] Bruce P. Smith, 'The Myth of Private Prosecution in England, 1750–1850' in Markus D. Dubber and Lindsay Farmer (eds.), *Modern Histories of Crime and Punishment* (Stanford, 2007).

proceedings, as one scholar puts it, 'represented the latter or final stages of the policing process and were in many ways a reflection of it'. In the second half of the eighteenth century, almost half of all identifiable prosecutors in the City of London summary courts were officers.[35] The records of summary courts for the period before this are sparse, but some approximation of officers' activity as prosecutors can be made from the lists of plaintiffs given in records of committals to houses of correction after summary trial. These reveal a long-term pattern, from the mid-sixteenth century through to the early eighteenth, in which about two-thirds of plaintiffs who sent offenders to the London and Middlesex houses of correction were officers.[36] If most of these officers had arrested the people they prosecuted, the figures suggest that a majority of those tried at summary courts were arrested by constables, watchmen, and their official colleagues.

Two scholars who have studied summary procedure in this period, Robert Shoemaker and Faramerz Dabhoiwala, suggest that law enforcement was becoming increasingly 'professionalised' in the capital. Beginning in the 1690s, London-based Societies for the Reformation of Manners promoted the arrest of moral offenders – especially 'lewd women' – by offering rewards for successful prosecutions. At the same time, parliament began to offer rewards for the prosecution of certain felonies by statute. In both cases, rather than galvanising the practice of popular policing, rewards were generally claimed by particular groups of men who became specialists in catching one kind of offender or another. Informers and 'reforming constables' trawled the streets in search of immorality while 'thief-takers' set off in pursuit of highway robbers, both groups motivated by the profits available to those who secured convictions. As Dabhoiwala has explained, the efforts of Societies for the Reformation of Manners served 'to reduce the involvement of ordinary people in the enforcement of the law and to accelerate its professionalization'.[37]

Data from the Old Bailey and Middlesex Sessions suggest these developments were part of a wider tilting of the balance between popular and specialised law enforcement. In the late seventeenth and early eighteenth centuries, official involvement in arrests was increasing. The data are

---

[35] Drew Gray, 'Summary Proceedings and Social Relations in the City of London, c.1750–1800' (University of Northampton PhD thesis, 2006), 53, 102.
[36] Paul Griffiths, *Lost Londons: Change, Crime, and Control in the Capital City 1550–1660* (Cambridge, 2008), Appendix, Table 8b; Robert B. Shoemaker, *Prosecution and Punishment: Petty Crime and the Law in London and Rural Middlesex, 1660–1725* (Cambridge, 1991), 216–8.
[37] Faramerz Dabhoiwala, 'Sex and Societies for Moral Reform, 1688–1800', *Journal of British Studies* 46.2 (2007), 291; Tim Hitchcock and Robert Shoemaker, *London Lives: Poverty, Crime and the Making of a Modern City, 1690–1800* (Cambridge, 2015), 29.

Table 2 *Official involvement in arrests by decade, 1681–1750*

Decade[a]	Old Bailey		Middlesex Sessions	
	Arrests where arrestor/s identifiable	Arrests involving officer/s	Arrests where arrestor/s identifiable	Arrests involving officer/s
1681–90	29	6 (20.7 per cent)		
1691–1700	12	3 (25 per cent)	78	21 (26.9 per cent)
1701–10	11	4 (36.4 per cent)	41	13 (31.7 per cent)
1711–20	114	38 (33.3 per cent)		
1721–30	165	72 (43.6 per cent)		
1731–40	97	48 (49.5 per cent)		
1741–50	67	31 (46.3 per cent)	24	10 (41.7 per cent)

[a] Cases from the 1670s are excluded as the OBP only began to be printed in 1674. Decades for which fewer than ten cases with identifiable arrestors survive in the Middlesex Sessions records are excluded.

unevenly spread, but Table 2 shows an increasing proportion of arrests by officers in both the Old Bailey and the Middlesex Sessions records. In the last decades of the seventeenth century, officers appear to have been involved in around a quarter of the arrests described in the records of these courts. By the middle of the eighteenth century, the proportion of official arrests was closer to half. As well as the Reformation of Manners and the rise of thief-takers, it seems likely that this trend was partly driven by the increasing deputisation among constables and watchmen discussed in the previous chapter. As the same people began to serve in the offices of law enforcement year after year, developing a collective sense of official identity, a growing number of Londoners turned to them rather than making arrests themselves. One indicator of this shift was a growing reluctance among some non-officers to act without official support. Shoemaker has made a similar argument about the second half of the eighteenth century, and there is evidence of hesitation and uncertainty among unofficial arrestors at least as early as the 1730s.[38] In 1734, in response to one Londoner's desire to call a constable to make an arrest rather than do it himself, another declared that 'any Man might take a Thief', but others were not so sure. In 1737, a victim of theft was asked by Old Bailey judges why he had not arrested the woman he suspected when he saw her in the

---

[38] Shoemaker, *London Mob*, 42, 46–9.

street: 'I had no Warrant; so I thought I had no Power to apprehend her'. Another man, asked much the same question in 1744, answered that 'I did not know I could take him up without a warrant, and I thought it was the safest way to take him with a Constable'. In the same year, a shopkeeper sent for a beadle to arrest someone who stole from his shop rather than doing it himself. A group of men who tracked down a counterfeiter in 1745 called a constable to make the arrest, 'for we did not care to apprehend him ourselves'.[39]

This reluctance to act without officers went hand in hand with a growing sense that arrests made by officers were in some sense more legitimate than those made by others. In the 1730s, a number of magistrates began to refuse to examine suspects who were 'not brought by a proper Officer' or 'did not come before him in charge of a Constable'. In the same decade, some judges began to presume that victims of crime would turn to officers to carry out arrests: in one Old Bailey trial, the judges asked a woman who had been raped 'Why did not you apprehend the Prisoner then? Was there ne'er a Constable in the Town?'[40] Even those who committed crimes increasingly associated arrests with officers, like the man who tried to turn himself in for murder, asking 'that an Officer might be got to apprehend me'. Some suspects would not submit to arrests made by non-officers. One victim of theft arrested the man he suspected, but 'when he found I had not a proper officer, he said, you little saucy dog, let me go'. In 1732, a woman apprehended for pickpocketing asked her arrestors 'Where's your Constable then?' This may have been a particular problem for anyone arresting a person of higher social status than themselves. When a journeyman tried to arrest a master artisan for homicide, 'He made a Punch at me, and said I was not a proper Officer – I should not hold him.'[41]

The increasing importance of officeholding to the practice of arrest was also reflected by the growing numbers of people who were sworn in as supernumerary constables. From the 1660s onward, the Court of Aldermen ordered almost anyone charged with keeping order in the City of London to take the oath of office and become a constable. In 1667, as the city was rebuilt after 'the late dismall fire', every beadle was made a

---

[39] *OBP*, Jan 1734, trial of Thomas Rowland (t17340116-2); *OBP*, May 1737, trial of Jane Clark (t17370526-11); *OBP*, Dec 1744, trial of Samuel Goodman (t17441205-41); *OBP*, Feb 1744, trial of Thomas Keate (t17440223-23); *OBP*, Feb 1745, trial of Robert Catherall (t17450227-21).

[40] *OBP*, Dec 1732, trial of Jane Gale, Eleanor Walker (t17321206-40); *OBP*, Apr 1738, trial of William Linton (t17380412-43); *OBP*, Jul 1734 (t17340710-33).

[41] *OBP*, Jul 1739, trial of Thomas Bridge (t17390718-16); Jan 1748, trial of William Matthews (t17480115-17); Dec 1732, trial of Jane Gale, Eleanor Walker (t17321206-40); Jan 1740, trial of Abraham Benbrook (t17400116-24).

constable 'for the better Execucon of my Lord Maiors Proclamation for redresse of disorders comitted by Workemen'. By the 1700s, the beadles of the Corporation of the Poor were frequently sworn in as constables and in 1763 it became official City policy that 'every Beadle shall be admitted and sworn as an Extra Constable, in order the better to enable him to discharge the Duties of the said Office'.[42] City marshals, charged with patrolling the City during the daytime, began to be made constables in the 1670s, a practice which continued into the eighteenth century.[43] Beginning the 1680s, the keepers of Moorfields,[44] the porters of Christ's, Bethlem, and Bridwell hospitals,[45] the men 'imployed for the regulation of Hackney Coachmen in the Streetes',[46] and those charged with the maintenance of order in markets[47] and at the Royal Exchange were all regularly sworn in as constables 'the better to enable them' to 'Correct and suppress disorders' or clear the streets of 'Lewd Women and other idle Persons' in their respective jurisdictions.[48] Some parishes and wards appointed men 'to keep of[f] & disperse the beggars frequently thronging about the door of their p[ar]ish church' or to 'keep the said Ward cleare from Beggers', and these too were made constables. In 1735, an informer working for the one of the Societies for the Reformation of Manners was sworn constable at the Society's request.[49]

This wave of constable-appointing suggests there were significant differences between the powers of officers and non-officers (and between those of constables and other officers) when it came to enforcing law. This goes against much of the established historiography on policing before the nineteenth century. Constables are said to have possessed 'only the most limited powers of arrest' so that 'unless he actually saw a crime committed

---

[42] LMA, COL/CA/01/01/73, f.261; LMA, COL/CA/01/01/112, f.44; LMA, COL/CA/01/01/113, f.166; LMA, COL/CA/01/01/114, f.96; LMA, CLA/048/PS/02/015, Corporation order, 26 Oct 1763.
[43] LMA, COL/CA/01/01/80, f.305; LMA, COL/CA/01/01/107, f.19; LMA, COL/CA/01/01/118, f.238; LMA, COL/CA/01/01/140, ff.232, 286; LMA, COL/CA/01/01/141, f.208; LMA, COL/CA/01/01/143, f.189.
[44] LMA, COL/CA/01/01/84, f.18; LMA, COL/CA/01/01/115, f.357; LMA, COL/CA/01/01/142, f.299.
[45] LMA, COL/CA/01/01/87, f.2; LMA, COL/CA/01/01/89, f.163; LMA, COL/CA/01/01/92, ff.134, 238; LMA, COL/CA/01/01/95, f.84; LMA, COL/CA/01/01/95, f.298; LMA, COL/CA/01/01/96, f.30.
[46] LMA, COL/CA/01/01/90, f.74; LMA, COL/CA/01/01/92, f.220; LMA, COL/CA/01/01/96, f.30; LMA, COL/CA/01/01/112, f.62; LMA, COL/CA/01/01/114, f.59; LMA, MJ/SP/1723/01/62, Letter from commissioners for licensing and regulating Hackney Coaches, 17 Jan 1723. See also J. M. Beattie, *Policing and Punishment in London, 1660–1750: Urban Crime and the Limits of Terror* (Oxford, 2001), 125–6.
[47] LMA, COL/CA/01/01/93, f.40; LMA, COL/CA/01/01/95, ff.46, 266; LMA, COL/CA/01/01/99, f.131; LMA, COL/CA/01/01/142, f.47; LMA, COL/CA/01/01/151, f.283.
[48] LMA, COL/CA/01/01/93, f.89; LMA, COL/CA/01/01/97, f.235; LMA, COL/CA/01/01/108, f.238; LMA, COL/CA/01/01/113, f.142.
[49] LMA, COL/CA/01/01/91, f.50; LMA, COL/CA/01/01/102, f.168; LMA, COL/CA/01/01/140, f.168.

he could arrest without warrant only at his peril'. There is said to have been so little that distinguished officers from others in matters of law enforcement that 'distinctions between state and popular responses [to crime] are artificial'.[50] If this were the case, the reluctance shown by some Londoners to make arrests without officers and the practice of swearing in various people as supernumerary constables would make little sense. John Beattie provided an alternative view, arguing that constables 'wielded authority not available to ordinary citizens in ordinary circumstances', including 'powers to arrest and imprison'. He offered no details about the nature of these powers but suggested that they were useful to thief-takers, government messengers, and later Bow Street Runners who took the constable's oath to enhance their ability to make arrests.[51]

One aspect of the difference between official and unofficial powers of arrest had to do with obligation. Officers were liable to be fined for failing to arrest offenders and had greater powers than other people to compel bystanders to assist them. This, according to the barrister William Hawkins, was 'the chief Difference between the Power and Duty of a Constable and a private Person'. Failure to assist an officer in the pursuit or apprehension of a felon had been punishable by fines for many centuries, and eighteenth-century legislation mandated similar penalties for neglecting to help arrest other kinds of offenders.[52] This deterrent was not always effective. A Yorkshireman asked by a constable to help him detain a suspected cow thief in 1648 'would not obaye' and allowed the man to escape. In 1722, when a Kentish constable 'demanded the Assistance' of John Sisley to arrest a man accused of getting an unmarried woman pregnant, Sisley 'Answerd Him the s[ai]d Officer of the Peace, in the Execution of His Office That He Coud not nor wou'd not go with Him'. In 1740, a Norwich constable called on bystanders to help him arrest a woman who had attacked someone. One man did, but another 'swore he would not' and set his dog on the officer's assistant. In the middle decades of the eighteenth century, as Shoemaker has shown, London officers sometimes

---

[50] Paul Rock, 'Law, Order and Power in Late Seventeenth- and Early Eighteenth-Century England' in Stanley Cohen and Andrew Scull (eds.), *Social Control and the State* (Oxford, 1983), 196; Patrick Pringle, *Hue and Cry: The Birth of the British Police* (London, 1955), 51; Gaskill, *Crime and Mentalities*, 250.
[51] Beattie, *Policing and Punishment*, 121, 244–7; J. M. Beattie, *The First English Detectives: The Bow Street Runners and the Policing of London, 1750–1840* (Oxford, 2012), 56, 78.
[52] William Hawkins, *A Treatise of the Pleas of the Crown II* (2nd edition, London, 1726), 80–1; 1275 Statute of Westminster I (3 Edw. I c.9); Joseph Shaw, *Parish Law, or, a Guide to Justices of the Peace* (London, 1733), 327. Failing to assist arrests under the 1744 Vagrancy Act (17 Geo. II c.5) was punishable by fine.

faced a similarly reluctant public, who could be as hesitant to help constables make arrests as they sometimes were to make arrests without any officer at all.[53]

The power to demand assistance and the threat of fines go some way to explaining why a growing number Londoners, including those who governed the city, saw officers as critical to the process of arrest. But officers also possessed other, more significant powers. Above all, they could make arrests on the basis of suspicion alone where others could not. These powers were strengthened over the course of the seventeenth and eighteenth centuries. They were sometimes controversial among lawyers but widely used on the streets of the capital, especially against women.

The Law of Suspicion

Powers of arrest depended on the type of crime in question. Arrests for misdemeanours were not governed by the same set of rules as arrests for felonies. According to a long-established principle, 'everyone is an officer of the law to arrest felons'. The category of felony covered homicide, rape, and most forms of theft. As Michael Dalton put it, 'every private man may arrest another, whom hee knoweth to have committed a Robbery, Manslaughter, or other felony'. The power to arrest for breach of the peace was similarly universal, provided the person making the arrest had actually seen the peace broken.[54] The law on arrests for other misdemeanours was less clear. There was some precedent to suggest that non-officers could make arrests for night-walking, but in practice this seems to have been left to constables and night watchmen.[55] Some vagrancy statutes granted powers of arrest specifically to officers, others gave such powers to 'any Person whatsoever'.[56] Amid this jumble of slightly confused distinctions there was one area in which the law became increasingly clear: officers' powers to make arrests on the basis of suspicion.

Those who peddled myths of English liberty claimed that arrests on suspicion did not happen. 'In England', wrote the French novelist Abbé Prévost, 'people are not arrested on vague suspicions and mere

---

[53] TNA, ASSI 45/2/2/32, Deposition of Thomas Drings, 5 Oct 1648; KHLC, Q/SB/1722/examinations, Information of Samuel Battam, 4 Apr 1722 (unnumbered); NRO, Case 12b/7, Information of Robert Bussey, 7 Aug 1740 (unnumbered); Shoemaker, *London Mob*, 45–48.
[54] John Baker, *The Oxford History of the Laws of England vol IV 1483–1558* (Oxford, 2003), 88; Michael Dalton, *The Countrey Justice* (London, 1618), 295; *Law of Arrests*, 183–4.
[55] *Seipp's Abridgementi*, 1488.047 (Mich. 4 Hen. VII 12 f.18b); Hawkins, *Pleas of the Crown*, vol. 2, 77.
[56] For example: 7 Jac. I c.4 s.5 (1609); 13 Anne c.26 s.2 (1714); 17 Geo. II c.5 s.5 (1744).

probabilities'.[57] According to William Paley, writing later in the eighteenth century,

> neither the spirit of the laws, nor of the people, will suffer the detention or confinement of suspected persons, without proofs of their guilt ... nor men to be apprehended upon the mere suggestion of idleness or vagrancy ... or, lastly, entrust the police with such discretionary powers, as may make sure of the guilty, however they involve the innocent.[58]

This was at best a distortion of the truth. Chapter 29 of Magna Carta supposedly guarded against the arrest or imprisonment of any free person without due process.[59] But 'in some cases', a fifteenth-century lawyer explained, 'a man may be taken and imprisoned without process of law, as where a man is taken and arrested on suspicion of felony'.[60] From the late fifteenth century, judges held that anyone could arrest a person suspected of felony on the basis of 'common fame'.[61] A series of rulings around 1600 affirmed that unexplained possession of stolen goods also provided good grounds for arrest on suspicion of theft.[62] Legal treatises provided lists of 'sufficient causes of suspition', which typically included: indictment for the felony; strong circumstantial evidence, such as being present at the time of a murder with a sword drawn; 'evill fame'; vagrancy; being found in possession of stolen goods; being found in company with known offenders; the information of an accomplice under oath; flight from the scene of the crime; being pursued by hue and cry.[63]

Both officers and non-officers could make arrests on suspicion of felony, but not on the same terms. Officers were permitted to use force, including

---

[57] Quoted in Pringle, *Hue and Cry*, 50.
[58] William Paley, *The Principles of Moral and Political Philosophy* (London, 1785) vol. VI, 385.
[59] John Baker, *The Reinvention of Magna Carta 1216–1616* (Cambridge, 2017), 32–35. This provision came under clauses 39–40 of the original 1215 charter but was listed as Chapter 29 in the 1225 charter and most later iterations, so it is generally referred to as such. The clause was extended to protect unfree villeins in the fourteenth century.
[60] Reading of Magna Carta at Lincoln's Inn, c.1455/60, translated and reproduced in Baker, *Reinvention*, 453–4.
[61] *Seipp's Abridgement*, 1467.057 (Mich. 7 Edw. IV 19 f.20a); 1471.008 (Trin. 11 Edw. IV 8 ff.4b–5a); 1477.022 (Mich. 17 Edw. IV 1 ff.5a–b); 1489.041 (Mich. 5 Hen. VII ff.4a–5a).
[62] Varrell v Wilson (1594), Moore (KB) 600, 72 *ER* 785; Chambers v Taylor (1602), Cro. Eliz. 900, 78 *ER* 1123; Dogatte v Lawry (1607), Cro. Jac. 190, 79 *ER* 166; Weal v Wells (1616), Bridgman 60, 123 *ER* 1200.
[63] See, for example: Ferdinando Pulton, *De Pace Regis et Regni* (London, 1609), 12v–13; Dalton, *Countrey Justice*, 266–7; William Sheppard, *The Offices of Constables* (London, 1641), 51–2; Edward Coke, *The Second Part of the Institutes of the Laws of England* (6th edition, London, 1681), 51–2; Hawkins, *Pleas of the Crown*, vol. 2, 76; Richard Burn, *The Justice of the Peace and Parish Officer* (London, 1755) vol I, 68; Henry Fielding, 'A Treatise on the Office of Constable' in John Fielding, *Extracts from Such of the Penal Laws, as Particularly Related to the Peace and Good Order of the Metropolis* (London, 1761), 262–3; Joseph Ritson, *The Office of Constable* (London, 1791), 8.

lethal force, in order to overcome suspected felons who resisted arrest. They were also allowed to break down doors to enter premises where suspected felons might be found. Non-officers who made similar use force to arrest suspected felons could be charged with assault, homicide, or housebreaking. The reason for the last of these distinctions, according to Matthew Hale, was that 'it would be a great inconvenience if every private man upon pretense of suspicion should break open houses'.[64] The contrasting degrees of legal protection in making arrests on suspicion may help to explain why, as we shall see, officers were considerably more likely to make such arrests than non-officers.

Another distinction, perhaps an even more important one, was developed by common lawyers over the seventeenth and eighteenth centuries. Under a long-established rule, arrests on suspicion of felony were limited by the principle that suspicion was not transferable. Suspects could only be arrested by the people who suspected them, not by third parties who had been informed of those suspicions. As one late medieval chief justice put it, 'I do not arrest anyone for suspicions that someone else has, but because I myself who arrest him have suspected him'. This applied equally to officeholders and private individuals: 'no king's officer nor anyone else can arrest for suspicion of a felony except those who have the suspicion; because it has been said, the suspicion does not extend to others'.[65] Elizabethan judges applied the same logic to arrests for peace-breaking. Citing a fifteenth-century case on the non-transferability of suspicion as precedent, one justice argued that 'A constable cannot arrest one to finde surety of the peace upon a complaint made to him, unless he himself sees the peace broken'.[66]

In the seventeenth century, legal thinking began to shift on this issue, generally in the direction of expanding official powers.[67] In 1618, Michael

---

[64] Matthew Hale (1609–76), *Historia Placitorum Coronae* (London, 1736), vol. 2, 92. See also Blackstone, *Commentaries*, vol. 4, 289–90.

[65] *Seipp's Abridgement*, 1480.044 (Trin. 20 Edw. IV 8 f.6b); 1487.024 (Hil. 2 Hen. VII 1 ff.15b–16a); 1495.017 (10 Hen. VII 17 ff.17a–18a).

[66] Scarret v Tanner (1593), Owen 105, 74 *ER* 933. Also reported as Skarret v Tanner (1595), BL Add. MS 25223 f.32; Scarlett v Hammer (1595), BL Add. MS 25211 f.88v; Skarett v Hanmer (1595), CUL MS Ii.05.24 f.41v; Sharrock v Hannemer (1595), Cro. Eliz. 375, 78 *ER* 622. The judges in these cases ignored, or were unaware of, an opposing precedent from 1370/1 in which one man informed a constable that another had threatened to kill him, the constable arrested the second man to find sureties for good behaviour, and this arrest was deemed justifiable though the constable had not seen any breach of the peace himself: Anthony Fitzherbert, *La Graunde Abridgement* (London, 1516), 'Barre', 202, 44 Edw. III.

[67] Barbara Shapiro has traced an analogous shift in magistrates' powers to issue arrest warrants on suspicion of felony without prior indictment by a jury: *'Beyond Reasonable Doubt' and 'Probable Cause': Historical Perspectives on the Anglo-American Law of Evidence* (Berkeley, 1991), 134–7.

Dalton could still write, as was traditional, that 'the party that shal arrest such suspected person, must have a suspition of him himselfe'. But in 1636, judges at the Assizes in York ruled that a constable who arrested a man for theft on the basis of the victim's suspicions had acted lawfully, in spite of the fact that he (the constable) had found nothing in a search of the suspect's house. The arrest 'was good though none of the goods were found in the hous, because the party whose goods were gone, did charge the Plaintiffe to have taken them, & to have them'. The absence of any cause for suspicion in the mind of the constable himself was no obstacle. The judges only remarked that 'the Constable in discretion might have refused to arrest him upon such request for that he himself found no cause of suspicion upon his search'.[68] According to this judgement, constables had a discretionary power to arrest on the basis of other people's suspicions as and when they saw fit. It was left to individual officers to decide whose suspicions merited action and whose should be ignored.

At first, legal commentators struggled to absorb this into their discussions of arrest on suspicion. William Sheppard, for example, wrote in 1641 'that if any man doth suspect another man of any Felony ... and doe declare the same to any one of these officers', such an officer 'may if the party suspect[ed] be within the limits of his office, arrest him'. He went on, however, to argue exactly the opposite, stating that 'one cannot imprison another man upon the suspition of a third man for felony, unless he himself have some cause of suspition also. And that one man, albeit he be an officer, cannot justifie the imprisonment of another man, suspected by a third man'. To reiterate this point, he concluded that 'if I suspect another man for felony, and give notice hereof to the Constable ... he cannot arrest him upon my suspition'.[69]

An escape from this contradiction was provided in the 1670s by Matthew Hale. Unlike his predecessors, Hale was firmly convinced that 'the constable may execute his office upon information and request of others, that suspect and charge the offenders, nay tho it be but with suspicion thereof'. It was, he wrote, 'not material, whether he saw the felony committed, or hath it only by complaint and information'. The reason for this was that 'such an information may carry over the suspicion even to the constable, whereby it may become his suspicion ... And if the constable should not be allowed this latitude in cases of this nature,

---

[68] Dalton, *Countrey Justice*, 296; Ward's Case (1636) in John Clayton, *Reports and Pleas of Assises At Yorke* (London 1651), 44.
[69] Sheppard, *Offices of Constables*, 49–50.

many felons would escape'. Hale's work was not printed until the 1730s, but these two justifications – that suspicion could be transferred from an informant's mind to the constable's mind and that this was necessary to ensure that felons were caught – became the basis of much subsequent writing on the subject. In 1692, Robert Gardiner agreed with Hale that 'if any man will lay Murther or Felony to anothers charge, he may declare it to a Constable and the Constable ought upon such Declaration, or Complaint, to carry him before a Justice'. In the early eighteenth century, Hawkins persisted in arguing that 'the Law hath so tender a Regard to the Liberty and Reputation of every Person, that no Causes of Suspicion whatsoever ... will justify the Arrest of an innocent Man, by one who is not himself induced by them to suspect him to be guilty'.[70] Later writers on the subject, however, suggested that a constable presented with another person's grounds for suspicion might be 'induced to suspect from what had been laid before him', making the suspicion his own. If this led to the arrest of innocent suspects, so be it. 'Many an innocent man has and may be taken up upon such suspicion', Lord Mansfield admitted in 1783, 'but the mischief and inconvenience to the public in this point of view is comparatively nothing. It is of great consequence to the police of the country'.[71]

Once established in law, officers' power to arrest on the basis of reported suspicions gave them broad discretion in the policing of potential felons, especially people accused of theft. There was, in theory, still another safeguard against arbitrary arrest: nobody was supposed to be arrested on suspicion of felony unless it was certain that a felony had actually taken place. As Dalton warned, 'for the arresting of such suspitious persons, note, that there must be some felony committed in deed' so 'suspicion only without a felonie committed, is no cause to arrest another'.[72] Judges overturned this protection in the late eighteenth century, but it had long been undermined in both common law and statute.[73] First, anyone could pre-emptively arrest people who 'intend, and goe about to commit a felony', who they saw 'on the Point of committing a Treason or Felony', or who they 'have

---

[70] Hale, *Placitorum Coronae*, vol. 2, 89–92; Robert Gardiner, *The Compleat Constable* (London, 1692), 22–3, 66; Hawkins, *Pleas of the Crown*, vol. 2, 76.
[71] *Law of Arrests*, 174, 182; Samuel v Payne (1780), 1 Dougl. 359, 99 *ER* 230; Ledwith v Catchpole (1783) in Thomas Caldecott, *Reports of Cases Relative to the Duty and Office of a Justice of the Peace* (London, 1786), 295.
[72] Dalton, *Countrey Justice*, 296, 268; Sheppard, *Offices of Constables*, 59–60; Hawkins, *Pleas of the Crown*, vol. 2, 76; Burn, *Justice of the Peace*, 69.
[73] Samuel v Payne (1780), 1 Dougl. 359, 99 *ER* 231; Ledwith v Catchpole (1783) in Caldecott, *Reports*, 292.

Cause to suspect of evil Designs'.[74] Second, the laws against night-walking granted broad discretionary powers to arrest people when no particular offence had been committed. The 1285 Statute of Winchester instructed night watchmen to arrest any 'stranger' walking the streets of a town after dark. Subsequent confirmations of this law specified 'any Stranger ... of whom any have suspicion' and added that anyone who was the subject of 'evil Suspicion' should be 'incontinently arrested by the Constables of the Towns'. As Henry Fielding explained, these statutes made it 'lawful to arrest a Night-walker, at a prohibited Time of Night, though no Felony hath been committed'.[75]

Legal writers paid far less attention to the lawfulness or otherwise of arresting night-walkers than they did to arresting suspected felons. As discussed in Chapter 1, some elites felt that their social status placed them above suspicion in this context. Such claims had some basis in law: in 1626, King's Bench judges ruled that Matthias Wheelhorse, though undoubtedly guilty of walking the streets after dark, was not 'a suspicious night-walker' but rather 'a man of good fame' and therefore should have been left to go on his way.[76] In general, however, watchmen and constables were given free rein at night to arrest whoever they suspected of wrongdoing. Discussion of what constituted grounds for suspicion in this context was hampered by confusion about who, at what stage, was responsible for deciding whether or not a night-walker was suspicious. According to some writers, 'Watchmen are to apprehend and examine all strangers that pass by them in the night, and if they find cause of suspition in them, then they may secure them till morning'. Others, by contrast, thought that watchmen should arrest and bring night-walkers to the watch-house indiscriminately for constables to decide whether or not they were suspicious and either release them or take them to a magistrate accordingly.[77]

Vagrancy law gave officers similarly broad discretionary power to arrest its loosely defined targets. Successive statutes ordered officers, under justices' warrants, to arrest 'Rogues Vagabonds wandring and idle p[er]sons'

---

[74] Dalton, *Countrey Justice*, 295; Sheppard, *Offices of Constables*, 62; Hawkins, *Pleas of the Crown*, vol. 2, 77; *Law of Arrests*, 195.

[75] 13 Edw. I c.4 (1285); 5 Edw. III c.14 (1331); Fielding, 'A Treatise', 269. See also *Seipp's Abridgement*, 1497.021 (13 Hen. VII 10 f.10b).

[76] R v Wheelhorse (1626), Popham 208, 79 *ER* 1297.

[77] R Turner, *Duty and Office of a High Constable* (London, 1671), 23; *The Universal Officer of Justice* (London, 1730), 299; Shaw, *Parish Law*, 363; Blackstone, *Commentaries*, vol. 4, 389. The possibility of constables making quasi-judicial decisions in this context continued to unsettle judges into the nineteenth century: Watson v Carr (1823), 1 Lewin 6, 168 *ER* 939.

or 'idle and disorderly Persons'.[78] The meanings of these labels were taken to be self-evident, though even senior lawyers noted their essential vagueness. Matthew Hale criticised seventeenth-century vagrancy law on the grounds that 'It is a difficult thing to determine who shall be said an idle Person'.[79] Some were alarmed by the threat vagrancy legislation posed to English liberty, but these protests tended to focus on the power of magistrates to summarily commit people to whipping and hard labour in houses of correction, rather than the discretionary arrest of 'vagrants' in the first place. Edward Coke, for example, saw summary justice as contrary to the 'ancient, and fundamentall Law' of Magna Carta's chapter 29. Over a century later, Blackstone still insisted that 'the common law is a stranger' to summary proceedings, which 'threaten the disuse of our admirable and truly English trial by jury'. For the most part though, elites were happy to accept laws which only threatened the liberties of the poor. In 1733, the author of a polemic against the summary powers of excise commissioners acknowledged that such powers already existed under various statutes, but asked 'to what Cases do these Laws extend? Only such as related to Vagabonds, Hedge-Stealers and other disorderly Persons, who are known to live by pilfering, or can give no Account of Themselves'.[80] According to Christopher Brooks, summary justice was generally tolerated by lawyers in spite of chapter 29 because its targets 'fell outside the normal definitions of freemen, or indeed, freewomen'.[81]

In combination, statutes against vagrancy and night-walking provided a legal basis for the policing of sex work. Before the nineteenth century, no legislation specifically criminalised the selling of sex. John Fielding complained to a House of Commons committee in 1770 of 'the great difficulty, as the law now stands, to punish those offenders, they being, as common prostitutes, scarce, if at all, within the description of any Statute now in being'.[82] Instead, suspected women were charged in large numbers

---

[78] Major legislation included: 7 Jac I c.4 (1609); 11 Wm III c.18 (1700); 13 Anne c.26 (1714); 13 Geo II c.24 (1740); 17 Geo II c.5 (1744). On vagrancy law in general, see Audrey Eccles, *Vagrancy in Law and Practice under the Old Poor Law* (Farnham, 2012); David Hitchcock, *Vagrancy in English Culture and Society, 1650–1750* (London, 2016).
[79] Matthew Hale, *A Discourse Touching Provision for the Poor* (London, 1683), 12.
[80] Coke, *Second Part of the Institutes*, 51; Blackstone, *Commentaries*, vol. 4, 277–8; Caleb D'Anvers [Nicholas Amhurst], *The Second part of an Argument Against Excises* (London, 1733), 11.
[81] Christopher W. Brooks, *Law, Politics and Society in Early Modern England* (Cambridge, 2008), 419. See also A. L. Beier, *Masterless Men: The Vagrancy Problem in England 1560–1640* (London, 1985), 157.
[82] Quoted in Tony Henderson, *Disorderly Women in Eighteenth-Century London: Prostitution and Control in the Metropolis 1730–1830* (London, 1999), 144. The first piece of legislation to refer explicitly to 'prostitutes' was the Vagrancy Act of 1822 (3 Geo IV c.40).

as night-walkers or as 'lewd, idle and disorderly persons' under vagrancy law. In London, in the late seventeenth and early eighteenth centuries, both of these offences were firmly gendered. Over the course of the seventeenth century, London was transformed from a majority-male to a majority-female city. This was largely driven by the immigration of large numbers of young women from other parts of the country in search of work. Many of these women found apprenticeships or employment in the textile trades, but many more entered domestic service, working under insecure verbal contracts that left them vulnerable to sudden changes of circumstance.[83] When things went wrong, some turned periodically to less legitimate ways of making a living, including sex work.[84] The loose legal categories of vagrancy and suspicious night-walking left it to officers to differentiate women selling sex from those running lawful errands for their families or employers.[85]

In the first decade of the eighteenth century, chief justice John Holt tried to restrict the scope of officers' discretion in arresting women on these terms. He was not the first judge to attempt this, though his efforts are by far the best documented.[86] In the spirit of Magna Carta, he demanded the protection of liberty by due process. In 1701, he argued that a woman had been wrongly incarcerated in London's New Prison as a 'lewd, idle and disorderly person' for simply being in the wrong place. 'What is it makes a lewd person?' he asked, 'It is not being catched in a house of bawdry, or a disorderly house at a seasonable time.' It is worth noting, however, that Holt accepted magistrates' powers to decide who counted as 'lewd and disorderly' according to their own discretion and without providing any particular justification. The problem in this case was that a justification

---

[83] Roger Finlay, *Population and Metropolis: The Demography of London 1580–1650* (Cambridge, 1981), 139–42; Laura Gowing, *Ingenious Trade: Women and Work in Seventeenth-Century London* (Cambridge, 2021).

[84] Eleanor Hubbard, *City Women: Money, Sex, & the Social Order in Early Modern London* (Oxford, 2012), 79–110; Faramerz Dabhoiwala, 'The Pattern of Sexual Immorality in Seventeenth- and Eighteenth-Century London' in Paul Griffiths and Mark S. R. Jenner (eds.), *Londinopolis: Essays in the Cultural and Social History of Early Modern London* (Manchester, 2000).

[85] On official attitudes to mobile women in an earlier period, see Laura Gowing, '"The freedom of the streets": women and social space, 1560–1640' in Griffiths and Jenner (eds.), *Londinopolis*.

[86] In 1521 a London constable sued a man for defamation when the latter suggested he might be 'rebuked' by the justices of King's Bench for arresting women 'without any offence' and setting them in the stocks: Fyfield v Hodgeson (1521) in R. H. Helmholz (ed.), *Select Cases in Defamation to 1600* (London, 1985), 14. In 1588, the court of Star Chamber punished the sheriffs of London for sending two noblewomen to Bridewell 'w[i]thout anie iust grounde … as women of Lewde behavior': Attorney-General v Skynner & Catcher (1588), BL Add. MS 48064 f.207, BL Harley MS 2143 f.44. The latter case is also reported in Richard Crompton, *L'Authoritie et Iurisdiction des Courts de la Maiestie de la Roygne* (London, 1594), f.31.

had been provided, and it was insufficient. After 'affidavits were read of her lewdness', Holt raised no objections to committing the woman to the Marshalsea.[87]

The chief justice made a more substantial effort to limit the arbitrary arrest of women suspected of sex work in 1709. The issue arose in connection with the trials of three soldiers for the murder of a London constable, discussed in some detail in Chapter 2. At around 9 pm one spring evening, constable Thomas Bray arrested Anne Dickins near Drury Lane playhouse, a woman he described as 'a reputed Common whore and a loose Idle disorderly Person plying there'. As the case progressed through the courts, it became clear that Bray had arrested Dickins before. His justification for this second arrest was that 'We knew her to be a very common Woman of the Town, and in a common plying Place for such People, therefore we took her up.' In legal terms, Bray's claim was that his personal knowledge of Dickins' life, combined with her reputation and her presence in 'a common plying Place', justified her arrest under vagrancy law. In the early stages of the case, the political diarist Narcissus Luttrell referred to Dickins straightforwardly as 'a lewd woman'. By the time it was discussed by senior judges at Serjeant's Inn, he had switched to a more cautious legal formulation, stating that Dickins was apprehended 'under pretence of being an idle and disorderly person'.[88]

Holt, who heard the case at Queen's Bench and gave the final ruling at Serjeant's Inn, refused to accept this justification. 'Why does this Man meddle with this Woman', he asked, 'when she was walking about civilly? What! must not a Woman, tho' she be lewd, have the liberty to walk quietly about the Streets?' The arrest of Dickins, he argued, was a violation of fundamental rights: 'a light Woman hath a right of Liberty as well as another to walk about the Streets. The Life of a Man, and the Liberty of the Subject, is a tender thing'.[89] Another justice laid out the arguments against Bray's conduct more prosaically. The constable, he argued,

> hath Invaded the Liberty of the Subject. 1st: He hath Seized this Woman Anne Deakins without any Cause or Ground; for the Woman did no ill thing, but only M[aste]r Constable had an ill Opinion of her and conceived

---

[87] Elizabeth Claxton's Case (1701), Holt (KB) 406, 90 *ER* 1124; R v Symonds (1701), 1 Ld. Raym. 699, 91 *ER* 1366.
[88] LMA, MJ/SP/1709/04/010, Information of Samuel Bray, 19 Mar 1709; Thomas Bray, *The Tryals of Jeremy Tooley, William Arch, and John Clauson* (London, 1732), 6; Narcissus Luttrell, *A Brief Historical Relation of State Affairs from September 1678 to April 1714*, 6 volumes (Oxford, 1857), vol. 6, 420, 463, 510.
[89] Bray, *Tryals*, 18–19.

her to be Lewd, what reason he hath doth not appear Unless it was that she was Walking first between the Play house and Rose Tavern, but neither came from nor was going to the other. 2ndly: He had taken her before as an Idle and Enormious [deviant/wicked] person, but that She was so or that he had any reason to take her as such doth not appear. But 3dly he could have no reason to take her as an Idle and Disorderly Person Virtute Officii for Idle and Disorderly Persons are not breakers of the Peace.

The arrest made by Bray, according to these objections, was legally groundless. Constables could arrest peace-breakers without a warrant, but Dickins had not broken the peace. Under vagrancy law, they could arrest suspected idle and disorderly persons, but not without a magistrate's warrant to search for such people, which Bray did not have. Under common law, constables could arrest suspected felons without warrant, but this required them to show 'a Sufficient ground for Suspition, and not as Mr Bray hath done to Shew that he had Arrested the Woman once and therefore for the same reason Arrested her again'. As one of the lawyers in the case argued, Dickins was not a suspicious person 'for she was very decent at the time, and therefore no cause of suspicion' could be held against her. This lawyer suggested that the officers should, instead, 'have found her to be a night-walker, as is usual in those cases' – no warrant or specific grounds for suspicion would then have been required.[90]

The central problem with the arrest, as Holt and others saw it, was that Dickins 'did no ill thing', 'had done no Crime', or 'any unlawful Action'. The suspicions of an officer were not reason enough in themselves. As Holt argued, 'it is not a Constable's suspecting a Man to do an evil Thing, that will entitle him to take him up, but there must be some Fact done ... It is a hard Case if the Liberty of the Subject shall depend upon the good Opinion of the Constable'. In his final ruling, Holt invoked the ultimate authority: 'Bray took this Woman up upon a bare Suspicion that she was lewd; and is not that against Magna Charta?'[91] This line of constitutional argument was allied to a more direct attack on Societies for the Reformation of Manners. Constable Bray was 'a Reformer' who, as Shoemaker has shown, often worked with these societies in the pursuit and prosecution of vice.

---

[90] BL, Add. MS 35979, 'Law Reports, being cases tried before Sir John Holt, Chief Justice', 69–v; R v Tooley (1709), 11 Mod. 242, 88 *ER* 1015. Holt had vindicated a constable who arrested a prominent physician for nightwalking in 1691, stating that 'the Constable had done what was his duty, and could do no lesse': Mark Knights (ed.), *The Entring Book of Roger Morrice*, vol. 5 (Woodbridge, 2017), 562.

[91] *A Report of All the Cases Determined by Sir John Holt, Knt. from 1688 to 1710, during Which Time He Was Lord Chief Justice of England* (London, 1738), 488–9, 491; Bray, *Tryals*, 29–30.

Holt complained that under their influence 'Constables now a days make a comon practice of taking up People only for walking the Streets. I dont know whence they have this Authority; its more than they can justify'. He did not object to the motives of the constables like Bray but could not approve of their methods: 'No man ought to think himself so far more righteous than his Neighbours as to enter into such Voluntary Societys for Reformation of Manners, as contradict the Laws & endanger our Rights & Liberties.'[92] Holt was portrayed as an enemy to the Societies in *The Tatler* in the same year as the Anne Dickins case, and one contemporary later wrote that he 'did not approve … of voluntary combinations for putting laws into execution'.[93]

For the most part, however, Holt's call for due process and higher evidentiary standards fell on deaf ears.[94] Tim Hitchcock and Robert Shoemaker found a dip the number of offences prosecuted by the reforming Societies in 1709, but this was only temporary and the overall rate at which allegedly 'lewd' women were arrested and incarcerated remained high.[95] Dabhoiwala has argued that by the mid-eighteenth century 'the idea had become firmly established that street-walking by prostitutes was not itself punishable'.[96] Whether or not this was true, 'street-walking' remained a tolerated (albeit legally vague) justification for arrest. In 1759, judges upheld the arrest of Margaret Prince by a watchman in St Martin's in the Fields for 'behaving herself riotously, and walking the streets there to pick up men'. One judge commented that 'The peace of this city can never be preserved, unless watchmen are supported in doing their duty'. No questions were asked about the watchman's grounds for labelling Prince 'a common street-walker' and

---

[92] BL, Add. MS 35994, 'Law Reports 1722–3 and Miscellaneous', 94, 96v, 99; Shoemaker, *Prosecution and Punishment*, 244 n.27.

[93] *The Tatler*, ed. Donald Bond (Oxford, 1987), vol. 1, no. 14, 119–21; *Bishop Burnet's History of His Own Time: With Suppressed Passages of the First Volume, and Notes by the Earls of Dartmouth and Hardwicke, and Speaker Onslow, Hitherto Unpublished* ed. Martin Joseph Routh (Oxford, 1823), vol. 5, 18–19.

[94] The most recent assessment of Holt's jurisprudence casts him as a proceduralist committed to authority of the courts and the letter of the law, rather than a champion of liberty: G. E. Artley, 'Law and politics under the later Stuarts: Sir John Holt, the courts, and the constitutional crisis of 1688' (University of Oxford D.Phil thesis, 2019).

[95] Hitchcock and Shoemaker, *London Lives*, 60, 107; Faramerz Dabhoiwala, 'Summary Justice in Early Modern London', *English Historical Review* 121.492 (2006), 813.

[96] Faramerz Dabhoiwala, *The Origins of Sex: A History of the First Sexual Revolution* (London, 2012), 73. A number of other historians have taken Holt's words in the Dickins case as evidence of a general respect for women's right to walk the streets freely, rather than a challenge to existing practices of policing: Penelope J. Corfield, 'Walking the City Streets: The Urban Odyssey in Eighteenth-Century England', *Journal of Urban History* 16.2 (1990), 134.

no reference was made to the arrest of Anne Dickins or Holt's ruling in her case.[97]

The experiences of Anne Dickins and Margaret Prince were far from unusual. London's fraternities of male officers routinely made arrests on the basis of suspicion alone, often targeting women they considered likely to sell sex or commit theft. These assumptions were guided by social status as well as gender. To fully understand them requires a detailed reconstruction of the practice of arrest on suspicion.

Suspicion in Action

Historians of policing have only recently begun to appreciate the importance of suspicion in pre-nineteenth century practices of law enforcement. Eleanor Bland has argued that arrests on suspicion were a key part of the activities of London officers in the decades both preceding and following the creation of the Metropolitan Police in 1829.[98] The sample of arrests recorded in the Old Bailey *Proceedings* and Middlesex Sessions papers shows that this was equally true in the late seventeenth and early eighteenth centuries. Among those cases described in sufficient detail to establish what prompted an arrest, suspicion provided the immediate grounds for action more often than anything else (Table 3). Prosecutors, defendants, and witnesses frequently stated that one person had arrested another for some 'suspected' offence, or that an arrest had been made 'upon suspicion' of crime.[99] Suspicion also lay behind many arrests which appeared to be prompted by other things, meaning the figures in Table 3 probably underestimate the proportion of arrests made on this basis. Some offenders were only caught in the act because witnesses or victims already suspected them and so watched their movements closely.[100] Arrests of people who

---

[97] R v Bootie (1759), 2 Burr. 864, 97 *ER* 605.
[98] Eleanor Bland, *Policing Suspicion: Proactive Policing in London, 1780–1850* (Abingdon, 2021).
[99] The phrase 'upon suspicion' occurs 133 times in the Old Bailey Proceedings between 1674 and 1750, often in connection with arrests, including the following: Oct 1677, trial of J.S., W.F (t16771010-3); Jul 1685, trial of John Williams, John Sparrow (t16850716-21); Oct 1707, trial of John Timms (t17071015-3); Jan 1708, trial of Francis Read (t17080115-2); Dec 1709, trial of Mary Haynes (t17091207-4); Apr 1710, trial of Mary Boreman (t17100418-43); Feb 1723, trial of Richard Evans, Edward Lewis (t17230227-30); Feb 1725, trial of John Bavan (t17250224-18); Jan 1735, trial of Jane Heybourn (t17350116-47). Examples from the Middlesex Quarter Sessions include: MJ/SP/1696/05/020, Information of Samuel Poulson, undated; MJ/SP/1697/07/035, Examination of Edward Davis, 7 Jun 1697; MJ/SP/1699/05/041, Information of Mary Temple, 28 Apr 1699; MJ/SP/1699/07/055, Information of Thomas White, 27 Jun 1699; MJ/SP/1704/09/023, Information of John Kingsbury, 22 Aug 1704.
[100] *OBP*, Aug 1723, trial of Elizabeth Doyle, Frances Doyle (t17230828-2); *OBP*, May 1730, trial of Rowland Friend (t17300513-4); *OBP*, Sep 1731, trial of Edward Martin (t17310908-39).

Table 3 *Prompts for arrests recorded at the Old Bailey and Middlesex Quarter Sessions, 1674–1750*

Prompt for arrest	Old Bailey	Middlesex Sessions
Suspicion	209 (31.9 per cent)	63 (42.6 per cent)
Caught in the act or pursued from the scene	207 (31.6 per cent)	57 (38.5 per cent)
Caught selling stolen goods or using counterfeit coins[a]	128 (19.5 per cent)	7 (4.7 per cent)
Information from others[b]	63 (9.6 per cent)	17 (9.5 per cent)
Recognised by witness or from circulated description[c]	49 (7.5 per cent)	4 (2.7 per cent)
Total no. arrests where sufficient detail recorded	656	148

[a] These cases typically involved a pawnbroker or shopkeeper 'stopping' goods which someone offered to sell them on the suspicion they might be stolen, then making enquiries about rightful ownership. The relative prominence of this activity in the OBP compared to the Middlesex Sessions records reflects the large numbers of high value theft cases heard at the Old Bailey.
[b] In these cases, an officer or victim of crime received 'information' about a suspect's identity or whereabouts, typically from a witness, accomplice, or thief-taker, then made the arrest themselves.
[c] These cases involved either coincidences (in which victims or witnesses who had seen a crime committed later encountered suspects elsewhere) or the operation of crime advertising, as described in John Styles, 'Sir John Fielding and the Problem of Criminal Investigation in Eighteenth-Century England', *Transactions of the Royal Historical Society* 33 (1983); John Styles, 'Print and Policing: Crime Advertising in Eighteenth-Century Provincial England' in Hay and Snyder (eds.), *Policing and Prosecution*.

tried to sell stolen goods were sometimes made on suspicion when it was unclear whether or not the goods were in fact stolen.[101] Information provided by others could – under the common law powers discussed above – provide grounds for an officer to make an arrest on suspicion as well as details of a suspect's identity or whereabouts.[102] It is also possible that substantial numbers of people arrested on suspicion were discharged by magistrates on grounds of insufficient evidence, leaving no trace in any court records.[103]

[101] *OBP*, Sep 1722, trial of Charles Palmer (t17220907-44); *OBP*, Sep 1722, trial of James Sparry, Edward Raymund (t17220907-63); *OBP*, Jan 1725, trial of Alexander Warren (t17250115-53); *OBP*, Jul 1730, trial of James Brennan (t17300704-63); *OBP*, Jan 1735, trial of Jane Heybourn (t17350116-47).
[102] LMA, MJ/SP/1708/07/059, Information of William Wood, 23 Jul 1708; *OBP*, May 1724, trial of Thomas Winter (t17240521-23).
[103] Magistrates were technically obliged to send all alleged felons to trial, but increasingly chose to dismiss those accusations they deemed groundless: Beattie, *Crime and the Courts*, 274–5.

Table 4 *Prompts for arrests by officers and non-officers, 1674–1750*[a]

Prompt	Old Bailey		Middlesex Sessions	
	Officers	Non-officers	Officers	Non-officers
Suspicion	47 (43.1 per cent)	70 (30.7 per cent)	19 (51.4 per cent)	32 (36.0 per cent)
Caught/pursued	17 (15.6 per cent)	96 (42.1 per cent)	6 (16.2 per cent)	43 (48.3 per cent)
Goods/coins	10 (9.2 per cent)	31 (13.6 per cent)	2 (5.4 per cent)	4 (4.5 per cent)
Information	19 (17.4 per cent)	15 (6.6 per cent)	9 (24.3 per cent)	7 (7.9 per cent)
Recognised	16 (14.7 per cent)	16 (7.0 per cent)	1 (2.7 per cent)	3 (3.4 per cent)
Total	109	228	37	89

[a] These figures exclude arrests in which it is impossible to tell whether the arrestor/s held any office.

Officers put their greater powers of arrest on suspicion to extensive use. As shown in Table 4, they were considerably more prone to making arrests on these grounds than other people. This was sometimes a response to commands from magistrates, who periodically issued warrants for the arrest of anyone suspected of particular crimes. In 1695, for example, Middlesex JPs attempting to crack down on theft ordered officers to arrest 'any person of whom you shall have just cause of suspition'. The following year, after an attempt to assassinate the king, they ordered the arrest of 'all Papists, reputed Papists, and other Disaffected Persons … and all other Suspected Persons, who can give no good Account of themselves'.[104] More broadly, arresting on suspicion was part of many officers' ordinary duties. A charge to newly sworn London constables instructed them to arrest 'all Night-Walkers, Malefactors, and suspected Persons' and called on watchmen to arrest 'all disorderly Persons whom you shall find disturbing the Publick Peace, or that you shall have just Cause to suspect of any evil Designs'. The same charge explained that constables should arrest suspected felons on the basis of suspicions brought to them by others: 'if any man doe suspect another of murder or felony, and declare it unto you, or if the comon fame bee that such a one hath co[m]itted a felony, you ought to take into ward, or search for & arrest such malefactor or suspected p[er]son'.[105] Table 4 confirms that arrests made by officers were substantially more likely to be prompted by information from third parties than arrests made by private individuals.

[104] LMA, MJ/SP/1695/12/015; LMA, MJ/SP/1696/04/029.
[105] LMA, CLA/048/PS/01/009/2, undated charge to constables, possibly given in 1697.

In almost half of the arrests on suspicion recorded at the Old Bailey (101 of 209), no specific cause of suspicion was mentioned. People were simply 'suspected' and 'apprehended upon suspicion'. Some provided more detail, like the watchman who told judges in 1733 that he had recognised a suspect's horse from a robbery committed the previous week, then noted the suspect's clumsiness in handling a possibly stolen watch ('I thought by the Manner of his handling it, that he had not been much us'd to a Watch'), and spotted a pistol in the suspect's pocket, all of which 'made me conclude' the man was a highway robber.[106] In general, however, officers were particularly unlikely to explain why they deemed a person suspicious or to have their explanations recorded by the court. Of the forty-seven cases of arrest on suspicion by officers, thirty-three (70.2 per cent) included no particular justification.

In her work on law enforcement in Sussex, Cynthia Herrup argued that arrests were made on the basis of 'ad hoc evidentiary standards' which amounted to 'a flexible, but relatively consistent, definition of probable cause in larceny'.[107] In fact, grounds for arrest on suspicion – at least as they were recorded in the courts – may have been less ad hoc than at first appears. The law of suspicion developed by common law judges specified a particular set of legitimate grounds for arrest.[108] Many of the causes of suspicion outlined in depositions and trial reports adhere to these standards. Suspects were arrested for keeping company with known felons, for fleeing the scene of the crime, or on the basis of strong circumstantial evidence, like the man who, in 1718, was found covered in blood beside the body of a murdered woman.[109] There were many cases of suspicion based on common fame. This was the single most frequent justification given for arrests on suspicion in the Middlesex Sessions papers (accounting for ten of the sixty-three cases). Officers and others described suspects as a 'reputed Comon Theife', 'a person of very ill fame and reputation', 'p[er]sons of very Evill fame [who] are knowne to be Comon Theeves', or simply 'a notorious theif'.[110] Reputations of this kind may have originated in the opinions of the middling sort, whether or not they were shared by the

---

[106] *OBP*, May 1733, trial of John Davis (t17330510-9).
[107] Herrup, 'New Shoes', 830.
[108] See note 64, above.
[109] LMA, MJ/SP/1696/10/077, Informations of John Day and Elizabeth Day, 30 Sep 1696; *OBP*, Jun 1692, trial of Richard Johnson (t16920629-12); *OBP*, Apr 1718, trial of John Price (t17180423-24).
[110] LMA, MJ/SP/1696/10/073, Informations of James Frimley and John Steward, 26 Sep 1696; MJ/SP/1697/12/038, Informations of Mary Derrickson and Dorothy Martin, 30 Oct 1697; MJ/SP/1699/09/019, Information of Ann Oswald, 14 Aug 1699; MJ/SP/1708/10/092, Information of Mary Dodd, 16 Sep 1708.

majority. In a case from Bradford, a woman was arrested on suspicion of counterfeiting coin because 'div[er]s substantiall Inhabitants in Bradford, hath a suspicon of' her.[111]

Possession of suspicious goods, another justifiable cause of suspicion under common law, was also mentioned frequently. Typically, suspects were spotted carrying bags, boxes, or bundles and required to provide an explanation of how these things came into their possession, which the arrestor might or might not deem satisfactory.[112] In 1699, a Whitechapel woman saw Dorothy Martin with a large bundle in her apron and 'suspecting that the said Martin had Stolen the said Goods in her Apron questioned her ab[ou]t the same, who giving noe good Account thereof, caused her to be Apprehended by an Officer'.[113] In this case and in many others, the victims of the supposed theft were 'persons unknown'. Arrestors simply did not believe that suspects could have acquired the goods they were carrying by any means other than theft. There was, as Bruce Smith has written of summary prosecutions for property crime in the later eighteenth century, a 'presumption of guilt'.[114]

The logic of this presumption, insofar as it can be discerned, was the logic of social status. Suspicion attached itself to a woman who wore clothes 'farr above her Condition', a man who was 'not any wayes suitable to his Horse'.[115] The poor were suspected if they appeared to have become richer. Londoners were arrested on the grounds that they were 'fuller of Money than usual' or 'very full of Money, fared sumptuously, went to Plays, bought new Cloaths, and liv'd merrily, treating all the Company'. Any previously poor person engaged in such performances of prosperity was likely to be asked 'how he came by it'. As one witness at the Old Bailey explained, when a servant and his friend 'had been very lavish in spending their Money ... this giving us sufficient Reason to suspect him, he was apprehended'. Servants and lodgers seem to have been especially vulnerable to this line of suspicion. One woman suspected her lodger of stealing from her because he was 'a poor man' who suddenly 'had got mony'. An

---

[111] TNA, ASSI 45/2/1/130, Deposition of Samuel Holmes, 29 May 1647.
[112] LMA, MJ/SP/1697/12/039, Information of John Barnes, 5 Nov 1697; LMA, MJ/SP/1699/01/058, Information of Oliver Clarke, 20 Dec 1698; LMA, MJ/SP/1704/04/045, Information of John Satchwell, 11 Mar 1704; LMA, MJ/SP/1705/01/009, Information of Susan Matton, 16 Dec 1704; LMA, MJ/SP/1749/07/134, Information of John Thompson, 23 May 1749.
[113] LMA, MJ/SP/1699/02/035, Information of Mary Fainty, 31 Jan 1699.
[114] Bruce P. Smith, 'The Presumption of Guilt and the English Law of Theft, 1750–1850', *Law and History Review* 23.1 (2005); LMA, MJ/SP/1699/07/061, Information of John Begarley, 28 May 1699.
[115] LMA, MJ/SP/1696/10/073, Informations of James Frimley and John Steward, 26 Sep 1696; LMA, MJ/SP/1708/07/059, Information of William Wood, 23 Jul 1708.

Table 5 *Grounds for suspicion in arrests recorded at the Old Bailey, 1674–1750*

Grounds for suspicion	Common fame or character	Seen carrying something	Opportunity to commit crime	Disappeared soon after crime	Other	Total
No. of cases	14 (13.0 per cent)	21 (19.4 per cent)	17 (15.7 per cent)	22 (20.4 per cent)	34	108

innkeeper suspected one of his guests 'for that he had little or no money by his own Confession the night before and the next day he was furnished with Money'.[116]

Servants, lodgers, and anyone else who lived in another person's house could easily be suspected of theft. They had constant access to their hosts' homes and often knew where the valuables were kept. These facts alone could prompt an arrest, so those who attracted more suspicion to themselves (by, e.g., leaving to find work or lodgings elsewhere soon after a theft was committed) stood little chance of escape. As shown in Table 5, disappearing shortly after a crime took place and simply having had the opportunity to commit a crime were among the most common grounds for arrest on suspicion mentioned in the *Proceedings* of the Old Bailey. Almost half (eight out of seventeen) of the suspects arrested on the grounds of opportunity were people who lived or worked in the houses of others: five servants, a day labourer, a charwoman, and a groom. People in similar positions accounted for sixteen of the twenty-two arrests made on the grounds of disappearance: thirteen servants, two apprentices and a lodger.

The concentration of suspicion around servants served to criminalise people on the basis of gender as well as social status. By the late seventeenth century, London's servant trade was dominated by young female migrants. This was especially true of domestic service, which brought these women close to other people's property.[117] In the Old Bailey records, almost two thirds of the arrestees who can be identified as servants were female (41 out of 65). The broader relationship between gender and suspicion is complex. In both the Old Bailey and Middlesex Sessions records, arrests on suspicion were slightly more likely to target women than arrests in general, as

---

[116] *OBP*, May 1724, trial of Thomas Winter (t17240521-23); *OBP*, May 1717, trial of William Collins, Rose Chapman (t17170501-6); *OBP*, Jan 1680, trial of Peter Richardson (t16800115-12); *OBP*, Apr 1741, trial of George Lancaster (t17410405-1); KHLC, Q/SB/9/18, Information of Agnes Lamb, 4 Oct 1663; LMA, MJ/SP/1699/09/035, Information of Robert Nicholls, 8 Sep 1699.

[117] Tim Meldrum, *Domestic Service and Gender 1660–1750: Life and Work in the London Household* (Harlow, 2000).

Table 6 *Gender of arrestees in general and on suspicion in the records of the Old Bailey and Middlesex Quarter Sessions, 1674–1750*[a]

	Old Bailey			
	Arrests of women	Arrests of men	Arrests of mixed groups	Total arrests
All arrests	273 (24.8 per cent)	793 (72.0 per cent)	35 (3.2 per cent)	1,101
Arrests on suspicion	56 (26.8 per cent)	144 (68.9 per cent)	8 (3.8 per cent)	209

	Middlesex Sessions			
	Arrests of women	Arrests of men	Arrests of mixed groups	Total arrests
All arrests	69 (35.6 per cent)	121 (62.4 per cent)	4 (2.1 per cent)	194
Arrests on suspicion	26 (41.3 per cent)	36 (57.1 per cent)	1 (1.6 per cent)	63

[a] In three of the Old Bailey cases and one of the Middlesex Sessions cases the gender of the arrestee/s cannot be identified.

shown in Table 6. This may reflect the tendency of some suspicions – like those of disappearing servants – to attach themselves to women more often than to men. The higher proportion of female arrestees in the Quarter Sessions records, however, points to a complicating factor. Women were charged with some crimes more often than men, and vice versa, so the proportions of women and men who appeared as defendants varied from court to court depending on the types of crime they dealt with.[118] The relatively small numbers of women whose arrests were recorded in the Old Bailey *Proceedings* may reflect the predominance of men among those charged with crimes of serious violence, which made up a considerable part of the business of that court.[119]

---

[118] On gender and crime in general, see Walker, *Crime, Gender and Social Order*; Jennine Hurl-Eamon, *Gender and Petty Violence in London, 1680–1720* (Columbus, 2005); Deirdre Palk, *Gender, Crime and Judicial Discretion 1780–1830* (Woodbridge, 2006). For an older historiography concentrated on changes in the rate at which women were prosecuted, see John M. Beattie, 'The Criminality of Women in Eighteenth-Century England', *Journal of Social History* 8.4 (1975); Malcolm M. Feeley and Deborah L. Little, 'The Vanishing Female: The Decline of Women in the Criminal Process, 1687–1912', *Law & Society Review* 25.4 (1991).

[119] On gender and violence in the Old Bailey records, see Robert B. Shoemaker, 'Reforming Male Manners: Public Insult and the Decline of Violence in London, 1660–1740' in Tim Hitchcock and Michèle Cohen (eds.), *English Masculinities 1660–1800* (London, 1999); Robert Shoemaker, 'Male Honour and the Decline of Public Violence in Eighteenth-Century London', *Social History* 26.2 (2001).

At the other end of the judicial spectrum, summary courts dealt with offences which were increasingly attributed to women. Accounts of law enforcement based exclusively on the records of Assizes or Quarter Sessions rather than summary proceedings risk overlooking many women's experiences of criminal justice. In London, the fraternalisation of law enforcement coincided with a feminisation of the crimes of night-walking and vagrancy, both of which were dealt with by magistrates at a summary level. In the sixteenth century, most of the people prosecuted for these offences in London and elsewhere had been men. This continued to be true across most of the country throughout the seventeenth and eighteenth centuries. In the capital, however, more and more of those charged with night-walking were women accused of sex work, so that by the mid-seventeenth century almost all alleged night-walkers were female. The same was increasingly true of vagrancy, with women making up two-thirds to three-quarters of those brought before London magistrates in the late seventeenth and eighteenth centuries. The numbers committed to various carceral institutions – Bridwell, county houses of correction, workhouses – for these offences was generally several times greater than the number of people tried in the higher courts for crimes against property and the person.[120] Summary records provide minimal details about the circumstances behind these charges, but it seems likely that many journeys to a magistrate's court began with an arrest by an officer on the basis of suspicion. As Shoemaker has explained, officers made 'hasty judgements concerning suspects' characters', especially the moral characters of women.[121]

It does not seem to have taken much to prompt an officer to suspect a woman of theft or selling sex, especially a woman walking the streets alone. Encouraged by Societies for the Reformation of Manners, officers arrested women on vague suspicions of being 'loose' or 'disorderly'.[122] From there it was only a short step to arresting women on suspicion of other offences, especially theft. In 1696, a headborough and four men who held no office broke into a house in Wapping, 'having a susp[i]con' that it was 'a disorderly house'. Inside, they found linen and a glass kettle 'w[hi]ch they suspect to be stolen from some p[er]sons unknown'.

---

[120] Nicholas Rogers, 'Policing the Poor in Eighteenth-Century London: The Vagrancy Laws and Their Administration', *Social History* 24.47 (1991), 133–5; Paul Griffiths, 'Meanings of Nightwalking in Early Modern England', *The Seventeenth Century* 13.2 (1998); Shoemaker, *Prosecution and Punishment*, 169–73, 185–6; Dabhoiwala, 'Summary Justice'; Kiran Mehta, 'Summary Justice in Eighteenth- and Nineteenth-Century Southwark', *Crime, History & Societies* 24.1 (2020), 60, 70–75.
[121] Shoemaker, *Prosecution and Punishment*, 179–80.
[122] Hitchcock and Shoemaker, *London Lives*, 34–41.

They also found three women, who they arrested on the suspicion that they 'stole the said Goods & brought them thither'. In court, the women denied stealing anything and called several witnesses to show that the goods were their own.[123] Many cases like this may have gone unrecorded. Most of the wrongful arrests which reached the courts involved arrestees of relatively high status. Writs of habeas corpus and civil suits of false imprisonment were technically available to anyone, but the costs of such proceedings put them out of reach for most of those arrested for vagrancy, night-walking, or on suspicion of theft.[124] Even those who could afford such remedies may have been put off by the prospect of paying double or even triple legal costs should an officer successfully plead the general issue (see Chapter 2).

In one very unusual case, an officer was charged with defamation after arresting a woman he incorrectly suspected of selling sex. On 2 March 1704, Mary Taylor, a milliner's wife from Bath, was in London staying with friends. At about 8 pm, she went for a walk by the theatre in Covent Garden. At some point, a man began to follow her. She broke into a run. He pursued her. In desperation, she turned into the shop of Margaret and John Langley, a young couple who made mirrors. John later deposed at the Bishop of London's Consistory Court that Taylor wanted him 'to lett her continue there in order to rescue her from a Fellow who came after & whom she thought would use rudeness to her'. Immediately after this, Thomas Row, the local constable, burst into the shop, 'pulled out a Constable staff and demanded her the said Mary Taylor to come out of this Dep[onen]ts said Room in order to be carried by him to the Roundhouse as a Night Walker'. As John Langley explained, Taylor tried to resist:

> the said Mary Taylor refused to come out of the s[ai]d Room saying That shee was an honest woman & that shee could bring severall persons that would give an account of her reputation & honesty & then offered to send the Depon[en]t for some persons (whom this Depon[en]t knowes to be men of Reputation) to speak for her honesty, but the said Thomas Row refused to give the producent [Taylor] time to send for such persons, & said that shee the said producent was a Whore & an Irish Whore & that he knew her to be a Whore, and then imediately he the s[ai]d Thomas Row

---

[123] LMA, MJ/SP/1696/04/053, Informations of Daniel Dier, Griffin Crane, John Carter, John Starling, Peter Johnson, Jane Burton, Elizabeth Downes, Elizabeth Lee, Jane Gibbs, Jane Woodcock, Ellen Branch, Ruth Brookes, 2 Apr 1696.

[124] Shoemaker, *Prosecution and Punishment*, 182; Paul Halliday, *Habeas Corpus: From England to Empire* (Cambridge, MA, 2010), 84–5.

charged the Depon[en]t to assist him to carry her the s[ai]d producent to the Round house, & the Depon[en]t went with her to the Round house & left her there.

Row's declaration that Taylor 'was a Whore & an Irish Whore' provided grounds to sue for defamation in the Consistory Court.[125] Witnesses on the constable's behalf maintained that he had been justified in making such an assumption because 'the lewd women who walke late in the night about the Play house & Covent Garden when they have any notice of the near approaches of the Constables fly & run away & shelter themselves in any shops or houses'.[126] Mary Taylor had inadvertently replicated this suspect behaviour. As a reputable married woman, she was not a typical object of officers' suspicions. In the constable's eyes, however, she was simply a woman walking alone in the wrong place at the wrong time who, when she noticed a man following her, made the wrong move.

Litigation in the ecclesiastical courts was expensive. Many women who had similar experiences to Mary Taylor could not have afforded to leave such a mark on the historical record. Many more could not call on 'men of Reputation' to rescue them from the roundhouse when they were arrested. A pamphlet published in 1754 told the story of three aristocratic women who, pursuing their wayward husbands through London's streets at 3 am, were arrested by a constable who presumed they were 'three of the bettermost sort of Street-Walkers'. Detained in an alehouse, they sent for a prominent local lace-maker who arrived and reprimanded the constable 'very severely for taking People of Distinction into Custody, without a sufficient Warrant or Cause for so doing'.[127] Women lacking 'distinction' might be arrested every night in the capital without 'sufficient cause', but that was not the pamphlet's concern.

Those who were arrested in late seventeenth- and early eighteenth-century London encountered the state in a variety of gendered forms. Many of them were 'knocked down' by men who held no office but who took part in law enforcement as an activity shared by all adult males. More research is needed to establish the precise nature and chronology of this particular convergence between manhood and state authority, but it was certainly no novelty. Unofficial men had participated in making

---

[125] LMA, DL/C/0248, Deposition of John Langley, 7 Oct 1704, ff.231–2; LMA, Deposition of Margaret Langley, 12 Oct 1704, ff.232v–3v.
[126] LMA, DL/C/0248, Deposition of John Crosby, 14 Feb 1704/5, ff.234–5; LMA, Deposition of William Hutchinson, 22 Feb 1704/5, ff.235v–6v.
[127] *The Midnight-Ramble: Or, The Adventures of Two Noble Females* (London, 1754), 20–22.

arrests long before this period and continued to do so long after it. At the same time, however, the capital was increasingly policed by constables and watchmen. These officers possessed distinctive powers to arrest on suspicion, powers which expanded in this period and which they used to the full, especially against poorer women. This was a different kind of gendered policing; the identities of the individual officers who made arrests on suspicion were, in principle, irrelevant. Their authority came not from their manhood but directly from the state, as conjured by Thomas Row's 'Constable staff'. In practice, the way they used that authority was powerfully influenced by the fact that all of them were men. These men treated some groups of people as more suspicious than others. Gender and social status were key factors in many arrests on suspicion. As the following chapter demonstrates, these categories also had a powerful effect on the way in which officers treated suspects before, during, and after an arrest. Those who were most easily suspected were also the least protected against invasive official power.

CHAPTER 5

Searches

Many of the themes of this book come together around searches for evidence of crime. Different kinds of searches illustrated different aspects of the relationship between gender and policing. In searches of houses, impersonal authority granted by the law of office collided with the old valorisation of the household. The rise of 'ministerial' models of officeholding meant that households no longer provided the key source of authority in office, but they retained a special position in other areas of law. In the context of searches, households were the primary obstacle to officers' intrusive powers. Common law and a growing number of statutes authorised forcible entry into houses to search for a wide variety of illicit objects, but doors and walls remained legal and cultural barriers as well as physical ones. Those who could take refuge behind such barriers were far better protected from searches than those who could not. Searches of people, by contrast, were entirely unregulated by law. Here officers and other searchers possessed total discretion. In London in the late seventeenth and early eighteenth centuries, constables and watchmen used that discretion – as they used their discretionary powers of arrest – according to assumptions about gender and social status. The same groups of poorer women who officers saw as almost inherently suspicious were subjected to especially invasive searches. In the absence of any legal protection, such women had to fight for boundaries based on modesty and propriety to protect their bodies from physical intrusions carried out in the name of the state.

Like arrests, searches were integral to the everyday functioning of the criminal law. Successful prosecutions required evidence, and much evidence was secured by searching places and people. The results of searches provided 'the most material Circumstances' at trial; suspects were often condemned or acquitted on the basis of what was or was not found in their possession. The discovery of stolen goods, weapons, contraband, or any other incriminating items in the custody of a suspect was said to supply 'full proof of the Fact'.[1] Cynthia Herrup noted that searches were 'the most common type of investigation' in the criminal process, but scholarship on this subject remains in its infancy.[2] Little work has been done on who or what was searched, by whom, in what manner, and under what circumstances. This chapter, like the previous one, reconstructs the law and practice of these routine procedures and the ways in which they were shaped by gender. It moves from a general account of house-searching in early modern England to a detailed analysis of how different people and places were searched in London's emerging culture of highly gendered policing.

Searching Houses

On the face of it, searching a house for evidence of crime violated two of this period's most cherished ideological constructs: property and the bounded household. In the seventeenth and eighteenth centuries, a growing number of political writers (and property-owners) believed that one of the central purposes of the state was to protect property. If this was true, how could that purpose be served by allowing outsiders to enter a person's property and conduct a search? Statutes mandated brutal punishments for crimes against property, and the prosecution of all kinds of theft made up the bulk of proceedings at Quarter Sessions and Assizes. But protecting property in this way required that officers and others be granted powers to search for thieves and stolen goods. Paradoxically, when their searches took them over the threshold of a house, they invaded the householder's own property. In pursuit of stolen goods, searchers forced their way into suspected houses and hunted for valuables in a manner strikingly similar to that of burglars and housebreakers. As we shall see, this comparison was not lost on contemporaries. The risk that searching could in fact be stealing heightened the need for impersonal authority in the form of officers and warrants, which made searching houses one of the most highly regulated aspects of law enforcement.

Such regulation also had to account for the sensitivities of householders, many of whom saw the boundaries of the house as the borders of their independent domain. Historians of domestic space have shown that

---

[1] *OBP*, Oct 1727, trial of Sarah Griffiths (t17271017-6); Oct 1731, trial of John Everett (t17311013-37).
[2] Cynthia Herrup, 'New Shoes and Mutton Pies: Investigative Responses to Theft in Seventeenth-Century East Sussex', *Historical Journal* 27.4 (1984), 819. See also Cynthia B. Herrup, *The Common Peace: Participation and the Criminal Law in Seventeenth-Century England* (Cambridge, 1987), 74–9.

doors, walls, and windows were often extremely permeable in practice, especially in towns and cities, but many people felt what Lena Orlin calls 'a frustrated yearning for clear boundaries and impregnable perimeters'.[3] That yearning was strongly supported by law. In Amanda Vickery's words, 'the domestic threshold was sacrosanct; in fact, the law had erected a fortification around it'. It was a well-established principle that householders could use serious force to protect their homes from invasion by outsiders but, as Christopher Brooks noted, 'the question of how far officials of one kind or another might be permitted to enter was more debatable'.[4] Such an entry could be construed as trespassing into a householder's territory, which might well be met with violence.

The protection of houses runs deep in both English and continental European law. Tenth-century law codes made violence within a house more punishable than violence outside it, while the Roman law maxim *domus sua cuique titussimum refugium* (everyone's house is their safest refuge) was a commonplace among English lawyers from at least the late fifteenth century.[5] The most influential statement of this principle was made by Edward Coke in his commentary on the early seventeenth-century King's Bench case of Semayne v Gresham: 'the House of every man is to him as his Castle, and Fortresse, as well for his defence against injuries and violence, as for his repose'. In accordance with this idea, he affirmed the longstanding principle that it was lawful to beat or even kill a person who tried to force entry into a house. The details of the case, however, present a more complex picture. Semayne had sent a sheriff and a jury of appraisers to value and confiscate goods from Gresham's house in lieu of unpaid debts, but 'Gresham perceiving, before the sheriff had enter'd the house, shut the door of the said house, and would not suffer the sheriff nor the jury to enter to view and praise the goods'. According to two of the King's Bench judges, 'Gresham has done nothing but what he may lawfully justify, viz. shut his own doors'. Others were not so sure, suggesting that 'by

---

[3] Lena Cowen Orlin, 'Boundary Disputes in Early Modern London' in Lena Cowen Orlin (ed.), *Material London ca. 1600* (Philadelphia, 2000), 372; Lena Cowen Orlin, *Private Matters and Public Culture in Post-Reformation England* (Ithaca, 1994); Jennifer Melville, 'The use and organisation of domestic space in late seventeenth-century London' (University of Cambridge PhD thesis, 1999); Vanessa Harding, 'Space, Property and Propriety in Urban England', *Journal of Interdisciplinary History* 32.4 (2002); Christoph Heyl, 'We Are Not at Home: Protecting Domestic Privacy in Post-Fire Middle-Class London', *The London Journal* 27.2 (2002).
[4] Amanda Vickery, 'An Englishman's Home Is His Castle? Thresholds, Boundaries and Privacies in the Eighteenth-Century London House', *Past & Present* 199 (2008), 155–6; Christopher W. Brooks, *Law, Politics and Society in Early Modern England* (Cambridge, 2008), 357.
[5] T. B. Lambert, 'Theft, Homicide and Crime in Late Anglo-Saxon Law', *Past & Present* 214 (2012), 27; Brooks, *Law, Politics and Society*, 355.

this means justice is hinder'd'. Eventually, the judges ruled unanimously in favour of Gresham, but only after agreeing that if the sheriff had been acting for the crown rather than a private individual, he could have lawfully broken down the door to enter. In Coke's words, 'in all cases where the King is party, the Sheriffe may breake the House (if the Doores be shut) and make Execution of his Writ'.[6] This distinction between private and crown suits was upheld in subsequent rulings and soon entrenched in influential legal treatises.[7] In the words of one justice, 'the law gives the house many privileges, yet the law does not privilege houses against itself'. Or, as Michael Dalton commented on Coke's report of Semayne's case, 'no mans house shall bee a Castle against the king'.[8]

Statute and common law laid out the specific causes for which officers could force their way into houses under royal authority. Elizabethan and Jacobean legislation allowed constables to break down doors in search of vagrants or poaching equipment.[9] Under the 1601 poor law, parish officers could force entry to distrain goods in lieu of unpaid poor rates or to take inventories – and inspect the moral quality – of paupers' homes.[10] Royal charters granted guild officials the power to search houses for substandard wares and unregulated manufacturing.[11] For a brief period in the

---

[6] *An Exact Abridgement in English of the Eleven Books of Reports of the Learned Sir Edward Coke* (London, 1650), 221–3. The case was first heard in 1602, then reviewed two years later: Semayne v Gresham (1602), Yelverton 29, 80 *ER* 21; Semayne v Gresham (1602), Moore (KB) 668, 72 *ER* 828; Semayne v Gresham (1604), 5 Co. Rep. 91a, 77 *ER* 194. Also reported piecemeal at BL Add. MS 25213 ff. 41, 43v, 55, 58. Killing in defence of a house was similarly justifiable under German law: B. Ann Tlusty, *The Martial Ethic in Early Modern Germany: Civic Duty and the Right of Arms* (Basingstoke, 2011), 58.

[7] Rape v Girlin (1607) in William Paley Baildon (ed.), *Les reportes del cases in Camera Stellata, 1593 to 1609: from the Original MS. of John Hawarde* (London, 1894), 324–6; White v Whitshire (1619), Cro. Jac. 555, 79 *ER* 476, Palmer 52, 81 *ER* 973, Harvey v Oldfield (1674), 1 Freeman 339, 89 *ER* 252.

[8] White v Whitshire (1619), 2 Rolle 137, 81 *ER* 709; Michael Dalton, *The Countrey Justice* (London, 1618), 177. Semayne's case followed two earlier rulings which held that it was unlawful for officers to break into houses 'unless for felony or treason': Smith v Smith (1600), Cro. Eliz. 741, 78 *ER* 974; South v Whitewit (1600), Owen 145, 74 *ER* 963.

[9] 14 Eliz I c.5 (1572); 7 Jac I c.4 (1609); 7 Jac I c.11 (1609).

[10] 43 Eliz I c.2 (1601); Steve Hindle, *On the Parish? The Micro-Politics of Poor Relief in Rural England c.1550–1750* (Oxford, 2004), 259; Joseph Harley, 'Pauper Inventories, Social Relations, and the Nature of Poor Relief under the Old Poor Law, England, c.1601–1834', *Historical Journal* 62.2 (2019). On distraint more generally, see Sara Pennell, 'Happiness in Things? Plebeian Experiences of Chattel "Property" in the Long Eighteenth Century' in Michael J. Braddick and Joanna Innes (eds.), *Suffering and Happiness in England 1550–1850: Narratives and Representations* (Oxford, 2017).

[11] Michael Berlin, '"Broken all in pieces": Artisans and the Regulation of Workmanship in Early Modern London' in Geoffrey Crossick (ed.), *The Artisan and the European Town, 1500–1900* (Abingdon, 1997); Joseph P. Ward, *Metropolitan Communities: Trade Guilds, Identity, and Change in Early Modern London* (Stanford, 1997), Chapter 2; Patrick Wallis, 'Controlling Commodities: Search and Reconciliation in Early Modern Livery Companies' in Ian Anders Gadd and Patrick Wallis (eds.), *Guilds, Society and Economy in London 1450–1800* (London, 2002).

1650s, constables were granted the power to enter any house in search of prohibited activity during the sabbath, though this was soon restricted to alehouses.[12] After the Restoration, powers to force entry into houses were dramatically extended by a long barrage of statutes. Parliament licensed officers to breach domestic boundaries under Conventicle Acts, Excise Acts, Vagrancy Acts, Impressment Acts, and many others.[13] If, as one legal writer claimed, 'the Law never allows such Extremities but in Cases of Necessity', then it would seem that 'necessity' covered a broad range of legislative concerns.[14] In the words of legal scholar William Cuddihy, 'everything from the food that an Englishman put into his mouth and the cap that he wore on his head to the thoughts circulating in his mind came to furnish legal pretexts for the government to inspect his home'. Looming behind all of these new powers was the common law endorsement of forcible entries to search for suspected felons or stolen goods.[15] Taken together, the various laws of entry substantially undermined householders' defences against official intrusion.

Nonetheless, many householders did resist attempts to enter their homes, resorting to a range of measures from locking doors to full-scale armed opposition.[16] The records of Southwark and Middlesex Quarter Sessions contain numerous presentments from constables complaining that alehouse-keepers and others refused to open their doors to let them search for vagrants, drunks, and gamblers. In 1721, in an attempt to strengthen their campaign against 'disorderly houses', Middlesex justices petitioned the Lord Chancellor to create a new offence of refusing to open the door to a constable.[17] The widely despised officers of excise often met

---

[12] Bernard Capp, *England's Culture Wars: Puritan Reformation and Its Enemies in the Interregnum, 1649–60* (Oxford, 2012), 29–30.
[13] 12 Car II c.19, s.1 (1660); 14 Car II c.11, s.4 (1662); 15 Car II c.11 (1663); 22 Car II c.1, s.8 (1670); 10 Wm III c.4, s.7 (1698); 3&4 Anne c.10 (1704); 4&5 Anne c.6 (1705); 10 Anne c.18, s.103 (1711); 13 Anne c.26, s.3 (1713); 10 Geo I c.10, s.13 (1723); 9 Geo II c.23, s.9 (1736); 15&16 Geo II c.32, s.2 (1742); 17 Geo II c.5, s.6 (1744); 25 Geo II c.36, s.2 (1752).
[14] *The Law of Arrests in Both Civil and Criminal Cases* (Savoy, 1742), 235. On the law of 'necessity', see John M. Collins, 'The Long Parliament and the Law of Necessity in Seventeenth-Century England', *Past & Present* 247.1 (2020).
[15] William J. Cuddihy, *The Fourth Amendment: Origins and Original Meaning 602–1791* (Oxford, 2009), 44; Matthew Hale, *Historia Placitorum Coronae*, vol. 2 (London, 1736), 92, 95, 150.
[16] For comparable clashes over searches by guild officials in an early modern German town, see Philip R. Hoffmann, 'In Defence of Corporate Liberties: Early Modern Guilds and the Problem of Illicit Artisan Work', *Urban History* 34.1 (2007).
[17] LMA, Southwark Quarter Sessions Papers, CLA/046/03/001, Presentments of the constables of St Olaves, St Saviours, St Thomas, 1684–1712, unnumbered; Robert B. Shoemaker, *Prosecution and Punishment: Petty Crime and the Law in London and Rural Middlesex, c.1660–1725* (Cambridge, 1991), 167–8.

with similar hostility over domestic thresholds. Minutes of meetings of the Board of Commissioners contain repeated references to fines levied on brewers, distillers, and others for 'obstructing an officer in the due execucion of his Office', generally by shutting the door in his face, sometimes by beating him until he went away. Such resistance could even receive judicial endorsement, as when Kentish magistrates ruled that a man had acted justifiably in chasing excisemen off his farm with a pitchfork. Another Kentishman was so confident in his right to defend his house that when a constable came to arrest him for theft he 'made fast the door & looked out of the Window … & bid defiance to his power & bid him break open the Door at his perill'.[18]

Those who opposed searches acted on the assumption that there was no real distinction between lawful and unlawful attempts to enter a house. Like those who confused officers with criminals, as discussed in Chapter 2, they claimed that a person searching for illicit goods was no different to a thief searching for goods to steal, and that forceful resistance to either was mandated by law. In 1706, two wardens of the Norwich worsted weavers company tried to search a house for 'Defective Yarnes' but were obstructed by the owner, who 'Told them that they were no better then Highwaymen & that they came to Robb him & take away what he had', insisting that 'he could Crowd theives out of his house at any time'. In the same spirit, a Whitechapel publican stopped a customs officer leaving his house with what he claimed was a contraband punch-bowl: 'I ask'd him if he had a Deputation to go a Thieving, and not finding that he did, I carried him before a Justice, and the Justice committed him to Newgate'. One London householder told a constable who came to search that 'if he went up Stairs, she would fetch a Warrant for him'. Another similarly threatened the woman who searched her house for stolen goods: 'Touch the Things out of my Room, and I'll send you to Newgate'. A third 'threatned to swear a Robbery against' the churchwarden who 'came to search her House for Disorderly Persons'.[19] These concerns were not new: in 1600, a judge had argued that without significant constraints on the power to force entry 'a man may be robb'd in his house'.[20]

---

[18] TNA, CUST 47/1/11, 47/45/37, 47/46/99, 47/159/130, 47/184/26; *The Kentish Post: or Canterbury News-Letter* no.1526 (Weds 10 Jan – Sat 13 Jan 1733), 4; KHLC, Q/SB/32/19, Information of Richard Evans, 30 Mar 1713.
[19] NRO, NCR Case 12b/4, Informations of John Money and Joseph Cubitt, 24 Feb 1706; *OBP*, May 1733 (t17330510-20); *OBP*, May 1741, trial of Francis Piggot, John Johnson (t17410514-16); *OBP*, Sep 1747, trial of Judith Lomas (t17470909-39); *OBP*, Feb 1719 (t17190225-28).
[20] South v Whitewit (1600), Owen 45, 74 *ER* 963.

Comparisons between searching and stealing had real legal significance. In the first place, the law on searching houses was shaped by categories of wrongdoing under both civil and criminal law. Any search made without proper authority was, by definition, a tort or civil wrong. The position was summarised by one eighteenth-century chief justice as follows:

> By the laws of England, every invasion of private property, be it ever so minute, is a trespass. No man can set his foot upon my ground without my license, but he is liable to an action, though the damage be nothing ... If he admits the fact, he is bound to shew by way of justification, that some positive law has empowered or excused him.[21]

To forcibly enter a house without authority from above was to trespass. To take goods out of it was to steal. To search for and confiscate illicit objects was to commit a kind of authorised theft. In fact, different kinds of searches were defined by the different categories of theft they most resembled. In 1663, King's Bench judges determined that bailiffs looking for moveable property to distrain need not announce themselves or their intentions before breaking open a barn unattached to a dwelling house because 'the breaking it is not burglary'. Searches like this, which targeted outhouses or other buildings separate from living quarters, resembled petty larceny rather than serious crimes like burglary or housebreaking. As such, they did not require such elaborate rituals of legitimation. More straightforwardly, jurists worried that searchers in pursuit of stolen property might take the opportunity of entering a house to steal whatever they liked. This was the reason, according to Matthew Hale, that searches for stolen goods ought to be made during daylight, 'for many times under pretense of searches made in the night robberies and burglaries have been committed'.[22]

Such fears were not groundless. Some of those who hunted down coin-clippers, for example, stole as they searched. A customs officer stole plate and jewellery 'under pretence of looking for Prohibited Goods'; an exciseman slipped a pound of tea into his pocket 'in the exercise of his office'.[23] According to a resident of Wye (Kent) whose goods were distrained by

---

[21] Entick v Carrington (1765) in T. B. Howell, *A Complete Collection of State Trials and Proceedings for High Treason and other Crimes and Misdemeanors from the Earliest Period to the Present Time*, vol. 19 (London, 1813), 1066.

[22] Penton v Brown (1663), 1 Keble 698, 83 *ER* 1193; Hale, *Placitorum Coronae*, vol. 2, 150.

[23] *OBP*, Oct 1693, trial of Walter Batson, Jeremy Bedford, William Dando (t16931012-1); Oct 1693, trial of Walter Batson (t16931012-53); May 1694, trial of John Connel, Elizabeth Connel (t16940524-42); Feb 1695, trial of Matthew Coppinger (t16950220-35); Oct 1692, trial of John Connyers, John Price (t16921012-33); Dec 1747, trial of Benjamin Jewks (t17471209-54).

creditors and bailiffs in 1660, 'the intent and purpose of their comming was to seize on certaine writings concerning the title of the house for which there hath bin a suite at law betwixt them these three years'. In 1690, a group of Norwich watchmen broke into the house of a silk-winder and stole some of his tools, claiming – somewhat absurdly – that they had orders 'to search for King James', who had fled to Ireland the previous year.[24]

Just as some searchers became thieves, some thieves took advantage of powers of entry by pretending to be searchers. In 1722, a man approached a house in London and 'knockt at the Kitchen door and said, he was high Constable, that he had the Lord Chief Justice Prats Warrant, and would break open all the doors in the House'. When the householder refused to let him in, the thief asked 'What are you afraid of Justice Madam?' and kicked down her door, then proceeded to steal large quantities of valuable textiles.[25] This was not an isolated incident; as shown in Chapter 2, impersonation of officers was a useful technique for gaining access to a house and its valuables. Theft under colour of searching worked because officers were widely understood to possess special powers of entry. If they had not, there would have been no point in impersonating them.

Officeholders had substantially greater powers to search houses than other people did, and these powers grew greater still in the early eighteenth century. This has made house searching a tricky subject for historians who emphasise the extent of unofficial participation in law enforcement, something to be glided over rather than analysed in detail. Several scholars have noted that constables were especially important to this kind of searching, but there has been no focused assessment of how different legal powers overlapped and diverged.[26] The default position was that entering a house without the householder's consent was something that could only be done by an officer – or at least in the presence of an officer – with a warrant to search that specific house during daylight hours. These were the requirements for most searches under statute until the early eighteenth century. For example, legislation granting excisemen the power to search

---

[24] KHLC, Q/SB/8/2, Examinations of John Tompson and William Kingsford, 23 Feb 1660; NRO, NCR Case 12b/2, Information of Edward Quintin, 11 Jul 1690.
[25] *OBP*, May 1722, trial of Charles Johns, James Bradshaw (t17220510-38).
[26] Herrup, 'New Shoes and Mutton Pies', 820; Herrup, *Common Peace*, 74–5; Tim Wales, 'Thief-Takers and Their Clients in Later Stuart London' in Paul Griffiths and Mark S. R. Jenner (eds.), *Londinopolis: Essays in the Cultural and Social History of Early Modern London* (Manchester, 2000), 75; J. M. Beattie, *Policing and Punishment in London, 1660–1750: Urban Crime and the Limits of Terror* (Oxford, 2001), 121.

for concealed stocks of taxable goods conformed to this pattern until the 1720s and 1730s, when new statutes authorised night-time searches with a constable and daytime searches without one.[27] More strikingly, the 1705 Impressment Act allowed constables with general warrants to search any house where they suspected sailors might be found at any time of night. This paralleled the 'general privy searches' for 'rogues and vagabonds' demanded by vagrancy law, which also took place at night and involved constables with warrants searching one house after another as they saw fit.[28] Even these expanded powers, however, constrained searches more tightly than the common law. Searches for stolen goods required the standard combination of constable, daylight, and a specific warrant, but anyone could enter a house to search for a person known to have committed a felony, and constables could do the same (without a warrant) in cases where the felony was only suspected.[29]

Court records suggest these rules were taken seriously by some and flouted by others. People about to embark on a search often called an officer to accompany them.[30] Many were unwilling to proceed without a constable, including other officeholders, like the London beadle who refused to pursue thieves into an alehouse 'he not having a proper Officer'.[31] Constables themselves were sometimes reluctant to make searches without a warrant, especially where the search involved breaking down doors.[32] Forcing entry without an officer was legally risky, as one Kentishman discovered to his cost in 1672, when he found himself before a justice who demanded to know 'wherefor he did committ such an outrage & Misdemeanour as to breake a door without either Calling the Constable or the Bayliffe of the Hundred to bee present as a witness to what he did'. In the eyes of one common lawyer, searchers who entered a house without a constable could not 'justify what they have done, by any plea whatever'.[33]

---

[27] Compare 10 Wm III c.4, s.7 (1698) to 10 Geo I c.10, s.13 (1723) and 9 Geo II c.23, s.9 (1736).
[28] 4&5 Anne c.6, s.1 (1705); 13 Anne c.26, s.3 (1714); 17 Geo II c.5, s.6 (1744).
[29] Dalton, *Countrey Justice*, 176; Hale, *Placitorum Coronae*, vol. 2, 92, 95, 150; P.S., *A Help to Magistrates, and Ministers of Justice: Also a Guide to Parish and Ward-Officers* (London, 1721), 92–3; Richard Burn, *The Justice of the Peace and Parish Officer* (London, 1755), 72.
[30] KHLC, Q/SB/9/18, Information of Agnes Lamb, 4 Oct 1663; KHLC, Q/SB/1750/Informations/1, Information of Isabella Hawkes, undated; *OBP*, Apr 1676, trial of John Smith (t16760405-3).
[31] *OBP*, Oct 1732, trial of Elizabeth Yates, Henry Richardson, Isaac Coxen (t17321011-13). In 1710 a Kentish aletaster called a constable to accompany his search of a baker's shop for under-weight bread: KHLC, Q/SB/30/166, Information of John Curtis and John Rayden, 10 Jun 1710.
[32] LMA, CLA/046/03/001, Information of Walter Manning, 13 Jun 1684; LMA, MJ/SP/1714/01/016, Petition of Jacob Burton, undated; *OBP*, Feb 1739, trial of Mary Davis (t17390221-15).
[33] KHLC, Q/SB/12/10, Examination of John Alfrey, 7 Nov 1672; Entick v Carrington (1765) in Howell, *State Trials*, vol.19, 1038.

Even when searches were conducted by officers with warrants, however, the precise prescriptions of law were not always followed. For example, no front door was supposed to be broken without a clear request for entry and announcement of authority beforehand. Those who searched for – and claimed rewards for finding – coin-clippers and counterfeiters sometimes skipped this procedure, breaking into houses 'on a sudden' without giving 'any Intimation of their coming' in an attempt to find the offenders 'at worke', surrounded by evidence of their crime.[34] A violation with broader consequences was perpetuated by magistrates, who frequently issued constables with general warrants in cases where no such warrants were allowed by common law or statute. Middlesex JPs ordered constables 'to goe from house to house & search for Papists' or, more regularly, to search 'all houses and places that you shall have just cause to suspect' for stolen goods.[35] Some jurists were sceptical about the legality of any general search warrant, and in 1725 one such warrant was ruled unlawful at the Westminster Quarter Sessions, but many magistrates continued to issue them regardless.[36]

Whether or not they were strictly legal, searches made by officers with warrants usually met with less resistance than searches made by non-officers without warrants. There were exceptions, like the Wapping pawnbroker who told a group of men searching for stolen goods they 'should not search her House, no, not if we had my Lord Chancellor's Warrant'.[37] In general, however, even people who initially opposed searchers opened their doors at the sight of an officer or warrant.[38] This was at least partly due to the

---

[34] TNA, ASSI 45/2/2/72, Deposition of Robert Frear, 26 Mar 1648; LMA, MJ/SP/1695/07/033, Informations of Richard Portlock and John Bonner, 6 Jun 1695; LMA, MJ/SP/1695/07/065, Information of John Lerrey, 1 May 1695; *OBP*, Oct 1717, trial of Mary Hunt, Joanna Wood (t17171016-23).

[35] LMA, MJ/SP/1692/10/026, Hounslow constable's return, 13 Oct 1692; MJ/SP/1696/05/004, Order dated 21 May 1696; MJ/SP/1696/04/015, Undated printed warrant; MJ/SP/1696/12/015, Undated printed warrant; MJ/SP/1703/05/003, Warrant dated 21 May 1703; MJ/SP/1715/07/083, Undated draft order.

[36] Edward Coke, *The Fourth Part of the Institutes of the Laws of England* (1644), 176–8; Henry Care, *English Liberties: Or, The Free-Born Subject's Inheritance* (London, 1680), 198; Shoemaker, *Prosecution and Punishment*, 263–5. For a broader discussion of general warrants and opposition to them, see Cuddihy, *Fourth Amendment*, 106–48, 268–97, 433–86.

[37] *OBP*, Apr 1726, trial of Miriam Keys (t17260425-5). See also *OBP*, Aug 1692, trial of Thomas Martyn, Susanna Martyn, John Basdell (t16920831-16).

[38] *OBP*, Jan 1698, trial of William Sickes, Mary Sickes, Thomas Barker, Elizabeth Stanley, Jane Greek (t16980114-31); *OBP*, Apr 1721, trial of John Phillips (t17210419-64); *OBP*, Feb 1724, trial of Lewis Hussare (t17240226-71); *OBP*, Oct 1747, trial of John Lamb, William Bilby, John Chandler, Charles Hooper (t17471014-11). Sometimes the threat of fetching a constable was enough to make someone open their house to a search: *OBP*, Oct 1726, trial of John Thomson (t17261012-7).

threat of force. One London constable, when he met resistance in a search for coin-clippers, explained that 'he must come in, having a Warrant, and therefore if Opposition was made, must use Violence'. Another searcher, asked during a trial at the Old Bailey if he had encountered any opposition, simply said 'They could not; I had a Search-Warrant'.[39] The same court often heard accounts of searches in which officers forced, broke through, or kicked down doors.[40]

In London, in the late seventeenth and early eighteenth centuries, most house searches involved either an officer or a warrant or both. Patterns of searching can be reconstructed in much the same way as patterns of making arrests. Depositions from Middlesex Quarter Sessions and trial reports in the Old Bailey *Proceedings* contain enough incidental mentions of searches to build up a picture of ordinary practice.[41] As Table 7 shows, officers were involved in more than half of the house searches recorded in this way. The real proportion was probably greater. Witnesses in both courts sometimes claimed to have carried out searches which, as other witnesses made clear, were in fact carried out by or alongside officers. The passive voice in which many searches were recorded – illicit goods were 'found in the Custody of' a suspect – sometimes obscured official involvement which was made apparent in other testimony.[42] Warrants were used in 221 of the searches recorded at the Old Bailey, accounting for 39.2 per cent of the total. The proportion was higher in searches carried out without officers – 103 out of 166 (62.4 per cent) – meaning only 63 of the 564 house searches mentioned in total (11.0 per cent) involved neither an officer nor a warrant. It seems likely that at least some of these searches also took place in the presence of officers or warrants, and that this was such a routine occurrence that those who wrote up the Old Bailey trial reports did not think it worth mentioning. Searching houses was a fraught activity, not to be undertaken lightly without people or pieces of paper embodying legal authority.

---

[39] *OBP*, Sep 1717, trial of Thomas Panting alias Panton (t17170911-5); *OBP*, Sep 1740, trial of Elizabeth Fisher, Rebecca Holden, George Holden (t17400903-19).
[40] *OBP*, Apr 1676, trial of John Smith (t16760405-3); *OBP*, Jul 1713, trial of Sarah Williams, Elizabeth White (t17130708-15); *OBP*, Oct 1731, trial of William Vaughan (t17311013-41); *OBP*, Apr 1741, trial of John Storer (t17410405-32); *OBP*, May 1743, trial of Gabriel Beaugrand, Lewis Brunet (t17430519-9).
[41] The Old Bailey sample represents every house search mentioned in 1494 instances of the word 'search' between 1674 and 1750. The Middlesex Sessions sample represents every house search mentioned in surviving depositions over the same period: LMA, MJ/SP/1674–1750.
[42] LMA, MJ/SP/1699/01/064, Informations of Richard Cooksey and Roger Morris, 9 Jan 1699; LMA, MJ/SP/1748/10/123, Informations of William Draper and John Mason, 15 Sep 1748; *OBP*, Nov 1716, trial of Elizabeth Hart (t17161105-66).

Table 7 *Official involvement in house searches recorded at the Old Bailey and Middlesex Quarter Sessions, 1674–1750*

Court	Total house searches	House searches where searcher/s identifiable	House searches involving officer/s
Old Bailey	564	358	193 (53.9 per cent)
Middlesex Sessions	65	53	30 (56.6 per cent)

Most of the house searches mentioned in these sources were searches for suspected thieves or stolen goods.[43] Property was invaded in pursuit of property. To gain the consent of reluctant householders – and to avoid the appearance of trespass and theft – it was safest to conduct these searches in as official a manner as possible. The presence of officers and warrants transformed the invasion of a person's home into an authorised and lawful act, one which could if necessary be carried out with legitimate violence. It was also, as we shall see, a gendered act and one which was far more likely to target the poor than the rich. Every house was a castle, but some were better fortified than others.

Castles and Cottages

In her work on parenthood under the poor laws, Patricia Crawford argued that officeholders acted as 'civic fathers' to intervene in the households of poor mothers and fathers. Intrusions that were unthinkable for wealthy families – up to and including the removal of children – were unremarkable when parents were deemed morally or economically incapable of conforming to the norms of patriarchal child-rearing.[44] Something similar can be said of searches. Lawyers and politicians who were outraged by the idea of rich people's houses being searched, who described such searches as violations of property, propriety, and the inalienable rights of householders, were strikingly unconcerned about the routine searching of poorer people's houses under statute and common law. Intersecting hierarchies of gender and social status meant different people experienced searches in very different ways.

---

[43] 421 (74.6 per cent) of the searches in the Old Bailey sample were part of theft investigations. Ninety-one (16.1 per cent) were searches for coin-clippers or counterfeiters, sixteen (2.8 per cent) were searches for evidence of infanticide, and no other crime accounted for more than ten searches.

[44] Patricia Crawford, *Parents of Poor Children in England, 1580–1800* (Oxford, 2010).

Table 8 *Gender of house searchers in the records of the Old Bailey and Middlesex Quarter Sessions, 1674–1750*

Court	Searches by women only	Searches by mixed groups	Searches by men only	Total cases where gender of searcher/s identifiable
Old Bailey	32 (7.9 per cent)	26 (6.5 per cent)	345 (85.6 per cent)	403
Middlesex Sessions	2 (3.8 per cent)	8 (15.1 per cent)	43 (81.1 per cent)	53

House searching was generally done by men (Table 8). This was partly due to the involvement of large numbers of male officers, but even discounting those cases, searches by men were far more frequent in the Old Bailey and Middlesex Sessions records than searches by women or by mixed groups. Women who had been robbed sometimes told their husbands or male servants to fetch an officer or search warrant and investigate suspected houses on their behalf.[45] Like making arrests, searching houses seems to have been understood as a particularly masculine activity.

Gender was equally important on the other side of the threshold. For patriarchal men whose identities were, as Karen Harvey puts it, 'grounded in the physical and emotional space of the house', searches were a profound challenge to their gendered power. 'Invasions of household space', Nicola Whyte argues, constituted 'an attack upon patriarchal order and dominance, and the honour and reputation of the husband and father'.[46] Married women were in a similar position as mistresses of households. Several scholars have noted the prominence of wives and widows in preventing officers and others from entering their houses to distrain their goods.[47] According to Garthine Walker, these women 'derived their authority from patriarchal discourses' about responsible householding – what Alexandra

---

[45] *OBP*, Oct 1720, trial of Thomas Paine (t17201012-16); *OBP*, Mar 1721, trial of Ann Westwood, Philip Brice (t17210301-2).
[46] Karen Harvey, *The Little Republic: Masculinity and Domestic Authority in Eighteenth-Century Britain* (Oxford, 2012), 167; Nicola Whyte, '"With a Sword Drawne in Her Hande": Defending the Boundaries of Household Space in Seventeenth-Century Wales' in Bronach Kane and Fiona Williamson (eds.), *Women, Agency and the Law, 1300–1700* (London, 2013), 141.
[47] Jennine Hurl-Eamon, *Gender and Petty Violence in London, 1680–1720* (Columbus, 2005), 118; Garthine Walker, 'Keeping It in the Family: Crime and the Early Modern Household' in Helen Berry and Elizabeth Foyster (eds.), *The Family in Early Modern England* (Cambridge, 2007), 80–92; Amanda Flather, *Gender and Space in Early Modern England* (Woodbridge, 2007), 44–5.

Shepard has labelled 'the moral authority of wives and mothers'. There was also, Walker suggests, a sexualised dimension to male entries into houses defended by women. A 'conflation of household and bodily boundaries' made this 'at once an invasive masculine act and one that suggested woman's sexual availability and desire for occupation'.[48] Descriptions of sexual assault – by officers, as discussed in Chapter 3, or otherwise – often involved forced entry into a house.[49]

In the first half of the eighteenth century, these gendered discourses aligned with complaints from merchant elites about what they saw as undue meddling by the state and its representatives. In 1733, during the political upheaval prompted by proposals to extend the Excise to wine and tobacco, pamphleteers portrayed the threatened tax as an assault on the patriarchal rights of male traders and the chastity of their wives and daughters. In the first place, 'a Man who deals in exciseable Goods, is so far from being able to call his House his Castle, that every Excise Officer is Lord and Master over him in his own House, and can command him as if he was his Servant'. When the government withdrew the proposals, a jobbing poet proclaimed the rescue of female honour: 'no new EXCISE / With Five hundred Eyes, / Shall henceforth your Wives or Daughters surprise; / For if they had License to gage all your Stocks, / May also pretend to gage under their Smocks'. This analogy gained brief notoriety, presenting the exciseman as an inveterate sexual predator: 'Then sometimes he stoops / To take up the Hoops / Of your Daughters as well as your Barrels'.[50]

These sexualised anxieties, whether genuine or conjured for polemical effect, were heavily inflected by status. The great fear, according to the author of another pamphlet, was that newly empowered officers 'may in the Middle of the Night enter the Bed-Room of the Lady of the highest Quality in the Nation'. This was especially alarming because an excisemen, as opponents of the tax saw it, was not only sexually dangerous but also 'a scurvy little Fellow', 'a pert Rascal', an 'unknown petty Officer' whose lowly social position made his power to enter the

---

[48] Garthine Walker, *Crime, Gender and Social Order in Early Modern England* (Cambridge, 2003), 111, 52–3; Alexandra Shepard, 'Provision, Household Management and the Moral Authority of Wives and Mothers in Early Modern England' in Michael J. Braddick and Phil Withington (eds.), *Popular Culture and Political Agency in Early Modern England* (Woodbridge, 2017).

[49] Garthine Walker, 'Rereading Rape and Sexual Violence in Early Modern England', *Gender & History* 10.1 (1998), 14–16.

[50] *Observations upon the Laws of Excise* (London, 1733), 20; *Excise Elegy* (London, 1733), 5–6; *Britannia Excisa* (London, 1733), 5.

houses of reputable traders all the more outrageous.⁵¹ Similar arguments were made in 1741 against an Impressment Bill which, one member of the House of Lords declared, would subject every house to a search at 'the caprice and insolence of every dirty little officer' – in this case a constable. In the 1760s, during the controversy over general warrants issued by secretaries of state to search the houses of John Wilkes and his associates, an opposition periodical warned that such warrants were a means 'to empower mean, Low-lif'd ignorant men to enter, and to act at discretion'.⁵²

Supporters of search powers were quick to point out the selective blindness in these arguments. As one wrote of the 1733 Excise Bill, 'this is no more oppressive and unreasonable than a Constable's searching for stol'n Goods, or a Custom-house Officer's for prohibited Ones, since they have but the same Power under the same Circumstances'. The government's lawyer in one of the general warrant cases involving Wilkes pointed out that vagrancy statutes allowed general warrants but these were never 'esteemed an infringement of our constitution'.⁵³ The Wilkes trials came close to turning this point on its head when chief justice Camden suggested that warrants to search for stolen goods might, like the secretarial warrants in dispute, be unlawful subversions of liberty. In support of this position, he cited Edward Coke's brief comment on warrants to search houses on the mere suspicion that they contained stolen goods. According to Camden, Coke 'denied its legality'. This was true, but Coke's reasoning was based on the same double standard that pervaded most discussions of search powers in print. 'Though commonly the Houses or Cottages of poore and base people be by such Warrants searched', Coke wrote, 'yet if it be lawfull, the houses of any subject, be he never so great, may be searched, &c. by such Warrant upon bare surmises'.⁵⁴ The frightening possibility was that powers ordinarily used to enter the houses of the poor could be turned on those of the rich.

---

⁵¹ *The Late Excise Scheme Dissected* (London, 1734), 60; *Second Review of the Late Excise Scheme* (London, 1734), 26–7; William Pulteney, *The Budget Opened* (London, 1733), 25; Caleb D'Anvers [Nicholas Amhurst], *The Second Part of an Argument Against Excises* (London, 1733), Appendix II, 11.

⁵² Cuddihy, *Fourth Amendment*, 275; *The Monitor, or British Freeholder*, vol. 6 no.445 (Sat 11 Feb 1764), 2595. On the secretarial warrant controversy, see John Brewer, 'The Wilkites and the Law' in John Brewer and John Styles (eds.), *An Ungovernable People: The English and Their Law in the Seventeenth and Eighteenth Centuries* (London, 1980).

⁵³ *A Dialogue Between Sir Andrew Freeport and Timothy Squat, Esquire, On the Subject of Excises* (London, 1733), 16; Wilkes v Wood (1763) in Howell, *State Trials*, 493.

⁵⁴ Entick v Carrington (1765) in Howell, *State Trials*, 1067; Coke, *Fourth Part*, 178.

The greatest inequality in protections against searching, however, was between householders and those who lived in the houses of others. Internal doors to rooms rented by lodgers did not have the same legal status as the external doors of a house: once inside a house, searchers could lawfully force their way into any room with impunity.[55] Servants and apprentices who kept prized possessions in boxes and trunks struggled to prevent their being broken open by searchers. According to Vickery, these 'personal receptacles stood proxy for individuality, so the taboo around violating them was powerful', but unlike households they lacked any status in law.[56] The strength of the taboo is made clear by those cases in which mistresses, masters, landladies and landlords fetched constables and warrants before searching the box of a servant or lodger, just as they might before searching a house. In legal terms, however, this was entirely unnecessary. In a sample of thirty searches of boxes or trunks mentioned in the Old Bailey *Proceedings*, only six involved officers and three more warrants; the remaining 21 (70 per cent) were carried out by householders with no authority beyond their own.[57]

Servants who protested against searches had no legal resources to draw on. In 1709, an Edmonton mistress 'Demanded to Search' her servant's trunk, which the servant 'att First refused to admitt of, and denied the Key &c: but at length was Forced to Comply and did open her s[ai]d Trunk'. In a similar case in Twickenham, a householder who suspected his servants of poisoning him declared he would 'search all your Boxes'. One woman answered 'He should not search hers, if he did he should pay for it. But he going to break it open with a Hammer, she opened it her self'.[58] As most live-in servants were female, searches like these targeted women disproportionately. Of the twenty-five identifiable owners of trunks or boxes in the Old Bailey sample, seventeen were women. In the hierarchy of searching, female servants were the opposite of elite male householders. To enter the house of a propertied patriarch, searchers had to negotiate a

---

[55] Harvey v Oldfield (1674), 1 Freeman 399, 89 *ER* 252; Browning v Dann (1735), 95 *ER* 107.
[56] Vickery, 'An Englishman's Home', 172.
[57] This sample represents all instances of the word 'search' in which boxes or trunks were searched in the OBP between 1674 and 1750. The cases involving officers are: *OBP*, Dec 1717, trial of Ann Woodburn (t17171204-43); Jan 1728, trial of Sarah Dickenson (t17280117-43); Jul 1740, trial of Elizabeth Davis (t17400709-4); Jul 1742, trial of Anna Maria Neale (t17420714-24); Feb 1743, trial of Dorothy Roberts (t17430223-1); Sep 1750, trial of Francis Keys (t17500912-36). Those involving warrants are: *OBP*, May 1719, trial of Ruth License (t17190514-22); Jan 1742, trial of George Lavan (t17420115-38); Dec 1746, trial of Mary Johnson (t17461205-24).
[58] LMA, MJ/SP/1709/07/073, Information of Mary Cocker, 16 Jul 1709; *OBP*, Apr 1720, trial of Elizabeth Cranbery (t17200427-43).

complex set of legal barriers and restrictions; to open servant's trunk, they simply had to insist. This inequality of protections was even more apparent in searches of people. Like house-searching, person-searching was a gendered activity. Like trunks and boxes, and unlike houses, bodies were not defended by law. As such, they were almost entirely open to the touch of the state.

Searching People

Until the late eighteenth century, according to many historians and philosophers, individual bodies were not considered autonomous, inviolable, and separated from the world around them.[59] Personal boundaries were fluid, uncertain, and often transgressed. Crimes against the person were often punished less severely that crimes against property.[60] Clothes and skin were more permeable barriers than doors and walls, if they were barriers at all. According to physicians, bodies – especially women's bodies – were porous, fluctuating, lacking clear lines of distinction.[61] In this context, there was little to guard a person against intimate searching. As historians of sex have shown, those who did not conform to either side of a binary gender divide had their bodies probed, prodded, and paraded in courtrooms and marketplaces across western Europe from the sixteenth century to the eighteenth.[62] More routinely, the bodies of unmarried women were closely examined for signs of illegitimate pregnancy by neighbours,

---

[59] The two most influential (and contrasting) versions of this argument are: Michel Foucault, *Discipline and Punish: The Birth of the Prison* tr. Alan Sheridan (London, 1991); Lynn Hunt, 'The 18th-Century Body and the Origins of Human Rights', *Diogenes* 203 (2004). The latter is expanded in *Inventing Human Rights* (New York, 2007).

[60] This began to change in the late eighteenth century: J. M. Beattie, *Crime and the Courts in England 1660–1800* (Princeton, 1986), 457–60, 609; Peter King, 'Punishing Assault: The Transformation of Attitudes in the English Courts', *The Journal of Interdisciplinary History* 27.1 (1996).

[61] Natalie Zemon Davis, 'Boundaries and the Sense of Self in Sixteenth-Century France' in T. C. Heller, S. Morton, and D. E. Wellbery (eds.), *Reconstructing Individualism: Autonomy, Individuality, and the Self in Western Thought*, ed. (Stanford, 1986); Gail Kern Paster, *The Body Embarrassed: Drama and the Disciplines of Shame in Early Modern England* (Ithaca, 1993); Ulinka Rublack and Pamela Selwyn, 'Fluxes: The Early Modern Body and the Emotions', *History Workshop Journal* 53 (2002).

[62] Lorraine Daston and Katherine Park, 'The Hermaphrodite and the Orders of Nature: Sexual Ambiguity in Early Modern France' in Louise Fradenburg and Carla Freccero (eds.), *Premodern Sexualities* (New York, 1996); Palmira Fontes da Costa, 'Mediating Sexual Difference: The Medical Understanding of Human Hermaphrodites in Eighteenth-Century England' in Willem de Blécourt and Cornelie Usborne (eds.), *Cultural Approaches to the History of Medicine: Mediating Medicine in Early Modern and Modern Europe* (Basingstoke, 2004); Cathy McClive, 'Masculinity on Trial: Penises, Hermaphrodites and the Uncertain Male Body in Early Modern France', *History Workshop Journal* 68 (2009); Patricia Simons, *The Sex of Men in Premodern Europe* (Cambridge, 2011), 25–33.

relatives, mistresses, midwives, and hospital matrons. 'The body of the single woman', Laura Gowing writes, 'was barely her own'.[63]

These activities took place in a legal vacuum. Nothing in statute or common law regulated who could search or examine who, for what reason, or in what way. In 1636, a case heard at the York Assizes briefly touched on this subject before moving on to better trodden ground. A constable with a warrant to search a house on the suspicion it contained stolen goods was brought to trial because 'in the search [he] did pull the clothes from off a womans bed then in her bed, to search under her Smock'. This was considered a misdemeanour, but the case was only treated as precedent in discussions of arresting people on suspicion, as described in the previous chapter.[64] In statute, searches of persons as opposed to property were rarely mentioned explicitly until the early nineteenth century.[65] Nonetheless, officers and others frequently searched people for evidence of offences against the criminal law. Often, such searches took place before, during, or after an arrest on the basis of suspicion. As a result, they played a large part in the gendered policing of suspects which characterised much London law enforcement in the late seventeenth and early eighteenth centuries. Without legal recourse, those subjected to searches tried – sometimes successfully – to lay down bodily boundaries based on notions of modesty and decency.

One indicator of the lack of legal regulation around searches of people is that, unlike house searches, many were conducted without warrants or the involvement of any officer. Between 1674 and 1750, 620 person searches were mentioned in Old Bailey trial reports and 139 in depositions given to the Middlesex Sessions. As with house searches, most of these were searches for stolen goods.[66] According to the author of one handbook for constables, 'a thorough search of the felon is of

---

[63] Laura Gowing, *Common Bodies: Women, Touch and Power in Seventeenth-Century England* (New Haven, 2003), 73; Paul Griffiths, *Lost Londons: Change, Crime, and Control in the Capital 1550–1660* (Cambridge, 2008), 269–75.

[64] Ward's case (1636) in John Clayton, *Reports and Pleas of Assises at Yorke* (London, 1651), 44.

[65] Seizure of Arms Act 1819 (60 Geo III c.2, s.1); Metropolitan Police Act 1839 (2&3 Vict c.47, s.66). One exception is the Woollen Manufacture Act 1726 (13 Geo I c.23 s.8) which allowed constables with magistrates' warrants to search 'End Gatherers' for pilfered scraps of cloth. According to Patrick Colquhoun, the Criminal Law Act 1782 (22 Geo III c.58 s.3) allowed constables 'to stop and search all suspicious persons conveying goods after dark', though no searches are explicitly mentioned in the statute: *A Treatise on the Functions and Duties of A Constable* (London, 1803), 13. On the legislative history of stop and search, see Geoff Monaghan's articles in *Criminal Law & Justice Weekly* 179.42, 179.47–48, 180.46 (2015–16).

[66] In the Old Bailey sample, 517 (83.4 per cent) were searches for stolen goods. No other object of searching accounted for more than 5 per cent of the sample. There were 28 (4.5 per cent) searches

Table 9 *Official involvement in person searches recorded at the Old Bailey and Middlesex Quarter Sessions, 1674–1750*

Court	Total person searches	Person searches where searcher/s identifiable	Person searches involving officer/s
Old Bailey	620	415	204 (49.2 per cent)
Middlesex Sessions	139	93	28 (30.1 per cent)

the utmost consequence to your own safety, and benefit of the public, as by this means he will be stripped of instruments of mischief, and evidence may probably be procured to convict him'.[67] As shown in Table 9, however, officers were far from being the only ones to carry out person searches.

These figures are quite similar to those for official involvement in arrests recorded in the same courts (Table 1, above), which may reflect the fact that many searches were carried out shortly before or after a person was arrested. As with the data on arrests and house searches, official involvement was probably greater than these numbers suggest, given the tendency to describe searches by officers in passive or indirect language.[68] Some non-officers felt unable to search suspects themselves and sought out officeholders (usually constables or watchmen) to do it for them.[69] One gentleman 'ordered my Servants one on each Side to search' a man he suspected of picking his pocket, but only after sending a friend 'to enquire whether we could answer so doing' – that is, whether such a search was legally defensible. The victim of another alleged pickpocket regretted that he 'had not Sense to search to search her my self, but left it all' to the constable, who failed to produce his stolen watch.[70]

---

for evidence of rape, 25 (4.0 per cent) for weapons, 24 (3.9 per cent) for counterfeit coins, and 11 (1.8 per cent) for evidence of infanticide. The remaining fifteen searches were for evidence of forgery, extortion, 'sodomy', seditious libel, and Catholic devotional practice.

[67] Saunders Welch, *Observations on the Office of Constable* (London, 1754), 19.

[68] For example: LMA, MJ/SP/1697/01/037, Informations of Josias Pearson and Timothy Jeffs, 27 Dec 1696; MJ/SP/1698/06/019, Informations of Samuel Barrock and Edward Chandler, 20 May 1698; MJ/SP/1699/02/035, Informations of Robert Thorne and Mary Fainty, 31 Jan 1699; MJ/SP/1748/10/124, Informations of John Anderson and Henry French, 19 Sep 1748.

[69] LMA, MJ/SP/1696/09/055, Informations of Humphrey Buckle and Anthony Buckmaster, 31 Aug 1696; LMA, MJ/SP/1709/12/020, Information of Charles Lacy, 24 Nov 1709; *OBP*, Jun 1715 (t17150602-9); *OBP*, Jan 1718, trial of Mary Betts (t17180110-61); *OBP*, Apr 1720, trial of Zephaniah Martin (t17200427-8); *OBP*, May 1741, trial of James Gardner (t17410514-34).

[70] *OBP*, May 1738, trial of Joseph Hodson (t17380518-10); Oct 1726, trial of Mary Sample (t17261012-50).

Suspects sometimes refused to be searched 'without a Constable'.[71] Others demanded an even greater authority, like the suspected thief who declared 'he would not be search'd but before higher Powers; whereupon he was carried before the Justice'.[72] Unofficial searchers of people could be accused of planting evidence or – like searchers of houses – of theft. In 1747, a suspected highwayman complained to the Old Bailey that 'it was not a proper Officer that search'd me; I don't know what they might put into my Pocket'. When a tavern drawer found a watch under the armpit of a suspected pickpocket, she said 'if you take it, I'll swear a Robbery against you'. Cases of actual theft in this manner were not unheard of: in 1730, one man accused another of picking his pocket, insisted on searching him, 'unbuttoned his Breeches, took from him his Money, Handkerchief, and Knife', then 'ran away'.[73]

The reservations expressed by some Londoners about unofficial searches of people suggest that, in the absence of any legal framework, this activity was governed by informal notions of what was or was not a legitimate search. Warrants, which featured in so many house searches, only appeared in eleven of the person searches in the Old Bailey sample and just two of those mentioned in the Middlesex Sessions material. The power to search a person was instead shaped by the identities of the searchers and the searchees. In this extra-legal context, the question of who could justify searching who was determined by hierarchies of gender and social status.

Suspect Bodies

Most straightforwardly, elite men considered any attempt to search them an outrageous violation of privilege. This was a rare occurrence and tended to provoke a furious response. Searching the body, these men felt, was an insult to their status, a treatment fit for those who broke the law, not those who made and administered it. In 1640, as tensions grew between crown and parliament, royal servants searched the pockets of several MPs and two lords. This was done, Harbottle Grimston wrote, 'as if they had been Felons and Traitors'; it was 'contrary to the Law, and the Subjects

---

[71] LMA, MJ/SP/1702/07/047, Information of Elizabeth Crane, 27 Jul 1702; *OBP*, Sep 1737, trial of Joan Cogan (t17370907-59).
[72] *OBP*, Jul 1730, trial of David Dickson (t17300704-46). A group of soldiers who arrested a man for treason in 1739 'did not think proper to search him till he came before a Magistrate': *OBP*, Dec 1739, trial of Loglin Rennells (t17391205-51).
[73] *OBP*, Feb 1747, trial of Henry Simms (t17470225-18); *OBP*, Jan 1732, trial of Elizabeth Caton (t17320114-39); *OBP*, Apr 1730, trial of Bartholomew Nicholson (t17300408-2).

Table 10 *Gender of searchees in the records of the Old Bailey and Middlesex Quarter Sessions, 1674–1750*

Court	Searches of women	Searches of men	Searches of mixed groups	Total identifiable searchees
Old Bailey	277 (44.8 per cent)	334 (54.0 per cent)	7 (1.1 per cent)	618
Middlesex Sessions	84 (60.9 per cent)	54 (39.1 per cent)	0	138

Liberty'. William Laud crowed over 'how odious it was to Parliament and some of themselves to have the pockets of men searched', though he was not slow to complain when, imprisoned in the Tower, he had 'my very Pockets searched'.[74] In more ordinary circumstances, a baronet threatened 'Satisfaction for such Scandal' when he was searched by a group of Londoners on suspicion of theft 'as is usual to common Criminals'. It was not only titled aristocrats who claimed to be above such treatment; gentlemen and men of the middling sort who laid claim to that title sometimes expected the same privilege of not being searched. A man involved in the search of a suspected highway robber at an alehouse recalled that 'While we were searching him, the Landlady seem'd to take the Prisoner's part; What! are you going to rob the Man? says she – He's a substantial Innkeeper – and as he is a gentleman, use him like one'.[75]

This kind of informal regulation of searching was shaped by gender in a more complex way. First, women may have been disproportionately likely to be subjected to searches of the person. As Table 10 shows, women were the targets of 44.8 per cent of the searches recorded at the Old Bailey and 60.9 per cent of those mentioned in the Middlesex Sessions papers. Both of these figures are higher than the proportion of female defendants indicted at each court in this period: 36 per cent and 27.2 per cent, respectively.[76] Searches of women seem to have been, on average, conducted with less formal authority than searches of men. In the Old Bailey *Proceedings*, in

---

[74] John Rushworth, *Historical Collections from the Year 1638 to the Year 1641 Abridg'd and Improved*, vol. 3 (London, 1706), 265; William Laud, *The History of the Troubles and Tryal of the Most Reverend Father in God and Blessed Martyr, William Laud* (London, 1695), 205; *The Complete Collection of State Trials and Proceedings for High-Treason and Other Crimes and Misdemeanours*, vol. 1 (London, 1730), 912.

[75] *OBP*, May 1717, trial of Charles Burton (t17170501-33); Apr 1733, trial of William Gordon (t17330404-44).

[76] Shoemaker, *Prosecution and Punishment*, 208.

cases where both searcher and searchee can be identified, 57.5 per cent of searches of men involved officers, compared to just 40.5 per cent of searches of women. In the Middlesex records, officers were involved in 39.5 per cent of searches of men but only 24.1 per cent of searches of women.[77] This suggests a greater degree of reluctance to search men without officers present, or, to put it the other way around, a greater degree of confidence in searching women without any particular authority. In the extra-legal hierarchy of searches of the person, women were afforded less protection than men.

Searches of women were also more invasive than searches of men. Most of the searches mentioned in court records were not described in detail, but an overall picture of routine practices can be drawn from those accounts which noted where illicit objects were found on a person. This information appears in 237 of the cases in the Old Bailey sample. The most common locations were in bosoms, breeches, pockets and under people's clothes. Table 11 breaks the figures down according to gender. Pockets, generally worn on strings outside a person's clothes, were one of the least intimate hiding places and accounted for a large majority of objects discovered on men. Searchers who found things in men's breeches sometimes came closer to their bodies; stolen goods were 'found concealed between his Breeches and his Skin' or 'between the Lining of his Breeches, and his Flesh, near his Garter'.[78] For the most part though, searches of men were relatively unobtrusive. One searcher told the Old Bailey 'we searched him every where; all his Pockets, his Coat, Shoes and Stockings'. Another claimed a suspect 'was so strictly searched, that it was impossible it should be about him, for his Shoes and Stockings were taken off'.[79] As we shall see, for a woman to be thoroughly or 'strictly' searched meant something very different.

Pockets may have been the most common location of objects found in searches of women, but almost as many were discovered under their clothes or in their bosoms. Searchers also looked between women's legs and around their 'privy parts', places which did not feature in searches of men. Law enforcement officers seem to have been especially likely to search these parts of women's bodies. The groups of men who policed

---

[77] The figures for the Old Bailey sample are: 79 of 195 searches of women involved officers, compared to 123 of 214 searches of men. In the Middlesex sample, thirteen of fifty-four searches of women involved officers, compared to fifteen of thirty-eight searches of men.

[78] *OBP*, Apr 1730, trial of Hugh Horton (t17300408-66); *OBP*, Oct 1740, trial of George Coates (t17401015-5).

[79] *OBP*, Apr 1734, trial of Daniel Cook (t17340424-13); *OBP*, Dec 1746, trial of John Poulter, Elizabeth Bradbury (t17461205-11).

Table 11 *Location of goods found on people as recorded in the Old Bailey Proceedings, 1674–1750*

Where objects found	On women	On men	Total
Apron	7	1	8
Armpit	1	3	4
Between legs	5	0	5
Bosom	15	9	24
Breeches	0	19	19
Lap	2	1	3
Mouth	2	2	4
Pocket	21	101	122
'Privy parts'	5	0	5
Stocking	1	1	2
Under clothes	17	12	29
Other[a]	5	7	12
Total	81	156	237

[a] There were individual instances of objects being found in hats, shoes, codpieces, knife-sheathes, and various other accessories.

London's streets appear to have thought that women – perhaps especially those women they arrested on suspicion of theft, vagrancy, or night-walking – tended to hide things in the most private parts of their bodies. One watchman, searching a woman accused of pickpocketing, said he 'believed she had hid it in a particular Place, which is easy to guess at without naming, for I knew such things had been done by other Gentlewomen on the like Occasion'. A beadle thought that 'these Creatures very often hide Things in their Stockings'.[80] Some women were accused of concealing goods in specially designed compartments of their petticoats which, Shelley Tickell has suggested, turned female thieves into 'walking storage systems'.[81] To the extent that this was more than a figment of male officers' imaginations, it seems likely that women resorted to these hiding places in response to intrusive searches. For example, when Mary Pearse and Sarah Cook were arrested on suspicion of stealing holland cloth in 1717, the constable began to search Cook, who promptly 'convey'd the Holland to Mary Pearse, who endeavour'd to put it under her Coats and

---

[80] *OBP*, Dec 1733, trial of Margaret Webb (t17331205-7); *OBP*, Jan 1740, trial of Alice Cook alias Taper (t17400116-51).
[81] Shelley Tickell, *Shoplifting in Eighteenth-Century England* (Woodbridge, 2018), 80. For example: *OBP*, Feb 1716, trial of Jane Bartwick (t17160222-30); *OBP*, Dec 1748, trial of Hannah Christian, Hannah Raductin, Hannah Mildred (t17481207-54).

conceal it between her Legs, but was not Mistress of Dexterity enough to do it unperceiv'd'.[82]

Female suspects were far more likely than their male counterparts to be strip-searched. The Old Bailey sample includes twenty-five strip searches of women and just two of men.[83] Stripping did not necessarily mean the removal of all clothes; one woman was said to have 'readily stripp'd off all her Cloaths to her Shift', while a group of officers searching another suspect 'stripped her naked, all but her Shift'. But other strip searches did go beyond shifts and smocks. Barbara Hewsly told the Old Bailey that when she and Mary Jones were taken to a constable's house on suspicion of highway robbery 'he stript us stark naked, and found nothing about us but what was our own'. The man who prosecuted them denied this, insisting that Hewsly 'was searched slightly, but not stript stark naked', but Jones confirmed Hewsly's account, claiming the constable 'search'd me from Top to Toe, and found nothing'.[84]

The conflicting accounts of how Jones and Hewsly were searched suggest that strip-searching could be controversial. There were no legal grounds to object, but appeals to modesty could sometimes offer a degree of protection. In a rare instance of a searcher being called to account for their actions, Middlesex magistrates issued a recognisance against a night watchman who arrested and searched a nightwalker in 1705; he had 'offer[ed] to put his hand up her coats' and was summoned to answer the vague charge of 'using her in an Undecent manner of rudeness'. Some officers only searched women 'as far as Decency would permit' or, in the case of another watchman, 'as far as Modesty would let me (for I am a little modest)'. Some were reluctant to search women at all, like the constable called to arrest a suspected pickpocket who 'had not Impudence enough to search her'.[85] Women were sometimes taken to private rooms where they could be searched away from prying eyes, to kitchens or parlours where blinds could be drawn over the windows. In 1727, a woman was strip-searched in a private room in a London playhouse, 'the Constable promising to look out at the Window'.[86]

---

[82] *OBP*, Jan 1717, trial of Mary Pearse, Sarah Cooke alias Downs (t17170111-3).

[83] One of the two men was an apprentice stripped by his master, the other a suspected highway robber: *OBP*, Oct 1730, trial of Joseph Isles (t17301014-28); *OBP*, Jan 1722, trial of John James (t17220112-40).

[84] *OBP*, Aug 1729, trial of Ann Cragg (t17290827-41); *OBP*, Dec 1743, trial of Elizabeth Miller (t17431207-24); *OBP*, Dec 1732, trial of Barbary Hewsly, Mary Jones (t17321206-14).

[85] Hurl-Eamon, 'Westminster Imposters', 464; *OBP*, Feb 1741, trial of Ann Lucas (t17410225-28); *OBP*, May 1740, trial of Martha Harding, Rachel Bowling (t17400522-7); *OBP*, Jan 1727, trial of Elizabeth Roberts (t17270113-11).

[86] *OBP*, Sep 1737, trial of Joan Cogan (t17370907-59); *OBP*, Dec 1738, trial of Constance James (t17381206-15); *OBP*, Oct 1739, trial of Elizabeth Ward (t17391017-17); *OBP*, Jan 1727, trial of Elizabeth Burgis (t17270113-18).

The barriers of propriety were erected by searchees themselves. Gowing has shown that despite the vulnerability of their position, female servants remained determined 'to assert bodily boundaries against the assumptions and intrusions of masters'. The same was true of women suspected of theft. These women invoked modesty and decency as justifications for resistance to searches, particularly searches by men. In one unusual case, a suspect 'would let no Body search her but a Man, so the Constable did'. For the most part, however, women preferred to be searched by other women. Mary Clark, suspected of pickpocketing, reportedly said that 'she'd let any Woman search her, but no Man'. When Susannah McKensey realised she was going to be searched 'she desir'd it might be by one of her own Sex'. Some went beyond words of protest. In 1724, Susanna Hutchins was brought before a justice after she refused to be searched by a constable. 'The Justice bidding him to search her by Violence, if she would not permit him by fair Means; he attempting it, she pull'd out a clasp'd Knife, threatning to stick him if he did attempt it'. All three of these efforts to resist were, one way or another, successful: the justice decided 'to get some Women to search' Hutchins, a constable's wife was called to search McKensey, and Clark was not searched at all (not coincidentally, she was later acquitted).[87]

The notion that it might be indecent for women to be searched by men was widespread. In his work on the policing of theft in late eighteenth-century Bristol, Matthew Neale suggested that 'there were gendered constraints on who could and could not search'.[88] In London, male householders, officers, and magistrates often asked their wives, female servants, or other women of their acquaintance to search female suspects.[89] A witness at the Old Bailey described how a married couple, 'Green and his Wife', carried out parallel searches of a man and woman suspected of stealing from them: 'Mrs. Green searched her, and he searched him'. This practice echoed the traditional involvement of officer's households in official business, as described in Chapter 1. But it was also closely connected to the new culture of policing in which certain groups of women, especially if they encountered officers in the streets late at night, were treated as inherently suspect. In 1737, a constable charged with searching Mary Lee at 2

---

[87] Gowing, *Common Bodies*, 64; *OBP*, Aug 1727, trial of Hannah Wittermore (t17270830-12); *OBP*, Jun 1725, trial of Mary Clark alias Brown (t17250630-38); *OBP*, Sep 1746, trial of Susannah McKensey (t17460903-13).
[88] Matthew Neale, 'Property Crime in late eighteenth-century Bristol: Contexts of theft in a pre-modern city' (University of Leicester PhD thesis, 2013), 203.
[89] *OBP*, Feb 1731, trial of Elizabeth Panton (t17310224-41); *OBP*, Jun 1738, trial of Ann Holden (t17380628-32); *OBP*, Dec 1738, trial of Constance James (t17381206-15); *OBP*, Oct 1739, trial of Elizabeth Ward (t17391017-17); *OBP*, Jun 1743, trial of Ann Chaloner, Ann Poole (t17430629-49).

am wondered 'where ... shall I get Women to search you now, except they are Whores, – like your self'.⁹⁰ Sometimes men searched women up to a certain point but no further. One suspect recalled how 'The men searched us in the Kitchen, as far as Modesty would permit, and then the Women carried us thro' a Passage into a back Room and searched us to our Shifts'. Searches of female suspects could be less thorough when there were no women available to do the searching. One night in 1730, Mary Gardener 'was carried to the Watch-house, and was indeed searched there; but the Watch was not found there, being none but Men to search her'. By contrast, a constable who searched a woman for a stolen jewellery box testified that 'he search'd her as far as Modesty would permit, and not finding it, he charg'd Jane Jewell to search her further'. The trial report does not explain who Jewell was, but her search was considerably more invasive than the constable's. She stripped the suspect and 'felt the Box in a Place not to be mention'd with Modesty; and calling the Constable, with shaking and disturbing the Box fell from her'. Modesty failed to protect Ann Munford from a similarly invasive search by other women. When the men who had arrested her left the room, she 'stript herself to her Under Petticoat; and then told them, that her Modesty would not let her go any farther to expose her Nakedness; but they not being satisfy'd with such a Pretence, she lifted up her Petticoat and Smock together'.⁹¹

The insistence of some suspects that modesty required they be searched by people of the same gender may explain why more women were involved in searching people than in searching houses or making arrests. The data presented in Table 12 show that this was still – like other aspects of law enforcement – a male-dominated activity, but a substantial minority of the searches of people described in the London court records were carried out by women. Almost all of these were searches of other women (forty-nine of the fifty-three Old Bailey cases and twenty-five of the twenty-seven Middlesex Sessions cases). In part, this represents the examinations carried out by midwives and others of women and girls involved in cases of infanticide and rape.⁹² Searching bodies for signs of pregnancy and penetration

---

⁹⁰ *OBP*, Dec 1732, trial of Jane Murphey (t17321206-38); *OBP*, Jul 1737, trial of Mary Lee (t17370706-14).
⁹¹ *OBP*, Jun 1733, trial of Mary Brian, Ann Atkinson (t17330628-6); *OBP*, Apr 1730, trial of Mary Gardener (t17300408-18); *OBP*, May 1728, trial of Mary Jenkyns (t17280501-10); *OBP*, Aug 1725, trial of Ann Munford (t17250827-16).
⁹² For example: *OBP*, Oct 1695, trial of Nicolas Oliver, Henry Sharpe (t16951014-22); *OBP*, Jul 1715, trial of Daniel Bonnely (t17150713-35); *OBP*, Jan 1723, trial of Mary Radford (t17230116-38); *OBP*, Oct 1733, trial of Frances Deacon (t17331010-5); *OBP*, Apr 1749, trial of James Pomeroy (t17490411-22).

Table 12 *Gender of searchers in the records of the Old Bailey and Middlesex Quarter Sessions, 1674–1750*

Court	Searches by women	Searches by men	Searches by mixed groups	Total identifiable searchers
Old Bailey	53 (12.7 per cent)	345 (82.7 per cent)	19 (4.6 per cent)	417
Middlesex Sessions	27 (29.0 per cent)	63 (67.7 per cent)	3 (3.2 per cent)	93

required sexual knowledge which, as Gowing has shown, was generally attributed to wives and widows, whether they worked as midwives or not.[93] But many of these cases were searches for stolen goods, in which female suspects demanded to be searched by women rather than men, or the men who wanted them searched felt unable to do it themselves.

This should not obscure the fact that most of the women searched in these records were searched by men. These searches were also shaped by the condition of women's bodies and by (men's) sexual knowledge. Searching women of different ages, for example, seems to have been understood differently. A man who accused Sarah Martin and Sarah Mullenux – 'a young Whore and an old Bawd' – of stealing his watch called a friend to help him look for it. They stripped Martin naked, 'but did not search Mullenux, for she's an old Woman'. The thinking behind this distinction is not clear, but it may be relevant that the man who accused these women was described by one witness at the Old Bailey as 'a common Whoremonger' who, as he acknowledged in his own testimony, had just been 'very close together' with Martin on a bed in Mullenux's house. If young women could be subjected to sexualised searches, those who were pregnant could sometimes draw on the protection of propriety, like Mary Jackson, who warded off a search on suspicion of shoplifting in 1717: 'telling them she was with Child and threatning them, they did not make a thorough search'.[94]

Just as married women searched for signs of rape or pregnancy on the basis of their presumed sexual knowledge, intimate searches of women by men were sometimes legitimated by male knowledge of women's bodies, specifically the knowledge of female anatomy which married men were

---

[93] Gowing, *Common Bodies*, 40–51.
[94] *OBP*, Aug 1727, trial of Sarah Martin, Sarah Mullenux (t17270830-40); *OBP*, Sep 1717, trial of Mary Jackson (t17170911-34). See also *OBP*, Feb 1733, trial of Sarah Malcolm (t17330221-52).

thought to possess. In 1750, a male lodger in the house of a burgled woman helped to search the prime suspect. As he explained to the Old Bailey, 'I happened to bob my hand against her belly, and feeling something hard, asked her what it was; she replied, it is only my two bones; said another man, if you are going to feel, we are all married men; I took out of a private place under her petticoats all of the things'.[95] The sense that married men were particularly well-qualified to search women was shared by some female suspects themselves. Barbara Hewsly, arrested on suspicion of a property offence for at least the second time in 1732, was taken to the St Giles roundhouse to be searched. Searches of women that took place in roundhouses and watch-houses, spaces dominated by fraternities of male officers, seem to have been especially intrusive and coercive. On this occasion, one of the men who had arrested Hewsly recalled seeing her stoop to hide something under her petticoats and challenged her:

> Bab, you have certainly got this Watch about you. Where have I got it? Says she. I told her in what Place. Why then, says she, as you are a married Man, you may search; and with that as she sat in the Chair, she parted her Feet, and remov'd the Covering, I refus'd to search, and so did Mr. Cross; but we told the Governor [the keeper of the roundhouse] it was his Business, and at last he agreed to do it. When she found we were come to a Resolution, she made some Resistance; but I and Mr. Cross kept her Feet in a proper Situation, while the Governor examin'd the Premises; after some search he call'd out, and told us, that he had got hold of the Chain at last; but says he, I had much ado to reach it, and with that he drew the Watch out, and in a sad Condition it was; we cleansed it, and carried it to the Gentleman, who own'd it.[96]

Did Hewsly change her mind about having her body searched because the governor of the roundhouse was not 'a married Man'? Or was she attempting to prove her innocence by showing a willingness to be searched, not thinking the men would actually go through with it? Regardless, her experience shows that London officers were willing, perhaps especially within the confines of watch-houses, to sweep aside the unwritten rules about who could search who. Ideas of modesty and sexual knowledge were weak defences against determined policing.

Accounts of men searching women by force can easily be read as narratives of sexual assault. For example, in a study of Inquisitorial encounters with Morisco women in sixteenth-century Spain, Ronald Surtz labels

---

[95] *OBP*, Dec 1750, trial of Jane Faulkner (t17501205-57).
[96] *OBP*, Jan 1733, trial of Barbara Hewsley (t17330112-4).

searches for Arabic texts hidden under women's skirts or in their bodices 'a kind of symbolic rape'.[97] Before making any such claim about searches of suspects in late seventeenth- and eighteenth-century London, it is worth pointing out that some suspects, both women and men, consented to searching or even asked to be searched. For those who were confident of their innocence, or of the fact that they had hidden illicit objects elsewhere, submitting to a search was a good way to dispel suspicion. In 1697, a soldier accused of robbery 'answered I have done noe Robbery & you may search mee' and was subsequently allowed to go on his way. In an effort to prove she had not picked a man's pocket, one Londoner was said to have 'stript her self quite naked, that he might search her'.[98] This practice was common enough that it sometimes backfired, causing victims of theft to suspect those who were willing to be searched even more vehemently. A publican whose house was robbed in 1748 announced he would search everyone in the house, but his suspicions soon came to focus on one man 'Because he was more ready to strip and be searched than the rest'.[99]

There is also evidence, however, of considerable fear of searching among suspects. This was not simply the fear of being caught; women and men confessed to theft and handed over stolen goods, condemning themselves to whipping, transportation, or even hanging, just to avoid being searched.[100] Officers and others used the dread of searching to their advantage. When Ann Davis was arrested in 1726, 'she at first deny'd the having any Money about her', but when the constable 'threaten'd to have her stript and searched, she confest that she had 6 Guineas about her'. Another constable told a woman 'I would search her to her Smock, if she would not confess', which produced the desired result.[101]

These fears were not unfounded, especially not for women. The level of violence involved in searching a person varied from case to case. Many

---

[97] Ronald E. Surtz, 'Morisco Women, Written Texts, and the Valencia Inquisition', *The Sixteenth Century Journal* 32.2 (2001), 430.

[98] LMA, MJ/SP/1697/12/039, Information of John Barnes, 5 Nov 1697; *OBP*, Apr 1722, trial of Alice Phenix (t17220404-14). See also LMA, MJ/SP/1707/09/022, Information of Elizabeth Lowde, 17 Jul 1707; *OBP*, Jan 1717, trial of William North, John Neal (t17170111-13); *OBP*, Jan 1727, trial of Elizabeth Travers (t17270113-6); *OBP*, Feb 1728, trial of Benjamin Branch (t17280228-43); *OBP*, Apr 1733, trial of Catherine Tracey (t17330404-46).

[99] *OBP*, Apr 1748, trial of Thomas Middleton (t17480420-14).

[100] *OBP*, Aug 1723, trial of John Sturt (t17230828-11); *OBP*, Jan 1724, trial of Sarah Matthews (t17240117-28); *OBP*, Aug 1728, trial of Sarah Darvill, Margaret Bristow (t17280828-3); *OBP*, Aug 1728, trial of Ann Wichard (t17280828-7); *OBP*, Oct 1729, trial of Alice Haley, Judith Smith (t17291015-40); *OBP*, May 1743, trial of Joseph Ward (t17430519-1); *OBP*, Sep 1749, trial of Mary Dimer (t17490906-84).

[101] *OBP*, Jul 1726, trial of Ann Davis (t17260711-2); *OBP*, Feb 1743, trial of Ann Bradford (t17430223-23).

accounts of searching elided the use of force to overcome resistance. One searcher recalled in court that 'She damn'd me and would not be search'd; but I search'd her'. Another noted parenthetically that '(she was very unwilling to be search'd), from under the left bosom I took out this box'.[102] Others mentioned violence explicitly but without comment: 'the said Sarah Stibbs in searching of the said Turner did strike the said Turner as also did Elizabeth Johnson'.[103] Officers often reported their own use of force in more detail, apparently without any hesitation or sense of wrongdoing. At one Old Bailey trial in 1722, 'The Constable depos'd, that the Watchman putting his Finger in her Mouth, she bit a piece of it off; but squeezing her hard by the Throat, forced 5s. 6d. out of her Mouth'. Another officer recalled how 'I asked her for the watch, but she would not give it me; I was forced to thumb screw her before I could get it, and I found it in a leather pocket under her petticoats'. In 1740, a watchman who claimed to have been restrained by modesty in his first search of a female suspect was perfectly willing to coerce her in his second attempt: 'I would have searched Harding, but she resisted, and we were forced to get three Watchmen to hold her; then I got one Leg over my Knee, as the Farriers shoe Horses, and just by the left Side of her Ancle-Bone, I found Half a Crown'.[104]

Almost all of the women on the receiving end of these forceful searches had been accused of pickpocketing. Searches by officers of women suspected of this crime seem to have been particularly violent and invasive. This may have something to do with the fact that small objects stolen out of pockets could be hidden in the most intimate parts of the body. But it may also be related to the context in which accusations of pickpocketing arose. Many suspected pickpockets were sex workers, or women who men assumed were selling sex.[105] Some took the opportunity to pick their clients' pockets. Others refused to have sex with men, who then retaliated by claiming their pockets had been picked. As one defendant put it, 'the Prosecutor would have done what she would not let him, and because she would not comply, [he] charged her with picking his Pocket'. In 1718, when Mary Betts resisted a man's attempts, first to rape her, then to have her 'Flog' him with feathers and a whipcord, 'he tax'd her with picking

---

[102] *OBP*, Feb 1736, trial of Grace Williams (t17360225-5); *OBP*, Sep 1749, trial of Lucy Lake (t17490906-69).
[103] LMA, MJ/SP/1701/09/002, Examination of Francis Turner, 13 Aug 1701.
[104] *OBP*, Apr 1722, trial of Jane Behn alias Macopny (t17220404-12); *OBP*, Feb 1748, trial of Ann Thomas (t17480224-7); *OBP*, May 1740, trial of Martha Harding, Rachel Bowling (t17400522-7).
[105] Beattie, *Crime and the Courts*, 180–1.

his Pocket'. Women who consented to sex for money could be accused of pickpocketing by men frustrated at their own impotence. Samuel Bonamy charged two women with picking his pocket in 1735 after, as one of them put it, 'he was in Carnal Copulation with Nan Taylor, and because he could not do it according to his mind, he swore he would be revenged upon us'.[106]

Men who took this path to vengeance assumed that these women had no right to refuse access to their bodies. When they took their accusations of pickpocketing to officers, those accusations became legally transferrable suspicions. As discussed in the previous chapter, from the later seventeenth century onward an officer could make arrests on the basis of suspicions reported by others: 'such an information may carry over the suspicion even to the constable, whereby it may become his suspicion'.[107] The women accused of picking pockets were often the same women who most readily attracted London officers' own suspicions: poor, walking alone, associated (or presumed to be associated) with selling sex. This made the transfer of suspicions all too easy. Moreover, prosecutors' assumptions of access to female bodies also seem to have been transferred to the officers who searched them for evidence. The shield of modesty with which others were able to prevent unwelcome searches offered suspected pickpockets little protection.

One evening in November 1733, the year of outraged protests against the Excise and its alleged intrusions, Margaret Webb was approached by a man in the street near the parish church of St Giles. In his version of events, she 'begg'd for a Pint of Beer', took him to an alehouse and stole his watch while they were drinking in a private room. In Webb's version, he 'overpersuaded' her to go to the alehouse and 'wanted to have to do with me, but having no Money he gave me the Watch to pawn for a Guinea, and then, because I refus'd to let him have his Will, he charged me with picking his Pocket'. A constable took her to the parish round-house where, after an initial search 'in the common Way' revealed no sign of the timepiece, the officers present 'concluded she had put it in a certain private Place'. One of the watchmen recounted what happened next:

> we propos'd to search her, but she refusing to let us, Mr. Hazeldine, the Governor of the Round house, desir'd his Wife to do it; but she bid him do it himself, for she would not be concern'd in any such Jobb. Whereupon he

---

[106] *OBP*, Sep 1719, trial of Rose Knight (t17191903-44); *OBP*, Jan 1718, trial of Mary Betts (17180110-61); *OBP*, Sep 1735, trial of Ann Maund, Rachel Needham (t17350911-10).
[107] Hale, *Placitorum Coronae*, vol. 2, 92.

undertook it, and I and the Constable of the Night, assisted in holding the Prisoner, while he examin'd her.

Another watchman, who turned his head away from Webb as he held down her hands, 'heard one of them say, that he felt it, and soon after, that he had got it out, and then I venture[d] to look back, and saw the Watch in his hand'. In Webb's own testimony, she said the officers 'stumbled and stumbled, and trowd me about till the Watch was found'.[108]

Like many others, Margaret Webb encountered the state in the form of a search by London's male officers. A legal framework which protected property and the household left her without resources to defend her body. The informal rules of decency made Mistress Hazeldine, Master Hazeldine, and the other officers reluctant to search her at first, but those restraints fell away once they had begun. The watchman who turned to look away protected his own modesty as he helped to violate hers. The whole episode was emblematic of the kind of specialised fraternal policing which had emerged out of the old officeholding system. Here was a group of male officers, working together in the watch-house under the impersonal authority of the criminal law, pursuing their suspicions of a woman by whatever means that law allowed. In the case of Margaret Webb, state authority took physical form in the hands that searched her and the hands that held her down.

[108] *OBP*, Dec 1733, trial of Margaret Webb (t17331205-7).

Conclusion

The emergence of policing as a distinct form of state activity was a process profoundly shaped by gender. It began with the separation of certain kinds of officeholding from the patriarchal household. This was accomplished by defining those offices as impersonal, not bound up with the individual identity of the officeholder. In practice, however, notions of impersonal officeholding allowed such offices to become more closely aligned with manhood than ever before. In London, constables and watchmen developed a fraternal culture of aggressive masculinity. One element of that culture was the targeted use of discretionary powers to arrest and search suspects, especially women accused of theft and sex work. Law enforcement in the capital became gendered in ways which persisted for centuries to come.

Uncovering this story contributes to several areas of historiography in a number of different ways. Most straightforwardly, it brings the history of policing into dialogue with histories of officeholding and, through them, histories of the early modern state. The early modern analogy between household and state is well known. This analogy was made manifest at a local level by householders who were also officeholders, combining domestic and state authority in a single person. What is less well known is how this pattern was perpetuated, especially by the notion of 'independence' and its relationship to gendered, social, and economic hierarchies. In laying out these connections, Chapter 1 provides a counterpoint to the picture of early modern officeholding drawn by Mark Goldie, while at the same time following his observation that the subject 'comes to life when we draw together the insights of social historians and historians of political thought'.[1] It also highlights the previously neglected role of the officeholding household in allowing some domestic subordinates to participate in

---

[1] Mark Goldie, 'The Unacknowledged Republic: Officeholding in Early Modern England' in Tim Harris (ed.), *The Politics of the Excluded, c.1500–1850* (Basingstoke, 2001), 154.

the process of government. This offers a more sophisticated way of thinking about how office was gendered and extends the findings of recent work on the authority of married women into the arena of local government.[2]

The separation of office from household is a forgotten feature of early modern state formation. This was, as Chapters 2 and 3 show, an uneven and complex process of legal, administrative, and social change. In the case of the Excise, it was the intended result of a deliberate attempt to detach offices from local society. In the case of law enforcement officers, it was the unintended result of an earlier set of policies. Judges and legislators in the early years of the seventeenth-century were engaged in a sustained effort to define, control, and reinforce officers' authority. Many decades later, the 'ministerial' model of officeholding produced by these efforts played a key role in facilitating the withdrawal of London householders from the offices of law enforcement and their replacement by paid deputies. Ministerial officers did not have to be householders because their authority came from above, not from their social position. As discussed below, separation from the household continued to be a key feature of urban policing well beyond the early modern period.

The legal distinction between ministerial and judicial offices has not been studied before. Nor have the numerous clauses in seventeenth-century legislation allowing officers to plead the general issue and give special matter in evidence. Both were designed by judges and legislators to address specific contemporary problems, but they were also part of a wider legal effort to draw clearer lines between the official and the personal, a central theme in the history of the state.[3] This is not to say that Jacobean judges were advocates of a Weberian bureaucracy. Rather, the construction of the law of office shows how distinctions between person and office were made in order to regulate and reinforce the everyday exercise of authority, to supervise officers' activities and strengthen their position as conduits of state power.

More broadly, this book emphasises the importance of law as a vehicle of state formation. Many scholars have discussed the importance of civil litigation in this regard. In the Elizabethan and early Stuart periods, people

---

[2] Garthine Walker, 'Expanding the Boundaries of Female Honour in Early Modern England', *Transactions of the Royal Historical Society* (1996); Alexandra Shepard, 'Provision, Household Management and the Moral Authority of Wives and Mothers in Early Modern England' in Michael J. Braddick and Phil Withington (eds.), *Popular Culture and Political Agency in Early Modern England: Essays in Honour of John Walter* (Woodbridge, 2017).

[3] Michael J. Braddick, 'The Early Modern English State and the Question of Differentiation, from 1550–1700', *Comparative Studies in Society and History* 38.1 (1996).

increasingly turned to the courts to resolve or escalate interpersonal disputes, bringing the state into their relations with each other and thereby expanding its reach.[4] Here, following the example set by Paul Halliday, David Chan Smith, and Krista Kesselring, the focus has been on the law writ large, as disseminated from the central courts and in legal literature.[5] The seventeenth-century remaking of the law of office made the state a more powerful presence in interactions between officers and others. By conjuring state authority, officers laid claim to powerful legal protections which licensed them to use force, further criminalised resistance, and restricted the possibilities of legal redress for official actions. In the later seventeenth and early eighteenth centuries, these advantages formed a potent combination with wide and widening powers to arrest and search people on the basis of suspicion alone. The minutiae of legal changes can sometimes disappear in wide-ranging discussions of the relationship between state and society, but they played a crucial role in shaping the everyday experience of the state in early modern England.

Each of these points helps to address the larger question of the relationship between gender and state authority in early modern England. One way to think about this is to focus on a key feature of much recent writing about the early modern state: participation. Paying attention to gender reframes popular participation in officeholding, law enforcement, and other areas of government. The vast majority of people taking part in these activities were men. This does not, however, invalidate the claim that the early modern state depended on widespread participation. Rather, it highlights the need to consider the specific qualifications required for different kinds of participation and the ways in which they shaped access to state authority. Where householding and economic independence were the basic requirements, as in much local officeholding, only the heads of middling households – mostly though not exclusively men – participated in government directly.

Thinking about participation in this way makes it possible to analyse the gender-state relationship as a dynamic historical process. Male domination

---

[4] There is a large literature on this subject. Key works include: Christopher W. Brooks, *Pettyfoggers and Vipers of the Commonwealth: The 'Lower Branch' of the Legal Profession in Early Modern England* (Cambridge, 1986); Craig Muldrew, 'The Culture of Reconciliation: Community and the Settlement of Economic Disputes in Early Modern England', *The Historical Journal* 39.4 (1996); Steve Hindle, *The State and Social Change in Early Modern England, 1550–1640* (Basingstoke, 2000).
[5] Paul Halliday, *Habeas Corpus: From England to Empire* (Cambridge, MA, 2010); David Chan Smith, *Sir Edward Coke and the Reformation of the Laws* (Cambridge, 2014); K. J. Kesselring, *Making Murder Public: Homicide in Early Modern England, 1480–1680* (Oxford, 2019).

of official positions was produced by ideas and practices which might be adapted, contested, or displaced. The entanglement between officeholding and householding was caused by the combination of three factors: a legal category (*idoneus homo*), hierarchical employment and family structures, and a widespread notion that wealth correlated with the capacity for independent action. The latter two factors persisted throughout the early modern period, but their combined power to bind officeholding to householding was substantially weakened by changes to the law. Ideas of impersonal or 'ministerial' officeholding undermined the ideal of the *idoneus homo* and allowed the partial disentangling of office from household. The question of who might serve as a ministerial officer was determined by a different set of factors. From the 1690s onward, London householders who were chosen to serve as constables or watchmen could appoint anyone they liked to act as a deputy in return for relatively meagre pay. The pool from which they chose, however, was shaped by the emerging culture of fraternal law enforcement and patterns of poverty based on the life cycle. Deputies were always male and tended to be either young and unmarried or beyond what contemporaries considered middle age. This mode of selection, rooted in very different ideas about the nature of officeholding, forged links between state authority and a non-householding form of masculinity.

The relationship between gender and policing can be seen in a similar light. Most work on this subject has concentrated on a particular time and place, revealing the many and complex ways in which gender shaped practices of law enforcement or the identities of the officers involved.[6] What is often missing is a sense of how one form of gendered policing transformed into another. Understandably, 'a strong narrative of continuity' arises from what Susan Broomhall and David Barrie describe as 'the deep and abiding relationship of power to masculinity within policing'.[7] The obvious exception is in histories of policing by women from the late nineteenth to the twenty-first century, which show how incorporating female officers was closely related to substantial changes in the overall nature of law enforcement.[8] One of the central aims of this book is to provide a

[6] For example: David G. Barrie and Susan Broomhall, 'Policing Bodies in Urban Scotland, 1780–1850' in Susan Broomhall and Jacqueline Van Gent (eds.), *Governing Masculinities in the Early Modern Period: Regulating Selves and Others* (Farnham, 2011); David G. Barrie and Susan Broomhall (eds.), *A History of Police and Masculinities, 1700–2010* (Abingdon, 2012).
[7] Barrie and Broomhall, 'Introduction' in Barrie and Broomhall (eds.), *A History of Police and Masculinities*, 22.
[8] Louise A. Jackson, *Women Police: Gender, Welfare and Surveillance in the Twentieth Century* (Manchester, 2006). Another exception is the work of Haia Shpayer-Makov: 'Shedding the Uniform

preliminary account of an earlier shift from one kind of gendered policing to another: from local government by middling heads of household to law enforcement by fraternities of poorer and often unmarried men. Like scholarship on policing by women in more recent times, it argues that this gendered transition was linked to important developments in the nature of law enforcement, in this case the legal construction of an impersonal model of state authority.

The patterns of policing which arose from this transition are described in Chapters 4 and 5. Here, the book follows the work of David Churchill and Eleanor Bland in reconstructing past practices of law enforcement – specifically arrests – by assembling material scattered across court records. What emerges is a quantitative picture of who made arrests in London from the later seventeenth to the mid-eighteenth century, one which captures the shifting balance between official and unofficial involvement. Participation in this aspect of law enforcement was widespread but qualified in two ways. First, a large majority of those who made arrests were men. Second, most of the thousands of people brought to summary trial had been arrested by officers, and officers accounted for a growing proportion of the arrests which resulted in trials at Quarter Sessions or the Old Bailey. There is no need to view these findings through the ahistorical lens of what Churchill calls the 'state monopolisation thesis'.[9] In the first place, even in the 1730s and 1740s the proportion of arrests by officers mentioned in the records of the regular courts was only about half. More importantly, increasing official involvement in arrests was the result of several specific circumstances, not some inexorable march to modernity. Arrests by officers were made more likely by the rise of deputisation, the offer of rewards by statute and by associations for moral reform, and the shift in the law of suspicion to grant officers greater capacities to apprehend people who they had no reason to suspect themselves. As Bland has made clear, data on arrests derived from court records can also be used to explore how powers to arrest on suspicion were used in practice. In the period studied here, officers made discretionary judgements about suspects based on a mixture of gender, social status, and legally justifiable grounds for suspicion.

---

and Acquiring a New Masculine Image: The Case of the Late-Victorian and Edwardian English Police Detective' in Barrie and Broomhall (eds.), *A History of Police and Masculinities*.

[9] David C. Churchill, *Crime Control and Everyday Life in the Victorian City: The Police and the Public* (Oxford, 2017); Eleanor Bland, *Policing Suspicion: Proactive Policing in London, 1780–1850* (Abingdon, 2021); David C. Churchill, 'Rethinking the State Monopolisation Thesis: The Historiography of Policing and Criminal Justice in Nineteenth-Century England', *Crime, History & Societies* 18.1 (2014).

Arrests which resulted in summary trial – a far larger number than ever reached the regular courts – appear to have been especially gendered, with officers routinely targeting women they found in the wrong place at the wrong time.

Applying the same methodology to searches – both of houses and of people – yields striking results. Searches have received some attention from legal scholars but very little from historians before the later twentieth century.[10] The history of searches – both of houses and people – encapsulates the complex interplay between gender, policing, and individual rights (or the lack of them). Households may have become less central to officeholding, but they lost none of their legal status as protected spaces. Householders were far better protected from searches than people whose notionally private territory consisted of a room in someone else's house or, worse still, a locked box or trunk. Most notably, in the absence of any legal constraints, searches of clothing and bodies were only regulated by such informal notions of propriety as the people being searched were able to assert. These could not prevent male officers from conducting highly invasive searches of women, especially women accused of pickpocketing and sex work. Encounters like this make it clear that officers' personhood, especially their masculinity, could never be entirely detached from their exercise of authority, regardless of how 'ministerial' they were supposed to be.

The ideas and practices of policing established in this period had significant consequences in the long term. Much of the old officeholding regime survived: churchwardens, for example, never appointed deputies on a large scale and remained amateur householders for centuries to come. In the offices of law enforcement, however, London's fraternal model of policing was increasingly institutionalised and subsequently reproduced in other parts of the country.

Rotational amateur officeholding became little more than a distant memory. Deputisation among Westminster constables was given statutory approval in 1756, by which time Henry Fielding had created a group of full-time salaried constables to pursue thieves and claim the rewards granted to those who prosecuted them successfully.[11] Fielding's Bow Street Runners provided the model for further organisational innovations towards the end

---

[10] The most extensive treatment is a teleological legal history of the Fourth Amendment of the U.S. Constitution: William J. Cuddihy, *The Fourth Amendment: Origins and Original Meaning 602–1791* (Oxford, 2009).

[11] 29 Geo. II c.25 (1756); J. M. Beattie, *The First English Detectives: The Bow Street Runners and the Policing of London, 1750–1840* (Oxford, 2012).

of the century: the 1792 Middlesex Justices Act and the creation of the Marine Police (1798) and Thames River Police (1800). By this time, the notion that salaries made officers dangerously dependent on their paymasters had all but disappeared. A handbook for constables announced that 'every man who serves the public ought to be paid by the public', a statement that would have been met with incredulity by early eighteenth-century opponents of the Excise. The spread of professional police forces only confirmed this change, beginning in Dublin in 1786, spreading to Scottish cities around the turn of the century, and becoming widely established in England several decades later.[12] By the early twentieth century the connection between regular wages and dependence had been wholly reversed. Ezekiel Polsted's satirical attempts to make a virtue of excisemen's salaries were echoed without irony by a Manchester chief constable in 1930, who insisted that his officers received 'pay and allowances of a sufficiently high standard to ensure independent and faithful service'.[13]

Institutional reforms in the late eighteenth and nineteenth centuries had little impact on the discretionary powers wielded by officers. A series of statutes authorised constables and watchmen to arrest people who they suspected of committing or intending to commit theft and various other offences, but this legislation only codified longstanding practices and powers granted by common law.[14] As a legal advisor to the Metropolitan Police put it, the new police officers had been 'expressly invested with the powers and duties of the old parish constables' and 'the possession of them is so essential that however they may be supplemented by modern legislation without them no police force could exist for a day'.[15] There was no change of comparable significance to the legalisation of transferred suspicions discussed in Chapter 4. Sporadic challenges were launched, in print and in the courts, to what one critic

---

[12] As F. W. Maitland recognised in 1885, 'A Full History of the New Police Would Probably Lay Its First Scene in Ireland': *Justice and Police* (London, 1885), 108. On these institutional developments, see Stanley H. Palmer, *Police and Protest in England and Ireland, 1780–1850* (Cambridge, 1985); David Barrie, *Police in the Age of Improvement: Police Development and the Civic Tradition in Scotland, 1775–1865* (Cullompton, 2008).
[13] Joseph Ritson, *The Office of Constable* (London, 1791), xii; Clive Emsley, *The English Police: A Political and Social History* (2nd edition, Harlow, 1996), 245.
[14] 25 Geo. II c.36 s.12 (1751); 11 Geo. III c.54 s.15 (1771); 14 Geo. III c.90 (1774); 32 Geo. III c.53 s.17 (1792); 39&40 Geo. III c.87 s.12 (1800); 52 Geo. III c.17 s.30 (1812); 2&3 Vict. c.47 s.66 (1839); 25&26 Vict. c.110 (1862); Paul Lawrence, 'The Vagrancy Act (1824) and the Persistence of Pre-Emptive Policing in England since 1750', *British Journal of Criminology* 57 (2017).
[15] Quoted in Carolyn Steedman, *Policing the Victorian Community: The Formation of English Provincial Police Forces, 1856–80* (London, 1984), 158. See also H.B. Simpson, 'The Office of Constable', *English Historical Review* 10.40 (1895), 636.

called the 'hideous power' to arrest on suspicion, but these were no more effective than the appeals to due process made by chief justice Holt in the early eighteenth century.[16]

What may have changed, however, was who officers tended to suspect. Bland argues that between 1780 and 1850, London officers who made arrests on suspicion of felony generally targeted young men, contributing to the Victorian notion of a poor and predominantly male 'criminal class'. This suggests a move away from the discretionary policing of female suspects, but further research is needed to firmly establish changing patterns of arrest on suspicion over the long term.[17] Any straightforward narrative of shifting targets is complicated by differences in the gender distribution of arrests for different offences. Londoners arrested on suspicion of night-walking or vagrancy, for example, remained predominantly female at least until the early nineteenth century.[18] Poor women, especially those suspected of sex work, continued to face frequent official interference. According to a 1785 poem, one of a constable's primary activities was 'consigning poor devils of female prostitutes in dark holes'. In 1803, the watchmen of Castle Baynard in the City of London were instructed 'particularly, to keep the Ward clear of Harlots, or Common Women'.[19] The 1824 Vagrancy Act formalised the long-established link between sex work and prosecutions for vagrancy; anyone suspected of being a 'Common Prostitute' could be arrested as 'an idle and disorderly Person'. In 1900, as one woman wrote to an MP, police were still 'prone to take the bad character of women who are out at night very easily for granted'.[20]

More research is also needed to trace racialised aspects of policing by suspicion. For the seventeenth and eighteenth centuries, this is hampered by the fact that most court records give few details about suspects'

---

[16] Robert Holloway, *The Rat-Trap* (London, 1773), 21; Tim Hitchcock and Robert Shoemaker, *London Lives: Poverty, Crime and the Making of a Modern City 1690–1800* (Cambridge, 2015), 310–14.

[17] Bland, *Policing Suspicion*. Bland's methodology is different to the one used in Chapter 4, complicating any attempt to compare or combine the two datasets. The later period offers more extensive source material, so Bland is able to focus exclusively on arrests made on the basis of suspicion, rather than setting such arrests in the context of a broader analysis of arresting practices. Nonetheless, there is clear agreement between Bland's work and the material presented in Chapter 4 on the long-term importance of suspicion in the history of London law enforcement.

[18] Nicholas Rogers, 'Policing the Poor in Eighteenth-Century London: The Vagrancy Laws and Their Administration', *Social History* 24.47 (1991), 133; Kiran Mehta, 'Summary Justice in Eighteenth- and Nineteenth-Century Southwark', *Crime, History & Societies* 24.1 (2020), 60, 70–75.

[19] *Daily Universal Register* (11 Apr 1785), 2; Andrew T. Harris, *Policing the City: Crime and Legal Authority in London, 1780–1840* (Columbus, 2004), 15.

[20] 5 Geo. IV c.83 s.3 (1824); David Taylor, 'Cass, Coverdale and Consent: The Metropolitan Police and Working-Class Women in Late-Victorian London', *Cultural and Social History* 12.1 (2015); *Hansard* HC Debates, 4th series, vol. 85, col. 1545.

identities beyond their names, which can be used with reasonable accuracy to identify Irish or Jewish people, but not members of the growing African and African-American populations.[21] In a rare and suggestive case heard by Middlesex magistrates in 1699, 'a Moore' named John Adams was arrested by two bystanders when he was seen running in the Strand shortly after a white gentleman was beaten and robbed. The gentleman was not certain about who had attacked him, and when Adams was charged with committing the robbery he insisted 'he did not, nor knoweth that any Gentleman was knockt downe or Robb'd'.[22] More straightforward evidence of arrests based on racialised suspicions is available from the late eighteenth century onward. In 1771, in the aftermath of a widely reported murder by a Jewish 'gang' in Chelsea, Jews who had no connection to the case were arrested on suspicion as far away as Truro.[23] Irish Londoners were similarly overpoliced, a pattern which also appeared in other cities and which only intensified over the course of the nineteenth century.[24]

The officers who used their discretionary powers in this way were mostly young unmarried men who participated in a culture of official fraternity. Deputisation and detachment from the household had allowed both older and younger men to serve in the offices of law enforcement, but the stereotype of the 'superannuated watchman' did not survive the period of major institutional reform. An 1821 statute banned the employment of watchmen aged over forty and county police forces created in the mid-nineteenth century recruited on the same basis. Officers in the Metropolitan Police were even younger: the maximum recruitment age was thirty-five in 1829

---

[21] Norma Myers, *Reconstructing the Black Past: Blacks in Britain c.1780–1830* (London, 1996); Karen A. Macfarlane, 'Ethnic Minorities and Criminal Justice in Eighteenth-Century London' (York University Toronto PhD thesis, 2008); Adam Crymble, 'A Comparative Approach to Identifying the Irish in Long Eighteenth-Century London', *Historical Methods* 48.3 (2015).

[22] LMA, MJ/SP/1699/01/067–68, Informations of Richard Wiseman, Samuel Jewell, John Adams, 30 Dec 1698. Peter King and John Carter Wood have shown that in terms of prosecutions and jury verdicts there was 'little, if any, systematic prejudice towards black people' at the Old Bailey in the late eighteenth and early nineteenth centuries, though this does not rule out prejudice in policing, particularly at the level of offences dealt with summarily by magistrates: 'Black People and the Criminal Justice System: Prejudice and Practice in Later Eighteenth- and Early Nineteenth-Century London', *Historical Research* 88.239 (2015), 124.

[23] Todd M. Endelmann, *The Jews of Georgian England, 1714–1830: Tradition and Change in a Liberal Society* (Philadelphia, 1979), 199.

[24] Peter King, 'Ethnicity, Prejudice, and Justice: The Treatment of the Irish at the Old Bailey, 1750–1825', *Journal of British Studies* 52 (2013); Peter King, 'Immigrant Communities, the Police and the Courts in Late Eighteenth and Early Nineteenth-Century London', *Crime, History & Societies* 20.1 (2016); David C. Churchill, 'Crime, Policing and Control in Leeds, c.1830–1890' (Open University PhD thesis, 2013), 155–56; Jennifer Davis, 'From "Rookeries" to "Communities": Race, Poverty and Policing in London, 1850–1985', *History Workshop Journal* 27.1 (1989).

and fell to twenty-seven by the end of the nineteenth century. Across the country, most of the men who became police officers were in their early or mid-twenties, the vast majority of them single. Some recruitment posters stated that 'No Married Men Need Apply' and many nineteenth-century forces required two or three years of service (rare in a period of extremely high officer turnover) before permitting an officer to marry. Robert Peel had considered barring married men from the capital's constabulary altogether.[25] In 1833, a member of London's Common Council called for a return to law enforcement by mature heads of household, at least at night, 'for his experience told him that at night young men were thinking of something else'. Officers of the new police forces lived together in section houses which bore some resemblance to the 'offices' inhabited by excisemen: shared male spaces in which 'a rough, masculine culture' took shape. Here, constables talked, gambled, played pranks, and fought together, boasted and gossiped about sex, and above all drank to excess. Four-fifths of dismissals from the Metropolitan Police in 1834 were for drunkenness, and this was not atypical. As Carolyn Steedman noted, 'most policemen were assumed to have a drinking problem'. In recognition (or support) of this hard-drinking masculine culture, single women were not permitted to enter some section houses until well into the twentieth century. Officers in urban forces seem, like some excisemen, to have been prone to sexually assaulting the women they encountered in the course of their duties, particularly women they assumed were selling sex. Disciplinary records suggest these assaults were more frequent in periods when higher proportions of constables were young and unmarried.[26]

The situation was slightly different in rural areas, at least in southern England, where some attempt was made to reconstitute the official households described in Chapter 1. The wives of married constables in county constabularies were expected to take messages, receive lost property or reports of crime, and generally act as informal auxiliaries to their husbands. This helps to explain why some forces prevented their officers' wives engaging in full-time employment, taking lodgers, or running premises licensed

---

[25] 1&2 Geo. IV c.118 (1821); Haia Shpayer-Makov, 'A Portrait of a Novice Constable in the London Metropolitan Police, c.1900', *Criminal Justice History* 12 (1990), 138–9; Emsley, *English Police*, 191, 212; Steedman, *Policing the Victorian Community*, 80–81; Ruth Paley, 'An Imperfect, Inadequate and Wretched System? Policing London before Peel', *Criminal Justice History* 10 (1989), 130 n.61.

[26] Donald Rumbelow, *I Spy Blue: The Police and Crime in the City of London from Elizabeth I to Victoria* (London, 1971), 121; Emsley, *English Police*, 208–9, 217–18, 62, 239; Steedman, *Policing the Victorian Community*, 151; Joanne Klein, *Invisible Men: The Lives of Police Constables in Liverpool, Manchester and Birmingham, 1900–1939* (Liverpool, 2010), 222–7, 241–47.

to sell alcohol.[27] More broadly, officers in rural forces were closer to the old ideal of the substantial local householder, governing his neighbours as he governed himself and his family. Most were born in the county they served, whereas constables in London and other towns and cities tended to come from elsewhere in the country or from Ireland.[28] Like the excisemen of the early modern period, these outsiders were not warmly welcomed. In 1839, a Norfolk clergyman who opposed the creation of a centralised force in his own county called police constables 'a race without fathers and mothers, without habitation and home, coming from a distance, perhaps Ireland'. The following year a Leicestershire MP expressed fears of policing by 'strange hired functionaries, with no ... allowance for the circumstances of individual or locality, no appeal to the sympathies of the neighbourhood'. The fact that the police officers lived in barracks-like section houses and wore distinctive uniforms did nothing to dispel this impression. As Ruth Paley observed of the Metropolitan Police, 'the new institution was deliberately divorced from the local community'.[29] Arguments made against the expansion of the Excise in 1733 reappeared in claims that the new police were, as one Tory put it, 'a blue army' of 'servile instruments of the Executive' which 'will continually increase its encroachment on popular rights and the liberty of the subject'.[30] Widespread hostility to urban police officers continued into the late nineteenth century.[31]

In the face of this opposition, officers relied on impersonal authority of the kind developed by seventeenth-century judges and legislators. The constable's staff was replaced by a uniform and baton, but these new props sent much the same message: officers were representatives of the state who

---

[27] Malcolm Young, 'Police Wives: A Reflection of Police Concepts of Order and Control' in Hillary Callan and Shirley Ardener (eds.), *The Incorporated Wife* (London, 1984).

[28] Emsley, *English Police*, 197–99; Steedman, *Policing the Victorian Community*, 74–79.

[29] Robert D. Storch, 'Policing Rural Southern England before the Police: Opinion and Practice, 1830–1856' in Douglas Hay and Francis G. Snyder (eds.), *Policing and Prosecution in Britain, 1750–1850* (Oxford, 1989), 238–9; Paley, 'An Imperfect, Inadequate and Wretched System?', 118.

[30] David Philips, '"A New Engine of power and Authority": The Institutionalization of Law-Enforcement in England 1780–1830' in Vic Gatrell, Bruce Lenman, and Geoffrey Parker (eds.), *Crime and the Law: The Social History of Crime in Western Europe Since 1500* (London, 1980), 155–6. Similar concerns about dependent officers exercising a disproportionate influence in parliamentary elections led to the exclusion of police constables from voting, even those who met suffrage requirements, until the passage of the Police Disabilities Removal Act: 50&51 Vict. c.9 (1887).

[31] Robert D. Storch, 'The Plague of the Blue Locusts: Police Reform and Popular Resistance in Northern England, 1840–57', *International Review of Social History* 20.1 (1975); Robert D. Storch, 'The Policeman as Domestic Missionary: Urban Discipline and Popular Culture in Northern England, 1850–1880', *Journal of Social History* 9.4 (1976); David Churchill, '"I am just the man for Upsetting you Bloody Bobbies": Popular Animosity towards the Police in Late Nineteenth-Century Leeds', *Social History* 39.2 (2014).

commanded obedience in its name, and could, if necessary, overcome resistance with legitimate violence. As *The Times* put it in 1853, 'the sworn professional policeman, attired as such, and acting in a known and recognised capacity ... paralyses the opposition by the power which is felt to be at his back'. An essay in the *Quarterly Review* made the point even more clearly: 'The baton may be a very ineffective weapon of offence, but it is backed by the combined power of the Crown, the Government, and the Constituencies ... The mob quails before the simple baton of the police officer, and flies before it, well knowing the moral as well as physical force of the Nation whose will, as embodied in law, it represents'. As in the early modern period, officers' authority was bolstered by the useful fiction that their individual identities were subsumed by the power they represented. Another often-quoted *Quarterly Review* essay described the police constable as 'an institution rather than a man. We seem to have no more hold of his personality than we could possibly get hold of his coat buttoned up to the throttling-point. Go, however, to the section-house ... and there you will no longer see policemen, but men ... they are positively laughing with each other!'[32]

The authority wielded by these men of the section-house had much the same legal status as that of their predecessors in the watch-house. In fact, the most influential judicial ruling on the nature of a police constable referred explicitly to seventeenth-century precedents. In 1930, justice McCardie stated in King's Bench that police officers derived their authority from the highest power in the land, not the local authorities which paid their wages. 'It is clear from Mackalley's Case', he said, 'that a constable, watchman or the like person was regarded as a servant or minister of the King'. This applied no less to modern constables, who he described as 'public servants and officers of the Crown'. In language reminiscent of rulings given at King's Bench three hundred years earlier, McCardie labelled the police officer 'a servant of the State, a *ministerial* officer of the central power'.[33]

By the time of McCardie's judgment, officeholding was undergoing another gendered transformation. Small numbers of women had begun to serve as police constables, albeit without full powers. The origins of this development lay, in part, in the gendered practices of searching described

---

[32] *The Times* (7 Dec 1853), 8; 'The Police of London', *London Quarterly Review* (July 1870), 48; A. Wynter, 'The Police and the Thieves', *London Quarterly Review* (July 1856), 93.

[33] Fisher v Oldham Corporation (1930), 2 KB 364, All ER Rep 96. Italics added. On the context in which this judgment was given, see Graham Smith, *On the Wrong Side of the Law: Complaints against Metropolitan Police, 1829–1964* (London, 2020), 133–52.

in Chapter 5. Throughout the eighteenth century and for most of the nineteenth, female suspects continued to experience invasive, unregulated searching by male officers. Some were able to assert the claims of modesty and decency with enough force to prompt the fetching of a married officer's wife or female servant to search them instead. In the late nineteenth century, this practice began to be formalised. In Liverpool in the 1870s, the Watch Committee began to pay the wives of Bridwell keepers an annual salary for searching female prisoners, while the wife of the Cambridge head constable earned £10 a year as a 'female searcher'. In the following decade, Metropolitan Police Commissioners began hiring women as 'visitors' to search and generally supervise female detainees, and in 1889 the force hired its first police matrons, most of whom were married or otherwise related to serving officers.[34] Increasing the number of police matrons became a priority for some feminist campaigners. Florence Balgarnie, a suffragist and trade union leader, called (with some success) for the appointment of police matrons in every station to carry out searches of female suspects.[35] Feminists drew links between male officers' searches of women's bodies and the 'instrumental rape' of women suspected of sex work when they were checked by doctors for signs of venereal disease under the Contagious Diseases Acts.[36]

The CD Acts could be – and eventually were – repealed. Searches of women suspected of theft or other crimes could only be rendered less offensive by making sure the searcher was a woman. The rise of the female police officer was inextricably tied to the policing of women, including intrusive searches of women's bodies.[37] During the First World War, women were employed by the government to search female munitions workers as they entered and left factories. At the end of the war, along with volunteers who had monitored the sex lives of young women near military bases, some of these women became the first female police officers in Britain. Centuries of everyday resistance to being searched by male

---

[34] Philippa Levine, '"Walking the Streets in a Way No Decent Woman Should": Women Police in World War I', *Journal of Modern History* 66.1 (1994), 35–7; Steedman, *Policing the Victorian Community*, 118.

[35] Florence Balgarnie, *A Plea for the Appointment of Police Matrons at Police Stations* (London, 1894); Florence Balgarnie and Louisa Twining, *Police Matrons* (London, 1899).

[36] Judith Walkowitz, *Prostitution and Victorian Society: Women, Class, and the State* (Cambridge, 1983), 109–10, 130, 201–2; Philippa Levine, *Prostitution, Race, and Politics: Policing Venereal Disease in the British Empire* (New York, 2003).

[37] This is especially clear in the work of Louise Jackson: 'Care or Control? The Metropolitan Women Police and Child Welfare, 1919–1969', *Historical Journal* 46.3 (2003); '"The Coffee Club Menace": Policing Youth, Leisure and Sexuality in Post-War Manchester', *Cultural and Social History* 5.3 (2008); *Women Police*.

officers, and decades of feminist campaigning on the issue, at last created a system in which searcher and searchee were persons of the same gender.[38] The sense that this was a pyrrhic victory, and that invasive searches remain a problem whoever carries them out, is a feature of what Philippa Levine has called 'the schizophrenia of the women's police movement', its pursuit of equality for some women through intrusion into the lives of others.[39]

All of these developments – the prolonged fraternalisation of law enforcement, the persistent use of discretionary powers against poor women, the Victorian idea of the police officer as 'an institution rather than a man' – were products of particular contingencies. But they were also, in some respects, among the legacies of the early modern separation of office from household and the related emergence of a legal framework which treated certain officers as bearers of an impersonal authority. The changes described in this book constituted a crucial turning point in the much longer history of entanglement between male power and state power. The officers of the seventeenth and eighteenth centuries, along with the lawyers who defined their authority and the many women and men who encountered and resisted them, were the architects of a new kind of gendered policing, some elements of which remain with us to this day.

---

[38] This was never an absolute rule: only searches of inner clothing and strip searches were (and are) required to be carried out by officers of the same gender as the suspect. Searches of outer clothing were (and are) still permissible by officers of a different gender.

[39] Levine, '"Walking the Streets"', 78; Alison Woodeson, 'The First Women Police: A Force for Equality or Infringement?', *Women's History Review* 2.2 (1993).

Appendix A
Officeholding in Earls Colne

Source: Sarah Harrison, Charles Jardine, Tim King, Jessica King, and Alan Macfarlane, *Earls Colne, Essex. Records of an English Village 1375–1854* (2008) [dataset], www.dspace.cam.ac.uk/handle/1810/195838.

Every year, Earls Colne chose two constables, two overseers of the poor, and two churchwardens. The survival of documents relating to these people is uneven, but there is enough material to draw some provisional conclusions, summarised in Chapter 1. I established officeholders' names by examining vestry minutes, indentures of pauper apprenticeship, removal orders, overseers' accounts, settlement certificates, and poor rate books. I then searched the baptism and marriage registers for corresponding names, disregarding those cases in which two people shared a name and it was impossible to determine who the records referred to.

My primary concern is with the age and marital status of those who held office as constable, overseer of the poor, and churchwarden. For a discussion of Earls Colne officeholders in terms of their property ownership, see Henry French and Richard Hoyle, *The Character of English Rural Society: Earls Colne, 1550–1750* (Manchester, 2007), 255–66.

Constables 1603–1750

Where possible to find, the average age of constables upon entry to office across the period was 35.5 ($n = 55$). Broken down into four periods, the figures suggest a slight decline in the average age of constables:

1601–50 ($n = 11$), 37.5
1651–1700 ($n = 15$), 38.1
1701–25 ($n = 12$), 33.5
1726–50 ($n = 17$), 33.4

Of 212 terms of constableship, 152 (71.7 per cent) were served by men who were married before they entered office (probably an underestimate, accounting for cases where the marriage date can only be determined as before birth of a child or death of a wife, and for officers who married outside the parish). The proportion fluctuated over time, but this may be the result of unevenly spread records rather than any real shifts in the level of officeholding by married men:

1601–50, 75.4 per cent married before office
1651–1700, 68.5 per cent married before office
1701–25, 58.7 per cent married before office
1726–50, 83.0 per cent married before office

141 (66.5 per cent) terms of constableship were served by men who were married and had children before they entered office. On average, constables with a traceable marriage or baptism of a child first served 7.3 years after that event.

Repeat service as constable was fairly frequent but not the norm. Altogether, 70 of 212 terms (33.0 per cent) were served by men who had served as constable before. Repeat constableship became more common in the early eighteenth century. Between 1603 and 1700, only 27.7 per cent of those who served as constable had served before, whereas between 1701 and 1750, 39.8 per cent had served before.

Overseers of the Poor 1681–1749

Where possible to find, the average age of overseers upon entry to office across the period was 39.8 (n = 25). Split into two periods, the figures suggest a substantial decline in the average age of overseers, albeit on the basis of a very small sample:

1681–1715 (n = 7), 47.0
1716–49 (n = 18), 37.0

Of 152 terms, 108 (71.1 per cent) were served by men who were married before they entered office (probably an underestimate, as above). The proportion of married overseers may have increased over time, though again this may be an illusion produced by patterns of record survival:

1681–1715, 56.8 per cent married before office
1716–49, 75.7 per cent married before office

Appendix A

One term of overseership was served by a widow, Ann Sandall. At least 103 terms (67.8 per cent) were served by men who were married and had children before they entered office. On average, overseers with a traceable marriage or baptism of a child first served 9.4 years after that event.

Repeat service was more common than among constables. Altogether, 74 of 152 terms (48.7 per cent) were served by men who had served before (Ann Sandall only served once). There seems to have been a substantial change in this regard in the first half of the eighteenth century. Between 1681 and 1715, only seven of thirty-seven terms of overseership (18.9 per cent) were served by men who had served before and none of these was before 1700. Between 1716 and 1749, by contrast, 67 of 115 terms (58.3 per cent) were served by men who had served before. The lack of evidence for the years before 1681 means some instances of repeat service could be missing from the figures for the late seventeenth century, but the data suggest a steady increase in repeat service in the first five decades of the eighteenth.

	Total identifiable overseers	Overseers who had served before	Per cent
1681–90	6	0	0
1691–1700	9	0	0
1701–10	14	4	28.6
1711–20	18	7	38.9
1721–30	29	13	44.8
1731–40	40	23	57.5
1741–49	36	27	75.0

Churchwardens 1586–1756 (with large gaps)

Where possible to find, the average age of churchwardens upon entry to office across the period was 45.5 ($n = 16$). Of the fifty-four identifiable churchwardens serving in this period, 42 (77.8 per cent) were married before they entered the office (again, an underestimate) and 38 (70.4 per cent) were married and had children before they entered office.

The average length of service for these churchwardens was 3.7 years. Broken down into the four periods for which sufficient records have survived, there is a clear shift towards longer periods of service in the later seventeenth and early eighteenth centuries:

Starting year as churchwarden	Average length of service (years)
1586–1600	1.9
1601–11	1.3
1669–1700	3.1
1701–50	9.9

The average for the last period is distorted by three men who served eighteen, thirty-one, and twenty years each, though these exceptions are in themselves indicative; in previous periods no churchwarden served for more than eight years.

Appendix B
General Issue Clauses

The list below includes every seventeenth-century 'general issue' clause recorded in the *Statutes of the Realm* and several examples from the early eighteenth century. An exhaustive list of statutes including such clauses beyond this period is outside the scope of this book. They continued to be used in legislation of the late eighteenth and nineteenth centuries to give officers and others legal protection in the course of performing statutory duties. For example, under the Townshend Acts of the 1760s, anyone sued for actions carried out while collecting revenue or policing smuggling in Britain's North American colonies was permitted to plead the general issue and bring special matter in evidence (7 Geo. III c.46 s.11). Half a century later, officers acting under the notorious 'Six Acts', passed in the wake of the 1819 Peterloo Massacre, were granted the same protection: 60 Geo. III & 1 Geo. IV c.1 s.5, c.2 s.6, c.6 s.36, c.8 s.8.

- 7 Jac. I c.5 (1609–10) – An Acte for ease in pleading against troublesome and contencious Suites, p[ro]secuted against Justices of the Peace Maiors Constables and c[er]taine other his Majesties Officers, for the lawfull execution of their Office
- 21 Jac. I c.12 s.2 (1623–4) – An Acte for ease in Pleading, against troublesom and contencious Suits
- 3 Car. I c.2 (1627) – An Act for the further reformacon of sondry abuses com[m]itted on the Lords Day comonlie called Sunday
- 16 Car. I c.19 s.7 (1640) – An Act for the better ordering and regulating of the Office of Clarke of the Market … and for the reformation of false Weights and Measures
- 12 Car. II c.23 s.27 (1660) – A Grant of certaine Impositions upon Beere Ale and other Liquors for the encrease of His Majestys Revenue dureing His Life
- 13 Car. II St.2 c.1 s.12 (1661) – An Act for the well Governing and Regulating of Corporations

- 13 Car. II St.2 c.3 s.31 (1661) – An Act for granting unto the Kings Majestie twelve hundred and threescore pounds ...
- 14 Car. II c.2 s.27 (1662) – An Act for repairing the High wayes and Sewers and for paving and keeping clean of the Streets in and about the Cities of London & Westminster and for reforming Annoyances and Disorders in the Streets ...
- 14 Car. II c.5 s.22 (1662) – An Act for regulating the making of Stuffs in Norfolke and Norwich
- 14 Car. II c.6 s.10 (1662) – An Act for enlarging and repairing of Common High wayes
- 14 Car. II c.10 s.13 (1662) – An Act for establishing an additional Revenue upon His Majestie His Heires & Successors
- 14 Car. II c.11 s.17 (1662) – An Act for preventing Frauds and regulating Abuses in His Majesties Customes
- 14 Car. II c.12 s.20 (1662) – An Act for the better Releife of the Poore of this Kingdom
- 14 Car. II c.17 (1662) – An Act for Reliefe of Collectors of Publick Moneys
- 14 Car. II c.32 s.13 (1662) – An Act for the better regulating of the Manufacture of Broad Woollen Cloath within the West Riding of the County of Yorke
- 15 Car. II c.1 s.11 (1663) – An Act for repairing the Highwayes within the Countyes of Hertford Cambridge and Huntington
- 15 Car. II c.4 s.14 (1663) – An Additional Act for the better ordering the Forces in the severall Counties of this Kingdome
- 15 Car. II c.17 s.13 (1663) – An Act for settling the dreyning of the Great Levell of the Fenns called Bedford Levell
- 16 Car. II c.4 s.6 (1664) – An Act to prevent and suppresse seditious Conventicles
- 16&17 Car. II c.1 s.28 (1664–5) – An Act for granting Royall Ayd unto the Kings Majestie of Twenty fower hundred threescore and seaventeene thousand and five hundred Pounds ...
- 16&17 Car. II c.2 s.4 (1664–5) – An Act for regulateing the Measures and Prices of Coales
- 18&19 Car. II c.1 (1666) – An Act for raising Moneys by a Poll, and otherwise towards the Maintenance of the present Warr
- 19&20 Car. II c.12 s.7 (1667–8) – An Additional Act against the Importation of Forreign Cattel
- 22 Car. II c.1 s.11 (1670) – An Act to prevent and suppresse Seditious Conventicles

Appendix B

22 Car. II c.12 s.4 (1670) – An Additionall Act for the better repairing of Highwayes and Bridges

22&23 Car. II c.3 s.54 (1670–1) – An Act for granting a Subsidy to his Majestie for Supply of his Extraordinary Occasions

22&23 Car. II c.5 s.13 (1670–1) – An Act for an Additionall Excise upon Beere, Ale and other Liquors

22&23 Car. II c.8 s.15 (1670–1) – An Act for the regulateing the makeing of Kidderminster Stuffes

22&23 Car. II c.16 s.13 (1670–1) – An Act for the discovery of such as have defrauded the Poore of the Citty of London, of the Moneys given for their Releife at the times of the late Plague and Fire

22&23 Car. II c.26 s.4 (1670–1) – An Act to p[re]vent the planting of Tobacco in England, and for regulateing the Plantation Trade

25 Car. II c.1 s.23 (1672) [unnamed taxation Act for royal supply]

29 Car. II c.1 s.35 (1677) – An Act for raising the Summe of Five hundred eighty foure thousand nine hundred seaventy eight pounds two shillings and two pence halfe-penny for the speedy building Thirty Shipps of Warr

29 Car. II c.4 s.19 (1677) – An Act for erecting a Judicature to determine Differences touching Houses burnt and demolished by the late dreadfull Fire in Southwarke

29&30 Car. II c.1 s.48 (1677–8) – An Act for raising Money by a Poll and otherwise to enable His Majestie to enter into an actuall Warr against the French King and for prohibiting severall French Commodities

30 Car. II c.1 s.10 (1678) – An Act for granting a Supply to His Majestie ... for disbanding the Army and other uses therein mentioned

30 Car. II c.3 s.10 (1678) – An Act for burying in Woollen

31 Car. II c.1 s.31 (1679) – An Act for granting a Supply to His Majestie ... for paying off and disbanding the Forces raised since the Nine and twentyeth of September One thousand six hundred seaventy seaven

31 Car. II c.2 s.19 (1679) – An Act for the better secureing the Liberty of the Subject and for Prevention of Imprisonments beyond the Seas

1 Jac. II c.15 s.10 (1685) – An Act for Rebuilding Finishing and Adorning of the Cathedrall Church of St. Pauls London

1 W&M c.13 s.37 (1688) – An Act for Raising Money by a Poll and otherwise towards the Reduceing of Ireland

- 1 W&M c.32 s.8 (1688) – An Act for the better preventing the Exportation of Woole and Encourageing the Woollen Manufactures of this Kingdome
- 1 W&M c.34 s.13 (1688) – An Act for Prohibiting all Trade and Commerce with France
- 2 W&M c.2 s.24 (1689) [a poll tax to fund wars in Ireland and France]
- 2 W&M Sess.2 c.1 s.22 (1690) – An Act for Granting an Ayd to Their Majestyes of the Summe of Sixteene hundred fifty one thousand seaven hundred and two pounds eighteene shillings
- 2 W&M Sess.2 c.8 s.21 (1690) – An Act for Paveing and Cleansing the Streets in the Cityes of London and Westminster … and for Regulating the Markets therein mentioned
- 3 W&M c.6 s18 (1691) – An Act for raiseing money by a Poll payable quarterly for One year for the carrying on a vigorous War against France
- 3 W&M c.10 s.6 (1691) – An Act for the more effectual Discovery and Punishment of Deer Stealers
- 3 W&M c.12 s.24 (1691) – An Act for the better repairing and amending the Highways and for settling the Rates of Carriage of Goods
- 4 W&M c.23 s.7 (1692) – An Act for the more easie discoverie and conviction of such as shall destroy the Game of this Kingdome
- 5 W&M c.7 s.15 (1693) – An Act for granting to their Majesties certain Rates and Duties upon Salt and upon Beer Ale and other Liquors …
- 5&6 W&M c.22 s.12 (1694) – An Act for the lycenseing and regulateing Hackney-Coaches and Stage-Coaches
- 6&7 W&M c.3 s.25 (1694) – An Act for granting to his Majestie an Aide of Four shillings in the Pound … for carrying on the Warr against France with vigour
- 6&7 W&M c.6 s.25 (1694) – An Act for granting to his Majesty certaine rates and duties upon Marriages Births and Burials and upon Batchelors and Widowers for the terme of Five yeares for carrying on the Warr against France with Vigour
- 6&7 W&M c.11 s.4 (1694) – An Act for the more effectuall suppressing prophane Cursing and Swearing
- 7&8 Wm III c.9 (1695–6) – An Act for repairing the Highways betweene the City of London and the Towne of Harwich in the County of Essex

7&8 Wm III c.12 s.11 (1695–6) – An Act for Relief of Poor Prisoners for Debt or Damages

7&8 Wm III c.14 s.21 (1695–6) – An Act for making navigable the Rivers of Wye and Lugg in the County of Hereford

7&8 Wm III c.18 s.21 (1695–6) – An Act for granting to His Majesty severall Rates or Duties upon Houses for making good the Deficiency of the clipped Money

7&8 Wm III c.26 s.9 (1695–6) – An Act for repaireing the Highwayes betweene Wymondham and Attleborough in the County of Norfolk

7&8 Wm III c.28 s.10 (1695–6) – An Act for the more eff[e]cual preventing the Exportacon of Wooll and for the incouraging the Importation thereof from Ireland

8&9 Wm III c.6 s.43 (1696–7) – An Act for granting an Aid to His Majesty as well by a Land Tax as by several Subsidies

8&9 Wm III c.15 s.8 (1696–7) – An Act for repairing the High-way betweene Ryegate in the County of Surrey & Crawley in the County of Sussex

8&9 Wm III c.25 s.6 (1696–7) – An Act for licensing Hawkers and Pedlers for a further p[ro]vision for the Payment of the Int[er]est of the Transport Debt for the reducing of Ireland

8&9 Wm III c.27 s.17 (1696–7) – An Act for the more effectual Relief of Creditors in Cases of Escapes & for p[re]venting Abuses in Prisons and pretended priveledged Places

8&9 Wm III c.29 s.6 (1696–7) – An Act for the Repair of the Peers of Bridlington al[ia]s Burlington in the East-Riding of the County of York

9 WM III c.7 s.6 (1697–8) – An Act to prevent the throwing or firing of Squibbs Serpents & other Fire-works

9 WM III c.9 s.8 (1697–8) – An Act for rendring the Laws more effectual for preventing the Importation of Forreign Bone-Lace Loom-Lace Needle-work Point & Cutt-work

9 WM III c.13 s.8 (1697–8) – An Act for granting to His Majesty several Duties upon Coals and Culm

9 WM III c.18 s.8 (1697–8) – An Act for repairing the Highways from the Towne of Birdlipp and the Top of Crickley Hill in the County of Gloucester to the City of Gloucester

9 WM III c.19 s.18 (1697–8) – An Act for cleansing & making Navigable the Channel from the hithe att Colchester to Wivenhoe

9 WM III c.27 s.6 (1697–8) – An Act for licensing Hawkers and Pedlers for a further Provision of Interest for the Transport Debt for reduceing of Ireland

9 WM III c.38 s.18 (1697–8) – An act for granting to His Majesty an Aid by a Quarterly Poll for One Year

9 WM III c.39 s.6 (1697–8) – An Act for settling and adjusting the Proportion of Fine Silver Silk … to prevent the Abuses of Wire-Drawers

9 WM III c.40 s.7 (1697–8) – An Act for the Explanation and better Execution of former Acts made against Transportation of Wool Fullers Earth and Scouring Clay

9 WM III c.41 s.5 (1697–8) – An Act for the better preventing the imbezlement of His Majesties Sores of War and preventing Cheats Frauds and Abuses in paying Seamens Wages

9 WM III c.43 s.11 (1697–8) – An Act for the better Incouragement of the Royal Lustring Company and the more effectual preventing the fraudulent Importation of Lustrings and Alamodes

9 WM III c.44 s.13 (1697–8) – An Act for raising a Sum not exceeding Two Millions upon a Fund for Payment of Annuities … and for settling the Trade to the East Indies

10 Wm III c.8 s.8 (1698) – An Act for makeing and keeping the River Tone navigable from Bridgwater to Taunton in the County of Somersett

10 Wm III c.9 s.18 (1698) – An Act for granting to His Majesty the Sum of One Million four hundred eighty four thousand and fifteene one Shilling eleaven Pence three Farthings for disbanding the Army providing for the Navy and for other necessary Occasions

10 Wm III c.15 s.8 (1698) – An Act for opening the ancient and makeing any New Roynes and Water Courses in and neare Sedgmore in the County of Somerset for rendring the said Moor more healthfull and profitable to the Inhabitants

10 Wm III c.16 s.13 (1698) – An Act to prevent the Exportation of Wool out of the Kingdoms of Ireland and England into Forreigne parts and for the Incouragement of the Woollen Manufactures in the Kingdom of England

10 Wm III c.25 s.8 (1698) – An Act for the makeing and keeping navigable the Rivers of Aire and Calder in the County of Yorke

10 Wm III c.26 s.15 (1698) – An Act for makeing and keeping the River Trent in the Counties of Leicester Derby and Stafford navigable

- 11 Wm III c.2 s.93 (1698–9) – An Act for granting an Aid to His Majesty by Sale of the forfeited and other Estates and Interests in Ireland and by a Land Tax in England for the severall Purposes therein mentioned
- 11 Wm III c.15 s.8 (1698–9) – An Act for the ascertaining the Measures for retailing Ale and Beer
- 11 Wm III c.19 s.6 (1698–9) – An act to enable Justices of Peace to build and repair Gaoles in their respective Counties
- 11 Wm III c.21 s.11 (1698–9) – An Act for the Explanation and better Execution of former Acts made touching Watermen and Wherrymen rowing on the River of Thames and for the better ordering and governing the said Watermen Wherrymen and Lightermen upon the said River between Gravesend and Windsor
- 11 Wm III c.23 s.18 (1698–9) – An Act for the better preserving the Navigation of the Rivers Avon and Froome and for cleansing paving and inlightning the Streets of the City of Bristol
- 3&4 Anne c.6 s.10 (1704) – An Act for the effectual securing the Kingdom of England from the apparent Dangers that may arise from several Acts lately passed in the Parliament of Scotland
- 6 Anne c.70 s.9 (1707) – An act for the more effectual making and keeping the River Tone navigable from Bridgwater to Taunton in the County of Somerset
- 7 Anne c.34 s.24 (1708) – An Act for building a Parish Church and Parsonage House and making a new Church Yard and a new Parish in Birmingham in the County of Warwick to be called the Parish of Saint Philip
- 9 Anne c.28 s.12 (1710) – An Act for the better Preservation and Improvement of the Fishery within the River of Thames

Select Bibliography

Manuscript Sources

Borthwick Institute for Archives, York
    Diocese of York Cause Papers 1661–1720, GB 193 CP.H. 2618-4219, CP.I. 23-667

British Library, London
    Beale Papers, Add. MS 48064
    Hardwicke Papers, Add. MSS 35948, 35955, 35979-81, 35994
    Heath and Verney Papers, Egerton MS 2985
    Law reports, 16th and 17th centuries, Add. MSS 25203, 25211, 25213, 25223
    Law reports, Harley MSS 2143, 4814

Cambridge University Library
    Law reports, late sixteenth century, GBR/0012/MS Ii.05.24
    University Registry Guard Books, GBR/0265/UA/CUR

Kent History and Library Centre, Maidstone
    Quarter Sessions Books 1660–1714, Q/SB/8-33
    Quarter Sessions Papers 1714–50, Q/SB/1715-1750

Lambeth Palace Library, London
    Court of Arches Personal Answers 1661–1753, Ee 1-10
    Court of Arches Depositions, 1664–1750, Eee 1-15
    Vicar-General's Peculiar Jurisdiction: Cause Papers, VH 77

London Metropolitan Archives
    City of London Police Predecessors, CLA/048/PS/01-02
    Consistory Court Deposition Books 1669–1744, DL/C/0236-0273
    Court of Aldermen Repertories 1667–1750, COL/CA/01/01/073-154
    Middlesex Quarter Sessions Papers 1642–1750, MJ/SP/1642-1750
    Southwark Quarter Sessions Papers 1654–1784, CLA/046/03/001
    St Anne and St Agnes Parish and Vestry Books, P69/ANA
    St John Hackney Parish and Vestry Books, P79/JN1
    St Katherine Cree Parish and Vestry Books, P69/KAT2
    Westminster Quarter Sessions Papers, WJ/SP
    Westminster Quarter Sessions Rolls, WJ/SR

The National Archives, Kew
    Excise Board and Secretariat Minute Books 1695–1745, CUST 47/1-185

Indemnity Committee Books and Papers 1647–56, SP 24
Northern Assize Depositions, ASSI 45
Norfolk Record Office, Norwich
Mayor's Court and Quarter Sessions Papers 1660–1750, NCR Case 12b/1-7

Digitised Primary Sources

Bellany, Alastair and Andrew McRae, *Early Stuart Libels* (earlystuartlibels.net)
Harrison, Sarah, Charles Jardine, Tim King, Jessica King and Alan Macfarlane, *Earls Colne, Essex. Records of an English Village 1375–1854* (2008) [dataset] (http://dspace.cam.ac.uk/handle/1810/195838)
Hitchcock, Tim, Robert Shoemaker, Clive Emsley, Sharon Howard and Jamie McLaughlin et al., *The Old Bailey Proceedings Online, 1674–1913* (www.oldbaileyonline.org)
Seipp, David J., *An Index and Paraphrase of Printed Year Book Reports, 1268–1535* (bu.edu/law/faculty-scholarship/legal-history-the-year-books)

Printed Primary Sources

Allestree, Richard, *The Whole Duty of Man* (London, 1658)
Amhurst, Nicholas, *An Argument against Excises* (London, 1733)
Amhurst, Nicholas, *The Second Part of an Argument against Excises* (London, 1733)
Anglia Liberate, or, The Rights of the People of England, Maintained against the Pretences of the Scottish King (London, 1651)
An Attorney at Law, *The Law of Arrests in Both Civil and Criminal Cases* (Savoy, 1742)
An Ease for Overseers of the Poore (Cambridge, 1601)
An Exact Abridgement in English of the Eleven Books of Reports of the Learned Sir Edward Coke (London, 1650)
An Impartial Account of the Misfortune That Lately Happened to the Right Honourable Philip Earl of Pembrook and Montgomery (London, 1680)
Bailey, Nathan, *Dictionarium Britannicum: Or a More Compleat Universal Etymological English Dictionary* (London, 1736)
Battye, T., *A Concise Exposition of the Tricks and Arts Used in the Collection of Easter Dues* (Manchester, 1800)
The Birth and Burning of the Image Calls S. Michael (London, 1681)
Blackstone, William, *Commentaries on the Laws of England*, 4 vols (Oxford, 1768)
Blount, Thomas, *Nomo-Lexikon, a Law-Dictionary* (London, 1670)
Bracton, Henri de, *On the Laws and Customs of England*, trans. by Samuel E. Thorne (Cambridge, MA, 1968)
Brailsford, Humphrey, *The Poor Man's Help* (London, 1689)
Bray, Thomas, *The Tryals of Jeremy Tooley, William Arch, and John Clauson, Three Private Soldiers* (London, 1732)
Britannia Excisa (London, 1733)

Burn, Richard, *The Justice of the Peace and Parish Officer*, 2 vols (London, 1755)
Butler, Samuel, *Characters and Passages from Note-Books*, ed. A. R. Waller (Cambridge, 1908)
Butler, Samuel, *The Genuine Remains in Verse and Prose*, ed. Robert Thyer (London, 1759)
Callis, Robert, *The Reading of That Famous and Learned Gentleman, Robert Callis Esq; Sergeant at Law, Upon the Statute of 23 H. 8. Cap. 5. Of Sewers: As it was delivered by him at Gray's Inn, in August, 1622* (London, 1647)
Carey, Henry, *The Contrivances: Or, More Ways than One* (London, 1715)
Carey, Henry, *Cupid and Hymen: Or, a Voyage to the Isles of Love and Matrimony* (London, 1742)
Care, Henry, *English Liberties: Or, the Free-Born Subject's Inheritance* (London, 1680)
The Case of the Dissenters, and Others in Office, with Respect to the Laws Now in Force (London, 1712)
Chaloner, Thomas, *The Merriest Poet in Christendom* (London, 1732)
Cheat upon Cheat, OR, The Debaucht Hypocrite (London, 1664)
Clayton, John, *Reports and Pleas of Assises at Yorke* (London, 1651)
Cock, Charles George, *English-Law: Or, A Summary Survey of the Houshold of God on Earth* (London, 1651)
Coke, Edward, *The First Part of the Institutes of the Lawes of England. Or, A Commentarie Vpon Littleton* (London, 1628)
Coke, Edward, *The Fourth Part of the Institutes of the Laws of England Concerning the Jurisdiction of Courts* (London, 1644)
Coke, Edward, *The Second Part of the Institutes of the Laws of England*, 6th edn (London, 1681)
Coke, Edward, *The Third Part of the Institutes of the Laws of England* (London, 1644)
Collyn, Nicholas, *A Briefe Summary of the Lawes and Statutes of England* (London, 1655)
Colquhoun, Patrick, *A Treatise on the Functions and Duties of a Constable* (London, 1803)
The Counterfeit Constable, or, The Wicked Watch (London, 1674)
Cowell, John, *The Interpreter: Or Booke Containing the Signification of Words* (London, 1607)
The Cucking of a Scould (London, 1630)
Dalton, Michael, *The Countrey Justice* (London, 1618)
Dalton, Michael, *Officium Vicecomitum: The Office and Authority of Sherifs* (London, 1628)
A Dialogue between Sir Andrew Freeport and Timothy Squat, Esquire, On the Subject of Excises (London, 1733)
A Dialogue Betwixt an Excise-Man and Death (London, 1659)
Defoe, Daniel, *Augusta Triumphans: Or, The Way to make London the most flourishing City in the Universe* (London, 1728)
Defoe, Daniel, *Colonel Jack*, ed. Samuel Holt Monk (Oxford, 1989)

Select Bibliography

Defoe, Daniel, *An Effectual Scheme for the Immediate Preventing of Street Robberies* (London, 1731)

Defoe, Daniel, *The Family Instructor*, 8th edn (London, 1766)

Defoe, Daniel, *Parochial Tyranny: Or, The House-Keeper's Complaint against the Insupportable Exactions, and Partial Assessments of Select Vestries* (London, 1727)

Dekker, Thomas, and Thomas Middleton, *Blurt Master-Constable. Or the Spaniards Night-Walke* (London, 1602)

The Digest of Justinian tr. Alan Watson, 4 vols (Philadelphia, 1985)

Dod, John, and Robert Clever, *A Godly Forme of Household Government* (London, 1612)

Duncombe, Giles, *Salmasius His Buckler, or, A Royal Apology for King Charles the Martyr* (London, 1662)

Earle, John, Microcosmography; Or, A Piece of the World Discovered; in *Essays and Characters* (London, 1628)

Ellwood, Thomas, *The History of the Life of Thomas Ellwood* (London, 1714)

Excise Elegy (London, 1733)

Fielding, Henry, *The Coffee-House Politician: Or, the Justice Caught in His Own Trap* (London, 1730)

Fielding, Henry, *The History of Tom Jones*, 3 vols (Dublin, 1749)

Fielding, John, *Extracts from Such of the Penal Laws, as Particularly Relate to the Peace and Good Order of the Metropolis* (London, 1761)

Fitzherbert, Anthony, *La Graunde Abridgement* (London, 1516)

Forster, Thomas, *The Lay-Mans Lawyer: Or, The Second Part of the Practice of Law* (London, 1654)

Fortescue, John, A Learned Commendation of the Politique Lawes of Englande [De Laudibus Legum Angliae], trans. by Robert Mulcaster

The Frollicksome Wager: OR, The Ranting Gallant's Ramble through the City (London, 1683)

Gardiner, Robert, *The Compleat Constable* (London, 1692)

Gay, John, *The Mohocks. A Tragi-Comical Farce* (London, 1712)

Glapthorne, Henry, *Wit in a Constable* (London, 1640)

Gouge, William, *Of Domesticall Duties* (London, 1622)

Great and Bloody News from Turnham Green (London, 1680)

Grey, Enoch, Vox Coeli, *Containing Maxims of Pious Policy* (London, 1649)

Hale, Matthew, *Historia Placitorum Coronae*, 2 vols (London, 1736)

Hatton, Edward, *The Gauger's Guide; or, Excise-Officer Instructed* (London, 1729)

Hawarde, John, *Les reportes del cases in Camera Stellata, 1593 to 1609: from the Original MS. of John Hawarde* ed. William Paley Baildon (London, 1894)

Hawkins, William, *A Treatise of the Pleas of the Crown*, 2nd edn, 2 vols (London, 1724)

Howell, T. B., *A Complete Collection of State Trials and Proceedings for High Treason and Other Crimes and Misdemeanors from the Earliest Period to the Present Time*, 34 vols (London, 1809)

Hunt, William, *A Guide for the Practical Gauger* (London, 1694)

Jacob, Giles, *The Compleat Parish-Officer* (London, 1718)
Jacob, Giles, *A New Law-Dictionary*, 4th edn (London, 1739)
A Jest; Or, Master Constable (London, 1662)
Johnson, Samuel, *A Dictionary of the English Language* (London, 1755)
The Jolly Gentleman's Frolick. OR, The City Ramble (London, 1675)
Lambarde, William, *The Dueties of Constables* (London, 1582)
Lambarde, William, *Eirenarcha, or the Office of the Justices of Peace* (London, 1581)
The Lamentation of a New Married Man (London, 1619)
The Late Excise Scheme Dissected (London, 1734)
Laud, William, *The History of the Troubles and Tryal of the Most Reverend Father in God and Blessed Martyr, William Laud* (London, 1695)
Layer, John, *The Office and Dutie of Constables* (Cambridge, 1641)
Leigh, Edward, *A Philologicall Commentary* (London, 1652)
L'Estrange, Roger, tran., *Tully's Offices in Three Books* (London, 1680)
Lightbody, James, *The Measurer and Gauger's Guide* (London, 1709)
Luttrell, Narcissus, *A Brief Historical Relation of State Affairs from September 1678 to April 1714*, 6 vols (Oxford, 1857)
Mark Noble's Frollick (London, 1670)
Marriot, John, *A Representation of Some Mismanagements by Parish-Officers In the Method at Present Followed for Maintaining the Poor* (London, 1726)
Meriton, George, *A Guide for Constables* (London, 1669)
The Midnight-Ramble: Or, The Adventures of Two Noble Females (London, 1754)
Miege, Guy, *The New State of England* (London, 1691)
Money, John, ed., *The Chronicles of John Cannon, Excise Officer and Writing Master* (Oxford, 2010)
Morrice, Roger, *The Entring Book of Roger Morrice 1677–1692* ed. Mark Goldie (Woodbridge, 2007), 6 vols
The Night-Walkers; Or, The Loyal Huzza (London, 1672)
The Notebook of Robert Doughty 1662–1665 ed. James M. Rosenheim (Norwich, 1989)
Observations upon the Laws of Excise (London, 1733)
Osborne, Francis, 'Traditional Memoirs' in Walter Scott (ed.), *The Secret History of the Court of James the First* (Edinburgh, 1811)
P., J., *A New Guide for Constables, Headboroughs, Tything-Men, Churchwardens* (London, 1692)
Paley, William, *The Principles of Moral and Political Philosophy*, 4 vols (London, 1785)
Paul, John, *The Compleat Constable* (London, 1785)
Polsted, Ezekiel, *Kaloz Telonesantai or, The Excise-Man* (London, 1697)
Phipps, Joseph, *The Vestry Laid Open; Or, A Full and Plain Detection Of the Many Gross Abuses, Impositions, and Oppressions of Select-Vestries* (London, 1739)
Prynne, William, *The Soveraigne Power of Parliaments and Kingdomes* (London, 1643)
Pulteney, William, *The Budget Opened* (London, 1733)
Pulton, Ferdinando, *De Pace Regis et Regni* (London, 1609)

Reasons of the Present Judgment of the University of Oxford, Concerning the Solemne League and Covenant (London, 1647)
The Report of the Committee Appointed by a General Vestry of the Parish of St Botolph Without, Aldersgate (London, 1733)
Ritson, Joseph, *The Office of Constable* (London, 1791)
Rushworth, John, *Historical Collections From the Year 1638 to the Year 1641 Abridg'd and Improved* (London, 1706)
S., P., *A Help to Magistrates, and Ministers of Justice: Also a Guide to Parish and Ward-Officers* (London, 1721)
Saunders, Edmund, *Observations upon the Statute of 22 Car. II Cap. I* (London, 1685)
Second Review of the Late Excise Scheme (London, 1734)
The Select Vestry Justified (London, 1754)
Shaw, Joseph, *Parish Law, or, a Guide to Justices of the Peace* (London, 1733)
Sheppard, William, *An Epitome of All the Common & Statute Laws of This Nation Now in Force, Wherein More Then Fifteen Hundred of the Hardest Words or Terms of the Law Are Explained* (London, 1656)
Sheppard, William, *The Offices of Constables*, 3rd edn (London, 1650)
Sheppard, William, *A Sure Guide to His Majesties Justices of the Peace* (London, 1663)
A Short View of the Frauds, Abuses, and Impositions of Parish Officers (London, 1744)
Sidney, Algernon, *Discourses Concerning Government* (London, 1698)
Smith, Alexander, *The Comical and Tragical History of the Lives and Adventures of the Most Noted Bayliffs In and about London and Westminster* (London, 1723)
Smith, John, *The Constables Hue and Cry After Whores & Bawds* (London, 1701)
Smith, Thomas, *De Republica Anglorum: The Maner of Government or Policie of the Realme of England* (London, 1583)
Smollett, Tobias, *The Adventures of Roderick Random*, 2 vols (London, 1748)
Strange and Wonderful News from London: Or, A True Narrative of Several Most Remarkable Occurrences There (London, 1679)
A Strange and True Relation of a Wonderful and Terrible Earth-Quake (London, 1661)
Tis Not Otherwise: OR, The Praise of a Married Life (London, 1617)
A True and Sad Relation of Two Wicked and Bloody Murthers (London, 1680)
Turner, R, *Duty and Office of a High Constable* (London, 1671)
Twelve Ingenious Characters: OR, Pleasant Descriptions of the Properties Of Sundry Persons & Things (London, 1686)
The Universal Officer of Justice (London, 1730)
Vaisey, David, ed., *The Diary of Thomas Turner* (Oxford, 1985)
Ward, Edward, *The London Spy Compleat* (London, 1703)
Ward, Edward, *The London Terrae-Filius: Or the Satyrical Reformer* (London, 1708)
Warr, John, *The Priviledges of the People, or, Principles of Common Right and Freedome* (London, 1649)

Welch, Saunders, *Observations of the Office of Constable* (London, 1754)
The West-Country Dialogue: Or, A Pleasant Ditty between Anniseed-Robin the Miller, and His Brother Jack the Plough-Man (London, 1672)
Wingate, Edmund, *The Exact Constable* (London, 1660)
A Wonderful Prophesie, Declared by Christian James a Maid of Twenty Years of Age (London, 1684)
Woodward, Josiah, *A Sermon Preach'd at the Parish-Church of St. James's, Westminster, On the 21st of May, 1702. At the Funeral of Mr. John Cooper, A Constable* (London, 1702)

Secondary Sources

Amussen, Susan D., 'The Contradictions of Patriarchy in Early Modern England', *Gender & History*, 30.2 (2018)
Amussen, Susan D., *An Ordered Society: Gender and Class in Early Modern England* (Oxford, 1988)
Amussen, Susan D., 'Punishment, Discipline, and Power: The Social Meanings of Violence in Early Modern England', *Journal of British Studies*, 34 (1995)
Arnold, J. H. and S. Brady (eds), *What Is Masculinity? Historical Dynamics from Antiquity to the Contemporary World* (Basingstoke, 2011)
Baker, John, *Collected Papers on English Legal History*, 3 vols (Cambridge, 2013)
Baker, John, *The Oxford History of the Laws of England*, vol. VI 1483–1558 (Oxford, 2003)
Baker, John, *The Reinvention of Magna Carta 1216–1616* (Cambridge, 2017)
Barrie, David, *Police in the Age of Improvement: Police development and the Civic Tradition in Scotland, 1775–1865* (Cullompton, 2008)
Barrie, David G. and Susan Broomhall (eds), *A History of Police and Masculinities, 1700–2010* (Abingdon, 2012)
Barry, Jonathan and Christopher Brooks (eds), *The Middling Sort of People: Culture, Society and Politics in England, 1550–1800* (Basingstoke, 1994)
Beattie, J. M., *Crime and the Courts in England 1660–1800* (Oxford, 1986)
Beattie, J. M., *Policing and Punishment in London, 1660–1750: Urban Crime and the Limits of Terror* (Oxford, 2001)
Becker, Anna, *Gendering the Renaissance Commonwealth* (Cambridge, 2020)
Beier, A. L., *Masterless Men: The Vagrancy Problem in England 1560–1640* (London, 1985)
Bennett, Judith M., 'Confronting Continuity', *Journal of Women's History*, 9.3 (1997)
Bennett, Judith M., *History Matters: Patriarchy and the Challenge of Feminism* (Manchester, 2006)
Berry, H. and E. Foyster (eds), *The Family in Early Modern England* (Cambridge, 2007)
Bitomsky, Jane, 'The Jury of Matrons: Their Role in the Early Modern English Courtroom', *Lilith: A Feminist History Journal*, 25.4 (2019)
Bland, Eleanor, *Policing Suspicion: Proactive Policing in London, 1780–1850* (Abingdon, 2021)

Boswell, Caroline, *Disaffection and Everyday Life in Interregnum England* (Woodbridge, 2017)
Boulton, Jeremy, *Neighbourhood and Society: A London Suburb in the Seventeenth Century* (Cambridge, 1987)
Braddick, Michael J., *The Nerves of State: Taxation and the Financing of the English State, 1558–1714* (Manchester, 1996)
Braddick, Michael J. (ed.), *The Oxford Handbook of the English Revolution* (Oxford, 2015)
Braddick, Michael J., *Parliamentary Taxation in Seventeenth-Century England* (Woodbridge, 1994)
Braddick, Michael J., *State Formation in Early Modern England c.1550–1700* (Cambridge, 2000)
Braddick, Michael J. and Joanna Innes (eds), *Suffering and Happiness in England 1550–1850: Narratives and Representations: A Collection to Honour Paul Slack* (Oxford, 2017)
Braddick, Michael J. and John Walter (eds), *Negotiating Power in Early Modern Society: Order, Hierarchy and Subordination in Britain and Ireland* (Cambridge, 2001)
Braddick, Michael J. and Phil Withington (eds), Popular Culture and Political Agency *in Early Modern England* (Woodbridge, 2017)
Brewer, John, *The Sinews of Power: War, Money and the English State, 1688–1783* (New York, 1989)
Brewer, John and John Styles (eds), *An Ungovernable People: The English and Their Law in the Seventeenth and Eighteenth Centuries* (London, 1980)
Brooks, Christopher W., *Law, Politics and Society in Early Modern England* (Cambridge, 2008)
Brooks, Christopher W., *Pettyfoggers and Vipers of the Commonwealth: The 'Lower Branch' of the Legal Profession in Early Modern England* (Cambridge, 1986)
Broomhall, S. and J. Van Gent (eds), *Governing Masculinities in the Early Modern Period: Regulating Selves and Others* (Farnham, 2011)
Brown, Wendy, *Manhood and Politics: A Feminist Reading in Political Theory* (Totowa, NJ, 1988)
Butler, Sara M., 'More than Mothers: Juries of Matrons and Pleas of the Belly in Medieval England', *Law and History Review*, 37.2 (2019)
Capern, Amanda L., *The Historical Study of Women: England 1500–1700* (Basingstoke, 2008)
Chalus, Elaine, *Elite Women in English Political Life c.1754–1790* (Oxford, 2005)
Chalus, Elaine, '"Ladies Are Often Very Good Scaffoldings": Women and Politics in the Age of Anne', *Parliamentary History*, 28.1 (2009)
Chapman, Annie Beatrice Wallis and Mary Wallis Chapman, *The Status of Women under the English Law* (London, 1909)
Churchill, David, *Crime Control and Everyday Life in the Victorian City: The Police and the Public* (Oxford, 2017)
Clark, Alice, *The Working Life of Women in the Seventeenth Century* (London, 1919)

Clarke, Lucy J. S., '"I say I must for I am the kings Shrieve": Magistrates Invoking the Monarch's Name in 1 Henry VI (1592) and The Downfall of Robert Earl of Huntingdon (1598)', *Historical Research* 95.268 (2022).

Clawson, Mary Ann, 'Early Modern Fraternalism and the Patriarchal Family', *Feminist Studies*, 6.2 (1980)

Cockburn, J. S. (ed.), *Crime in England 1550–1800* (Princeton, 1977)

Cockburn, J. S. (ed.), 'Patterns of Violence in English Society: Homicide in Kent 1560–1985', *Past & Present*, 130.1 (1991)

Coffman, D'Maris, *Excise Taxation and the Origins of Public Debt* (London, 2013)

Collinson, Patrick, 'The Monarchical Republic of Queen Elizabeth I', *Bulletin of the John Rylands University Library of Manchester*, 69 (1987)

Collinson, Patrick, *De Republica Anglorum: Or, History with the Politics Put Back* (Cambridge, 1989)

Condren, Conal, *Argument and Authority in Early Modern England: The Presupposition of Oaths and Offices* (Cambridge, 2006)

Connell, R. W., *Masculinities*, 2nd edn (Berkeley, 2005)

Connell, R. W., 'The State, Gender, and Sexual Politics: Theory and Appraisal', *Theory and Society*, 19.5 (1990)

Connell, R. W. and James W. Messerschmidt, 'Hegemonic Masculinity: Rethinking the Concept', *Gender & Society*, 19.6 (2005)

Corfield, P. J., *Towns, Trade, Religion, and Radicalism: The Norwich Perspective on English History* (Norwich, 1980)

Corfield, P. J., 'Walking the City Streets: The Urban Odyssey in Eighteenth-Century England', *Journal of Urban History*, 16.2 (1990)

Craig, J. S., 'Co-Operation and Initiatives: Elizabethan Churchwardens and the Parish Accounts of Mildenhall', *Social History*, 18.3 (1993)

Crawford, Patricia, *Parents of Poor Children in England, 1580–1800* (Oxford, 2010)

Crossick, Geoffrey (ed.), *The Artisan and the European Town, 1500–1900* (Abingdon, 1997)

Cruickshanks, Eve, 'Ashby v. White: the case of the men of Aylesbury, 1701–4' in C. Jones (ed.), *Party and Management in Parliament, 1660–1784* (Lecester, 1984)

Dabhoiwala, Faramerz, *The Origins of Sex: A History of the First Sexual Revolution* (London, 2012)

Dabhoiwala, Faramerz, 'Sex and Societies for Moral Reform, 1688–1800', *Journal of British Studies*, 46.2 (2007)

Dabhoiwala, Faramerz, 'Summary Justice in Early Modern London', *English Historical Review*, 121.492 (2006)

Davis, Jennifer, 'From "Rookeries" to "Communities": Race, Poverty and Policing in London, 1850–1985', *History Workshop Journal* 27.1 (1989)

Davis, Natalie Zemon, *Fiction in the Archives: Pardon Tales and Their Tellers in Sixteenth-Century France* (Stanford, 1990)

Davis, Natalie Zemon, 'The Reasons of Misrule: Youth Groups and Charivaris in Sixteenth-Century France', *Past & Present*, 50 (1971)

Ditz, Toby, 'The New Men's History and the Peculiar Absence of Gendered Power: Remedies from Early American Gender History', *Gender & History*, 16 (2004)

Dixon, Simon, 'Quakers and the London Parish 1670–1720', *London Journal* (2007)

Dodsworth, Francis M., '"Civic" Police and the Condition of Liberty: The Rationality of Governance in Eighteenth-Century England', *Social History*, 29.2 (2004)

Dodsworth, Francis M., 'The Idea of Police in Eighteenth-Century England: Discipline, Reformation, Superintendence, c.1780–1800', *Journal of the History of Ideas*, 69.4 (2008)

Dodsworth, Francis M., *The Security Society: History, Patriarchy, Protection* (London, 2019)

Dolan, Frances E., *True Relations: Reading, Literature, and Evidence in Seventeenth-Century England* (Philadelphia, 2013)

Doran, Susan, '1603: A Jagged Succession', *Historical Research* 93.261 (2020)

Dyer, Christopher (ed.), *The Self-Contained Village? The Social History of Rural Communities, 1250–1900* (Hatfield, 2007)

Earle, Peter, *The Making of the English Middle Class: Business, Society and Family Life in London, 1660–1730* (Berkeley, 1989)

Eccles, Audrey, 'The Eighteenth-century Vagrant Contractor', *Local Population Studies* 85 (2010)

Eccles, Audrey, *Vagrancy in Law and Practice under the Old Poor Law* (Farnham, 2012)

Emsley, Clive, *The English Police: A Political and Social History*, 2nd edn (London, 1997)

Erickson, Amy Louise, 'Married Women's Occupations in Eighteenth-century London', *Continuity & Change* 23.2 (2008)

Erickson, Amy Louise, 'Mistresses and Marriage: Or, a Short History of the Mrs', *History Workshop Journal*, 79 (2014)

Feeley, Malcolm M. and Deborah L. Little, 'The Vanishing Female: The Decline of Women in the Criminal Process, 1687–1912', *Law & Society Review*, 25.4 (1991)

Flather, Amanda, *Gender and Space in Early Modern England* (Woodbridge, 2007)

Fletcher, Anthony, *Gender, Sex & Subordination in England 1500–1800* (New Haven, 1995)

Fletcher, Anthony, 'Manhood, the Male Body, Courtship and the Household in Early Modern England', *History* 84 (1999)

Fletcher, Anthony, *Reform in the Provinces: The Government of Stuart England* (New Haven, 1986)

Fletcher, Anthony and John Stevenson (eds), *Order and Disorder in Early Modern England* (Cambridge, 1985)

Foyster, Elizabeth, *Manhood in Early Modern England: Honour, Sex and Marriage* (London, 1999)

Foyster, Elizabeth, *Marital Violence: An English Family History, 1660–1857* (Cambridge, 2005)

French, Henry, *The Middle Sort of People in Provincial England 1600–1750* (Oxford, 2007)
French, Henry and Richard Hoyle, *The Character of English Rural Society: Earls Colne, 1550–1750* (Manchester, 2007)
French, Henry and Mark Rothery, *Man's Estate: Landed Gentry Masculinities, c.1660–c.1900* (Oxford, 2012)
French, Katherine L., *The Good Women of the Parish: Gender and Religion after the Black Death* (Philadelphia, 2008)
Froide, Amy M., *Never Married: Singlewomen in Early Modern England* (Oxford, 2005)
Gaskill, Malcolm, *Crime and Mentalities in Early Modern England* (Cambridge, 2000)
Gatrell, Vic, Bruce Lenman, and Geoffrey Parker (eds), *Crime and the Law: The Social History of Crime in Western Europe Since 1500* (London, 1980)
Gianoutsos, Jamie, *The Rule of Manhood: Tyranny, Gender, and Classical Republicanism in England 1603–1660* (Cambridge, 2020)
Gowing, Laura, *Common Bodies: Women, Touch and Power in Seventeenth-Century England* (New Haven, 2003)
Gowing, Laura, *Domestic Dangers: Women, Words, and Sex in Early Modern* (London, Oxford, 1996)
Gowing, Laura, *Ingenious Trade: Women and Work in Seventeenth-Century London* (Cambridge, 2021)
Gowing, L., M. Hunter, and M. Rubin (eds), *Love, Friendship and Faith in Europe, 1300–1800* (Basingstoke, 2005)
Graham, Rose, 'The Civic Position of Women at Common Law before 1800', *Journal of the Society of Comparative Legislation*, 17.1/2 (1917)
Gray, Drew, 'Summary Proceedings and Social Relations in the City of London, c.1750–1800' (unpublished PhD, University of Northampton, 2006)
Greenberg, Janelle, 'Our Grand Maxim of State, "The King Can Do No Wrong"', *History of Political Thought*, 12.2 (1991)
Griffin, Ben, 'Hegemonic Masculinity as a Historical Problem', *Gender & History*, 30.2 (2018)
Griffiths, Paul, *Lost Londons: Change, Crime, and Control in the Capital 1550–1660* (Cambridge, 2008)
Griffiths, Paul, 'Meanings of Nightwalking in Early Modern England', *The Seventeenth Century*, 13.2 (1998)
Griffiths, Paul, Adam Fox, and Steve Hindle (eds), *The Experience of Authority in Early Modern England* (Basingstoke, 1996)
Griffiths, Paul, and Mark S. R. Jenner (eds), *Londinopolis: Essays in the Cultural and Social History of Early Modern* (London, Manchester, 2000)
Halliday, Paul D., *Dismembering the Body Politic: Partisan Politics in England's Towns, 1650–1730* (Cambridge, 1998)
Halliday, Paul D., *Habeas Corpus: From England to Empire* (Cambridge, MA, 2010)
Harding, Vanessa, 'Controlling a Complex Metropolis, 1650–1750: Politics, Parishes and Powers', *The London Journal*, 26.1 (2001)

Harding, Vanessa, 'Families and Housing in Seventeenth-Century London', *Parergon*, 24.2 (2007)
Harding, Vanessa, *People in Place: Families, Households and Housing in Early Modern* (London, 2008)
Harding, Vanessa, 'Space, Property and Propriety in Urban England', *Journal of Interdisciplinary History*, 32.4 (2002)
Hardwick, Julie, *The Practice of Patriarchy: Gender and the Politics of Household Authority in Early Modern France* (Pennsylvania, 1998)
Harris, Andrew Todd, *Policing the City: Crime and Legal Authority in London, 1780–1840* (Columbus, 2004)
Harris, Barbara J., 'Women and Politics in Early Tudor England', *The Historical Journal*, 33.2 (1990)
Harris, Tim (ed.), *The Politics of the Excluded, c.1500–1850* (Basingstoke, 2001)
Harris, Tim (ed.), *Popular Culture in England, c.1500–1850* (Basingstoke, 1995)
Harris, Tim, Paul Seaward, and Mark Goldie (eds), *The Politics of Religion in Restoration England* (Oxford, 1990)
Hartley, T. E., 'Under-Sheriffs and Bailiffs in Some English Shrievalties, c.1580 to c.1625', *Bulletin of the Institute of Historical Research*, 47.116 (1974)
Hartman, J., J. Nieuwstraten, and M. Reinders (eds), *Public Offices, Personal Demands: Capability in Governance in the Seventeenth-Century Dutch Republic* (Newcastle-upon-Tyne, 2009)
Harvey, Karen, *The Little Republic: Masculinity and Domestic Authority in Eighteenth-Century Britain* (Oxford, 2012)
Harvey, Karen, 'Ritual Encounters: Punch Parties and Masculinity in the Eighteenth Century', *Past & Present*, 214.1 (2012)
Hay, Douglas and Paul Craven (eds), *Masters, Servants, and Magistrates in Britain and the Empire, 1562–1955* (Chapel Hill, 2004)
Hay, Douglas and Francis G. Snyder (eds), *Labour, Law, and Crime: An Historical Perspective* (London, 1987)
Hay, Douglas and Francis G. Snyder (eds), *Policing and Prosecution in Britain, 1750–1850* (Oxford, 1989)
Healey, Jonathan, *The First Century of Welfare: Poverty and Poor Relief in Lancashire 1620–1730* (Woodbridge, 2014)
Healey, Jonathan, 'The Fray on the Meadow: Violence and a Moment of Government in Early Tudor England', *History Workshop Journal*, 85 (2018)
Henderson, Tony, *Disorderly Women in Eighteenth-Century London: Prostitution and Control in the Metropolis 1730–1830* (London, 1999)
Henry, Wanda, 'Hester Hammerton and Women Sextons in Eighteenth- and Nineteenth-Century England', *Gender & History*, 31.2 (2019)
Henry, Wanda, 'Women Searchers of the Dead in Eighteenth- and Nineteenth-Century London', *Social History of Medicine*, 29.3 (2016)
Herrup, Cynthia, *The Common Peace: Participation and the Criminal Law in Seventeenth-Century England* (Cambridge, 1987)
Herrup, Cynthia, 'New Shoes and Mutton Pies: Investigative Responses to Theft in Seventeenth-Century East Sussex', *Historical Journal*, 27.4 (1984)

Hindle, Steve, 'The Growth of Social Stability in Restoration England', *The European Legacy*, 5.4 (2000)

Hindle, Steve, *On the Parish? The Micro-Politics of Poor Relief in Rural England c.1550–1750* (Oxford, 2004)

Hindle, Steve, 'Power, Poor Relief, and Social Relations in Holland Fen, c.1600–1800', *The Historical Journal*, 41.1 (1998)

Hindle, Steve, *The State and Social Change in Early Modern England, c.1550–1640* (Basingstoke, 2000)

Hindle, Steve, Alexandra Shepard, and John Walter (eds), *Remaking English Society: Social Relations and Social Change in Early Modern England* (Woodbridge, 2013)

Hitchcock, David, *Vagrancy in English Culture and Society, 1650–1750* (London, 2016)

Hitchcock, Tim, *Down and Out in Eighteenth-Century London* (London, 2004)

Hitchcock, Tim and Michèle Cohen (eds), *English Masculinities 1660–1800* (London, 1999)

Hitchcock, Tim and Robert Shoemaker, *London Lives: Poverty, Crime and the Making of a Modern City, 1690–1800* (Cambridge, 2015)

Hitchcock, Tim and Heather Shore (eds), *The Streets of London: From the Great Fire to the Great Stink* (London, 2003)

Hodgkin, Katharine, 'Thomas Whythorne and the Problems of Mastery', *History Workshop Journal*, 29 (1990)

Howard, Sharon, 'Investigating Responses to Theft in Early Modern Wales', *Continuity & Change*, 19.3 (2004)

Hubbard, Eleanor, *City Women: Money, Sex, & the Social Order in Early Modern* (London (Oxford, 2012))

Hughes, Ann, *Gender and the English Revolution* (London, 2012)

Hughes, Ann, 'The King, the Parliament, and the Localities during the English Civil War', *Journal of British Studies* 24 (1985)

Hughes, Ann, 'Parliamentary Tyranny? Indemnity Proceedings and the Impact of Civil War: A Case Study from Warwickshire', *Midland History* 11.1 (1986)

Hunt, Lynn, 'The 18th-Century Body and the Origins of Human Rights', *Diogenes* 203 (2004)

Hunt, Lynn, *Inventing Human Rights* (New York, 2007)

Hunt, Margaret R., *The Middling Sort: Commerce, Gender, and the Family in England 1680–1780* (Berkeley, 1996)

Hurl-Eamon, Jennine, *Gender and Petty Violence in London, 1680–1720* (Columbus, 2005)

Hurl-Eamon, Jennine, 'Policing Male Heterosexuality: The Reformation of Manners Societies' Campaign against the Brothels in Westminster, 1690–1720', *Journal of Social History*, 37.4 (2004)

Hurl-Eamon, Jennine, 'The Westminster Imposters: Impersonating Law Enforcement in Early Eighteenth-Century London', *Eighteenth-Century Studies*, 38.3 (2005)

Innes, Joanna, *Inferior Politics: Social Problems and Social Policies in Eighteenth-Century Britain* (Oxford, 2009)

Jackson, Louise A., *Women Police: Gender, Welfare and Surveillance in the Twentieth Century* (Manchester, 2006)
Jordan, Constance, 'The Household and the State: Transformations in the Representation of an Analogy from Aristotle to James I', *Modern Language Quarterly*, 54.3 (1993)
Kane, Bronach and Fiona Williamson (eds), *Women, Agency and the Law, 1300–1700* (London, 2013)
Kent, Joan R., 'Attitudes of Members of the House of Commons to the Regulation of "Personal Conduct" in Late Elizabethan and Early Stuart England', *Bulletin of the Institute of Historical Research* 46.113 (1973)
Kent, Joan R., 'The Centre and the Localities: State Formation and Parish Government in England, circa 1640–1740', *The Historical Journal*, 38.2 (1995)
Kent, Joan R., *The English Village Constable 1580–1642: A Social and Administrative Study* (Oxford, 1986)
Kent, Joan R., 'The Rural "Middling Sort" in Early Modern England, circa 1640–1740: Some Economic, Political and Socio-Cultural Characteristics', *Rural History*, 10.1 (1999)
Kern Paster, Gail, *The Body Embarrassed: Drama and the Disciplines of Shame in Early Modern England* (Ithaca, 1993)
Kesselring, K. J., *Making Murder Public: Homicide in Early Modern England, 1480–1680* (Oxford, 2019)
King, Peter, *Crime, Justice, and Discretion in England 1740–1820* (Oxford, 2000)
King, Peter, 'Ethnicity, Prejudice, and Justice: The Treatment of the Irish at the Old Bailey, 1750–1825', *Journal of British Studies*, 52 (2013)
King, Peter, 'Immigrant Communities, the Police and the Courts in Late Eighteenth and Early Nineteenth-Century London', *Crime, History & Societies*, 20.1 (2016)
King, Peter, 'Punishing Assault: The Transformation of Attitudes in the English Courts', *The Journal of Interdisciplinary History*, 27.1 (1996)
King, Peter, 'The Summary Courts and Social Relations in Eighteenth-Century England', *Past & Present*, 183 (2004)
King, Peter and John Carter Wood, 'Black People and the Criminal Justice System: Prejudice and Practice in Later Eighteenth- and Early Nineteenth-Century London', *Historical Research*, 88.239 (2015)
Knepper, Paul and Anja Johansen (eds), *The Oxford Handbook of the History of Crime and Criminal Justice* (Oxford, 2016)
Knights, Mark, *Trust and Distrust: Corruption in Office in Britain and its Empire, 1600–1850* (Oxford, 2021)
Kümin, Beat A., *The Shaping of a Community: The Rise and Reformation of the English Parish, c.1400–1560* (Aldershot, 1996)
Landau, Norma, *The Justices of the Peace, 1679–1760* (Berkeley, 1984)
Langbein, John H., 'The Criminal Trial before the Lawyers', *University of Chicago Law Review* 45.2 (1978)
Langbein, John H., 'Shaping the Eighteenth-Century Criminal Trial: A View from the Ryder Sources', *University of Chicago Law Review* 50.1 (1983)

Langelüddecke, Henrik, '"I Finde All Men & My Officers All Soe Unwilling": The Collection of Ship Money, 1635–40', *Journal of British Studies*, 46 (2007)

Langelüddecke, Henrik, '"The Pooreste and Sympleste Sorte of People"? The Selection of Parish Officers during the Personal Rule of Charles I', *Historical Research*, 80.208 (2007)

Langford, Paul, *The Excise Crisis: Society and Politics in the Age of Walpole* (Oxford, 1975)

Lawrence, Paul, 'The Vagrancy Act (1824) and the Persistence of Pre-Emptive Policing in England since 1750', *British Journal of Criminology*, 57 (2017)

Lemmings, David, *Law and Government in England during the Long Eighteenth Century: From Consent to Command* (Basingstoke, 2011)

Levine, Philippa, *Prostitution, Race, and Politics: Policing Venereal Disease in the British Empire* (New York, 2003)

Levine, Philippa, '"Walking the Streets in a Way No Decent Woman Should": Women Police in World War I', *Journal of Modern History* 66.1 (1994)

Macfarlane, Karen A., 'The Jewish Policemen of Eighteenth-Century London', *Journal of Modern Jewish Studies*, 10.2 (2011)

Mackie, Erin, 'Boys Will Be Boys: Masculinity, Criminality, and the Restoration Rake', *The Eighteenth Century*, 46.2 (2005)

Mackie, Erin, *Rakes, Highwaymen, and Pirates: The Making of the Modern Gentleman in the Eighteenth Century* (Baltimore, 2009)

Mackinnon, Catherine A., *Toward a Feminist Theory of the State* (Cambridge, MA, 1989)

Matthews, Nancy L., *William Sheppard, Cromwell's Law Reformer* (Cambridge, 1984)

McCormack, Matthew, *The Independent Man: Citizenship and Gender Politics in Georgian England* (Manchester, 2005)

McCormack, Matthew (ed.), *Public Men: Masculinity and Politics in Modern Britain* (London, 2007)

McDiarmid, John F. (ed.), *The Monarchical Republic of Early Modern England: Essays in Response to Patrick Collinson* (Aldershot, 2007)

McGovern, Jonathan, *The Tudor Sheriff: A Study in Early Modern Administration* (Oxford, 2022)

McNamara, Jo Ann and Suzanne Wemple, 'The Power of Women through the Family in Medieval Europe: 500–1100', *Feminist Studies*, 1.3/4 (1973)

McShane, Angela and Garthine Walker (eds), *The Extraordinary and the Everyday in Early Modern England* (Basingstoke, 2010)

McSheffrey, Shannon, *Marriage, Sex, and Civic Culture in Late Medieval London* (Philadelphia, 2006)

Mehta, Kiran, 'Summary Justice in Eighteenth- and Nineteenth-Century Southwark (London)', *Crime, History & Societies* 24.1 (2020)

Meldrum, Tim, *Domestic Service and Gender 1660–1750: Life and Work in the London Household* (Harlow, 2000)

Mendelson, Sara and Patricia Crawford, *Women in Early Modern England 1550–1720* (Oxford, 1998)

Merry, M. and P. Baker, '"For the house her selfe and one servant": Family and Household in Late Seventeenth-century London', *The London Journal* 34.3 (2009)

Miller, John, *Cities Divided: Politics and Religion in English Provincial Towns, 1660–1722* (Oxford, 2007)

Miller, Pavla, *Transformations of Patriarchy in the West, 1500–1900* (Bloomington, 1998)

Munkhoff, Richelle, 'Searchers of the Dead: Authority, Marginality, and the Interpretation of Plague in England, 1574–1665', *Gender & History*, 11.1 (1999)

Muravyeva, Marianna G. and Raisa Maria Toivo (eds), *Gender in Late Medieval and Early Modern Europe* (New York, 2013)

Murray, Jacqueline (ed.), *Conflicted Identities and Multiple Masculinities: Men in the Medieval West* (New York, 1999)

Ogborn, Miles, *Spaces of Modernity: London's Geographies, 1680–1780* (New York, 1998)

Orlin, Lena Cowen (ed.), *Material London ca. 1600* (Philadelphia, 2000)

Orlin, Lena Cowen (ed.), *Private Matters and Public Culture in Post-Reformation England* (Ithaca, 1994)

Paley, Ruth, 'An Imperfect, Inadequate and Wretched System? Policing in London before Peel', *Criminal Justice History*, 10 (1989)

Palk, Deirdre, *Gender, Crime and Judicial Discretion 1780–1830* (Woodbridge, 2006)

Palmer, Stanley H., *Police and Protest in England and Ireland, 1780–1850* (Cambridge, 1985)

Pateman, Carole, *The Sexual Contract* (Cambridge, 1988)

Pearl, Valerie, 'Change and Stability in Seventeenth-Century London', *The London Journal*, 5.1 (1979)

Pearl, Valerie, *London and the Outbreak of the Puritan Revolution* (Oxford, 1961)

Peters, Christine, *Patterns of Piety: Women, Gender and Religion in Late Medieval and Reformation England* (Cambridge, 2003)

Pitman, Jan, 'Tradition and Exclusion: Parochial Officeholding in Early Modern England, A Case Study from North Norfolk, 1580–1640', *Rural History*, 15.1 (2004)

Poska, A. M., J. Couchman, and K. A. McIver (eds), *The Ashgate Research Companion to Women and Gender in Early Modern Europe* (Farnham, 2013)

Power, Eileen, 'The Position of Women', in Charles G. Crump and Ernest F. Jacob (eds), *The Legacy of the Middle Ages* (Oxford, 1926)

Reinke-Williams, 'Manhood and Masculinity in Early Modern England', *History Compass*, 12.9 (2014)

Reinke-Williams, 'Misogyny, Jest-Books and Male Youth Culture in Seventeenth-Century England', *Gender & History*, 21.2 (2009)

Reinke-Williams, *Women, Work and Sociability in Early Modern* (London and Basingstoke, 2014)

Reynolds, Elaine A., *Before the Bobbies: The Night Watch and Police Reform in Metropolitan London, 1720–1830* (London, 1998)

Robinson, Cyril D., 'Ideology as History: A Look at the Way Some Police Historians Look at the Police', *Police Studies*, 2 (1979)

Rogers, Nicholas, 'Policing the Poor in Eighteenth-Century London: The Vagrancy Laws and Their Administration', *Histoire Sociale/Social History*, 24.47 (1991)

Roper, Lyndal, 'Beyond Discourse Theory', *Women's History Review*, 19.2 (2010)

Roper, Lyndal, *The Holy Household: Women and Morals in Reformation Augsburg* (Oxford, 1989)

Roper, Lyndal, *Oedipus and the Devil: Witchcraft, Religion and Sexuality in Early Modern Europe* (London, 1994)

Rublack, Ulinka and Pamela Selwyn, 'Fluxes: The Early Modern Body and the Emotions', *History Workshop Journal*, 53 (2002)

Sabapathy, John, *Officers & Accountability in Medieval England 1170–1300* (Oxford, 2014)

Saunders, Elaine, '"Men of Good Character, Strong, Decent and Active": Hertfordshire's Petty Constables, 1730–1799' (Open University, 2017)

Schmidt, Ariadne and Manon van der Heijden, 'Public Services and Women's Work in Early Modern Dutch Towns', *Journal of Urban History*, 36.3 (2010)

Schochet, Gordon J., *Patriarchalism in Political Thought* (Oxford, 1975)

Shagan, Ethan, *The Rule of Moderation: Violence, Religion and the Politics of Restraint in Early Modern England* (Cambridge, 2011)

Shapiro, Barbara, *"Beyond Reasonable Doubt" and "Probable Cause": Historical Perspectives on the Anglo-American Law of Evidence* (Berkeley, 1991)

Sharpe, James, *Crime in Early Modern England 1550–1750*, 2nd edn (London, 1999)

Sharpe, James, *Early Modern England: A Social History 1550–1760*, 2nd edn (London, 1997)

Sharpe, James, *A Fiery & Furious People: A History of Violence in England* (London, 2016)

Shepard, Alexandra, *Accounting for Oneself: Worth, Status, and the Social Order in Early Modern England* (Oxford, 2015)

Shepard, Alexandra, 'Manhood, Credit and Patriarchy in Early Modern England', *P & P*, 167 (2000)

Shepard, Alexandra, *Meanings of Manhood in Early Modern England* (Oxford, 2003)

Shoemaker, Robert B., *Gender in English Society, 1650–1850: The Emergence of Separate Spheres?* (London, 1998)

Shoemaker, Robert B., *The London Mob: Violence and Disorder in Eighteenth-Century England* (London, 2004)

Shoemaker, Robert B., 'Male Honour and the Decline of Public Violence in Eighteenth-Century London', *Social History*, 26.2 (2001)

Shoemaker, Robert B., 'The Old Bailey Proceedings and the Representation of Crime and Criminal Justice in Eighteenth-Century London', *Journal of British Studies*, 47 (2008)

Shoemaker, Robert B., *Prosecution and Punishment: Petty Crime and the Law in London and Rural Middlesex, c.1660–1725* (Cambridge, 1991)

Shore, Heather, '"The Reckoning": Disorderly Women, Informing Constables and the Westminster Justices, 1727–33', *Social History*, 34.4 (2009)

Simons, Patricia, *The Sex of Men in Premodern Europe* (Cambridge, 2011)

Smith, Bruce P., 'The Myth of Private Prosecution in England, 1750–1850' in Markus D. Dubber and Lindsay Farmer (eds), *Modern Histories of Crime and Punishment* (Stanford, 2007)

Smith, Bruce P., 'The Presumption of Guilt and the English Law of Theft, 1750–1850', *Law and History Review*, 23.1 (2005)

Smith, Hilda, *All Men and Both Sexes: Gender, Politics, and the False Universal in England, 1640–1832* (Philadelphia, 2002)

Smith, Hilda (ed.), *Women Writers and the Early Modern British Political Tradition* (Cambridge, 1998)

Smith, Hilda and Melinda S. Zook (eds), *Generations of Women Historians: Within and Beyond the Academy* (London, 2018)

Spufford, Margaret (ed.), *The World of Rural Dissenters, 1520–1725* (Cambridge, 1995)

Statt, Daniel, 'The Case of the Mohocks: Rake Violence in Augustan London', *Social History*, 20.2 (1995)

Stephanson, Raymond, *The Yard of Wit: Male Creativity and Sexuality, 1650–1750* (Philadelphia, 2004)

Stopes, Charlotte Carmichael, *British Freewomen: Their Historical Privilege* (London, 1894)

Sweet, Rosemary and Penelope Lane (eds), *Women and Urban Life in Eighteenth-Century England: 'On the Town'* (Aldershot, 2003)

Tickell, Shelley, *Shoplifting in Eighteenth-Century England* (Woodbridge, 2018)

Turner, Janice, '"Ill-Favoured Sluts"?—The Disorderly Women of Rosemary Lane and Rag Fair', *The London Journal*, 38.2 (2013)

Vickery, Amanda, 'An Englishman's Home Is His Castle? Thresholds, Boundaries and Privacies in the Eighteenth-Century London House', *Past & Present*, 199 (2008)

Vickery, Amanda, 'Golden Age to Separate Spheres? A Review of the Categories and Chronology of English Women's History', *Historical Journal*, 36.2 (1993)

van der Heijden, Manon, *Civil Duty: Public Services in the Early Modern Low Countries* (Newcastle-upon-Tyne, 2012)

Waddell, Brodie, *God, Duty and Community in English Economic Life, 1660–1720* (Woodbridge, 2012)

Waddell, Brodie, 'Governing England through the Manor Courts, 1550–1850', *The Historical Journal*, 55.2 (2012)

Walby, Sylvia, *Theorizing Patriarchy* (Oxford, 1990)

Wales, Tim, '"Living at Their Own Hands": Policing Poor Households and the Young in Early Modern Rural England', *Agricultural History Review*, 61.1 (2013)

Walker, Garthine, *Crime, Gender and Social Order in Early Modern England* (Cambridge, 2003)

Walker, Garthine, 'Expanding the Boundaries of Female Honour in Early Modern England', *Transactions of the Royal Historical Society* (1996)

Walker, Garthine, 'Rereading Rape and Sexual Violence in Early Modern England', *Gender & History*, 10.1 (1998)
Walkowitz, Judith R., *Prostitution and Victorian Society: Women, Class, and the State* (Cambridge, 1983)
Ward, Joseph P., *Metropolitan Communities: Trade Guilds, Identity, and Change in Early Modern* (London (Stanford, 1997)
Ward, Joseph P. (ed.), *Violence, Politics, and Gender in Early Modern England* (London, 2008)
Webb, Beatrice and Sidney Webb, *English Local Government from the Revolution to the Municipal Corporations Act* (London, 1906–1929), 9 volumes
Weil, Rachel, *Political Passions: Gender, the Family and Political Argument in England 1680–1714* (Manchester, 1999)
Weil, Rachel, 'The Public, the Private, and Feminist Historiography', *Histoire Sociale/Social History* 40.80 (2007)
Weil, Rachel, 'Thinking about Allegiance in the English Civil War', *History Workshop Journal* 61 (2006)
Wiesner, Merry E., 'Guilds, Male Bonding and Women's Work in Early Modern Germany', *Gender & History*, 1.2 (1989)
Wiesner, Merry E., '"Wandervogels" and Women: Journeymen's Concepts of Masculinity in Early Modern Germany', *Journal of Social History*, 24.4 (1991)
Wiesner, Merry E., *Women and Gender in Early Modern Europe* (Cambridge, 2000)
Willen, Diane, 'Women in the Public Sphere in Early Modern England: The Case of the Urban Working Poor', *Sixteenth Century Journal*, 19.4 (1988)
Williamson, Fiona (ed.), *Locating Agency: Space, Power and Popular Politics* (Newcastle-upon-Tyne, 2010)
Williamson, Fiona (ed.), *Social Relations and Urban Space: Norwich, 1600–1700* (Woodbridge, 2014)
Wilson, Kathleen, *The Sense of the People: Politics, Culture and Imperialism in England, 1715–1785* (Cambridge, 1995)
Wood, Andy, *Faith, Hope and Charity: English Neighbourhoods, 1500–1640* (Cambridge, 2020)
Woodeson, Alison, 'The First Women Police: A Force for Equality or Infringement?', *Women's History Review*, 2.2 (1993)
Wright, S. J. (ed.), *Parish, Church and People: Local Studies in Lay Religion 1350–1750* (London, 1988)
Wrightson, Keith, 'Aspects of Social Differentiation in Rural England, c. 1580–1660', *The Journal of Peasant Studies*, 5.1 (1977)
Wrightson, Keith, *Earthly Necessities: Economic Lives in Early Modern Britain* (New Haven, 2000)
Wrightson, Keith, *English Society 1570–1680* (London, 1982)
Wrightson, Keith (ed.), *A Social History of England 1500–1750* (Cambridge, 2017)
Wrightson, Keith and David Levine, *Poverty and Piety in and English Village* (New York, 1979)
Zedner, Lucia, 'Policing before and after the Police: The Historical Antecedents of Contemporary Crime Control', *British Journal of Criminology*, 46.1 (2006)

Index

Abreu-Ferreira, Darlene, 54
Ågren, Maria, 54
alcohol, 125–7, 214
aldermen, 43, 116, 121, 148
Aldermen, 43
Amhurst, Nicholas, 114
arrests, 14, 45, 66, 81, 83, 134–72
    gendered, 140–3
    wrongful, 169–71
Assizes, 84, 154, 174, 190
    trials, 6, 32

bailiffs, 4, 73, 85, 88, 95, 98, 128–30
    family, 53
    long-serving, 109
    staff, 92
Baker, John, 65
Balgarnie, Florence, 217
Bancroft, Richard (archbishop), 70
Barrie, David, 208
Bath, 117
beadles, 4, 92
    attitudes to female suspects, 195
    family, 51, 54
    powers, 181
    salaried, 109
    sworn as constables, 149
Beattie, John, 8, 116, 120, 150
Birmingham, 117
Blackstone, William, 80, 157
Bland, Eleanor, 162, 209
Boswell, Caroline, 84
Bourdieu, Pierre, 93, 94
Bow Street Runners, 144, 150, 210
Braddick, Michael, 5, 9, 11, 63, 89, 109
Brewer, John, 109, 126
Bristol, 117, 197
Brooks, Christopher, 42, 157, 175
Broomhall, Susan, 208
Burn, Richard, 107
Butler, Samuel, 62, 92, 131

Cambridge, 17, 71
Cambridgeshire, 56
Cannon, John, 111, 114, 123, 126, 130
Carey, Henry, 94
Catholics, 4
Chaloner, Thomas, 110, 112, 115, 126, 130
Chan Smith, David, 65, 207
Cheshire, 41
Chester, 37
Churchill, David, 138, 139, 141, 209
churchwardens, 3, 70, 119
    age, 38
    amateur, 5, 210
    character, 40
    family, 52, 53
    marital status, 35, 36
    powers, 68, 176
    social status, 7, 33
civil wars, 46, 82–5, 108, 118, 125
Clarendon code, 118
Clarke, Lucy, 89
Coke, Edward, 17, 26, 75, 81, 96, 107, 157, 175, 187
Collinson, Patrick, 5
Colquhoun, Patrick, 31, 117
common law, 211
    on forcible entry, 177, 181
    on homicide, 101
    on officeholding women, 108
    on officers' powers, 46
    on protection of houses, 174–6
    on qualifications for office, 26
    on suspicion, 151–5, 160, 165
    on types of office, 72–82
    protecting officers, 72
Common Pleas, 18, 26, 73
    increasingly assertive, 65, 67
Condren, Conal, 64
consistory courts, 126, 171
constables, 1, 3, 115–23, 48, 69, 93, 131, 145, 148
    age, 37, 38, 120–2, 213

constables (cont.)
  amateur, 5, 8
  attitudes to female suspects, 173
  character, 39
  competence, 28
  family, 52, 53
  marital status, 36, 120–2
  ministerial officers, 13, 75, 78
  powers, 14, 151, 159–61, 164, 177, 180, 211
  qualifications, 26–7, 34, 208
  reforming constables, 42, 160
  social status, 7, 31, 33, 120
  supernumerary, 148
  violence, 203
Cornwall, 213
coroners, 4, 6
corruption, 9, 31–2
Cowell, John, 63
Crawford, Patricia, 103, 184
customs officers, 94, 178, 179

Dabhoiwala, Faramerz, 146, 161
Dalton, Michael, 27, 69, 74, 151, 154, 155, 176
Davies, Celia, 110
Defoe, Daniel, 31, 39, 117, 121, 123, 142
deputies, 14, 115–23, 79, 147, 208, 210
  long-serving, 122
Derbyshire, 56, 107
Devon, 55
Dissenters, 118
distraint, 66, 68–9, 176, 179
Dorset, 56

Ely, 36
Essex, 33–7, 56, 84, 85, 90
excise, 9, 13, 126–8, 178, 186, 215
excisemen, 215
  age, 110
  confiscating goods, 86, 180
  family, 110–11
  length of service, 109
  marital status, 110
  qualifications, 109

false imprisonment, 69, 72, 74, 84, 85, 87, 89, 170
Fielding, Henry, 45, 156, 210
Fielding, John, 131, 157
Filmer, Robert, 41
Foster, Michael, 101
fraternity, 2, 13, 123–7, 204
French, Henry, 34

Gardiner, Robert, 107, 155
Gay, John, 49, 93, 141

Gianoutsos, Jamie, 104
Goldie, Mark, 5, 205
Gouge, William, 53
Gowing, Laura, 190, 197, 199
Grimston, Harbottle, 192

Hale, Matthew, 17, 62, 97, 153, 154, 157, 179
Halliday, Paul, 65, 83, 207
Harvey, Karen, 185
Hawkins, William, 150
Healey, Jonathan, 89
Herbert, Philip (Earl of Pembroke), 47
Herrup, Cynthia, 6, 137, 165, 174
Hertfordshire, 33, 56
Hindle, Steve, 7
Hitchcock, Tim, 127, 161
Hobbes, Thomas, 76, 80
Holt, John, 80, 100, 158–62, 212
homicide, 47, 95–101, 153
  killing by officers, 97
  killing of officers, 98–101
households, 10, 13, 106, 174–89, 205, 210, 214
  physical space, 51
  subordinate members, 52–5, 197, 214
houserow (custom), 106–8
houses of correction, 145, 157, 169
hue and cry, 1
Hughes, Ann, 104
Hull, 52

idoneus homo, 56, 72–5, 80, 102, 106, 120
Indemnity Committee, 85
independence, 10, 13
  and social status, 30, 34
  in political thought, 23–4
  in the excise, 111–15
Irish
  officers, 215
  suspected criminals, 44, 171, 213

Jeffries, George, 78
Jewish
  officers, 119
  suspected criminals, 213
Johnson, Samuel, 92
judges, 12
  in central courts, 72–5, 78, 96, 100, 153, 158–62
  Old Bailey, 148
justices of the peace, 4, 67, 69, 89, 116, 196
  examining suspects, 148, 181
  orders to officers, 42, 48, 164
  receiving petitions, 35, 52
  social status, 7

Kent, 19, 33, 35, 37, 41, 51–3, 94, 128, 141, 142, 150, 178, 181
  Ashford, 45
  Hollingbourne, 86
  Wye, 179
Kent, Joan, 9, 28, 33, 65
Kesselring, Krista, 207
Knights, Mark, 9

Lambarde, William, 17, 74
Lancashire, 53, 90
Laud, William, 193
lawyers, 12, 14, 42, 62, 71, 100, 106, 153
legal knowlege, 28–9
legislation, 11, 116, 150
  on officers' powers, 157, 176, 177, 181, 211
  protecting officers, 68–72
  on qualifications for office, 27
Leicestershire, 53, 215
Levine, Philippa, 218
Liverpool, 141
Locke, John, 41, 88
lodgers, 120
  excluded from office, 24, 35
  as suspects, 166, 188
London, 50
  Castle Baynard, 212
  Chelsea, 86, 213
  Cornhill, 122
  Farringdon Without, 122
  law enforcement, 8, 14, 43, 90, 115–23, 134–204
  literacy, 28
  parishes, 149
  Queenhithe, 122
  St Botolph Aldersgate, 56
  St Botolph Aldgate, 52
  St Botolph without Aldgate, 29
  St Clement Danes, 131
  St John's Hackney, 55
  St Laurence Pountney, 54
  St Michael Bassishaw, 121
  St Paul's Covent Garden, 31
  St Paul's Shadwell, 119
  Whitechapel, 84, 166, 178

Mackalley's Case, 95–101, 216
Magna Carta, 152, 157, 158, 160
Manchester, 54, 117, 211
manors, 4
  manor courts, 6, 16
  officers, 55, 56, 73, 108
married women, 53–5, 185, 199, 206
  auxiliaries to officer husbands, 11, 53–5, 214, 217
  excluded from office, 11, 34, 110
  reputation, 171
marshals, City of London, 109, 149
Marvell, Andrew, 13
masculinity, 140, 141, 185, 210, 214
  alternative modes, 13, 25, 104, 123–33
  and officeholding, 2
Mendelson, Sara, 103
Meriton, George, 107
middling sort, 33, 40, 46, 165, 193
  officeholding, 7, 9, 24, 34, 45
  reluctance to hold office, 118
Miege, Guy, 31, 92, 117
misogyny, 30, 105, 110, 127
monarchs, 4, 9, 12, 76–7, 81, 94, 96
Murray, William (Lord Mansfield), 155

Neale, Matthew, 197
Newcastle, 34
night watchmen, 3, 49, 115–23, 144, 165, 180
  age, 213
  amateur, 8
  attitudes to female suspects, 173, 195
  clashes with gentlemen, 46–9, 86, 93
  corruption, 32
  deferential, 45, 46
  drinking, 125
  fraternal, 124
  marital status, 36, 120
  mocked, 44
  powers, 151, 161, 164, 211
  qualifications, 29, 208
  salaried, 123
  subject of mockery, 102
  violence, 131, 132, 196, 202, 203
night-walking, 46, 151, 156, 160
  gendered, 15, 169
Norfolk, 33, 36, 215
Northumberland, 55
Norwich, 19, 34, 42, 47, 50, 86, 94, 117, 127, 128, 131, 142, 150, 178, 180
Nottinghamshire, 56

officeholding, 9–10
  discharge, 27, 34–6
  handbooks, 29, 31, 32, 37, 45, 87, 107, 116, 190
  judicial, 12, 73–80, 206
  law, 58–102
  ministerial, 12, 56, 73–81, 102, 115, 120, 206, 208, 216
  participatory, 5, 24, 33, 207
  patriarchal, 21–57
  rotational, 12, 106, 122, 210
  synonymous with duty, 64

officers
  authority, 7, 12, 13, 89–102, 215
  committing crimes, 87–89
  female, 55–7, 79, 103, 106–8, 216
  impersonation, 1, 180
  legal protection, 67–72
  privileges in litigation, 71
  representing higher powers, 58–102
  resisted, 41–50, 83–7, 95–102
  stealing, 91, 178–80
  subject to lawsuits, 66–72, 7, 171
Old Bailey
  jurisdiction, 168
  published *Proceedings*, 20, 44, 51, 124, 132, 139, 144, 162, 183, 188, 190, 193
  trials, 88, 94, 98, 100, 102, 129, 141, 147
Olive v Ingram, 56–7, 79, 108
Orlin, Lena, 175
overseers of the poor, 4, 70, 79, 119
  age, 38
  amateur, 5
  family, 52, 53
  marital status, 35, 36
  powers, 68, 176
  social status, 7, 33
Oxford, 17
Oxfordshire, 114, 123

Paley, Ruth, 215
Paley, William, 152
parishes, 4
  parish clerks, 29, 52, 53, 109
  parish elections, 13, 29, 33, 35, 52, 108
Pateman, Carole, 2, 14, 123
patriarchs, 11, 34–41
patriarchy, 2, 123
  and officeholding, 25, 38
  and the state, 11
  clashing with younger men, 44–50
  contradictions, 41–2
  undermined, 102
  violence, 143
Paul, John, 131
Peel, Robert, 214
Phelps v Winchcombe, 74–5, 78
pickpocketing, 43, 51, 140, 192, 202–3
pleading
  general issue, 66–72
  justifications, 66–7
Polsted, Ezekiel, 112–13, 126, 132, 211
poor laws, 35, 176, 184
  protection of officers, 68
  rates, 33
Prévost, Abbé, 151
Prynne, William, 76

Quarter Sessions, 84, 174
  depositions, 20, 124, 139, 141, 142, 162, 183, 190
  discharges from office, 27
  jurisdiction, 168
  presentments, 177
  rulings, 107, 182
  trials, 6, 32
Queen's Bench, 18, 74–6
  cases, 56, 72, 77, 79, 95, 100, 106, 108, 156, 159, 175, 179, 216
  increasingly assertive, 65, 67

R v Stubbs, 79–80, 108
rakes, 46–50
reformation of manners, 160–1
  informers, 149
  involvement in policing, 146, 147, 169, 209
  judicial opposition, 161
  societies, 40, 44
  supportive magistrates, 42, 177
republicanism, 5, 63
rewards for prosecution, 123, 209, 210
  one-off, 43
  statutory, 87, 146, 182
  unofficial, 146
Reynolds, Elaine, 116
Rutherford, Samuel, 76

salaries/payment, 8, 13, 109, 122, 211
  via deputisation, 122
scavengers, 4
  marital status, 36
  salaried, 109
Scotland, 95, 96, 211
searches, 15, 173–204
  gendered, 185, 204, 217
  resisted, 174–9, 192, 197
  restrained by modesty, 198, 199, 204
  strip searches, 196–7, 201
  violent, 201–2
servants, 1, 11, 80, 127, 166–7, 188
  excluded from office, 24, 34
sex work, 158, 217
  legal status, 157–62, 212
  linked to other offences, 43, 202
  policing, 43, 71, 99, 146, 169, 205, 210, 212
sextons, 4
  family, 53, 54
  female, 55, 56
  poor householders, 51
  salaried, 109
sexual knowledge
  female, 199
  male, 200
Shakespeare, William, 28

Index

Shepard, Alexandra, 30, 37, 42, 186
Sheppard, William, 107, 154
sheriffs, 4, 73, 107, 175
Shoemaker, Robert, 14, 143, 146, 147, 150, 160, 161, 169
shoplifting, 43, 199
Sidney, Algernon, 78
single men, 13, 14, 35–6, 214
singlewomen, 11, 56
   idoneus homo, 106
   officeholding, 107
Smith, Alexander, 129
Smith, Bruce, 166
Smith, Sir Thomas, 6
Smollett, Tobias, 47, 51
soldiers, 85, 93, 99, 201
Somerset, 106, 114
specialisation, 2, 8, 109, 122, 146
Staffordshire, 79
Star Chamber, 67
staves, 12, 42, 92–3, 99–101, 215
   weapons, 142
Stopes, Charlotte Carmichael, 103
Suffolk, 56, 107, 110
summary courts, 169, 210
Surtz, Ronald, 200
surveyors of the highways, 4, 27
suspicion, 14, 151–72, 209
   gendered, 167–71, 212
   legal grounds, 151–2, 164–6
   social status, 166–7
   transferable, 153–5, 164, 203
Sussex, 137, 165

Tadmor, Naomi, 54
Tarbin, Stephanie, 40
Taylor, Hillary, 30
the state, 1–2, 4–7, 96, 204, 206
   abstraction, 15
   analogous to household, 23, 205
   differentiation, 3, 8, 62, 206, 215
   gendered, 3, 171, 218
   source of authority, 81, 95
theft, 174
   accusations against officers, 85, 86, 192
   arrests for, 147, 151
   associated with servants, 167
   association with sex work, 169
   attempted crackdown, 164
   by impersonating officers, 180
   by officers, 87, 179

   compared to confiscation, 94
   compared to distraint, 179
   gendered, 15
   suspected, 152, 154, 166
thief-takers, 87, 146, 147, 150
Tickell, Shelley, 195

vagrancy, 152, 156–7
   gendered, 15, 169
   legislation, 151, 176, 212
vestries, 31–4, 118
Vickery, Amanda, 175, 188
violence, 46–9, 129–33, 141–3
   against officers, 46
   by officers, 129, 130
   lawful, 12, 183
   sexual violence, 127–8, 186, 196, 214

Wales, 35, 67
Walker, Garthine, 185
Walpole, Horace, 88
Walpole, Robert, 86
Wapping, 169, 182
Ward, Ned, 44, 88, 93, 122
wards, 4, 120–2, 149
   ward elections, 13
warrants, 27, 84, 91, 182–4
   arrest, 53, 74, 148
   forged, 44, 90
   general, 164, 181, 182, 187
   search, 180, 192
watch-houses, 15, 125, 156, 200
watchmen
   powers, 156
Weber, Max, 8, 9, 109, 206
Welch, Saunders, 45, 125, 131, 132
Whyte, Nicola, 185
widows, 54, 185, 199
   idoneus homo, 106
   officeholding, 56, 79, 107, 108
Wilkes, John, 187
Wingate, Edmund, 107
Wood, Andy, 30
Worcestershire, 1
Wrightson, Keith, 7, 33

York, 53
Yorkshire, 56, 94, 107, 128, 150
   Bradford, 166
   Skipton, 29
   York, 84, 154

Printed by Printforce, United Kingdom